COMMITMENT TO EQUITY HANDBOOK

COMMITMENT TO EQUITY HANDBOOK

Estimating the Impact of Fiscal Policy
on Inequality and Poverty

Second Edition

VOLUME 2

Methodological Frontiers in Fiscal Incidence Analysis

Nora Lustig

EDITOR

CEQ INSTITUTE AT TULANE UNIVERSITY
New Orleans

BROOKINGS INSTITUTION PRESS
Washington, D.C.

Published by Brookings Institution Press
1775 Massachusetts Avenue, NW
Washington, DC 20036
www.brookings.edu/bipress

Co-published by Rowman & Littlefield
An imprint of The Rowman & Littlefield Publishing Group, Inc.
4501 Forbes Boulevard, Suite 200, Lanham, Maryland 20706
www.rowman.com

86-90 Paul Street, London EC2A 4NE

The Brookings Institution is a nonprofit organization devoted to research, education, and publication on important issues of domestic and foreign policy. Its principal purpose is to bring the highest quality independent research and analysis to bear on current and emerging policy problems.

The Commitment to Equity (CEQ) Institute at Tulane University, founded by Nora Lustig in 2015, works to reduce inequality and poverty through comprehensive and rigorous tax and benefit incidence analysis, and active engagement with the policy community.

British Library Cataloguing in Publication Information Available

Library of Congress Cataloging-in-Publication Data

ISBN: 978-0-8157-4046-9 (paperback)
ISBN: 978-0-8157-4047-6 (electronic)

∞™ The paper used in this publication meets the minimum requirements of American National Standard for Information Sciences—Permanence of Paper for Printed Library Materials, ANSI/NISO Z39.48-1992

To Anthony Atkinson (1944–2017), one of the most brilliant thinkers on the topics of inequality, poverty, and social injustice

For Antonio, my beloved husband and companion

For Carlos Javier and Liliana, our wonderful children

CONTENTS

Volume 1

PART I
Methodology

Chapter 3
Measuring the Redistributive Impact of Taxes and Transfers
in the Presence of Reranking   121
Ali Enami

Chapter 4

Can a Poverty-Reducing and Progressive Tax and Transfer System Hurt the Poor?

Sean Higgins and Nora Lustig (*reproduced from* Journal
of Development Economics)

Chapter 9

Analyzing the Impact of Fiscal Policy on Ethno-Racial Inequality   472
Rodrigo Aranda and Adam Ratzlaff

PART III
Applications
Included in First Edition

Chapter 10
Fiscal Policy, Income Redistribution, and Poverty Reduction in Low- and Middle-Income Countries
Nora Lustig

Chapter 11
Argentina: Taxes, Expenditures, Poverty, and Income Distribution
Dario Rossignolo

Chapter 15
El Salvador: The Impact of Taxes and Social Spending on Inequality and Poverty   693

Margarita Beneke de Sanfeliu, Nora Lustig, and Jose Andres Oliva Cepeda

Chapter 16

Ghana and Tanzania: The Impact of Reforming Energy Subsidies, Cash Transfers, and Taxes on Inequality and Poverty

Stephen D. Younger

Chapter 17

Fiscal Policy, Inequality, and Poverty in Iran: Assessing the Impact and Effectiveness of Taxes and Transfers

Ali Enami, Nora Lustig, and Alireza Taqdiri (*reproduced from* Middle East Development Journal)

Added to Second Edition

Chapter 20

China: The Impact of Taxes and Transfers on Income Inequality, Poverty, and the Urban-Rural and Regional Income Gaps in China

Nora Lustig and Yang Wang

Chapter 21
Argentina: Fiscal Policy, Income Redistribution and Poverty Reduction in Argentina   862
Juan Cruz Lopez Del Valle, Caterina Brest Lopez, Joaquin Campabadal, Julieta Ladronis, Nora Lustig, Valentina Martinez Pabon, and Mariano Tommasi

PART IV
The *CEQ (Commitment to Equity) Assessment* Tools
Available only online at www.ceqinstitute.org, under "Handbook."

1. Planning for a CEQ Assessment©: Data and Software Requirements
CEQ Institute

9. CEQ Assessment: Checking Protocol
Sandra Martinez-Aguilar, Adam Ratzlaff, Maynor Cabrera,
Cristina Carrera, and Sean Higgins

10. CEQ Training Tools
CEQ Institute

10.a CEQ Training PPT Presentations

10.b CEQ Training Videos

PART V
CEQ Data Center on Fiscal Redistribution
CEQ Institute
Available only online at www.ceqinstitute.org.

1. Description

2. CEQ Standard Indicators

3. CEQ Data Visualization

4. CEQ Indicators and the Sustainable Development Goals

5. CEQ Master Workbooks

6. CEQ Do Files and Replication Codes

6.a CEQ Assessments: Constructing Income Concepts and for Running CEQ Stata Package to Complete Master Workbook

6.b Frontier Topics

7. CEQ Harmonized Microdata

8. CEQ Metadata Table

9. Comparison of Income Concepts in Databases with Indicators of Fiscal Redistribution

PART VI
CEQ Microsimulation Tools
Available only online at www.ceqinstitute.org.

1. CEQ Desktop Tax Simulator
Ali Enami, Patricio Larroulet, and Nora Lustig

2. CEQ Markdown Statistical Code for Microsimulating the Short-run Impact of COVID-19 on Inequality and Poverty
Federico Sanz

3. CEQ Statistical Code for Microsimulating the Long-run Impact of COVID-19 on Human Capital and Intergenerational Mobility
Guido Neidhöfer and Patricio Larroulet

CONTENTS

Volume 2

**Alternative Methods to Value Transfers in Kind:
Health, Education, and Infrastructure**

Redistributive Impact of Contributory Pensions

Chapter 6
The Within-System Redistribution of Contributory Pension Systems: A Conceptual Framework and Empirical Method of Estimation

Carlos Grushka

Fiscal Redistribution and Sustainability

Chapter 7
Intertemporal Sustainability of Fiscal Redistribution: A Methodological Framework

Jose Maria Fanelli

Chapter 8
Fiscal Redistribution, Sustainability, and Demography in Latin America

Ramiro Albrieu and Jose Maria Fanelli

Political Economy of Redistribution

LIST OF ILLUSTRATIONS

Figures

Tables

ABSTRACTS

Alternative Methods to Value Transfers in Kind: Health, Education, and Infrastructure

Chapter 1. The Effect of Government Health Expenditure on Income Distribution: A Comparison of Valuation Methods in Ghana

Jeremy Barofsky and Stephen D. Younger

To assess how publicly funded in-kind health care affects the income distribution, we must estimate its monetary value to beneficiaries. We describe and compare three approaches to measuring the distributional consequences of government health spending: average cost of provision, willingness to pay, and health outcomes. We provide example applications for each of these methods using a national cross-section from Ghana for 2012–13. Estimates of a willingness-to-pay model for outpatient services show that, on average, users value those services at less than what the government pays for them. The estimated marginal effects of health spending for outpatient care on inequality are modest and somewhat smaller than those for the average cost approach. In contrast, the health outcomes method finds that the marginal effects of health spending for three causes of death and five health interventions are very large.

JEL Codes: I14, I15, I32, I13, H51, H40

Keywords: health, economic inequality, poverty, mortality, Ghana, full income

Chapter 2. The Market Value of Public Education: A Comparison of Three Valuation Methods

Sergei Soares

Publicly provided education is both an important public expenditure and a relevant in-kind transfer, often to the poorest households. This chapter compares three methods for valuing education services and their distributive impact in Brazil. The first method is cost of provision, according to which education is worth what it costs the state to provide it; the second values educational services using the labor market as the measure of their worth; and the third matches private educational expenditures, paid for by students or their parents, with equivalent public education services, and then values the latter according to the price of the former. The results from all three approaches do not fall far from each other. The imputed income from publicly provided education reduces inequality by between 3 and 4 Gini points and increases incomes by about 6 percent. The chapter concludes that the value of public education in Brazil is close to 6 percent of household income and that it is quite distributive, whatever the valuation method used.

JEL Codes: I24, D31, H44, I38

Keywords: educational service valuation, inequality, education, welfare, returns to education, hedonic pricing

Chapter 3. Redistribution through Education: Assessing the Long-term Impact of Public Spending

Sergio Urzua

This chapter assesses how publicly funded education affects income distribution and compares different approaches to measuring the consequences of government education spending. The empirical quantification of private returns to education, the estimation of the elasticity of school enrollment to public spending in the sector, and the identification of age-earnings profiles are the building blocks of the analysis. The text extends the conventional incidence analysis and incorporates behavioral responses to public subsidies. The methods are implemented using aggregate-level data and cross-sectional information from household surveys from Chile and Ghana. Real-world data limitations are taken into account. From the country comparison, we assess how public initiatives might shape income inequality in the short and long run.

JEL Codes: I26, I28, I22, J31

Keywords: public spending, education, incidence analysis, inequality

Chapter 4. The Market Value of Owner-Occupied Housing and Public Infrastructure Services

Sergei Soares

Owner-occupied housing and public infrastructure services are a relevant part of income distribution whose impacts have not yet been adequately studied, at least not from the distributive point of view. This chapter suggests a way to find the market value for these services using hedonic prices. While far from new, this methodology is nevertheless useful in assigning values to these services. The chapter uses Brazilian data from 1995, 2005, and 2015 to impute rental values for owner-occupied housing and associated infrastructure services. The results are that imputation of housing services considerably reduces inequality and that public infrastructure services have become more progressive as their expansion has brought these services to increasingly poorer households.

JEL Codes: H41, D31

Keywords: public infrastructure services, hedonic prices, imputed rent, concentration coefficients, income distribution

Fiscal Incidence of Corporate Taxes

Chapter 5. Taxes, Transfers, and Income Distribution in Chile: Incorporating Undistributed Profits

Bernardo Candia and Eduardo Engel

This chapter seeks to measure the distributive impact of fiscal interventions in Chile by applying the Commitment to Equity (CEQ) methodology, a standardized fiscal incidence analysis. In a methodological innovation, we incorporate income accrued and not received by Chilean taxpayers through their companies and corporations into the distribution of prefiscal income. We find that the difference between the distribution of accrued and received income turns out to be important—around 6 Gini percentage points for each main concept of income. In addition, when moving from the distribution of Market Income to the distribution of Final Income (after taxes and transfers) the distribution of income improves by 7 Gini percentage points. To assign the improvement in the distribution of income between the different fiscal interventions, we apply the Shapley value and observe that half of the improvement in the distribution of income is due to transfers in education, while direct taxes only explain 20 percent of the reduction of the Gini coefficient. Finally, based on the simulation of the impact of the 2014 tax reform carried out by the World Bank, we estimate that the reform would produce an additional reduction of 2.4 Gini percentage points when going from Market Income to Final Income.

JEL Codes: D31, H22

Keywords: fiscal incidence, inequality, poverty, undistributed profits, taxes, transfers, Chile

Redistributive Impact of Contributory Pensions

Chapter 6. The Within-System Redistribution of Contributory Pension Systems: Conceptual Framework and Empirical Method of Estimation

Carlos Grushka

When discussing the distributional impacts of pension systems, it is critical to understand the underlying rationale for considering them as either tax transfers or deferred wage schemes. The way that benefits are determined (usually with decreasing replacement rates by income level) plays a significant role in within-system redistribution. However, evaluating the overall effective redistribution requires incorporating the effects of coverage, or "selectivity," and the funding or financing of the benefits under payment. Within-system redistribution is greatly affected by rules that change over time, the specific ways that they apply in each country, the different approaches for data definition (on revenue, expenditure, and coverage), and data availability. After analyzing in detail the case of Argentina and all the variables involved, we propose a simplified redistribution index, defined as the difference of gross substitution rates by education levels (proxy of lifetime income). This index can be estimated from cross-sectional income surveys and works as an excellent complement to or a reasonable proxy for the significance of redistribution within contributory pensions systems in different countries and periods.

JEL Codes: H50, H55, D31, J14

Keywords: social security and public pensions, personal income distribution, economics of the elderly, Argentina

Fiscal Redistribution and Sustainability

Chapter 7. Intertemporal Sustainability of Fiscal Redistribution: A Methodological Framework

Jose Maria Fanelli

This chapter develops a methodological framework to study the linkages between fiscal redistributions, fiscal sustainability, and the government's wealth constraint. The framework includes demographic factors and income strata, shows the connections between the concepts used in the Commitment to Equity (CEQ) and National Transfer Accounts (NTA) databases, and suggests possible synergies and directions for further data collection and research efforts. We conclude that more research is needed, first, about the role of public wealth, including all assets in the government's balance sheet, and, second, about the distributional consequences—on income as well as wealth—of policies regarding fiscal sustainability, intergenerational transfers that finance the demand for life-cycle wealth, and the management of publicly owned natural resources. We also show that the framework is useful for connecting the two approaches to sustainability: one concerning fiscal soundness and one concerning development. With regard to policies, the implications indicate that sustainability tests should be part of the design of redistribution initiatives, that these initiatives must consider the demographic transition, and that fiscal redistributions may ultimately deplete the stock of natural resources without ensuring a compensatory accumulation of reproducible capital if they do not take adjusted government savings and capital gains into account.

JEL Codes: E62, J11

Keywords: fiscal policy, demographics

Chapter 8. Fiscal Redistribution, Sustainability, and Demography in Latin America

Ramiro Albrieu and Jose Maria Fanelli

This chapter investigates links between fiscal space, fiscal redistributions, and distributional outcomes for Latin America. It focuses on two factors: (1) the role of intertemporal restrictions and debt sustainability and (2) the demographic transition's influence on the fiscal redistribution structure. It also identifies some stylized facts that matter in designing distribution-friendly fiscal consolidation policies. Two findings deserve highlighting. First, the way in which a given fiscal adjustment is implemented matters to income distribution. As a general rule, the downward adjustment of expenditures is regressive, although the importance of the impact varies substantially according to the expenditure item and from one economy to another. Second, the demographic window of opportunity (DWO) is the key stage of the demographic transition regarding the fiscal space in Latin America. Younger countries are entering the DWO and the older ones have to prepare to abandon it and enter the aging stage. The exercises suggest that the DWO will create the fiscal space required to implement progressive policies in younger countries while the opposite will occur in the countries that will age. The simulations indicate that the demographic transition-driven effects on the items of fiscal redistributions are potentially very large and have substantial consequences for income distribution and debt sustainability.

JEL Codes: E62, J11

Keywords: fiscal policy, demographics.

Political Economy of Redistribution

Chapter 9. On the Political Economy of Redistribution and Provision of Public Goods

Stefano Barbieri and Koray Caglayan

We analyze the public provision of public goods and income redistribution in a median voter framework. We review existing related frameworks, devoting special attention to their implications for applied analysis. Motivated by empirical regularities discovered in the analysis of Commitment to Equity (CEQ) data linking the percentage of "net receivers" to the levels of provision of public goods, we present an extension of the classic framework of taxation and public goods provision that departs from the assumption of a simple proportional tax in favor of a flat tax with an exemption. Adjusting the exemption level, we capture tax schemes restricted to generating different numbers of net receivers. We then let voters decide on the tax rate and the quantity of public goods provided. In a standard framework, we find that the public goods level can increase or decrease in proportion to "net receivers" according to the relationship between the income of the decisive voter and the average income in the population conditional on income being larger than the exemption. This result suggests that to account for the richness of the comparative statics we observe, the framework should encompass additional considerations such as turnout and the presence of substitutes for government-provided public goods.

JEL Codes: H21, D31, D72

Keywords: public goods provision, income distribution, median voter, flat tax, exemption levels

Alternative Methods to Value Transfers in Kind

Health, Education, and Infrastructure

Chapter 1

THE EFFECT OF GOVERNMENT HEALTH EXPENDITURE ON INCOME DISTRIBUTION

A Comparison of Valuation Methods in Ghana

Jeremy Barofsky and Stephen D. Younger

Introduction

Health spending in developing nations has expanded rapidly since 2000. Health expenditure now constitutes 37 and 23 percent of total government expenditure in low- and low-middle income nations, respectively.[1] Many developing nations have expanded health insurance coverage, while the goal of universal health coverage for even the poorest countries has received increasing support among multilateral institutions and researchers (WHO, 2010; Jamison et al., 2013).[2] Clearly, any comprehensive attempt to understand the distributional consequences of government taxation and spending must come to grips with the benefit of publicly funded healthcare. This is more difficult than most other parts of the budget because the benefits are in-kind, not cash. We need a way to value those benefits in monetary terms.

A standard *Commitment to Equity (CEQ) Assessment* does this with an estimate of the government's cost of providing the health services people receive in-kind.[3] The motivation for this chapter is that the standard approach may not be very accurate. We discuss criticisms of the standard approach in section 1 and then turn to two alternative

---

[1] Authors' calculations using World Bank national accounts data (World Bank, 2018a; 2018b).

[2] Recent health coverage expansions include Mexico, Ghana, Thailand, China, and India. See Cotlear et al. (2015) for a summary.

[3] This is usually called the "average cost" approach, but we prefer "cost of provision" to include the possibility of the "insurance value" approach discussed in Lustig and Higgins (2022) (chapter 1 in Volume 1 of this Handbook).

methods for estimating the monetary value of in-kind health services to their beneficiaries. Throughout, we focus on methods that seem likely to be applicable in many
countries. In particular, we take as a constraint that we should be able to implement
the method with standard multipurpose cross-sectional survey data similar to what a
CEQ Assessment uses, perhaps along with other data that are readily available in most
countries.[4]

In addition to the standard average cost approach, we consider two alternative
methods to estimate the benefits that patients receive from publicly funded health services and a fourth method that is an add-on to the others rather than a substitute. The
first uses actual demand for health services to estimate the benefits consumers receive
from utilization; this is a revealed preference approach usually referred to as "willingness to pay." However, because consumers exhibit positive income elasticity for healthcare, if the poor and the rich exhibit the same level of health need, healthcare demand
will be higher among the rich than the poor. Observed healthcare demand therefore
reflects both an individual's willingness and ability to pay for care. Consequently, instead of referring to demand calculated using revealed preference as "willingness to
pay," throughout the text we emphasize this distinction by using the term "willingness
and ability to pay" (WATP). The demand estimates use survey respondents' choice of
healthcare provider along the lines of the seminal papers by Gertler, Locay, and Sanderson (1987) and Gertler and van der Gaag (1990).

Our second alternative estimates the monetary value of the improved health that
publicly funded healthcare services generate. In particular, we estimate the reduction
in mortality produced by government spending across five health interventions and
three causes of death and value this averted mortality in monetary terms using the approach of Jamison et al. (2013). We calculate mortality averted through government
action by comparing the mortality rate that obtains with Ghana's current level of health
intervention coverage against an assumed counterfactual mortality rate that would have
occurred had health intervention coverage been at the lowest level observed among
other West African nations. While it is also possible to generate such estimates for the
mortality effects of entire health systems, our example estimates the value of mortality reduction from several specific health interventions, including the two largest causes
of premature death in Ghana—malaria and HIV.

While each of these alternative methods addresses some of the limits of the average cost approach, they have shortcomings of their own, both conceptual and practical. We discuss these in turn. It is not clear that one of the three methods is superior
to the others, so we discuss situations in which researchers might want to use each of
them. Our goal is to provide a menu of options for valuing publicly funded healthcare
benefits and some guidance on how to choose among the methods.

---

[4] The term *CEQ Assessment* is used for the fiscal incidence studies that use the methodology described in Volume 1 of this Handbook. For details, see chapter 1 in Volume 1.

A common theme is that both new methods estimate the benefit of healthcare services to recipients rather than the cost to the government, thus addressing an important criticism of the standard approach (section 1). A more subtle point is that by divorcing the estimated benefit from the government's actual expenditure, we allow the expenditure to have positive (or negative) rates of return: our estimate of the monetary value of in-kind benefits can be more or less than the amount spent to provide it. This is not the case for most of the budget. When government makes a cash transfer, its monetary value to the recipient is the amount of the transfer, no more, no less. When government collects a tax, its monetary value is the amount paid to a first order approximation.[5] But as we will see, government spending on in-kind health services can have very large rates of return. Jamison et al. (2013), for example, estimate the benefit-cost ratio of a basic package of health services in low-income countries at between nine and 20. Such high returns provide considerable leverage for public health spending's effect on the ex-post welfare distribution.

Apart from the benefit of specific health services to their beneficiaries, the mere existence of publicly funded health services provides insurance against the financial risk of catastrophic healthcare expenditures.[6] Indeed, policymakers' rationale for Britain's National Health Service and Medicare in the United States was not so much to improve people's health, but to protect them from large financial losses (Finkelstein and McKnight, 2008). Note that this is different from the "insurance value" approach to measuring the value of health spending, which averages total health expenditures over all eligible beneficiaries rather than over actual users of publicly funded health services. The insurance here is financial and valuable for risk-averse individuals because it lowers the probability of catastrophically large health expenditures. We estimate the change in household health spending risk across the income distribution and then calculate the monetary value of this risk change (usually a reduction) from health insurance using an expected utility framework where value depends on an assumed degree of risk aversion. The benefit of this financial risk reduction is additional to any ex-post benefits associated with actual healthcare services received, so it can be added to any one of those benefit estimates to generate an overall benefit of public spending on healthcare.[7]

We apply each of these methods, along with the standard average cost of provision approach, to data for Ghana, the same data used in a *CEQ Assessment* for that

---

[5] See Box 1-1 by Stephen Younger in chapter 1, Volume 1 of this Handbook (Younger, 2022).

[6] See Alam and Mahal (2014) and Acharya et al. (2013) for reviews.

[7] In principle, many forms of government spending provide financial risk protection: disability insurance, unemployment insurance, retirement pensions, and targeted transfers for those with low income. The theoretical literature goes back as far as the 1960s (Arrow, 1963), and there are many empirical studies. See Feldstein (1973) on health insurance, Bernheim (1987) for retirement pensions, and Bound et al. (2004) for disability insurance. Even though the topic is not limited to health spending, we include it here because it has not yet been treated in a CEQ methodological publication.

country (Younger, Osei-Assibey, and Oppong, 2017). We find that the revealed preference method produces benefit estimates that are somewhat smaller and somewhat less progressive than the standard average cost approach. The methods based on the monetary value of health improvements produce a range of estimates, most of which are so large that they dramatically alter the ex-post income distribution, yielding enormous reductions in inequality.

This chapter proceeds as follows: section 1 describes the conceptual weaknesses of the current average cost method. These weaknesses constitute the basis for developing new methods to value in-kind government health spending. Section 2 describes the WATP approach for valuing healthcare using consumer observed behavior. The section applies the method to Ghana and summarizes results compared to the average cost method. Section 3 defines the health outcomes method, applies the method to Ghana, and summarizes results. Section 4 provides guidance on the circumstances in which each of the three methods should be used. Section 5 develops a method to estimate the value of insurance from reduced out-of-pocket (OOP) health spending risk. It then applies the method to calculate the value of Ghana's National Health Insurance Scheme (NHIS) across the income distribution. Section 6 concludes.

1 What's Wrong with the Cost of Provision?

Perhaps, nothing. Asking "How much does government spend to provide health service X to its beneficiaries and how is that spending distributed across the income distribution?" is a reasonable question. Call this "expenditure incidence." As long as the variation in expenditure per patient for service X is small,[8] using the average cost of provision for that service gives an estimate with which to calculate the expenditure incidence and allows governments to compare spending amounts across policy options.

In most instances, though, we are interested in the value of the service to the recipient, the "benefit incidence." This can be very different from the expenditure incidence because government can spend money inefficiently or corruptly (Gauthier and Wane, 2008). Government may pay public sector healthcare staff more than what comparable private sector staff are paid (Lindauer and Nunberg, 1994; Lakin, 2010), or those staff may not perform the duties for which they are paid (Das and Hammer, 2005; Das et al., 2012). In such cases, part of the benefit from public spending accrues to the staff, not patients. In addition, government may pad contracts with suppliers in exchange for kickbacks to functionaries, producing a similar effect. Or government may simply bungle the job for reasons of inattention or political economy, offering services of little value that patients nevertheless accept because they are free or because they assume that the healthcare staff know better. In all these cases, government expenditure

---

[8] Enami, Higgins, and Lustig (2022) (chapter 6, part 3.8.1 in Volume 1 of this Handbook) discusses ways to keep the variation small.

is greater than the benefit to patients and, if it is inefficient, greater than the benefit to anyone.

On the other hand, there are at least two reasons to believe that the benefits of publicly funded healthcare can be greater than what government spends to provide them. First, the marginal benefits for many health services are a step function. A first consultation to diagnose a sinus infection is valuable; a second is worth much less or nothing at all. The same is true for vaccinations, many surgeries, and infectious disease treatments. As a result, the demand for these services is discrete: high demand for one unit and usually zero demand for any further units. So even if the cost of provision is very low, patients will not demand more than one unit, and the marginal value to them of that one unit may be much greater than its cost. It may make sense, then, to estimate the service's value and use that estimate in a benefit incidence analysis. In essence, this approach captures the consumer surplus associated with that one unit demanded. In doing so, it diverges from standard practice in national income accounting and most incidence analyses, where we value all units consumed at the marginal cost (usually the market price), thus ignoring consumer surplus. But doing so in the case of many healthcare services seems more egregious than for most other goods and services, because, unlike most goods, health provides both intrinsic and instrumental value (Sen, 1988). Better health is valuable in itself as the basis for future utility, while also permitting individuals to achieve other goals they value such as education and greater labor productivity. In addition, there exists an objective and widespread way to measure this benefit since we can credibly assume that the marginal utility of health is positive and constant without resorting to revealed preference as is necessary with other goods.

A second argument applies to public services that are non-rivalrous, where one person's use of the service does not prevent another's use. These include natural monopolies such as water and sanitation systems and public goods such as information on good healthcare practices and vector control. Here, too, the marginal benefit of many such services is a step function, so Samuelson's (1969) standard efficiency condition— provide the public good until its marginal cost is equal to the sum of everyone's marginal benefits—may not apply. Spraying once for mosquitos may have joint benefits much greater than the cost, but once the mosquitos are dead, further spraying has no value, so again, the benefits are greater than the marginal cost.

If there are good reasons to believe that the benefit incidence of publicly funded health services differs significantly from their expenditure incidence, then we need methods to estimate that benefit incidence.

2 Using Healthcare Consumers' Choices to Estimate the Compensating Variation for Public Healthcare Expenditures

The compensating variation is the amount of money one would need to receive to keep utility constant in the face of a change in prices and/or quality. Public spending on healthcare usually reduces the price that patients pay for health services, so the compensating variation of that price change is an exact measure of what the public spending is worth to them in monetary terms. For a good or service with continuous demand, the compensating variation for a price change is the area under the demand curve between the old and new prices, so if we can estimate the demand function, we can calculate the compensating variation.

The demand for most healthcare services is discrete, not continuous. This complicates both the demand estimation and the calculation of the compensating variation, but both are still possible. Economists working on public transport first developed models to estimate the demand for any one of a few choices for commuting to work (walk, drive, take the bus, for example) using only the fact that if a consumer chooses one option over the others, her utility from that option must be greater than the utility she would derive from any of the others (McFadden, 1981).[9] Suppose that consumers can choose between J healthcare providers and define the utility derived from option j as

$$U_j = V_j + \varepsilon_j,$$

where V_j is a deterministic component of utility and a function of variables we observe, but ε_j is random and unobservable. McFadden (1981) calls this a "random utility model" (RUM). It is possible to estimate the demand for each option j as the probability that the consumer chooses that option, which is the probability that the $U_j > U_k$ for all $k \neq j$. Let y be the option chosen, then

$$\Pr[y=j] = \Pr[U_k - U_j < 0 \; \forall \, k \neq j] = \Pr[\varepsilon_k - \varepsilon_j < V_j - V_k \; \forall \, k \neq j].$$

If we specify the deterministic component of utility as a function of observed variables, say, $V_j = X_j \beta_j$, and we specify a joint distribution for the ε's, we can estimate these demand functions with maximum likelihood. If the ε's are distributed multivariate normal, this model is a multinomial probit.[10] If they are distributed type I extreme value, this is either a multinomial logit (if the X's are constant across the options, i.e., not option-specific), a conditional logit (if the X's are option-specific but the β's are constant across options), or a mixture of the two.[11] And if the ε's have the generalized extreme value distribution, this is a nested logit.[12]

The multinomial probit model is more general than the logit models because it allows for correlations among the random components, the ε's. But the logit models are usually easier to estimate and so are more often used in practical applications. Both

---

[9] Cameron and Trivedi (2005) provide a concise textbook exposition.

[10] Stata estimates this with `asmprobit`.

[11] Stata calls this "alternative-specific conditional logit" and estimates it with the command `asclogit`.

[12] Stata estimates this with `nlogit`.

multinomial and conditional logit models assume no correlation among the ε's. The nested logit model generalizes these models to allow some limited correlation among options' random components, assuming that options nested together are more similar to one another than are options outside their "nest."

The logit models have the additional practical advantage that calculating compensating variations is easier compared to the multinomial probit. The compensating variation for a price change for one option, i, is defined implicitly as

$$max_{\{j=1,...,J\}}U(y - p_j^0, X_j, \varepsilon_j) = max_{\{j=1,...,J\}}U(y - CV - p_j^1, X_j, \varepsilon_j),$$

where y is income and $y - p_j$ is net income after paying for option j, i.e., income available for consuming other goods and services that provide utility; X_j are other determinants of the utility associated with choosing option j, which includes the quality of option j but also characteristics of the consumer; and CV is the compensating variation. In this simple example with one price change, the only difference between p_j^0 and p_j^1 is when $j = i$, but the formula can be applied as well to multiple price (or quality) changes. The compensating variation depends on variables we can observe, but also on the unobservable errors. To get around this, we calculate the expected value of the compensating variation. In general, this requires integrating over the joint distribution of the ε's, something that is computationally intensive. But Herriges and Kling (1999) show how to approximate this expected value for these models, and Dagsvik and Karlström (2005) give another approach that reduces the integration to one dimension. Even more remarkably, if the marginal utility of income is constant, Small and Rosen (1981) derive a closed form solution for the expected value of the compensating variation.[13]

This procedure yields the expected value of the compensating variation for each observation (person or household), which we use as the value of the subsidy implicit in publicly funded health services to that person or household. An important criticism of the WATP method is that since there is a positive income elasticity for healthcare, the compensating variation will be lower for the poor than the rich because demand reflects willingness *and* ability to pay. To overcome this issue, we first estimate individual WATP for outpatient care (described in greater detail in section 2.1), but value that care to each beneficiary using the average WATP across the population in our estimated demand model. It is this average WATP value rather than the cost of provision that we use to estimate the benefit incidence of public spending on that service.[14]

---

[13] The solution is complicated; we give the specific formula for the case of two options in section 2.1 below, where we apply these methods to demand for health services in Ghana.

[14] For the particular case we estimate in Ghana, results using each observation's WATP are not very different from the results we present here using the average WATP across individuals.

2.1 Example Application: Demand for Healthcare Consultations in Ghana

We model the choice of seeking healthcare conditional on having been ill or injured in the previous two weeks.[15] We assume that utility for each care option is a separable function of consumption of non-health goods and services, the quality of healthcare received, and a random component:

$$U_j = V_C(C_j)_j + V_Q(Q_j)_j + \varepsilon_j = ln(Y - P_j) \cdot \alpha + X \cdot \beta_j + \varepsilon_j.$$

The second equality assumes that utility is logarithmic in consumption to ensure that the marginal utility of income is declining in income, but always positive.[16] It also imposes a budget constraint that consumption must equal income less the cost of the chosen healthcare option. We assume the latter includes user fees plus the time costs of getting to a healthcare facility and any time spent waiting for attention there. Specifically, net consumption C_j is defined in the following way where the term in parentheses defines the cost of care choice j:

$$C_j = Y - (OOP_j + wT_j + wH_j).$$

The price for the no care option is zero. OOP_j is the out-of-pocket (OOP) price for provider j, wT_j is the opportunity cost of time for travel to and from the health facility, and wH_j is the opportunity cost of wait time at the health facility. We use a combination of health system structure and self-reports to calculate the OOP price of outpatient care. For those with membership in the NHIS, no coinsurance, copayment, or deductible is required at the point of service (Nguyen, Rajkotia, and Wang, 2011). Therefore, OOP prices for NHIS members (66 percent and 61 percent of the self-reported sick or ill sample in urban and rural areas, respectively) are set to zero. This is consistent with what is observed empirically as approximately three-quarters of individuals accessing outpatient care report paying no OOP fees at the point of service. The data set used, the Ghana Living Standards Survey, 2012–13, round 6 (GLSS-6) (GSS, 2014), asks questions about outpatient price paid for care overall and the price by stage of care (registration, consultation, diagnosis, drugs, and treatment). Because the price paid for the stages of care does not always sum to the re-

---

[15] This is simpler than the usual approach that assumes people choose between no care, public care, and private care, as in Gertler, Locay, and Sanderson (1987). We do this because there is not a clear distinction between publicly funded and private healthcare in Ghana. Some private providers accept payment from the government for NHIS participants, and some public providers charge fees to those who are not NHIS participants, so we limit our model to the no care versus care decision.

[16] Estimates using a quadratic yielded a negative marginal utility of income at the highest incomes.

ported total, we use the maximum of these two measures. Once defined, we estimate prices for outpatient care using the median self-reported costs for those without NHIS coverage per cluster. We set OOP outpatient fees paid for those without NHIS coverage at the district median.

We calculate the opportunity cost of time as annual household income divided by the number of work hours in a year to obtain an hourly wage per household. For households that report zero total wages earned, we replace their opportunity cost of time with the minimum reported hourly wage in their district. For the other components of cost, the GLSS 2012–13 included a community survey for rural areas that asked about travel time to the nearest healthcare facility and wait time at the nearest facility; cluster level median values are used from this survey. For urban areas without the community survey, we use median self-reported travel and wait times by survey cluster and, if missing, by region.

We assume that quality depends on household characteristics X that are the same across options.[17] Because a logit model can identify only the β's relative to one option, those for the no-care option are assumed to be zero, and so quality is normalized such that it is zero for the no-care option. Note that the α coefficient is not subscripted. This constrains the marginal utility of income to be the same across options.[18]

Table 1-1 gives the results of the conditional logit demand model for outpatient care. Most of the coefficients have the expected sign, but few are statistically significant. Demand increases with income, for children under five years old, and as the number of days sick in the last two weeks increases. It is unusual for the coefficients on urban residence and the education variables to not be significantly different from zero. This reflects Ghana's considerable efforts to expand healthcare coverage in recent years, including through the NHIS.[19]

We use these demand estimates to calculate the compensating variation for a price change in the cost of a healthcare consultation equal to the average cost of provision used in the *CEQ Assessment* for Ghana, 33.6 cedis (Younger, Osei-Assibey, and Oppong, 2017). Given that this amount is small relative to income, we assume that the marginal utility of income is constant, which makes the calculation of the compensating variation straightforward, as given by Small and Rosen (1981):

---

[17] In theory, X could also include option-specific characteristics such as quality measures, but we have no such data in Ghana, nor is this type of data included in most income and expenditure surveys.

[18] Most statistical packages, including Stata's `mlogit` and `clogit` commands, normalize all the coefficients in the base option to zero which implies a different marginal utility of income for the base option. Stata's `asclogit` command allows us to constrain the marginal utility of income to be the same across all options.

[19] Figure 1A.1 shows the approximately equal access to NHIS coverage across income deciles in 2012–13.

TABLE 1-1

Conditional Logit Estimates of the Demand for Outpatient Health Consultations

Variable	Coefficient	Standard error
ln(consumption)	14.1	0.9
Urban	0.0361	0.0531
Age	−0.0043	0.0050
Age^2	4.15E-05	6.14E-05
Male	−0.0832	0.0518
Child < 5 years old	0.0674	0.0298
Older than 70 years	0.0653	0.0679
Days sick	0.0797	0.0067
Primary school	−0.0729	0.0908
Junior high	−0.0159	0.1090
Senior high	0.0114	0.1194
Above high school	0.2023	0.1739
Missing educ.	0.3228	0.0868
Use Mother's educ.	−0.2285	0.1121

Source: GSS (2014) and authors' calculations.

$$CV = \left(\frac{1}{\lambda}\right)(ln(exp(V_{no\ care}^{ex\ ante}) + exp(V_{care}^{ex\ ante}))$$
$$- ln(exp(V_{no\ care}^{ex\ post}) + exp(V_{care}^{ex\ post}))),$$

where λ is the marginal utility of income and the Vs are the estimated utility functions evaluated at the care and no-care options and before and after the price change. Table 1-2 gives distributional statistics for the compensating variation for a price change for outpatient consultations from zero to 33.6 cedis, the average cost of provision at public health centers in 2012. It also gives the estimated benefits using the average cost of provision, which is the standard approach in most *CEQ Assessments*. On average, the compensating variations are about 10 percent lower than the average cost estimates. This difference could reflect inefficiency or corruption in the provision of public health-care services, which affects demand for care, but it is also to be expected insofar as beneficiaries cannot value an in-kind benefit more than the cash required to provide that benefit.

The compensating variations are also distributed across all survey respondents in the regression sample (those reporting being sick or injured in the last two weeks) because the probability of using outpatient services among this population is almost always positive. The average cost method gives benefits only to actual users and so is more concentrated—note that the benefit for the average cost method at the 25th percentile and median are zero. Actual users, though, are more concentrated among the poor as demonstrated by the more negative concentration coefficient for the average

TABLE 1-2

Distributional Statistics for Estimated Compensating Variation and Average Cost of Provision for Outpatient Consultations

Method	Mean	25th	Median	75th	Min.	Max.	c.c.	Gini—marginal effect
Average cost of provision	311	0	0	830	0	966	−0.187	0.008
Compensating variation	264	157	365	365	0	365	−0.099	0.007

Sources: GSS (2014) and authors' calculations; Younger, Osei-Assibey, and Oppong (2017).

Notes: Values in 2012 Ghanaian cedis, annualized.

The quartiles in the column headers are for estimated benefits, not income.

All statistics are on the sample of those reporting an illness or injury in the past two weeks except the concentration coefficients which are on the entire GLSS sample.

The compensating variation is for a price decrease from 33.6 cedis, the average cost of provision, to zero.

c.c. = concentration coefficient.

cost method. So, in addition to lowering the overall estimate of total benefits, use of the compensating variation spreads the benefits away from the poorer people who actually used outpatient services in this sample to all those who reported themselves sick or injured.[20] The marginal effects[21] for both methods are relatively small, producing reductions of 0.8 and 0.7 percentage points for the Gini coefficient.

2.2 Discussion of the Revealed Preference Approach to Valuing Publicly Funded Healthcare

An important advantage of the compensating variation over the average cost of provision is that it anchors the estimate of the value of care in consumers' observed behavior. In addition, because the demand estimates can be conditional on consumers' characteristics, the value we estimate can vary across the population according to those characteristics, including need for health services. Perhaps most importantly, large discrepancies between what government pays for services and consumers' WATP for them may reflect inefficient or corrupt government spending. Using WATP avoids erroneously attributing that expenditure to beneficiaries.

---

[20] If the concentration coefficient for healthcare services using the average cost method were positive, we would also expect that the concentration coefficient for the compensating variation to be closer to zero.

[21] The "marginal effect" is the amount that this spending changes the Gini coefficient. See chapter 1 in Volume 1 of this Handbook (Lustig and Higgins 2022) for definition of the marginal contribution here called the "marginal effect."

But as with all the approaches, WATP has limitations. Conceptually, this approach is applicable only to services that are private goods because we must observe demand. Practically, using survey data to estimate the demand for healthcare services is an order of magnitude more effort than that of the average cost approaches. It is certainly possible to estimate the demand for healthcare services with the single cross-section of data used for a *CEQ Assessment* as we have done here. But a skeptical econometrician could easily cast doubt on whether this approach can successfully identify the demand function needed to calculate the compensating variation for a price change. In addition, as in the average cost approach, while it is theoretically possible to estimate WATP for many different publicly funded health services, in practice we are forced to aggregate those services into a few groups, which we assume have the same value. In our example, we aggregate all outpatient consultations into a single group.

Even the apparently attractive feature of relying on consumers' choices has been challenged in the literature because this approach assumes that consumers are rational in their healthcare decisions. But given the limits to consumer sovereignty in healthcare generally (Akerlof, 1995), and particularly in low-income settings, many of the rational model's assumptions do not hold. That is, revealed preference is limited because it relies on the assumption that individuals are able to accurately estimate the expected health benefit of obtaining care. Psychological biases such as overweighting low-probability events and tunneling to the present moment, as well as information asymmetry between patient and provider mean that individual decisions often differ systematically from utility optimization. Difficulties in accurately estimating the benefit of healthcare choices means that the observed price elasticity of demand is often high and the implied value of care is low, even when health technologies are highly effective and disease burdens are substantial. Moreover, for certain health choices, identifying benefits is more challenging than for others, making observed choice valuations lower. For highly effective health technologies for which effects are relatively difficult to observe, such as better water quality in protected springs (Kremer et al., 2011) and insecticide-treated bed nets (ITNs) in malaria-endemic areas (Cohen and Dupas, 2010), very high levels of price elasticity of demand are observed.[22] These results indicate that, particularly for healthcare services whose effects are difficult to observe (e.g., most preventive care), WATP will systematically underestimate expected health benefits. Noting this discrepancy, Greenstone and Jack (2015) observe that, because individuals in high disease burden areas do not exhibit high willingness to pay to avoid that burden, there is "hardly a more important topic for future study than developing revealed preference measures . . . that capture the aesthetic, health, and/or income gains from environmental quality [such as clean water]" (p. 21).

---

[22] See Cohen and Dupas (2010) who offered pregnant women in rural Kenya an ITN at prenatal clinics and find that net acquisition declines from 99 percent to 39 percent when price increases from 0 to $US0.60.

In addition, low-income households experience liquidity constraints that impede decision-making[23] about healthcare, and they lack information, or the education to process information, on the returns to healthcare. Even when individuals intend to use healthcare, they may have trouble fulfilling those intentions (Laibson, 1997). The limited studies in the developing world that measure WATP do indeed find values for reduced mortality risks lower by several orders of magnitude than estimates in high-income countries.[24] This contradiction between high health burdens (and therefore high returns to healthcare) and low WATP on the part of consumers challenges the rational model. Healthcare may be worth more than low-income consumers' observed behavior implies. That is the motivation for the health outcomes approach we address next.

3 The Health Outcomes Approach

Publicly funded health services should improve people's health, reducing both mortality and morbidity. This has instrumental value: healthier workers are more productive; healthier children learn better. But it also has intrinsic value: health is the basis upon which all other utility is enjoyed since extending life allows individuals to purchase additional utility (Hall and Jones, 2007).[25] Given that the primary goal of a health system is to improve health status, the health outcomes approach estimates a monetary value for those improvements derived from public healthcare spending.

The approach begins with an estimate of the effect of government healthcare spending on mortality.[26] We estimate this by comparing health outcomes in the nation under study against counterfactual health outcomes, which represent what would have occurred without government healthcare spending. We assume that this counterfactual is the mortality level that would have obtained if a country experienced the minimum level of health intervention coverage observed in peer countries over a similar time period. We use readily available epidemiological models to estimate how health

---

[23] See Mani et al. (2013). There is a response to Mani and others' argument, though. If the reason that consumers do not demand healthcare despite its high value is that they are liquidity constrained, then the problem is the liquidity constraint, not lack of demand for healthcare. If government were to relieve the liquidity constraint with a cash transfer, say, it is possible that beneficiaries would spend the money on something that provided even greater value than healthcare. To be consistent with the "consumer surplus" approach we take here, a CEQ Assessment would then need to value the cash transfer at greater than its monetary value, too.

[24] Examples include Kremer et al. (2011) and León and Miguel (2017).

[25] In addition to Hall and Jones (2007), the health outcomes approach is derived from an earlier literature that measures the social value of mortality and morbidity from 1970 to 1990 in the United States (Cutler and Richardson, 1998) and mortality across the twentieth century in the United States (Murphy and Topel, 2006).

[26] In principle, the approach could be expanded to consider the value of reducing morbidity as well. We are unaware of any applications that do that. Given that its benefits are larger and easier to measure across nations, we limit our discussion to mortality.

intervention coverage rates affect mortality. Because the mortality changes are usually small, Jamison et al. (2013) use standardized mortality units (SMUs), a change in the probability of death of 0.0001 (10^{-4}). Our estimate of the change in mortality for people of age a caused by a particular publicly funded healthcare intervention h is

$$\Delta SMU_{c,h,a} = M_{c,h,a} - M_{c_{cf},h,a}.$$

The change in mortality, $\Delta SMU_{c,h,a}$, is the difference in the mortality rate among age group a in country c for the nation's current coverage level of health intervention h minus the same mortality units in a comparator counterfactual country ("cf") that has the lowest level of health intervention h coverage among all comparator countries. We assume that this is the mortality that would occur if the government in the country of interest spent nothing for health intervention h.[27]

Data for the mortality estimates must come from a source other than the household survey used for *CEQ Assessments* because income/expenditure or living standards surveys do not usually ask about mortality, and even when they do, they do not ask about healthcare the deceased may or may not have received. The alternate data source is usually an epidemiological model or clinical trial whose main purpose is to identify the effect of the health service of interest. These include medical trials of very specific healthcare interventions—one drug or care practice, for example—but could also include estimates for entire health systems. Results for specific healthcare interventions may be few for any one country, but for many aspects of healthcare, it is reasonable to borrow results from studies done in other countries, particularly if the two countries share similar socioeconomic, environmental, and disease transmission characteristics.

One particularly useful example of an epidemiological modeling tool for developing countries is the Spectrum System of Policy Models, which allows researchers and policymakers to estimate the impact on mortality (but not morbidity) of health interventions for HIV, malaria, and a series of maternal, childhood, and noncommunicable diseases.[28] These models are based on demographic data and projection models combined with epidemiological disease transmission models across multiple conditions, adjusted for the specific demographic and health data from a country of interest.

Once we have estimates for the impact of publicly funded healthcare interventions on mortality, we must put a monetary value on those changes. We do this using an

---

[27] An alternative approach would assume that there would be no healthcare of type h at all in the absences of public spending on h, but this is unrealistic because there will always be some private provision of the health intervention unless it is a pure public good.

[28] Avenir Health (2018). Examples of Spectrum's use include Korenromp et al. (2015), Korenromp et al. (2016), and Stover, Brown, and Marston (2012). See appendix 1A.1 for further details on mortality calculations.

extensive literature that examines the behavior of people who systematically and voluntarily increase their mortality risk by, say, pursuing an occupation such as policing or coal mining, and the additional income they earn for accepting that risk. That additional pay divided by the increased mortality risk gives an estimate of the value of small changes in mortality risk, which can be understood as the sum of what a cohort would pay for risk reductions.[29]

While most survey data used for a *CEQ Assessment* are sufficient to estimate simple wage equations with variables to indicate the premium for risky professions, they do not have sufficient data to estimate the mortality probabilities associated with those professions, so here too, the health outcomes approach uses secondary sources. There are many such studies with a wide range of results for the value of an SMU, but most are for developed countries. One important and uncomfortable result in those studies is that people's willingness to accept higher mortality risk varies substantially with income. This is true within countries and also between them. Hammitt and Robinson (2011) review the literature and conclude that a reasonable value for a mortality risk reduction of one SMU (VSMU) at age 35 is 1.8 percent of annual GDP per capita.[30] To adjust this value for age, Jamison et al. (2013) suggest multiplying the value of an SMU for 35-year-olds by the ratio of life expectancy at one's current age to life expectancy at 35 years old. They also halve this value for children under five years old. We follow both these conventions in our examples, but as in Jamison et al. (2013), we hold the value of an SMU constant within any one country.

For a given health intervention h, the formula to value mortality change is the following:

$$V(e'(a), e(a), y) = 0.018y \cdot \int_0^\infty n(a) \cdot \frac{e(a)}{e(35)} \cdot \Delta SMU_{c,h,a}(e'(a), e(a))\, da,,$$

where

- $e(a)$ is life expectancy at age a before the health spending of interest;
- $e'(a)$ is life expectancy at age a after the health spending;
- $V(e'(a), e(a), y)$ is the monetary value of changing from the ex-ante to the ex-post life expectancies;

---

[29] This literature often aims to calculate the "value of a statistical life" (VSL), and it is still known by that name (Viscusi and Aldy, 2003). But for our calculations, we do not need to value an entire (statistical) life, but only small changes in mortality probabilities measured in SMUs. In this, we follow Jamison et al. (2013) and Hammitt and Robinson (2011).

[30] More commonly, the value placed on changes in micro-risk of mortality are expressed as the (VSL). A VSL is calculated as the aggregated value of 10,000 *VSMU. For reference, Ghana's GDP per capita in 2013 is US$1,730 using the World Bank Atlas Method, meaning the VSL used implicitly in this analysis is US$311,400.

- y is GDP per capita;
- $n(a)$ is the population density at age a; and
- $\Delta SMU_{c,h,a}$ $(e'(a), e(a))$ is the change in standardized mortality units—a change in mortality risk of 10^{-4}—at each age a for country c and health intervention h that results from government health expenditure.[31]

Note that the integral is across the age distribution at a point in time, not across a person's life. This is the value for one year of health spending that reduces mortality probability by 0.01 percent. In words, we estimate the monetary value of a health intervention by calculating for each age group the change in mortality probability it induces, adjust for life expectancy at each age, sum those changes, weight by the age-group population share, and multiply that sum by 0.018 times GDP per capita. Again, although the value of an SMU is assumed to be proportional to income per capita across nations, within a nation, we hold it constant. The implicit assumption is that from the policymaker's perspective, eliminating the death of one citizen is equally valuable irrespective of a citizen's income.

3.1 Example Application

We use the Spectrum System of Policy Models to estimate the mortality reduction due to five specific health interventions and three causes of death: indoor residual spraying (IRS) for mosquito control, distribution of insecticide-treated bed nets (ITNs), and distribution of antimalarial drugs (mainly artemisinin), all three of which are intended to reduce malaria mortality; the distribution of antiretroviral therapy (ART) to treat HIV/AIDS; and diabetes control. In each instance, we use the Spectrum software to predict the mortality reduction across the age distribution caused by government intervention defined as the difference in health intervention coverage rates in Ghana versus the minimum coverage counterfactual rate—the lowest health intervention coverage rate among peer nations between 2011 and 2015.[32] We then apply Jamison et al.'s (2013) calculation of the monetary value of that increased mortality risk.

Table 1-3 shows mortality averted by age group due to each of the five health interventions. Note in particular the large reductions due to the distribution of antimalarial drugs. For children up to four years old, this is almost a one-half percentage point per year reduction in mortality. While much smaller, the other malaria interventions

---

[31] Jamison et al. (2013). Although VSL is commonly used in the literature, we focus our discussion on the value of SMUs because the maximum change in mortality risk we investigate is 46 SMUs or 0.0046 of a VSL.

[32] Ghana's peer nations are based on geography and data availability. They include Benin, Togo, Ivory Coast, Guinea, Liberia, Sierra Leone, and Nigeria. Data on health interventions coverage levels for IRS, ITNs, antimalarial medication use, and diabetes prevalence come from Measure DHS (2018) and UNAIDS (2019).

TABLE 1-3

Change in Age-Specific Mortality Rates from Reducing Health Intervention Coverage Rates from Current Levels to the Minimum Rates in Peer Nations by Age Group and Health Intervention per 10,000 People

	IRS	ITNs	Antimalarial medication	Adult HIV treatment, male	Adult HIV treatment, female	Diabetes control
<1 year	0.37	4.98	46.44	−0.07	−0.07	0.00
1–4	0.37	4.98	46.44	−0.07	−0.07	0.00
5–9	0.29	3.06	35.94	0.00	0.00	0.00
10–14	0.29	3.06	35.94	0.00	0.00	0.00
15–19	0.22	1.32	13.33	0.05	0.08	0.00
20–24	0.22	1.32	13.33	0.13	0.13	0.00
25–29	0.22	1.32	13.33	0.58	0.65	0.00
30–34	0.22	1.32	13.33	1.11	0.97	0.05
35–39	0.22	1.32	13.33	2.75	2.18	0.05
40–44	0.22	1.32	13.33	4.27	2.48	0.05
45–49	0.22	1.32	13.33	4.24	1.94	0.05
50–54	0.22	1.32	13.33	3.64	1.38	0.10
55–59	0.22	1.32	13.33	2.44	0.92	0.10
60–64	0.22	1.32	13.33	1.69	0.64	0.25
65–69	0.22	1.32	13.33	1.23	0.46	0.25
70–74	0.22	1.32	13.33	0.99	0.38	0.30
75–79	0.22	1.32	13.33	0.85	0.32	0.30
80–84	0.22	1.32	13.33	0.61	0.14	0.20
85+	0.22	1.32	13.33	0.61	0.14	0.20
Total	**0.26**	**2.23**	**23.21**	**0.92**	**0.59**	**0.10**

Note: Age-specific mortality rate (per 10,000 population). Changes calculated using Spectrum System of Policy Models (Avenir Health, 2018).

also have substantial effects on mortality. For ART, the effects are smaller overall than ITNs or antimalarial medication, but comparable to ITNs for prime age adults. The effects of diabetes control on mortality are minimal.

Use of each of the modeled health interventions is not necessarily equal across the income distribution, so the next step in the analysis is to distribute the calculated reductions in mortality probability across the income distribution according to actual use. GLSS 2012–13 does not include sufficient information on use of these specific health interventions across the income distribution, so we use the 2014 Ghana Demographic and Health Survey (GSS, GHS, and ICF International, 2015), which does. Table 1-4 shows how the coverage of each health intervention or disease prevalence varies across the distribution of wealth. We take the distribution of wealth based on an index of asset ownership from the DHS as a proxy for the distribution of income. Individuals are much more likely to report receiving indoor residual spraying in the last 12 months in

TABLE 1-4

Access to Health Interventions or Disease Prevalence by Wealth Quintile, Percentage of Population

Wealth quintile	IRS[1]	ITN[2]	Antimalarial medication[3]	Malaria prevalence[4]	HIV prevalence (ages 15–49)			Diabetes prevalence[5]		
					Women	Men	Total	Women	Men	Total
Lowest	29.2	52.2	41.4	42.1	1.2	0.5	0.9	3.66	0.61	2.24
Second	8.7	53.6	46.4	39.5	3.1	1.8	2.5	1.7	2.27	1.97
Middle	8.1	43.3	54.6	24.6	3.2	1.7	2.5	3.11	1.88	2.49
Fourth	4.7	32.9	51.4	13.9	4	1	2.5	7.03	3.73	5.24
Highest	5.5	29.5	52.8	7.5	2.5	0.8	1.7	7.82	6.81	7.2
Total	**9.7**	**43**	**48.5**	**26.7**	**2.8**	**1.1**	**2**	**4.664**	**3.06**	**3.828**

Sources: GSS, GHS, and ICF International (2015); Gatimu, Milimo, and Sebastian (2016).

Notes: [1] Percentage of households that received indoor residual spraying in last 12 months.
[2] Percentage of children <5 who slept under a long-lasting insecticide treated net last night.
[3] Percentage of children <5 with fever who took any antimalarial medication in the last two weeks.
[4] Malaria prevalence using microscopy measurement.
[5] Diabetes prevalence for adults >50 by wealth quintile from Gatimu, Milimo, and Sebastian (2016, table 2).

TABLE 1-5

Distributional Statistics for the Value of Mortality Reduction Due to Specific Health Interventions in Ghana

Intervention	Mean	25th	Median	75th	Min.	Max.	c.c.	Gini— marginal effect
Antimalaria drugs	1890	845	1217	3131	0	4430	−0.020	0.117
IRS	23	9	15	27	0	97	−0.372	0.008
ITNs	175	71	125	286	0	417	−0.175	0.039
Antiretroviral drugs	41	0	7	58	−6	393	0.106	0.005
Diabetes	1	0	0	2	0	16	0.359	0.000

Source: GSS (2014) and authors' calculations.

Notes: Values in 2012 Ghanaian cedis per year.
Statistics in the first six columns are for the distribution of benefits, not income.

c.c. = concentration coefficient.

the poorest quintile compared to others, a consequence of the fact that this is mostly deployed in poor, rural areas with high malaria prevalence. Distribution of ITNs is also more common in the poorer quintiles. These two expenditures will thus have a strongly progressive impact on the income distribution. Coverage of antimalarial drugs is lower in the poorest two quintiles, so spending on them will be less progressive. It is also worth noting that the use of antimalaria drugs is approximately constant across the income distribution compared to measured malaria prevalence, which is highly skewed by income level.

For antiretroviral drugs and diabetes control, the Ghana 2014 DHS does not include information on actual use but does have information on disease prevalence. We also assume that use of the corresponding healthcare services is proportional to prevalence, though it seems likely that this will be biased toward being too equalizing since in practice we would expect that richer people with HIV or diabetes would be more likely to get treatment in the absence of government intervention. HIV prevalence is concentrated in the middle three quintiles, while diabetes is much more common at the two highest quintiles.

The last step in the analysis is to monetize the mortality reductions we have distributed across the income quintiles. We do this using the estimated probabilities of treatment from table 1-4 and the monetization formula from Jamison et al. (2013) defined above. Table 1-5 summarizes the result of applying this valuation method to the estimates of mortality averted through government health expenditure. To put the values in perspective, average expenditure per capita in the GLSS data was 2,261 cedis per year in 2012, and the official poverty line is 1,314 cedis per adult equivalent. Clearly, the estimated value of mortality reduction due to antimalaria drugs distribution is substantial. But the other malaria interventions and antiretroviral drugs also have high rates of return.[33]

The concentration coefficients in table 1-5 show distributions of benefits consistent with the assumptions based on table 1-4. The benefits of malaria drugs are spread evenly across the population.[34] Indoor spraying and bed nets are both highly progressive. To put these in perspective, the most progressive expenditures in the original *CEQ Assessment* for Ghana are a targeted school feeding program (concentration coefficient of −0.40) and the Livelihood Empowerment Against Poverty (LEAP) conditional cash transfer scheme (concentration coefficient of −0.29). The benefits of antiretroviral drugs and diabetes control go more to richer people than the poor, but neither is as concentrated as income itself.

The marginal contributions of the malaria interventions to inequality reduction are also huge. Those for indoor spraying are comparable to the largest marginal effects for any of the budget items considered in the original *CEQ Assessment*. Those for bed nets and antimalaria drugs dwarf other line items. In fact, the marginal effect for the entirety of government taxes and social spending in the *CEQ Assessment* is 0.025 for the Gini (Younger, Osei-Assibey, and Oppong, 2017). The marginal effects for antiretroviral drugs look smaller, but they are in fact similar to many of the marginal effects for social expenditures in the original *CEQ Assessment*. Only diabetes control has no perceptible effect on inequality. It is important to remember that what drives these results is the extraordinary rates of return from averted mortality through the malaria interventions, the validity of which we consider in the next section.

We do not explicitly estimate the change in headcount poverty rates when using the health outcomes approach to value in-kind health spending. We refrain from making this estimate because the monetized value of reduced mortality risk is sufficiently large to represent a substantial proportion of overall income. To make an accurate estimate of changes to poverty headcount rates would require redefining the poverty threshold inclusive of health value. Given uncertainty about what health need should be, we instead show the combined monetary income and the monetized value of health benefits by decile (figure 1-1). We observe that relative value of health benefits is more than three times income at the lowest decile and about two times income at the third decile. Monetary income and the monetized value of health become equal only at the seventh income decile. This relative distribution of monetized value from health versus income drives the significant inequality reductions we observe in table 1-5 when using the health outcomes approach.

---

[33] We do not have information on the costs of these programs, but given that public healthcare expenditure was less than 2 percent of GDP in 2012, the costs of these programs must be far less than the benefits calculated here.

[34] This might seem at odds with table 1-4, which shows somewhat higher use in richer quintiles. But the largest mortality gains are for children, and children tend to be concentrated in the poorer quintiles, equalizing the effect.

FIGURE 1-1

Final Income and Value of Health Using the Health Outcomes Method by Income Decile

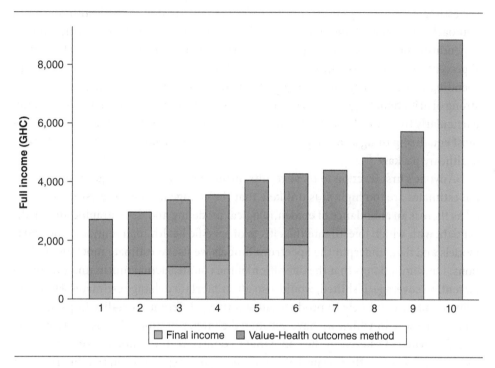

3.2 Discussion of the Health Outcomes Approach

Even though the estimated benefits in table 1-5 are enormous relative to other tax and spending programs,[35] we must start our discussion by noting that these are for just the few health interventions for which we can calculate effects on mortality probabilities. Although a comprehensive assessment of health interventions using the health outcomes approach would yield larger estimates of their value, this estimate includes both the first and second largest causes of premature death in Ghana in 2012: malaria and HIV, respectively (IHME, 2017).[36] In addition, Ghana has experienced rapid progress in reducing the burden of both diseases as malaria- and HIV-related mortality

---

[35] In principle, the mortality benefits of non-health policies should also be added to a benefit-incidence analysis using the health outcomes approach. However, given that the scope of this chapter is focused on health and the method is applied to a high-mortality, weak social safety net nation such as Ghana, we expect most health benefits to flow from health sector spending.

[36] Premature death refers to the total number of years of life lost (YLLs) per cause of death where YLLs are defined as the average number of years lost for a given death compared with what that person would have lived given Ghana's average life expectancy.

have declined by 28 percent and 43.5 percent, respectively, between 2005 and 2016. This means that the current analysis already includes a substantial proportion of Ghana's government-provided mortality gains. Nevertheless, given the overwhelming size of the estimated monetary effects, health spending measured with the health outcomes approach has a much larger effect on the income distribution than any other public expenditure or tax in Ghana. Antimalaria drugs alone reduce the Gini coefficient by 11 percentage points. So while Jamison et al.'s (2013) argument in favor of greater health spending is based solely on the high benefit/cost ratios, it is also clear that there is a strong distributional argument in favor of increased spending on certain types of health, particularly those that benefit rural areas and children. Indeed, it seems likely that the most equalizing thing a country could do is to put in place Jamison et al.'s (2013) basic healthcare package.[37]

Anyone's first reaction to these results, including our own, is to question whether the estimates are too high. It is unlikely that the change in mortality estimates is far off as there is an abundance of epidemiological modeling and demographic and medical data with which to estimate the effects of specific health interventions, and those models and data underpin the Spectrum models we use to estimate mortality reductions. One limitation is that the definition of the counterfactual minimum level of intervention coverage, if shifted, would also affect mortality change estimates. However, adjustments are unlikely to produce substantively different mortality impacts. And indeed, the way in which we have estimated changes in mortality risk may well be biased downward as even in the comparator country with the worst coverage for any specific intervention, there is probably still *some* public spending on that intervention while the appropriate counterfactual for a *CEQ Assessment* should be zero public spending.

The monetary value of mortality reduction, though, is a normative question and so open to more debate. Almost all studies to estimate the value of SMUs are done in developed countries. While estimates of the value of reduced mortality vary widely, they do not vary by more than an order of magnitude. A summary report from the OECD (2011) that provides practical guidelines for valuing reduced mortality from health, environmental, and transport policies in high-income nations notes that the US Office of Management and Budget (OMB) recommends a range of US$100 to US$1,000 per reduced SMU for all government agencies.[38] The US Environmental Protection Agency (EPA) has produced the most cost-benefit analyses of policies that affect mortality and uses a central estimate of 2007 US$750 per SMU. Other agencies in

---

[37] An explicit assessment of the equalizing effect of introducing this basic healthcare package is, however, beyond the scope of the current chapter.

[38] Throughout this chapter, we refer to the value of reduced mortality using the value of a micro-mortality risk of SMU instead of the more commonly used VSL. We translate guidance from the OECD (2011) in VSL terms to SMUs. Additional background on valuing change in mortality risk can be found in appendix 1A.2.

the US government use central estimates that vary between US$500 and US$680.[39] Given lower incomes in the European Union (EU) and the OECD overall, the OECD report also recommends a central SMU value of 2005 US$350 for the EU and 2005 US$290 for an analysis applied across the OECD. To compare these values with our analysis, valuing an SMU at 1.8 percent of GDP means that each SMU is equal to 2007 US$865.[40] The value we employ therefore is larger than the EPA's central estimate, but well within the US government's most frequently used value range for regulatory decision-making.

While ethically uncomfortable, it seems necessary for public policy decisions to adjust the value of reduced mortality risk by national income because of government budget constraints. Poor countries simply cannot spend money as if mortality reduction were as valuable as the rich countries' estimates given above. The challenge is how to make the adjustment across countries. Several authors have used cross-country regressions of SMU estimates on GDP per capita to estimate an elasticity that can then be used to predict the value of an SMU in countries for which there are no estimates. We have used the estimate of Hammitt and Robinson (2011) of 1.8 percent of annual GDP per capita for a mortality risk reduction of 0.01 percentage points at age 35.[41] Projecting that constant ratio from the income range of the countries for which we have studies that value reduced mortality risk to poor countries such as Ghana can be seen as problematic. But it is consistent with the recommendations and practice in both Jamison et al. (2013) and the OECD (2011) study, both of which apply a unit income elasticity for the value of mortality reduction to adjust across countries.

The other option would be to use estimates of SMU values from studies done in the developing world, but there are very few of those, and they produce estimates that vary by orders of magnitude from developed country estimates. One study looks at options for transport to the airport in Freetown, Sierra Leone, and finds values of reduced mortality only slightly lower than those from developed countries. But international airport users are on the wealthier end of the income distribution. Another study of WATP for improved water quality among the rural poor in Kenya finds an SMU value of $US0.077 from reduced micro-risk of child death from diarrheal disease. SMU estimates are calculated by comparing the health benefit of cleaner water against the opportunity cost of walking longer distances to obtain it. This estimate is four orders of magnitude smaller than developed country estimates, and the authors provide several reasons why those estimates are likely to be unreasonably low (Kremer et al., 2011).

Given this range of mortality risk values, we investigate how much we would need to reduce an SMU's value from 1.8 percent of GDP per capita to make aggregate

---

[39] These agencies include the Department of Transportation, Food and Drug Administration, and the Department of Homeland Security.

[40] Given US GDP per capita of $48,061 in 2007 current dollars.

[41] Other estimates are lower—Miller (2000) for example estimated a relation of 1.2—but again, not two or three orders of magnitude lower.

benefits from the health outcomes approach equal those from the average cost method. This calculation takes as given the estimated change in mortality risk from government health spending in Ghana and explores what SMU value would equalize total benefits using the health outcomes and average cost methods. Performing this analysis, we find that an SMU's value would need to be divided by 40 for the aggregate values of each method to be equal. In other words, the VSMU would need to be reduced to 0.045 percent of GDP per capita instead of 1.8 percent (2007 US$21.6) for the value of health spending to be equal under the health outcomes and average cost methods. A reduction in the value of averted mortality that large—almost 1.5 orders of magnitude—is outside of the plausible range, given valuations in the developed world. Put another way, an SMU of less than US$22 is small enough to be rejected on normative grounds. Thus, even though we acknowledge that uncertainty exists in what exact SMU should be used, our qualitative results remain the same, unless we reduce the SMU to a level too low to be credible.

Based on this robustness check and the magnitude of our results, it should be clear that even if we used the lowest value of reduced mortality risk in the OECD (2011) report and adjusted for Ghana's income, our qualitative results would not substantively change. The minimum SMU value mentioned in the OECD (2011) summary across all high-income nations is US$100, the low end of OMB guidance. Although to our knowledge no government agency has used an SMU value that low for policy analysis, if we had used that value instead of US$865, our estimates of the value of public spending for health would be reduced by almost 90 percent. However, even with that value, the three causes of death we analyze would still generate larger reductions in inequality than any other area of government expenditure. In addition, the provision of antimalaria medication alone would still represent the largest single contribution to reduced inequality among the budget items analyzed in CEQ's previous analysis in Ghana (Younger, Osei-Assibey, and Oppong, 2017).

One weakness of the health outcomes approach as applied here is that it addresses only individual health interventions for which we have readily available estimates of mortality effects. So even though the estimated benefits are sometimes quite large and represent the two largest causes of premature mortality in Ghana, they are partial. In a country where we do not have estimates for the link between publicly funded health spending and the main causes of mortality, this will be a more important limitation.

There is one further conceptual question to consider in this discussion. If government spends, say, a dollar to distribute an artemisinin tablet to a malaria patient and that tablet reduces mortality by an amount we estimate to be worth $1,000, should we count the benefit that government has transferred to the patient as $1 or $1,000? We have already mentioned that standard national income accounting would value this at its $1 cost, which is also the standard average cost approach of most incidence analyses. To justify the $1,000, we must argue that we should treat health benefits differently because more health is both utility-enhancing on its own and, crucially, allows the purchase of additional utility in the future.

Another consideration is that in the absence of government provision, patients could presumably buy artemisinin on their own for about $1. If government simply transferred cash of $1 and the patient used that dollar to buy artemisinin, we would not give government credit for the spectacular rate of return to artemisinin in an incidence analysis; we would count it as a dollar transferred. The question, then, is if government provides the good or service in-kind rather than the cash one could use to buy it, should we "credit" the government with the rate of return in an incidence analysis that aims to understand the overall distributional impact of taxation and spending? We argue that the value provided by government spending is actually two-fold: (1) the monetary value of antimalarial treatment itself and (2) the value of facilitating access to this technology when needed among patients without the information or education to do so otherwise. Finally, we note that this question would not pertain to genuine public goods provided by government because individual consumers could not buy those on their own in private markets. The case for using the health outcomes method is therefore stronger when incomplete provision of health-related public goods is a significant driver of national mortality.

In the end, the choice between the health outcomes approach and the other methods to valuing in-kind health services depends on a difficult normative question. We are persuaded that we should treat health differently, certainly for public goods, but probably also for most publicly funded health services. But we recognize that not everyone will be convinced. What our example in Ghana shows without doubt, though, is that where one comes out on this question has huge consequences for an incidence analysis. If we value health services at cost, they will have positive but modest distributional effects. If we value them based on reduced mortality, they may overwhelm the other line items in the budget and add a strong distributional argument in favor of universal provision of basic health services.

4 Summary: Choosing among the Options

We now turn to providing guidance on how and when each of these methods can be applied beyond the Ghana context we investigate here. Each of the three options presented has strengths and weaknesses and will be the best option depending on a nation's health system and the questions a particular analysis intends to answer. To judge which option is most appropriate in a given country, we describe the positive and negative attributes of each method along five dimensions: (1) conceptual validity, (2) comprehensiveness in health budget coverage, (3) ability to address the health budget in detail, (4) data requirements, and (5) ease of use.

4.1 Conceptual Validity

The motivation for this chapter is that the conceptual validity of the average cost of provision is weak. There is no reason to believe that what government spends on health services is anywhere close to the value of those services to beneficiaries. A particular concern is that government may spend money corruptly or incompetently so that the average cost of provision overstates the benefits to recipients of any healthcare provided. But it is also true that for some healthcare spending, the value in terms of life and health far outweighs what government spends to provide it.

Nevertheless, the average cost of provision does have the advantage of precedence, which includes comparability with the many existing studies on health spending incidence. In addition, the average cost of provision is consistent with the way national income accounting treats all government spending: in practice, the value of anything purchased by government is measured by its cost.

Another subtle way in which the average cost of provision approach is consistent with both national income accounting and most incidence analyses is that it ignores consumer surplus when valuing consumption of healthcare services. The other two methods we present explicitly try to capture that surplus. In national income accounting, all units of a good and service purchased are valued at the market price, so the total "value" is the marginal benefit of the last unit purchased multiplied by the quantity. In most incidence analyses, if government provides a free or subsidized good, we value that benefit at the quantity times the market price, just as in national income accounting. Both WATP and the health outcomes approach, on the other hand, estimate something closer to compensating variations, the integral under the demand curve. Given the possibility for extraordinarily large compensating variations for some healthcare services, this may well be appropriate. But using that estimate differs from existing accounting systems, which one might take as a conceptual advantage for the average cost of provision method.

Because the WATP approach relies on revealed preference it is considerably more attractive conceptually than the average cost of provision. Using people's own decisions in real circumstances to infer the value to them of the care they are buying is a natural approach for economists. But this approach assumes that people are rational consumers, and in healthcare there is significant evidence that individual behavior departs from optimality, especially for preventive care because there is not always an obvious (to the consumer) cause-and-effect relation between a healthcare choice and a health outcome. In addition, preventive care is an intertemporal and probabilistic decision: cost today versus expected future benefit. Experimental economists have shown that many people do not make utility-maximizing probabilistic or intertemporal choices. So, we might expect the WATP approach to significantly undervalue preventive care. Therefore, we recommend using this approach for curative care where its benefit is both immediate and obvious. Many surveys that form the basis of incidence studies provide such healthcare data on use of outpatient consultations and inpatient hospital stays. WATP is applicable in most practical circumstances to value these types of care despite the conceptual limitation of revealed preference.

Of course, WATP requires the ability to observe demand for publicly funded health services. This is not possible for non-rivalrous goods such as public goods and services provided by natural monopolies. Important aspects of health-related spending (not necessarily in the health sector budget) have these characteristics: provision of information about health and vector control are public goods; water and sanitation systems are natural monopolies. A revealed preference approach will not work for such services.

The conceptual validity of the health outcomes approach depends on whether we can put a monetary value on reductions in mortality probabilities.[42] If we can, then this approach responds well to the limitations of the other two approaches. It can capture the fact that healthcare spending may provide benefits that are much larger than their cost of provision, but if government provides services incompetently, this approach will capture that in the consequent lack of mortality reduction. Further, this approach does not rely on rational choice in healthcare demand. And because it does not rely on revealed preference for healthcare services, it is applicable to non-rivalrous goods and services.

While putting a monetary value on mortality is uncomfortable for some, it is a fact that governments must continuously make resource allocation decisions about health policies that affect mortality risk. Some of these choices are based on an explicit and public value for reduced mortality. And indeed, governments across the developed world use cost-benefit analysis as one input into the broader policy decision-making process. However, deciding not to use an explicit mortality valuation only means that health resources are allocated in a potentially ad-hoc way. One policy may implicitly value mortality reduction more than another (by, for example, spending more to achieve a similar result). Since these decisions are ultimately political, avoiding an explicit valuation increases the likelihood that spending to reduce mortality among the better off and more powerful will be valued more than spending on others.

There are three conceptual limitations to the health outcomes approach. The first objects to the use of consumer surplus from reduced mortality in an accounting exercise, as discussed above. The second challenges the possibility of finding a reasonable estimate of the monetary value of reduced mortality probability and/or the ethics of using such an estimate. And the third is the $1/$1,000 question: if government provides a service that costs $1 and reduces mortality probability by an amount worth $1,000, should we use $1 or $1,000 in the accounting of government-provided benefits if the beneficiary could have purchased that service herself? In any other aspect of incidence analysis, we would use $1. Each of these criticisms is addressed above in section 3. In low-income nations with a large rural population and incomplete coverage of health-related public goods the justification for using the health outcomes approach is particularly strong. This is recommended for two reasons: (1) neither of the other methods is able to include the benefits from public goods, and (2) the justification for using consumer surplus from reduced mortality is strongest when income and informational constraints limit citizens' ability to obtain needed healthcare on their own.

---

[42] The same question applies to morbidity, if that were to be included.

4.2 Comprehensiveness

CEQ Assessments aim to include as much of the budget as possible, so a comprehensive treatment of health expenditures is important. Each of the three options has the potential to be comprehensive, though in practice, data availability limits each one. Average cost of provision can certainly be comprehensive if the survey questionnaire asks about use of all types of publicly funded healthcare services. In practice, survey questions are limited mostly to consultations and hospitalizations, even though these represent the bulk of healthcare expenditures. The "insurance value" approach to average cost of provision avoids this problem by assigning benefits to all eligible beneficiaries whether they actually use publicly funded health services or not, so it is completely comprehensive.

The WATP approach is limited to private goods and services, which, again in practice, tend to be consultations and hospitalizations. The healthcare outcomes approach, as we have applied it, is limited to a few specific healthcare services that we can easily link to mortality reductions with epidemiological models. But, in principle, this approach could also compare overall mortality across time and countries with similar disease vulnerabilities to estimate the reduced risk of death associated with all publicly funded healthcare.

4.3 Detail

In principle, all three approaches can be quite detailed. We could calculate the average cost of provision for very precisely defined medical services and assign the benefits to users of those services. But the demand for administrative data on the cost of a very large number and many types of services would be daunting, something most ministries of health could not provide. And the demands on survey data would be similarly daunting. Sample sizes would need to be extremely large to have reliable samples of very specific healthcare services, and in any event these data are not collected in standard income and expenditure or health surveys. The same problems affect the WATP approach. While in principle we could estimate the demand for very precisely defined healthcare services, in practice, surveys do not collect sufficient information to do so reliably. We have seen that the health outcomes approach can be quite detailed. But in addition to the same demand for information about who actually uses publicly funded healthcare as the other two methods, the health outcomes approach also needs epidemiological models linking a specific service to mortality reductions. These models remain limited and focus, understandably, on infectious diseases.

4.4 Data Requirements

As mentioned above, to be both comprehensive and detailed, each method would require data that are not routinely available. All three methods require information on who uses publicly funded healthcare services.[43] All three generally suffer from lack of detail in this regard. The average cost of provision approach also requires information on the administrative cost of providing publicly funded healthcare services and suffer from lack of detail here, too. The health outcomes approach also needs information linking healthcare spending to mortality probabilities, something that is not available for all countries or for all healthcare services.

In preparing this chapter, we chose to limit ourselves to methods that can be applied with a single cross-sectional household survey since most CEQ studies accept that limitation. That survey clearly must ask about respondents' use of healthcare services or their affiliation with health insurance schemes (for the "insurance value" approach) in as much detail as possible. Beyond that, each method needs additional data. The average cost of provision approach needs administrative information on the cost of providing healthcare services at a level of detail consistent with the survey information. The WATP approach requires that the survey also include adequate information on factors that influence demand for publicly funded healthcare services and its substitutes, including measures of quality and the opportunity cost of using those services. This includes price, but also travel and waiting times. The health outcomes approach needs data that link specific healthcare services to reductions in mortality probabilities, which usually come from epidemiological models.

Which of these requirements is the least restrictive? Given the large number of existing studies of healthcare incidence, getting the administrative information for the average cost of provision seems to be generally feasible. Surveys certainly can ask about healthcare pricing and quality, but many do not, making the WATP approach less generally applicable. Estimates of the mortality reduction from healthcare services would seem to be the most difficult to find, but the Spectrum models are very helpful in this regard, and there is a wealth of medical and epidemiological research that remains to be tapped for such information.

4.5 Ease of Use

Assuming that one has the data required, the average cost of provision approach is clearly the easiest to apply. Estimating WATP models is more difficult. While such models are quite common, our experience is that their specification requires significant econometric expertise such that they converge to coefficient estimates consistent with their underlying behavioral models. The health outcomes approach also requires epidemiological knowledge about the drivers of disease burden in the nation under study. The Spectrum System of Policy Models was created to allow policy makers to project how health system change would impact mortality without extensive training. For this reason, the health outcomes approach can be applied without significant

---

[43] The "insurance value" approach is again an exception. It requires information only on who is covered by the insurance of interest.

specialized statistical knowledge as long as extensive health system background is also available.

4.6 Advice

We cannot make a blanket recommendation based on our experience to date. Clearly much depends on data availability, but even ignoring those limits, there are strong conceptual arguments for and against each method. Given this uncertainty, it probably makes sense to take the average cost of provision approach as a default if for no other reason than precedent. What is the strongest reason to override that default? Where government spends money corruptly or incompetently on mostly curative care services, there is a strong case to be made for switching to the WATP model. Because consumers will put little value on low-quality services, this approach will capture the lack of benefit from misspent funds.

The strongest case for the health outcomes approach occurs in nations where non-rivalrous health services are not provided universally and therefore generate a substantial impact on mortality. WATP cannot handle these, and the cost of provision may grossly underestimate the value of these services to beneficiaries. Given our stunning results in Ghana, we feel that any study that has access to reliable evidence on the impact of any healthcare expenditure on mortality probabilities should explore the health outcomes approach. Not doing so risks missing what may be by far the largest benefit government provides to its citizens.[44]

5 Insurance Value of Financial Risk Reduction

All public spending on health provides insurance to eligible beneficiaries. This is obvious in the case of social insurance schemes but is equally true of generally provided health services as well. Health services paid through general revenue require taxes from all taxpayers and provide benefits to those who draw unfortunate outcomes by falling ill. Since most people are risk averse, this insurance has value to them over and above the cost of providing health services or the value of their health outcomes because it reduces the variance of their ex-post income. As such, this approach identifies an additional value of public health spending that is ignored in benefit-incidence analysis and can be added to any of the previous methods.

We calculate the value of financial risk protection from health insurance in two steps. The first step calculates for each person a distribution of income after healthcare expenditures both with and without insurance. One way to do this is through matching methods that compare health expenditures for insured and uninsured people. In

---

[44] For practitioners interested in reproducing these estimates or applying them in a new context using this analysis as the starting point, we have posted all data and do-files used in the chapter. Additional details can be found in appendix 1A.5.

countries where only part of the population has access to publicly funded healthcare (as in a social insurance system limited to formal sector workers), we can estimate this difference by comparing the health spending of those inside and outside the system, usually using the same survey data from the *CEQ Assessment*. We show an example for Ghana in the next section. Another option is to examine changes in access to publicly funded health services over time to measure impacts on the distribution of health spending. This requires two separate surveys, one before and one after a significant change in health policy, but not necessarily a panel.

In either case, we first calculate the distribution of health expenditures for insured households compared with matched uninsured households using a quantile regression of OOP health expenditures on a dummy variable—for insurance, status at each percentile of the health expenditure distribution.[45] Second, we use a risk-averse utility function to evaluate household utility from reduced financial risk attributable to government health insurance. This approach has been used widely to estimate insurance value in the United States for Medicare (Finkelstein and McKnight, 2008) and Medicare Part D (Engelhardt and Gruber, 2011), Japan (Shigeoka, 2014), Thailand (Limwattananon et al., 2015), Ghana (Powell-Jackson et al., 2014), and Mexico (Barofsky, 2015), although the distributional consequences have not been a focus of this research. We assume that households satisfy a per period budget constraint of $c = y - m$ where y represents income, m household health spending, c non-health expenditure, and utility is determined under a constant relative risk aversion (CRRA) utility function:[46]

$$U(c) = \begin{cases} \left(\dfrac{c^{(1-\varepsilon)} - 1}{(1-\varepsilon)} \right) \ if \ \varepsilon \neq 1 \\ \ln(c) \ otherwise \end{cases}.$$

Call the distributions of health spending calculated with the quantile regressions $P_k(m)$ where $k = [1, 0]$ indexes those households with and without insurance, respectively. The difference between household income minus $P_0(m)$ or $P_1(m)$ determines the change in risk exposure from insurance. Household expected utility is

$$EU(y, \gamma, P_k(m)) = \int_0^m u(\max[y - m, \gamma y]) P_k(m) \, dm,$$

where γ represents an assumed minimum consumption value under which household expenditure does not fall irrespective of the cost of medical care. Previous studies set this limit between 20 and 40 percent of household expenditure in developed countries. But for a poor country that threshold seems far too low. It is unlikely that a poor

---

[45] Standard errors in the quantile regressions are clustered to adjust for correlation of outcomes within enumeration areas (Parente and Santos Silva, 2016).

[46] We vary the coefficient of relative risk aversion to check the sensitivity of the value of risk protection to this important parameter.

person in Ghana could spend 60 percent of her household's income on healthcare. So, in addition to the standard assumption, we also impose a lower limit on expenditures equal to Ghana's extreme poverty line.

The risk premium represents the quantity of money a risk-averse household would be willing to pay to completely insure against a given financial risk distribution. The risk premium for a household is

$$\pi_k = E_k(y-m) - CE_k = \left\{ \sum_{m=0}^{m} (\max[y-m,\gamma])P_k(m) \right\}$$
$$- \left\{ u^{-1} \left[\sum_{m=0}^{m} u(\max[y-m,\gamma])P_k(m)] \right] \right\},$$

where $E_k(y-m)$ represents the expected value of a household's non-health expenditure and CE_k is the household's certainty equivalent for the same distribution of health spending. The difference in risk premia between those with and without coverage, $\pi_1 - \pi_0$, represents the monetary value of financial risk protection provided by government health insurance.

5.1 Example Application: Financial Risk Reduction from Ghana's National Health Insurance Scheme

In Ghana, nearly all those with health insurance are covered through the NHIS. The NHIS began as separate district-based and mutual health insurance schemes and was rolled out nationally in 2004 (Duku et al., 2016). To increase access to care among the most vulnerable, statutorily the NHIS provides coverage without premiums to children under 18 years old, elderly aged 70 and above, pregnant women, and recipients of Ghana's conditional cash transfer program. In addition, formal sector workers pay into the system through payroll taxes but are exempt from paying any premium. Given that over 90 percent of total health insurance coverage in the 2012–13 GLSS is provided by the NHIS, this estimate is close to comprehensive for measuring financial risk protection from insurance coverage in Ghana. Figure 1A-1 shows health insurance coverage by income decile in Ghana in 2005 and 2012–13.

We match those without NHIS coverage to those covered using coarsened exact matching (Blackwell et al., 2009). This gives us a control group similar in a range of observable characteristics to those with coverage. Specifically, we match on the following variables: days sick in the last two weeks, days spent in the hospital in the last two weeks, the number of children under five and adults over 70 in the household, and the household's Disposable Income.[47] Because we expect income to be highly predictive of health expenditures, we divide the sample into household income quartiles, matching households covered by the NHIS to uninsured households separately for each one.[48]

---

[47] Disposable Income for CEQ is household consumption, the standard welfare variable for GLSS.
[48] NHIS coverage is defined as a household in which more than half of residents have insurance.

FIGURE 1-2

Effect of NHIS Insurance on Medical Expenditure by Income Quartile

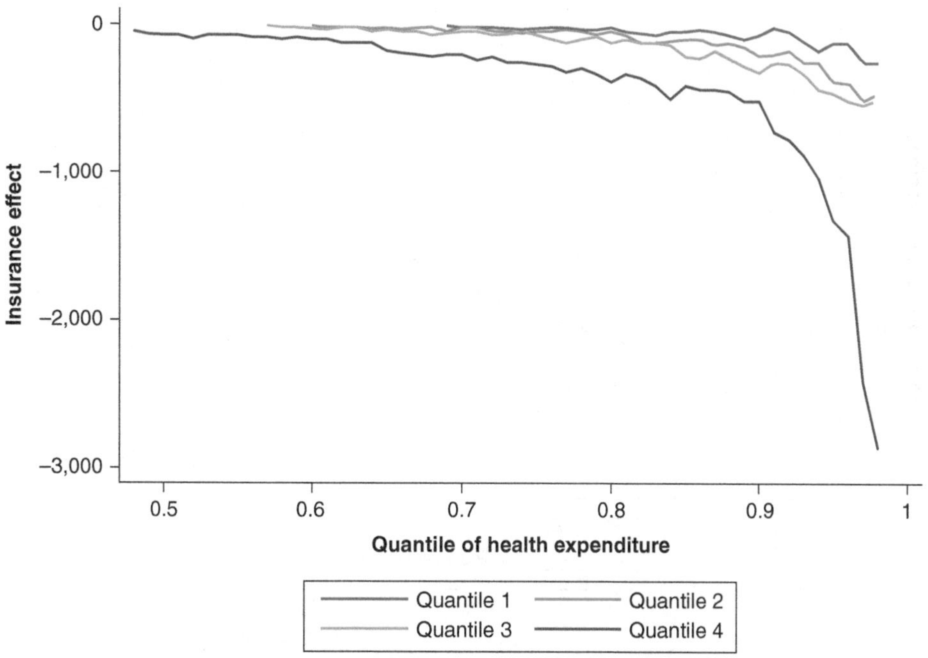

Note: "Insurance effect" refers to the difference in annual out-of-pocket health spending for households with NHIS coverage compared with those without coverage (units are 2013 GHC).

In all, then, we have $99 \times 4 = 396$ regressions, one for each percentile of the health expenditure distribution and each quartile of the income distribution.

Figure 1-2 summarizes the effect of NHIS insurance on OOP health expenditures for each income quartile using coarsened exact matching to create comparison groups without insurance. The horizontal axis is the quantile of health expenditure within each income quartile. Health spending is highly skewed within each quartile, so reductions in health spending from insurance coverage are small at lower centiles of health spending and rise rapidly above the 90th percentile, especially for the richest quartile. Even for the richest quartile, health spending in the 48th centile and below is zero, meaning that quantile treatment effects are mechanically zero below this level. For the highest spending groups, insurance provides increasingly important coverage against catastrophic expenditures due to health shocks. We should expect the benefits of NHIS financial risk protection to be skewed toward richer households even if the use of the NHIS is not so skewed because richer households would have been willing and able to spend significantly larger amounts on healthcare in the absence of NHIS insurance, making the risk reduction benefit of insurance correspondingly greater for those better-off households.

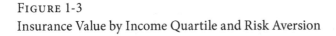

FIGURE 1-3

Insurance Value by Income Quartile and Risk Aversion

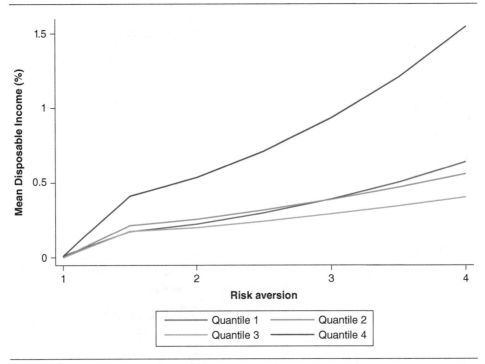

Note: The value of financial risk protection from the NHIS across income quartile is calculated using a consumption floor based on Ghana's extreme (food) poverty line adjusted for household size.

Figure 1-3 summarizes the value of financial risk protection from the NHIS by income quartile and by level of risk aversion. The consumption floor, y, is set to Ghana's extreme (food) poverty line adjusted for household size. The figure shows that financial risk protection benefits are greatest for the richest quartile, ranging from 0.5 percent to 1 percent of quartile annual income across the most plausible estimates of risk aversion. For comparison purposes, the health benefits calculated using the standard CEQ average cost approach average 10 percent, 6 percent, 3.5 percent, and 1.8 percent of quartile mean income for the poorest to richest income quartiles, so the insurance values captured in the analysis are relatively small. The value of financial risk protection increases as risk aversion levels increase, as we would expect. But the largest difference is between the top income quartile and the rest. The value of risk protection as a percent of quartile income for the top income quartile is more than double the lower three levels and also rises faster with increased risk aversion. So even though the NHIS has targeting mechanisms meant to include poorer households, the largest benefits in terms of financial risk protection go to richer households because their health spending in the absence of insurance is greater. The insurance benefits estimated when using the extreme poverty line consumption floor are more concentrated among the top three

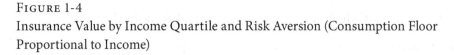

FIGURE 1-4

Insurance Value by Income Quartile and Risk Aversion (Consumption Floor Proportional to Income)

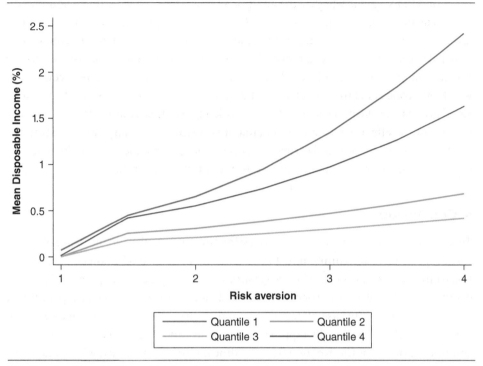

Note: The value of financial risk protection from the NHIS across income quartile is calculated using a consumption floor of 20% of household income.

income quartiles than income itself because the lowest quartile's insurance benefits are limited the most by this consumption floor assumption. Overall, however, insurance benefits with the extreme poverty consumption floor are less concentrated than income, with a concentration coefficient of 0.30 compared to an income Gini coefficient of 0.41.

In addition to using the extreme poverty line, we also calculate financial risk protection benefits using a consumption floor proportional to 20 percent of household income. This assumes that all households, including the poor, will spend up to 80 percent of their income for healthcare, which is implausible in a setting such as Ghana. However, using this assumption allows us to calculate results that are comparable to estimates of financial risk protection from insurance calculated elsewhere (Finkelstein and McKnight, 2008). Figure 1-4 shows the benefits by quartile and risk aversion as a percent of quartile income. The figure shows a similar pattern to those found with the extreme poverty line consumption floor, except benefits are larger for the poorest quartile. Consequently, the benefits are also relatively progressive compared with income with a concentration coefficient of 0.19.

5.2 Discussion of Methods to Value Financial Risk Reduction

Because this approach does not need to be traded off against the others, the only consideration in using it is whether the additional effort required to estimate households' counterfactual health spending is worthwhile. In a country such as Ghana, where there is one primary health insurance system and plausible comparison groups can be constructed because insurance eligibility criteria include multiple groups across the income distribution, this approach is feasible. It would be more challenging for a country in which everyone is insured or substantial differences exist between insured and uninsured groups (e.g., formal versus informal workers). Another consideration is whether the size of the effect is relevant. In Ghana, it is. While not as large as the estimated health benefits from the standard average cost method, the financial risk reduction benefits are of the same order of magnitude and so merit consideration.

6 Conclusion

This chapter compares three methods for estimating the benefits and incidence of health spending, while also defining how to measure the incidence of financial risk protection from government-provided health insurance. The average cost approach is the most common way to measure the benefits and incidence of government health spending. It is useful because of its ease of calculation and clarity. Most developing nations have sufficiently detailed nationally representative surveys and national health spending accounts data such that the average cost of healthcare can be calculated widely and compared across nations and over time. In addition, these methods are accessible to researchers and government officials without extensive training in econometrics. But the government's cost of providing a service may have little to do with its actual value to beneficiaries. Governments may spend more than a service is worth if its provision is corrupt, inefficient, or misguided. At the same time, the service may be worth much more than what government spends if it has an appreciable effect on beneficiary health, something that has important and large intrinsic value. Each of these possibilities leads us to consider other options for valuing in-kind health services.

The first, the WATP approach, is conceptually attractive for an economist because it relies on revealed preference. Especially in cases where we suspect that government is spending far more than a service is worth, low WATP for those services will flag the problem and perhaps give a better estimate of the service's value.

The method does have limitations. Conceptually, we can apply it only if we can estimate a demand function for in-kind services, which rules out any services that are public goods. When using income and expenditure surveys, as a CEQ Assessment does, that also excludes most types of preventive care. Practically, the demand estimation requires considerably more work than the average cost method. In our particular example of Ghana, that extra work does not seem worthwhile as the results for the two methods are not too different. But that is just one example. We recommend the method's use for situations in which one suspects large differences between government costs and patient benefits due to corruption, inefficiency, or incompetence, and especially if the analysis is most interested in valuing curative care only.

The second method we consider, health outcomes, takes a much different approach. It estimates the effect of government-funded health interventions on mortality probabilities and then monetizes those changes based on studies that look at how much money people will accept (pay) in exchange for small increases (reductions) in the probability of death.[49] This approach also estimates benefits rather than costs to government, but without relying on observed WATP for care. There are good reasons to be suspicious of WATP estimates for healthcare, especially preventive healthcare. People may have difficulty understanding the effect of healthcare services on their mortality and so undervalue them considerably. It is also true that the severe liquidity constraints common in developing countries cause people to shun expenditures that offer future, uncertain benefits when their focus is survival for themselves and their children today.

Unlike the WATP for healthcare we calculate, our estimates for health benefits are sometimes radically different from cost of provision estimates. Indeed, the benefits to malaria control and treatment are so large that they swamp the distributional consequences of any other budget line or combination of budget lines, and this despite the fact that we are able to analyze only a few publicly funded health interventions (albeit the two largest causes of premature death). If this is the right approach, it is of substantial importance for distributional analysis. Unfortunately, whether this is the right approach depends on a normative argument about how to value changes in mortality probabilities in developing countries. However, for our estimates of the value of malaria medication to be similar to those for the average cost method, we would need to reduce the value we place on reduced mortality by about two orders of magnitude: an implausibly low valuation. For bed nets provision on its own, we would need to reduce the value of mortality by about one order of magnitude. Clearly, our normative judgment (and most estimates of the value of mortality risk reduction) would need to be far off the mark for the health outcomes approach to be irrelevant.

There is a conceptual challenge to this approach: it is not consistent with how national income accounting treats publicly funded services. To accept the health outcomes approach, we must argue that health is different because of its intrinsic importance and so should be treated differently in our accounting.

In practical terms, the health outcomes approach is limited to instances for which we have ready access to estimates of the effect of publicly funded health interventions. The Spectrum models are very helpful in this regard, can be run for all developing nations, and include many but not all causes of death. Even though this approach requires more effort than the average cost approach, its results are so dramatic that the effort seems well worthwhile.

---

[49]These valuations are, to be clear, revealed preference of WATP for changes in mortality risk (instead of healthcare services) among adults in the developed world.

Lastly, we estimate the insurance value of reduced financial risk that comes from government health spending. This is an add-on to the other approaches discussed here because it is not valuing health services per se, but rather financial risk. The method does require an arbitrary assumption about risk aversion, but for a wide range of such assumptions, we find that the benefits are similar in value to average costs (and WATP). The effect of financial risk protection on the income distribution is somewhat less than average cost because its benefits tend to go more to richer households that spend more on healthcare in the absence of public funding.

Practically, our approach to financial risk requires us to match insured with un-insured households to compare their health expenditures. Ghana is a good case for such matching because the NHIS does not apply to everyone, but it is also not obviously cor-related with income. If the matching is feasible, this method is also worthwhile in an incidence analysis.

Acknowledgments

Thanks to Ian Heffernan for providing valuable research assistance for this research project. We also thank Henry Aaron, Gary Burtless, Sean Higgins, Carol Levin, Nora Lustig, Eric Osei-Assibey, John Quattrochi, and Marcia Weaver for helpful comments and suggestions. This research project was conducted for the Commitment to Equity (CEQ) Institute at Tulane University and was made possible by the generous support of the Bill & Melinda Gates Foundation. For more information on CEQ, visit www.commitmentoequity.org.

References

Acharya, A., S. Masset Edoardo, F. Taylor, E. Massett, A. Satija, M. Burke, and S. Ebrahim. 2013. *The Impact of Health Insurance Schemes for the Informal Sector in Low-and Middle-Income Coun-tries: A Systematic Review.* Policy Research Working Paper. Washington, DC: World Bank.

Akerlof, G. 1995. "The Market for 'Lemons': Quality Uncertainty and the Market Mechanism. In Saul Estrin and Alan Marin, eds, *Essential Readings in Economics.* London: Palgrave Macmillan.

Alam, K., and A. Mahal 2014. "Economic Impacts of Health Shocks on Households in Low and Middle Income Countries: A Review of the Literature." *Globalization and Health* 10, no. 21, pp. 1–18.

Arrow, K. J. 1963. "Uncertainty and the Welfare Economics of Medical Care." *American Economic Review* 53, pp. 941–73.

Avenir Health. 2018. *Spectrum Manual: Spectrum System of Policy Models.* Glastonbury, CT. http://avenirhealth.org/Download/Spectrum/Manuals/SpectrumManualE.pdf.

Barofsky, J. 2015. "Estimating the Impact of Health Insurance in Developing Nations: Evidence from Mexico's Seguro Popular." Cambridge, MA: Harvard School of Public Health.

Bernheim, D. B. 1987. "The Economic Effects of Social Security: Toward a Reconciliation of The-ory and Measurement." *Journal of Public Economics* 33, pp. 273–304.

Blackwell, M., S. M. Iacus, G. King, and G. Porro. 2009. "cem: Coarsened Exact Matching in Stata." *Stata Journal* 9, no. 4, pp. 524–46.

Bound, J., J. Berry Cullen, A. Nichols, and L. Schmidt. 2004. "The Welfare Implications of Increasing Disability Insurance Benefit Generosity." *Journal of Public Economics* 88, no. 12, pp. 2487–514.

Cohen, J., and P. Dupas. 2010. "Free Distribution or Cost-Sharing? Evidence from a Randomized Malaria Prevention Experiment." *The Quarterly Journal of Economics* 25, no. 1, pp. 1–45.

Cameron, A. C., and P. K. Trivedi. 2005. *Microeconometrics: Methods and Applications.* Cambridge: Cambridge University Press.

Cotlear, D., S. Nagpal, O. Smith, A. Tandon, and R. Cortez. 2015. *Going Universal: How 24 Developing Countries Are Implementing Universal Health Coverage from the Bottom Up.* Washington, DC: World Bank.

Cutler, D. M., and E. Richardson. 1998. "The Value of Health: 1970–1990." *American Economic Review* v. 88, no. 2, pp. 97–100.

Dagsvik, J. K., and A. Karlström. 2005. "Compensating Variation and Hicksian Choice Probabilities in Random Utility Models That Are Nonlinear in Income." *Review of Economic Studies* 72, no. 1, pp. 57–76.

Das, J., and J. Hammer. 2005. "Which Doctor? Combining Vignettes and Item Response to Measure Clinical Competence." *Journal of Development Economics* 78, no. 2, pp. 348–83.

Das, J., A. Holla, V. Das, M. Mohanan, D. Tabak, and B. Chan. 2012. "In Urban and Rural India, a Standardized Patient Study Showed Low Levels of Provider Training and Huge Quality Gaps." *Health Affairs* 31, no. 12, pp. 2774–84.

Duku, S., F. Asenso-Boadi, E. Nketiah-Amponsah, and D. Kojo Arhinful. 2016. "Utilization of Healthcare Services and Renewal of Health Insurance Membership: Evidence of Adverse Selection in Ghana." *Health Economics Review* 6, no. 43, pp. 1–12.

Enami, Ali, Sean Higgins, and Nora Lustig. 2022. "Allocating Taxes and Transfers and Constructing Income Concepts: Completing Sections A, B, and C of the *CEQ Master Workbook,*" chap. 6 in *Commitment to Equity Handbook: Estimating the Impact of Fiscal Policy on Inequality and Poverty,* 2nd ed., Vol. 1, edited by Nora Lustig. Brookings Institution Press and CEQ Institute, Tulane University. Free online version available at www.commitmentoequity.org.

Engelhardt, G. V., and J. Gruber. 2011. "Medicare Part D and the Financial Protection of the Elderly." *American Economic Journal: Economic Policy* 3, no. 4, pp. 77–102.

Feldstein, M. 1973. "The Welfare Loss of Excessive Health Insurance." *Journal of Political Economy* 81, pp. 251–80.

Finkelstein, A., and R. McKnight. 2008. "What Did Medicare Do? The Initial Impact of Medicare on Mortality and Out-of-Pocket Medical Spending." *Journal of Public Economics* 92, no. 7, pp. 1644–68.

Gatimu, S. M., B. W. Milimo, and M. S. Sebastian. 2016. "Prevalence and Determinants of Diabetes among Older Adults in Ghana." *BMC Public Health* 16, no. 1174, pp. 1–12.

Gauthier, B., and W. Wane. 2008. "Leakage of Public Resources in the Health Sector: An Empirical Investigation of Chad." *Journal of African Economies* 18, no. 1, pp. 52–83.

Gertler, P., and J. van der Gaag. 1990. *The Willingness to Pay for Medical Care: Evidence from Two Developing Countries.* Baltimore, MD: Johns Hopkins University Press.

Gertler, P., L. Locay, and W. Sanderson. 1987. "Are User Fees Regressive?: The Welfare Implications of Health Care Financing Proposals in Peru." *Journal of Econometrics*, 36, no. 1, pp. 67–88.

Greenstone, M., and B. K. Jack. 2015. "Envirodevonomics: A Research Agenda for an Emerging Field. *Journal of Economic Literature* 53, no. 1, pp. 5–42.

GSS (Ghana Statistical Service). 2014. *Ghana Living Standards Survey, Round 6 (GLSS-6): Main Report.* https://www.statsghana.gov.gh/gssmain/fileUpload/Living%20conditions/GLSS6 _Main%20Report.pdf.

———. 2018. *Ghana Population and Housing Census 2010.* http://ghana.opendataforafrica.org /vbbbbb/population-and-housing-census-of-ghana-2010 (accessed 03-03-2018).

GSS (Ghana Statistical Service), GHS (Ghana Health Service), and ICF International. 2015. *Ghana Demographic and Health Survey 2014.* Rockville, MD: Authors. https://dhsprogram.com/pubs /pdf/fr307/fr307.pdf.

Hall, R. E., and C. I. Jones. 2007. "The Value of Life and the Rise in Health Spending." *The Quarterly Journal of Economics* 122, no. 1, pp. 39–72.

Hamilton, M., G. Mahiane, E. Werst, R. Sanders, et al. 2017. "Spectrum-Malaria: A User-Friendly Projection Tool for Health Impact Assessment and Strategic Planning by Malaria Control Programmes in Sub-Saharan Africa." *Malaria Journal* 16, no. 1, p. 68. https://doi.org/10.1186 /s12936-017-1705-3.

Hammitt, J. K., and L. A. Robinson. 2011. "The Income Elasticity of the Value per Statistical Life: Transferring Estimates between High and Low Income Populations." *Journal of Benefit-Cost Analysis* 2, no. 1, pp. 1–29.

Herriges, J. A., and C. L. Kling. 1999. "Nonlinear Income Effects in Random Utility Models." *Review of Economics and Statistics* 81, no. 1, pp. 62–72.

Jamison, D. T., L. H. Summers, G. Alleyne, K. J. Arrow, S. Berkley, A. Binagwaho, . . . and G. Ghosh. 2013. "Global Health 2035: A World Converging within a Generation." The Lancet 382, no. 9908, pp. 1898–955.

Kremer, M., J. Leino, E. Miguel, and A. P. Zwane. 2011. "Spring Cleaning: Rural Water Impacts, Valuation, and Property Rights Institutions." *Quarterly Journal of Economics* 126, no. 1, pp. 145–205.

Korenromp, E. L., B. Gobet, E. Fazito, J. Lara, L. Bollinger, and J. Stover. 2015. "Impact and Cost of the HIV/AIDS National Strategic Plan for Mozambique, 2015–2019—Projections with the Spectrum/Goals Model." *PloS One* 10, no. 11, e0142908.

Korenromp, E., G. Mahiané, M. Hamilton, C. Pretorius, R. Cibulskis, J. Lauer, . . . and O. J. Briët. 2016. "Malaria Intervention Scale-Up in Africa: Effectiveness Predictions for Health Programme Planning Tools, Based on Dynamic Transmission Modelling. *Malaria Journal* 15, no. 1, pp. 1–14.

Laibson, D. 1997. "Golden Eggs and Hyperbolic Discounting." *Quarterly Journal of Economics* 112, no. 2, pp. 443–78.

Lakin, J. M. 2010. "The End of Insurance? Mexico's Seguro Popular, 2001–2007." *Journal of Health Politics, Policy and Law* 35, no. 3, pp. 313–52.

León, G., and E. Miguel. 2017. "Risky Transportation Choices and the Value of a Statistical Life." *American Economic Journal: Applied Economics* 9, no. 1, pp. 202–28.

Limwattananon, S., S. Neelsen, O. O'Donnell, P. Prakongsai, V. Tangcharoensathien, E. Van Doorslaer, and V. Vongmongkol. 2015. "Universal Coverage with Supply-Side Reform: The

Impact on Medical Expenditure Risk and Utilization in Thailand." *Journal of Public Economics* 121, pp. 79–94.

Lindauer, D., and B. Nunberg, eds. 1994. *Public Sector Wage and Employment Policies in Sub-Saharan Africa*, Washington, DC: The World Bank.

Lustig, N., ed. 2022. *Commitment to Equity Handbook: Estimating the Impact of Fiscal Policy on Inequality and Poverty*, 2nd. ed., 2 Vols. Brookings Institution Press and CEQ Institute, Tulane University. Free online version available at www.commitmentoequity.org.

Lustig, N. and S. Higgins. 2022. "The *CEQ Assessment*: Measuring the Impact of Fiscal Policy on Inequality and Poverty," chap. 1 in *Commitment to Equity Handbook: Estimating the Impact of Fiscal Policy on Inequality and Poverty*, 2nd ed., Vol. 1, edited by Nora Lustig. Brookings Institution Press and CEQ Institute, Tulane University. Free online version available at www.commitmentoequity.org.

Mani, A., S. Mullainathan, E. Shafir, and J. Zhao. 2013. "Poverty Impedes Cognitive Function." *Science* 341, no. 6149, pp. 976–80.

McFadden, Daniel. 1981. "Econometric Models of Probabilistic Choice." In *Structural Analysis of Discrete Data: With Econometric Applications*, edited by C. Manski and D. McFadden. Cambridge, MA: MIT Press.

Measure DHS. 2018. STATcompiler, The DHS Program. https://www.statcompiler.com/en/ (accessed 04/10/2018).

———. 2019. Service Provision Assessment Survey Overview. https://dhsprogram.com/methodology /Survey-Types/SPA.cfm (accessed 02/13/2022).

Miller, T. R. 2000. "Variations between Countries in Values of Statistical Life." *Journal of Transport Economics and Policy* 34, no. 2, pp. 169–88.

Murphy, K. M., and R. H. Topel. 2006. "The Value of Health and Longevity." *Journal of Political Economy*, 114, no. 5, pp. 871–904.

National Population Commission [Nigeria] and ICF International. 2014. *Nigeria Demographic and Health Survey 2013*. Abuja, Nigeria, and Rockville, Maryland: Authors. https://dhsprogram .com/pubs/pdf/fr293/fr293.pdf.

Nguyen, H. T., Y. Rajkotia, and H. Wang. 2011. "The Financial Protection Effect of Ghana National Health Insurance Scheme: Evidence from a Study in Two Rural Districts." *International Journal for Equity in Health* 10, no. 1, p. 1–12.

OECD. 2011. "Valuing Mortality Risk Reductions in Regulatory Analysis of Environmental, Health and Transport Policies: Policy Implications. Paris: OECD Publishing. www.oecd.org/env /policies/vsl.

Parente, P. M. D. C., and J. M. C. Santos Silva. 2016. "Quantile Regression with Clustered Data." *Journal of Econometric Methods* 5, no. 1, pp. 1–15.

Powell-Jackson, T., K. Hanson, C. J. Whitty, and E. K. Ansah. 2014. "Who Benefits from Free Healthcare? Evidence from a Randomized Experiment in Ghana." *Journal of Development Economics* 107, issue C, pp. 305–19.

Samuelson, P. 1969. "Pure Theory of Public Expenditure and Taxation." In *Public Economics: An Analysis of Public Production and Consumption and Their Relations to the Private Sectors*, edited by J. Margolis and H. Guitton. New York: MacMillan.

Sen, A. 1988. "Freedom of Choice: Concept and Content." *European Economic Review* 32, no. 2–3, pp. 269–94.

Shigeoka, H. 2014. "The Effect of Patient Cost Sharing on Utilization, Health, and Risk Protection." *American Economic Review* 104, no. 7, pp. 2152–84.

Small, K. A., and H. S. Rosen. 1981. "Applied Welfare Economics with Discrete Choice Models." *Econometrica: Journal of the Econometric Society* 49, no. 1, pp. 105–30.

Soares, Sergei. 2019. "The Market Value of Public Education. A Comparison of Three Valuation Methods." CEQ Working Paper 71, Commitment to Equity Institute, Tulane University.

Stover, J., T. Brown, and M. Marston. 2012. "Updates to the Spectrum/Estimation and Projection Package EPP Model to Estimate HIV Trends for Adults and Children." *Sex Transmitted Infections* 88, suppl. 2, pp. i11–i16.

UNAIDS. 2019. "People Living with HIV Receiving ART (%)." https://aidsinfo.unaids.org/ (accessed 06/09/2019).

Viscusi, K., and J. Aldy. 2003. "The Value of a Statistical Life: A Critical Review of Market Estimates throughout the World." *Journal of Risk and Uncertainty* 27, no. 1, pp. 5–76.

WHO. 2017. *World Malaria Report 2017.* Geneva: World Health Organization; 2017.

——. 2018. Global Health Observatory Data Repository. who.int/gho/data/?theme=main&vid=60630 (accessed 03-06-2018).

——. 2010. *The World Health Report: Health Systems Financing—The Path to Universal Coverage.* Executive Summary (No. WHO/IER/WHR/10.1). Geneva: World Health Organization.

World Bank Development Indicators. 2018a. "Domestic General Government Health Expenditure as Percentage of GDP." https://data.worldbank.org/indicator/SH.XPD.GHED.GD.ZS?locations=XM-XN (accessed 04/19/2019).

——. 2018b. "General Government Final Consumption Expenditure as Percentage of GDP." https://data.worldbank.org/indicator/NE.CON.GOVT.ZS?locations=XN-XM (accessed 04/19/2019).

Younger, Stephen D. 2022. "Box 1-1: Ignoring Behavioral Responses to Tax and Expenditure Policies," chap. 1 in *Commitment to Equity Handbook: Estimating the Impact of Fiscal Policy on Inequality and Poverty*, 2nd ed., Vol. 1, edited by Nora Lustig (Brookings Institution Press and CEQ Institute, Tulane University). Free online version available at www.commitmentoequity.org.

Younger, Stephen D., Eric Osei-Assibey, and Felix Oppong. 2017. "Fiscal Incidence in Ghana." *Review of Development Economics* 21, no. 4, pp. e47–e66.

Appendix 1A

1 Using the Spectrum Policy Models Software

Spectrum is a system of policy models used to examine the impact of changes in health interventions for use by researchers and policymakers. Each projection starts with results from an underlying country-specific demographic model that projects population change using data on fertility, mortality, and migration rates. The demographic model comes prepopulated with country-specific data and population estimates from the United Nations Population Division. Built on these demographic projections, disease-specific epidemiological models are used to estimate mortality from multiple causes of death, including malaria, HIV, and a range of child, maternal health, and non-communicable diseases. In our application, the System of Policy Models is used to project how disease-specific mortality rates will change across the age distribution when health intervention coverage rates change from their current level to their counterfactual minimum.

Each disease model combines our understanding of transition probabilities through different disease stages with measures of intervention efficacy using the scientific literature. Country-specific data on underlying prevalence and disease type, environmental conditions that lead to transmission (for example, the entomological infection rate for malaria which measures exposure to infectious mosquitoes throughout the year) are also used. Intervention coverage data come from nationally representative surveys such as the Demographic and Health Surveys. Data sources are updated annually or as frequently as nationally representative surveys are conducted in a given country, while research literature is reviewed frequently as well to ensure efficacy parameters are up to date.

To implement projections for changes to HIV-, malaria-, and diabetes-related mortality, we estimated mortality rates first using all health intervention rates set at their Spectrum-provided current level. Modules used are DemProj, the base model that reflects population change, the AIDS Impact Model (AIM), which projects the consequences of the HIV epidemic including AIDS deaths by age and sex, and Malaria, a module that permits countries with endemic malaria to project over-time malaria case load and malaria-attributable mortality, in three distinct age groups. The malaria transmission model underlying Spectrum's estimates is based on OpenMalaria, which was developed by researchers at the Swiss Institute of Tropical Hygiene and Medicine and simulates the dynamics of malaria transmission and epidemiology in mosquito and human populations, as well as the effects of malaria control. These statistical impact functions[50] are combined with a database of malaria endemicity and epidemiology at the subnational level to project future burden.

After mortality rates at current coverage are calculated, health intervention coverage levels are then changed one by one to reflect the counterfactual minimum coverage level, and intervention-related age-specific mortality rates are again calculated. The difference in projected age-specific mortality rates when intervention coverage changes from current to counterfactual minimum levels is used as the change in mortality attributable to government spending. Since the Spectrum software allows mortality rate projections only in the future, intervention coverage levels are changed in year 2018 and the effect is taken from the first year after that change occurs—2019.[51]

---

[50] As described in Korenromp et al. (2016).

[51] See Avenir Health (2018) for a detailed introduction on how to use the projection system and the contents of each module.

The counterfactual minimum level of health intervention coverage is estimated using DHS survey waves across other West African nations from 2011 to 2015 for malaria and diabetes interventions and UNAIDS for antiretroviral therapy coverage rates. The countries included are Benin, Togo, Ivory Coast, Guinea, Liberia, Sierra Leone, and Nigeria. For example, minimum reported use of ITNs for children five years of age and below among Ghana's peer nations is 16.6 percent using the Nigeria 2013 DHS survey (National Population Commission and ICF International, 2014). This compares with a rate of 55 percent in Ghana. In addition, UNAIDS reports that the minimum ART coverage rate among these West African nations is Liberia in 2013 with a coverage rate of 13 percent, compared with a rate of 65 percent in Ghana (UNAIDS, 2019).

To finish the valuations of change in mortality, data on the distribution of the population in Ghana by age group and life expectancy by age are needed. The former is obtained from the Ghana Population and Housing Census of 2010 (GSS 2018). To calculate total population in each age group in 2013, it is assumed that the distribution of population across age groups is constant from 2010 to 2013, and the GSS's total population projection for 2013 is used to estimate population in 2013 by age group (GSS 2018). Data on life expectancy in Ghana by five-year age group is obtained from the WHO's Global Health Observatory (WHO 2018).

2   Financial Risk Protection with Consumption Floor Proportional to Income

Figure 1A-1 displays the percentage of the population by income decile that is covered by the NHIS in both 2005 and 2013. Although in 2005 there was a clear income gradient for insurance access, by 2013 access was approximately equal across the income distribution.

Figure 1-4 shows the values of insurance protection from health shock risk through the NHIS across income quartiles and levels of risk aversion, where the consumption floor is assumed proportional to household income. The results show, as expected, that the value of insurance increases with risk aversion. In contrast to using the extreme poverty line consumption floor, this figure shows that when a consumption floor proportional to income is used, the value of insurance is relatively progressive as benefits (as a percentage of quartile mean disposable income) are largest for the lowest income group.

3   Concentration Curves by Valuation Method

This section of the appendix presents concentration curves for the benefits estimated with each health valuation method in the chapter. Comparing concentration curves is more general than comparing concentration coefficients (the area between the curve and the 45-degree line), though in these examples, the information is qualitatively similar.

FIGURE 1A-1
Insurance Coverage by Decile (Ghana), GLSS 2004–05 and 2012–13

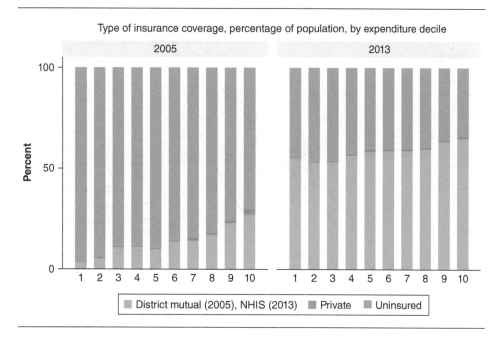

Figure 1A-2 shows concentration curves for the average cost method. It shows that these methods produce a more progressive estimate of healthcare's value than the compensating variation WATP method because WATP increases with income, but both methods show a progressive distribution of benefits. Figure 1A-3 shows concentration curves for each health intervention analyzed in the health outcomes approach. It indicates that interior spraying for mosquitoes is the most progressive public expenditure of this group, showing that, for example, almost 70 percent of the benefits from IRS goes to the bottom two income quintiles. The benefits from ITNs also goes disproportionately to the poor, although less than IRS, because this program focuses on families with young children. The distribution of benefits from antimalarial drugs is spread evenly across the population, though as noted in the chapter text, the need (as measured by malaria incidence) is greater among poorer households. The benefits of antiretroviral drugs and, especially, diabetes care go more to richer households, though both are still distributed more equally than income itself. Figure 1A-4 shows the concentration coefficients for two estimates of financial risk protection using a consumption floor proportional to income. Specifically, one scenario uses a high level of risk aversion ($\rho = 4$) and low consumption floor of $\gamma = 10$ percent, which would maximize the estimate of insurance value. The other scenario uses a moderate level of risk aversion ($\rho = 2.5$) and higher consumption floor $\gamma = 20$ percent. Even with these changes we see that the distributional effects are similar,

FIGURE 1A-2

Concentration Curves for Outpatient Care Value

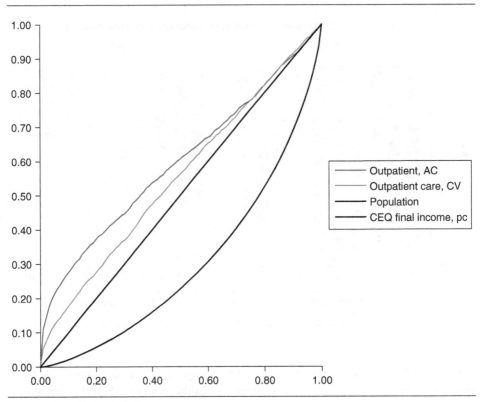

Source: GLSS-6 and authors' calculations.

Notes: Observations ranked by Final Income as defined by CEQ but *excluding* any benefits from public healthcare spending. AC = average cost approach; CV = compensating variation.

generating impacts that are more equal than income, but not absolutely progressive. In contrast, the concentration curve of insurance value with moderate risk aversion and a consumption floor γ equal to the extreme poverty line shows that benefits to the bottom 20 percent are lower than their proportion of income. However, the value is greater than their proportion of income for the middle 60 percent of the income distribution.

4 Using Willingness and Ability to Pay by Matching Publicly Funded Health Services to Private Health Services

A straightforward approach to valuing healthcare services is to look at what people actually pay for healthcare services at private providers of comparable quality to the public services we want to value. This also relies on revealed preference: the service is obviously worth at least as much to users as they are willing to pay for it in a private market. Soares (2019) uses this approach for schooling in Brazil.

FIGURE 1A-3

Concentration Curves for Health Outcome Benefits by Intervention Type

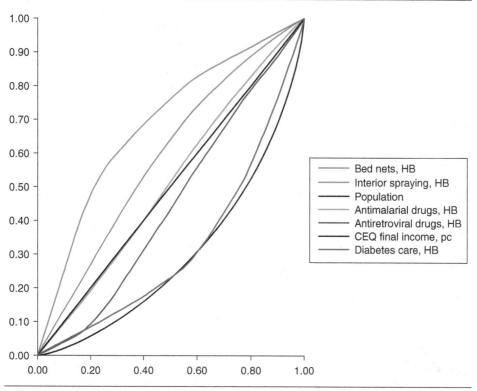

Legend:
- Bed nets, HB
- Interior spraying, HB
- Population
- Antimalarial drugs, HB
- Antiretroviral drugs, HB
- CEQ final income, pc
- Diabetes care, HB

Source: GLSS-6 and authors' calculations.

Notes: Observations ranked by "Final Income" as defined by CEQ but *excluding* any benefits from public healthcare spending. HB = health benefit; pc = per capita.

There are two challenges for this approach, one conceptual, the other practical. Conceptually, we need to control for different quality of services. We can do so by matching public to private services with one or more indicators of the quality of the service. Practically, we need data on the quality of services at public and private facilities and the fees charged at the private facilities. Relatively few surveys used for a *CEQ Assessment* include this information, which should be collected at the facilities level rather than at the household level. But the Demographic and Health Surveys' Service Provision Assessments, available in 15–20 countries, do provide the necessary facilities data (Measure DHS, 2019). There may be other special-purpose surveys in other countries done on an ad-hoc basis.[52]

---

[52] Unfortunately, the World Bank's Service Delivery Indicators surveys do not collect information on fees.

FIGURE 1A-4

Concentration Curves for Financial Risk Protection

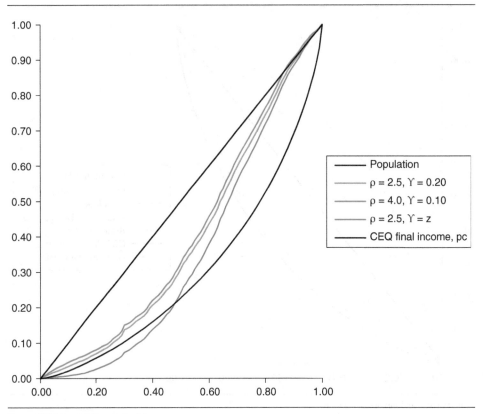

Source: GLSS-6 and authors' calculations

Notes: ρ = coefficient of relative risk aversion; γ = is percentage of household income used as a lower limit for nonhealth expenditures, except when γ = z, which indicates use of the extreme poverty line (792 cedis per adult equivalent per year) as the lower limit.
Observations ranked by "Final Income" as defined by CEQ but *excluding* any benefits from public healthcare spending.
pc = per capita.

Once facilities are matched, we would simply use the matching private facility's price to estimate the value of the matching public facility's service. These values can then be assigned to users of public health facilities, perhaps disaggregated by geographic area and type of facility.

4.1 Example Application

Although there has not been an example in the health sector of this method, it has been used in education to estimate the value of in-kind subsidies for schooling in Brazil. In the education context, there are clearer substitutes between private and public services than in health. However, there does exist a series of surveys called Service Provision

Assessments collected through the Demographic and Health Surveys that may be used for this purpose (Measure DHS, 2019). One exists for Ghana from 2002, outside of our timeframe of interest here.

4.2 Discussion of Public/Private Matching

The advantage of the matching approach is that, like the discrete choice demand estimation, it relies on patients' actual choices. It is also much easier to implement. An important disadvantage is that the data on facility quality and prices may not be available in many countries. In addition, because this approach relies on demand for private services, it is not applicable to health spending on public goods or natural monopolies, services that have some of the highest returns for public spending.

5 Data and Do-Files for Replication

The do-files and data required to replicate this analysis in its entirety have been posted in the CEQ Data Center on Fiscal Redistribution (part V, section 6.b of this Handbook, online only). These serve both to validate the results shown here and to provide a starting point for similar analysis to be undertaken in another country using the five criteria we describe in section 4 to assess which method should be used and based on that nation's health system structure.

Chapter 2

THE MARKET VALUE OF PUBLIC EDUCATION
A Comparison of Three Valuation Methods

Sergei Soares

Introduction

Public education has become widespread in most societies. Apart from failed states or nations in throes of civil war, the state in almost all countries provides schooling to children. This service is usually provided free of cost to families.[1] According to UNESCO, 80 percent of the world's 184 nations for which it has education statistics have laws that require the state to provide eight or more years of free education to their children. It is not, however, free of cost to the state. Again according to UNESCO, the median public education expenditure in those countries is close to 5 percent of GDP.[2] Worldwide school attendance is about 91 percent for primary education and 83 percent for secondary. Thus, that publicly provided education is both an important public expenditure and a relevant in-kind transfer, often to the poorest households. It is important to value this public effort adequately.

In this chapter, I compare three methods for valuing education services and their distributive impact. For each method, I calculate the total value of public educational services by level as well as their impact on income inequality, as measured by the Gini and concentration coefficients. I apply each method to Brazil, a country for which educational, expenditure, and income distribution data are both good quality and easily available.

By far the most common approach in recent times has been to value education according to its cost to the public sector. An OECD (2008) report on income distribution makes this clear:

---

[1] In some African countries, there are still school fees for public primary education.
[2] Data from UNESCO Institute for Statistics website: http://data.uis.unesco.org/.

Imputation of public educational expenditures to individuals based on actual use requires, first, determining whether or not an individual is participating in different levels of the educational system; and second, increasing the income of the household where they live by the average public spending per student at the relevant educational level. (p. 235)

The majority of the recent literature, such Atkinson (2005) and the *Commitment to Equity Handbook* (Lustig, 2022), follows this approach, which is to take how much it costs the state to provide the educational services and split it up evenly among the families with children in the public education system. I use this cost of provision method as well.

The second method I use to value educational services involves taking the labor market as the measure of their worth. The value of an additional year of education is calculated based on how much more individuals will earn if they study an additional year. This approach is based upon Sergio Urzua's proposal in chapter 3 of Volume 2 of this Handbook.

The third method is to use the market for private educational services to measure the value of public education services. This involves matching private educational expenditures, paid for by students or their parents, with equivalent public education services. The two are matched using test scores, which of course means that this approach presupposes that test score data are a good proxy for schooling quality.

None of the three methods is perfect; in fact, all suffer from serious conceptual problems, to be detailed below. However, I believe that looking at the results from all three may allow a reasonably complete picture of the distributive and welfare impacts of education.

1 First Method: Schooling Is Worth What It Costs the State to Provide It

The cost of provision approach has several advantages.

First, it is easy. To calculate the value of schooling and monetize it, take the cost per student at the lowest level of aggregation possible and divide it up equally among the families whose children are enrolled in public education, weighted by the number of children enrolled by family, of course. This value can then be added to the per capita income of households and all the distributive statistics can then be calculated.

Second, the data requirements are modest. All that is needed is per-student expenditures by level, ideally at a low level of aggregation. In many countries with centralized systems, this level of aggregation will be the whole county. In some it might be the municipality (or even the school). In the United States, it is the school district. For Brazil, I use states, since all municipalities in each state receive in principle the same per-student financing.[3]

---

[3] The Fundo de Manutenção e Desenvolvimento da Educação Básica e de Valorização dos Profissionais da Educação (Fundeb), which provides the base per capita funding to schools, is the same

Third, the cost of provision approach does not change the size of the welfare cake. The benefits of public education are by definition equal to the taxes used to finance it. I am not sure that this is really an advantage but it does keep things simple. Education is nothing more than a redistribution from those who pay to those who benefit; it neither creates nor destroys wealth.

On the other hand, the cost approach also suffers from various shortcomings.

First, it assumes that all students are receiving the same public education. This is clearly not the case even if the state spends the same on each student, which is also usually not the case. Even in a highly centralized system such as that of France, in which all students study the same subject matter on the same day, the differences in teaching quality between a school in a poor *banlieue* and a school in Paris's fifth district are quite evident. These differences are even higher for countries in which schools or municipalities are allowed to raise money for themselves.

Second, it is not consistent with the theory of provision of public goods (Samuelson 1955), according to which the welfare value of a public good is the sum of the marginal utilities of all its users (as opposed to the simple marginal utility in the case of private goods). While schools are definitely not pure public goods since one can only fit so many children into a classroom without hindering learning, allowing the marginal benefit of educational services to differ from their average cost allows for public education to be welfare enhancing (or welfare reducing). Whether the state is highly efficient or woefully inefficient in translating educational expenditure into learning and future wages makes no difference in the cost method.

2 Second Method: Schooling Is Worth What the Labor Market Says It Is Worth

The labor market method is conceptually a little more complicated than the cost of provision method, but not much. The idea is to take the difference in present values of lifetime earnings of men and women with and without an additional year of schooling as the value of that year of schooling. In symbols,

$$value_s = lifetime\ y_s - lifetime\ y_{s-1} = \sum_{t=16}^{70} d^{(t-16)} y_{s,t} - \sum_{t=16}^{70} d^{(t-16)} y_{s-1,t},$$

where $y_{s,t}$ represents the average earnings of someone with schooling level s at age t and d is a discount factor. The age range we consider goes from the legal working age of 16 to maximum retirement age of 70. Note that $y_{s,t}$ is the product of the probability of employment by the average wage if employed. $y_{s,t}$ must also be calculated at some level of aggregation since individual future wages cannot be observed for people in school today. My objective was to use individuals of a given race and sex born in the same state, but

---

for every school in a given state. Complementary expenditures by the federal government, states, and municipalities will vary from school to school, but these are less important than the Fundef.

sampling noise forced me to settle for individuals of a given race and sex born in the same region of the country (North, Northeast, Southeast, South, and Center-West).

But what if there is more than one schooling level? The calculation becomes a little more complicated. A child or young adult completing a given year of schooling opens to his or her future self not only the doors of higher earnings accruing to that year of schooling, but also the possibility of going further in his or her education and accessing the higher wages of subsequent schooling levels. This means that in addition to the future salary already contracted with an additional year of education s, the child or young adult has also added the option value of going to level $s+1$ to his menu. In symbols,

$$value_s = (lifetime\ y_s - lifetime\ y_{s-1}) + p_{s+1}\ value_{s+1},$$

where p_{s+1} is the probability of completing schooling level $s+1$, given that schooling level s has been completed.

The calculation is simple. Begin with the highest schooling level in the household survey and calculate $value_s$ for that level. Then work backward using the option value for $value_{s+1}$ for calculating each new $value_s$.

The incomes and probabilities of working can be found in any labor market survey. For Brazil, I used the 2015 Pesquisa Nacional por Amostragem de Domicilios (National Household Sample Survey—PNAD). For each region of Brazil, I calculated the mean earnings and employment probabilities for men and women by region and race. I used sex, race, and region because these variables change rates of return to education. Having the age-earnings profile for each type of person and educational level means that the net present value of all types of education can be calculated.

The transition probabilities can be calculated either using educational statistics or else just a cross-section of individuals who no longer go to school. Educational statistics will usually provide repetition, drop-out, and promotion rates, and then a flow model can be used to calculate the estimated future educational end states and their probabilities. An alternative (and much simpler) procedure is to use a household survey to observe the educational end states of individuals whose educational trajectories have been completed. This is what I did, using individuals age 25, since there are few people still in school at that age or older.

At this stage in the calculation, only the discount rate d needs to be determined. I used three values: 5 percent, 10 percent, and 15 percent. They are somewhat arbitrary but 5 percent is close to the long-run real prime rate for Brazil and 15 percent is close to the lowest interest rate for a personal loan in Brazil. I consider the 15 percent annual discount rate as the most adequate for individual decisions.

Precision of the estimates can be calculated using the variance of earnings for each age in the age-earnings profile. These variances can then be used to calculate the variance of the estimates of present value of future earnings for educational level and, therefore, of its distributional statistics.

The labor market approach, which uses the net present value of income, also has advantages and disadvantages.

Perhaps its main advantage is that it ties the value of schooling to its real world impacts. This allows for welfare-enhancing public schooling, particularly if labor market returns are elevated, as they still are in Brazil. This is a huge advantage over the cost approach.

I can think of four main disadvantages.

The first is that the results depend crucially on an arbitrary parameter, the discount rate d. Given that there is no uncontroversial way to calculate what should be the discount rate for a given country or person, this is indeed a problem.

The second is that the method reduces the impact of education to its future income component. Education has also been shown to enhance health (independently of income),[4] to reduce the probability of being murdered (which is also conditional on income),[5] and to increase the educational level of future generations. These are certainly important dimensions of welfare that are not included in the labor market approach. It would be possible to include them in an incomplete way by applying mortality and morbidity probabilities to the age-earnings profiles by schooling level, but I do not do so here.

A variation on this theme is that many educators maintain that education has intrinsic value, independent of its effect on other desirable outcomes. In other words, knowing about the world is a source of satisfaction in and of itself (this is certainly true for me). This is not captured looking at future earnings.

A third calculation problem is that the future labor market will almost certainly differ from today's labor market, which means that the values will be calculated with bias. In a country with an expanding education system, it is likely that this bias will be upward since more education will drive down educational premiums. Premiums will fall for obvious reasons if the returns to education reflect signaling, but they will also fall due to decreasing marginal returns to the more abundant factor of production even if returns to education reflect true increases in productivity. In Brazil over the last two decades, educational premiums have fallen so that a high school diploma would have been more highly valued ex ante in 1990 than if its holder had been followed throughout his or her life from graduation until today.

Finally, this method cannot be used to value pre school education with present data. Since household surveys contain only the highest educational level completed, we do not know how much additional income is gained from having attended preschool.

The net present value of income labor market approach ignores all these issues.

---

[4] Da Silva, Araujo Freire, and Pereira (2016) show that individuals age 15 who went on to higher education had life expectancy 6.3 years higher than those with incomplete primary education.

[5] According to Waiselfisz (2016), homicide rates in Brazil are 262 per 100,000 for youth with less than four years of schooling as opposed to 19 for those with a secondary education and 0.4 for those with higher education.

3 Third Method: Schooling Is Worth What the Private Education Market Says It Is Worth

The third method is to use the private education market to attribute a value to public education. One possibility would be simply to attribute the value of private education of the same level and in the same area to public schooling. The problem is that private schools are often considered better than public ones—which is why people put their hard-earned money into paying tuition instead of enjoying free public education. A way to take this into consideration is to attribute to public education at a given level and in a given geographical area the same value as private education of the same quality. But how does one measure the quality of schooling?

Faute de mieux, I consider quality as being measured solely by a score on a standardized test. This is certainly a problem as schooling quality may also refer to how welcoming a school is and how its students feel there. School quality may refer to the interpersonal and soft skills whose importance in the labor market is increasingly clear. The decision to put one's children in a private school may even answer to motives many will find lacking in legitimacy such as racial, religious, or cultural homogeneity. We cannot, however, measure any of these in a systematic way. So test scores it is.

How does the cost of equivalent private education method work? Three pieces of information are necessary: tuitions, test scores, and of course school enrollment data. Tuitions in private schools must be paired with test scores to find the hedonic price for school quality, and this price must then be matched with enrollment in public schools. The educational market value of public education is then whatever a student in a public school would have to pay to get the same education in a private one.

In Brazil, tuition can be found only in the Family Expenditures Survey (the Ministry of Education collects data on tuition by school but they are not made public). Test scores can be found in all the main tests: Prova Brasil / Sistema de Avaliação da Educação Básica (SAEB) for elementary and middle school, Exame Nacional do Ensino Médio (ENEM) for high school, and Exame Nacional de Desempenho dos Estudantes (ENADE) for higher education. In addition, I use the PNAD for incomes.

With five databases and no identifiers, the biggest challenge in this method is merging data. Luckily, all the school tests (Prova Brasil/SAEB, ENEM, ENADE) have good socio-economic questionnaires with plenty of variables that allow for matching keys to be made.

The steps I followed are as follows:

First, individual tuition from the 2009 Family Expenditures Survey was matched to test score data from the same year from SAEB, ENEM, and ENADE. The objective was to get a relation between tuition and quality as measured by test scores. Only private schools were included, and the matching codes on table 2-1 were used. This means that the average tuition of boys born in 1999 and enrolled in eighth grade in private schools in the state of Minas Gerais, whose parents both had completed higher education, and who lived in a household with four people with a computer, a car, and a DVD player, was matched to the average test score data of these same kids.

TABLE 2-1
Matching Codes and Regression Statistics

Schooling level	Match code	Number matched	R^2
Preschool	No regression		
Lower primary	State; sex; year born; mother's education; Father's education; household size; microcomputer; car; DVD	195 + 9	0.2792
Upper primary	State; sex; year born; mother's education; father's education; household size; microcomputer; car; DVD	122 + 26	0.2556
Secondary	State; sex; year born; income category; mother's education; father's education; microcomputer	151 + 11	0.2784
Higher	State; sex; year born; income category; household size; mother's education; father's education	1,637 + 270	0.0534

Sources: Family Expenditures Survey, 2009; SAEB, 2011; ENEM, 2009; ENADE, 2009.

Second, for each educational level (barring preschool, for which there are no test scores), a regression linking test scores to tuition was estimated. Unfortunately, the Family Expenditures Survey has few observations for private tuition and the numbers were typically in the low hundreds (also shown on table 2-1).[6] The end result is a test score–tuition converter.

The "Number matched" column in table 2-1 is expressed as the sum of two numbers. The first number shows the observations that were directly matched between the test scores and the Family Expenditures Survey. The second number represents observations for which there are tuition data in the consumption survey but no match with test score data. In order to use these observations, they had to be matched to the nearest observation in the test score data. The distance measure used is the predicted value of a regression in which test scores are the dependent variable and the match code variables above make up the independent variables.

The regression results in which test scores explain tuition can be found in the appendix to this chapter.

Having the test score–tuition converter, I turned back to the test scores and matched test score data to the PNAD using the same match codes as before. The data were different since 2015 data were used for both incomes and test scores. This time, only test results for public schools were used. In this case, the number of observations was much higher—typically in the low thousands—and the merges were almost perfect. With the match

---

[6] If many more observations were available, no regression would be needed, and test scores could be converted to tuition nonparametrically.

made, the coefficients from step 2 were used to predict the tuition that would have been paid by families for the same quality of education they obtained for free from the state. Since I used the 2015 PNAD Household Survey, the predicted values for tuitions had to be multiplied by 1.51067, which represents the inflation rate from 2009 to 2015.

Finally, this predicted value was added to family income, and the same standard distributional analysis undertaken for methods 1 and 2 were repeated.

The cells defined by each match code also define a variance in tuitions. These variances then can be used to calculate the variance of the different distributional statistics.

The private education market method also has advantages and shortcomings.

The biggest advantage is that it is anchored in what people are actually willing to pay for education. Gertler and Glewwe (1989) estimated willingness to pay for education in rural Peru in 1985 using the decisions of families to send or not to send their children to schools. Given that 38 percent of children in rural Peru did not go to school in 1985, that school places were not rationed, and that there were considerable costs in terms of time, the schooling decision could be used to uncover the value families placed on public schooling. However, this identification strategy no longer works in any but the poorest countries since in middle-income countries schooling is very close to universal and often compulsory. The private education market method will work anywhere that public and private schooling coexist.

The main disadvantage is assuming an equivalence of private and public education conditional on test scores. If public schooling exists as a free alternative to paid private schooling of the same quality, why do families part with their hard-earned money paying for private education?

The answer is that the common support for education is somewhat rationed. School places in the best public schools such as exam schools are limited and require exams or lotteries to get in. It may be argued that a public school of a quality comparable to an available private school is only available elsewhere or its places are rationed. The reason for private schooling that invalidates this approach is that some parents value class, religious, ideological, or racial homogeneity and may send their children to private schools for that reason. In this case there is no equivalence to what parents who pay for private schooling are paying for and what public schooling provides. I will leave it up to the reader to decide which alternative is true.

A second disadvantage is empirical. Test scores, private school tuition data, and enough additional data to allow matching are all necessary for computation. Whereas Brazil has exceptionally good test data, many countries may not count on an ENEM, an ENADE, and Prova Brasil. Most developing countries and even many developed ones do not have such good standardized test data. Nevertheless, tests such as those undertaken by the Programme for International Student Assessment (PISA), the Southern and Eastern Africa Consortium for Monitoring Educational Quality (SACMEQ), and the Laboratorio Latinoamericano de Evaluación de la Calidad de la Educación (LLECE) allow this method to be applied in various countries, at least for some grade levels.

4 Comparison of Results

The first question each method must answer is how much public education is worth. The answer varies according to the method used. The estimates go from 60.80 reais (R$) for every man, woman, and child in Brazil for the cost method to R$474.59 using the labor market method with a discount factor of 5 percent. As I said before, I am using a 15 percent discount rate for Brazilian individuals since they are willing to pay that amount, or even more, for personal credit. That having been said, one could make an argument that the social discount rate should be closer to 5 percent since the state can finance itself at close to 5 percent.

If we use the 15 percent discount factor for the labor market method, all three methods provide reasonably close estimates of the total value of public education to the public.[7] They vary from R$60.80 to R$74.09 per month, increasing incomes for the population as a whole by about 6 percent or 7 percent. All three methods provide estimates that are quite close to each other. Remember, though, that the labor market method does not value preschool.

The standard deviations are quite high. In the case of the labor market method, this is due to the fact that differences between variables add and do not subtract. In the case of the education market method, the reason is that small sample sizes are used to estimate the relations between standardized test scores and tuition. With the large standard deviations shown in table 2-2, it is clear that there are no statistical differences between the three methods in bold. The labor market estimates using discount rates of 10 percent and 5 percent, respectively, are different from the education market estimate with a probability of 32.0 percent and 99.7 percent.

In addition, the reduction in Gini points is about the same for all three methods. The Gini coefficient falls by about 3.5 Gini points with the addition of the value of public educational services to family incomes.

What is the breakdown by education level?

Table 2-3 shows that the labor market approach provides much higher estimates of educational value than the education market and the cost approaches. This is not clear in table 2-2 because the labor market approach cannot value preschool education, but one could argue that the benefits of preschool are included in later earnings. The labor market approach provides estimates that, compared with the cost approach, are 40 percent higher for primary school and 67 percent higher for secondary.

The cost approach and the education market approach, on the other hand, provide estimates that are quite close for all schooling levels except higher education. An argument can be made, however, that included in public higher education cost are items that are really not education, particularly research. While specific research budgets and research grants have not been included in education costs, the salaries of many higher education teachers also pay for their time as researchers.

---

[7] If we use the 5 percent discount rate, then the value of public education is much higher according to the labor market method.

TABLE 2-2

Impacts of Public Education Services on Global Income Distribution

Distribution	Income (in R$)	Δ Income (in R$)	Standard deviation Δ Income	Gini	Δ Gini
Income	1,056			0.514	
Cost approach	**1,117**	**61**	**n.a.**	**0.477**	**−0.037**
Labor market (5%)	1,531	475	157	0.446	−0.068
Labor market (10%)	1,220	164	82	0.455	−0.059
Labor market (15%)	**1,130**	**74**	**52**	**0.477**	**−0.037**
Education market	**1,118**	**62**	**32**	**0.479**	**−0.035**

Sources: Family Expenditures Survey, 2009; PNAD Household Survey, 2015; SAEB, 2011, 2015; ENEM, 2009, 2015; ENADE, 2009, 2015.

Note: Education values are per person; calculated using the entire population, not only students.

n.a. = Not applicable

TABLE 2-3

Value of Public Education by Level, per Student

Educational level	Number of students (millions)	Avg. cost approach	Labor market (15%)	Education market
Preschool	5.19	248	none	296
Lower primary	14.09	250	352	233
Upper primary	11.32	272		291
Secondary	8.08	302	504	414
Higher	1.87	917	883	502
All levels	**40.55**	**297**	**415**	**305**

Sources: Family Expenditures Survey, 2009; PNAD Household Survey, 2015; SAEB, 2011, 2015; ENEM, 2009, 2015; ENADE, 2009, 2015.

The last table, table 2-4, shows distributive impacts of public schooling by level. That is, it shows both the ex-ante impacts (concentration coefficients calculated with no imputation of public schooling value into incomes—across the ex-ante distribution) and ex-post impacts (concentration coefficients calculated with educational values included in incomes). Once again, there are no preschool impacts for the labor market approach because the method cannot estimate them with the data available.

The distributive results are more varied than the averages. The cost approach yields an ex-ante concentration coefficient in the −30s—highly distributive—for preschool and primary education. The labor market and education market approaches yield concentration coefficients in the −20s—still quite distributive but less so than the labor market approach. The same relation holds true for secondary education. For higher education, concentration coefficients from all three approaches are in the +30s.

TABLE 2-4
Concentration Coefficients of Public Education by Level, Ex Ante and Ex Post

Level	Ex ante			Ex post		
	Cost approach	Labor market	Education market	Cost approach	Labor market	Education market
Preschool	−0.302	none	−0.257	−0.240	none	−0.150
Lower primary	−0.388	−0.290	−0.279	−0.319	−0.048	−0.162
Upper primary	−0.332		−0.257	−0.251		−0.116
Secondary	−0.181	−0.139	−0.141	−0.093	0.071	0.018
Higher	0.321	0.378	0.350	0.532	0.592	0.459
All Levels	**−0.216**	**−0.173**	**−0.188**	**−0.122**	**0.057**	**−0.055**

Sources: Family Expenditures Survey, 2009; PNAD Household Survey, 2015; SAEB, 2011, 2015; ENEM, 2009, 2015; ENADE, 2009, 2015.

This discrepancy is probably due to heterogeneity of schools. While the cost approach assigns to all schools in a given state the same expenditures, the education market approach assigns higher value to better public schools, thus negating some of its distributive impacts.

The ex-post results are always less distributive because the recipients of education spending all move up the income distribution once educational spending is imputed to their incomes. Additional spending on higher education is regressive as shown by ex-post concentration coefficients, which are higher than the ex-post Gini coefficient. Also for comparison purposes, the most distributive government program in Brazil, Bolsa Familia, has an ex-post concentration coefficient of about −0.6. This means that public education falls quite short of targeted social welfare programs, which should not be a surprise since it is a universal service.

The six panels of figure 2-1 show the ex-ante and ex-post concentration curves for all educational levels for all three methods.

5 Conclusion

In this chapter I compare different methods for providing an estimate of how much public education is worth to those who benefit from it. Apart from the tried and true cost method, I also applied the labor market method invented by Sergio Urzua (2017) and the education market method I pioneered (Soares, 2017). I find that the results from the three methods do not fall far from each other (although the labor market approach requires high discount rates to yield results similar to the other two).

That cost and education market methods yield similar estimates of value should not be a surprise. The private system is heavily influenced by the public schooling supply since it uses many of the same inputs—particularly teachers. The labor market valuation of public education, however, depends a lot on the discount rate chosen.

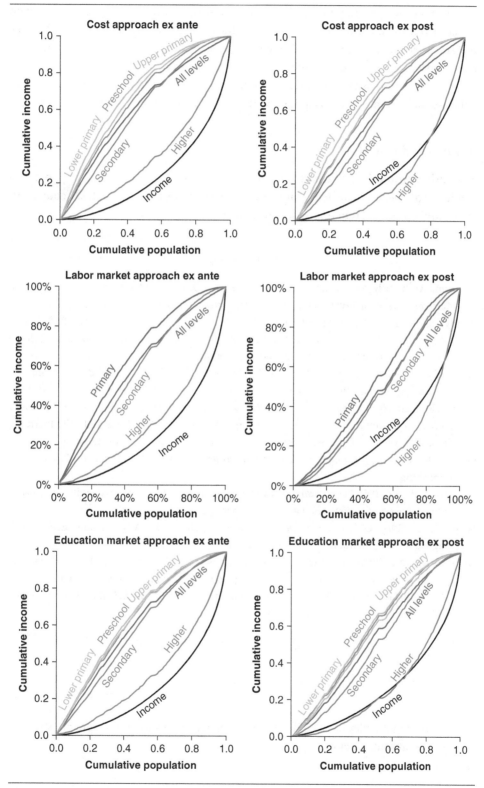

FIGURE 2-1
Concentration Curves

Cost approach ex ante

Cost approach ex post

Labor market approach ex ante

Labor market approach ex post

Education market approach ex ante

Education market approach ex post

Sources: Family Expenditures Survey, 2009; PNAD, 2015; SAEB, 2011, 2015; ENEM. 2009, 2015; ENADE, 2009, 2015.

All methods provide similar distributive results ex ante because the children who benefit from them are more or less in the same position in terms of income distribution. Furthermore, if the value each assigns to public education is not too different, then the ex-post distributive results will not fall too far from each other either.

My conclusion is that the value of public education in Brazil is close to 6 percent of household income, and it is quite distributive, whatever the valuation method used.

Acknowledgments

The author would like to thank Commitment to Equity for financial support and Stephen Younger for excellent comments on earlier drafts of the text. Of course, all errors and omissions remain my sole responsibility.

References

Atkinson, Anthony B. 2005. *Measurement of Government Output and Productivity for the National Accounts. Atkinson Review: Final Report.* Basingstoke, England: Palgrave MacMillan.

da Silva, Lariça Emiliano, Flavio Henrique Miranda de Araujo Freire; Pereira, and Rafael Henrique Moraes. 2016. "Mortality Differentials According to Schooling in Brazilian Adults in 2010." *Cadernos de Saúde Pública* 32, no. 4, p. e00019815.

Gertler, Paul, and Paul Glewwe. 1989. *The Willingness to Pay for Education in Developing Countries: Evidence from Rural Peru.* Living Standards Measurement Study Working Paper No. 54, July.

Lustig, Nora, ed. 2022. *Commitment to Equity Handbook: Estimating the Impact of Fiscal Policy on Inequality and Poverty,* 2nd ed., 2 Vols. Brookings Institution Press and CEQ Institute, Tulane University. Free online version available at www.commitmentoequity.org.

OECD. 2008. *Growing Unequal? Income Distribution and Poverty in OECD Countries.* Paris: OECD Publishing.

Samuelson, Paul A. 1955. "Diagrammatic exposition of a Theory of Public Expenditure." *Review of Economics and Statistics* 37, no. 4 (November), pp. 350–56.

Soares, Sergei. 2017. "O Valor de mercado da educação pública." IPEA Discussion Text no 2324. August. Rio de Janeiro: Instituto de Pesquisa Economica Aplicada.

Urzua, Sergio. 2017. "Estimating the Value of Education Services: A Comparison of the Average Cost versus Private Rate of Returns to Education." Presentation at CEQ Workshop, Buenos Aires.

Waiselfisz, Julio Jacobo. 2016. *Educação: Blindagem contra a violência homicida?* Caderno Temático No 1. Mapa da Violência. Flasco, Brasil.

Appendix 2A

Additional tables on school tuition regressions and standard errors of estimates are presented below.

Table 2A-1
School Tuition Regressions

Variable	Lower primary		Upper primary		Secondary		Higher education	
	Coefficient	p-value (%)	Coefficient	p-value (%)	Coefficient	p-value (%)	Coefficient	p-value (%)
Test Score	**18.31**	**0**	**9.88**	**10**	**9.21**	**5**	**18.89**	**1**
Acre	548	82	1692	63	−918	66	2135	4
Amazonas	−2459	14	−782	84	−2624	39	642	52
Roraima	0		0		0		−113	97
Pará	417	76	849	80	−1069	58	624	47
Amapá	836	65	1528	65	−23	99	1	100
Tocantins	−1276	36	0		−1131	63	176	83
Maranhão	−1359	33	771	79	155	92	1710	4
Piauí	−593	63	1256	67	−209	90	747	36
Ceará	−958	47	−2	100	−1159	53	−414	63
Rio Grande do Norte	−551	65	148	96	−1032	57	−344	70
Paraíba	817	53	3761	21	759	68	−35	97
Pernambuco	−505	69	1817	56	−718	68	655	39
Alagoas	−925	46	848	77	−480	78	−277	72
Sergipe	−105	93	1362	64	3003	7	587	45
Bahia	−1411	30	−231	94	3016	10	845	25
Minas Gerais	−118	93	608	84	−191	90	1601	2
Espírito Santo	−1909	13	2343	43	−1553	35	348	64
Rio de Janeiro	1250	36	2160	49	−1125	49	2137	1

(continued)

TABLE 2A-1   (continued)

Variable	Lower primary		Upper primary		Secondary		Higher education	
	Coefficient	p-value (%)	Coefficient	p-value (%)	Coefficient	p-value (%)	Coefficient	p-value (%)
São Paulo	1091	40	2541	41	1964	19	1932	1
Paraná	−360	80	928	76	867	65	629	39
Santa Catarina	−311	82	6476	7	1240	47	153	83
Rio Grande do Sul	−908	53	632	85	−365	84	1872	1
Mato Grosso do Sul	−1578	25	209	95	711	71	325	66
Mato Grosso	−1378	34	−451	88	3123	19	−166	83
Goiás	293	83	47	99	−155	92	876	22
Distrito Federal	−557	69	6292	5	5473	8	2325	0
Constant	−5544	1	−3794	32	−1763	55	1777	2

Sources: Family Expenditures Survey, 2009; PNAD Household Survey, 2015; SAEB, 2011, 2015; ENEM, 2009, 2015; ENADE, 2009, 2015.

TABLE 2A-2

Standard Deviations for Monthly Value of Education Estimates

Educational level	Number of students (millions)	Labor market (15%)		Education market	
		Value	Standard error	Value	Standard error
Preschool	5.19	none		296	
Lower primary	14.09	352	44.38	233	30
Upper primary	11.32			291	31
Secondary	8.08	504	25.26	414	39
Higher	1.87	883	11.47	502	21

Sources: Family Expenditures Survey, 2009; PNAD Household Survey, 2015; SAEB, 2011, 2015; ENEM, 2009, 2015; ENADE, 2009, 2015.

Chapter 3

REDISTRIBUTION THROUGH EDUCATION

Assessing the Long-Term Impact of Public Spending

Sergio Urzua

Introduction

Education can be a powerful policy instrument to redistribute resources. On the one hand, by equipping individuals with relevant abilities and skills, human capital policies affect future poverty and inequality (Heckman and Krueger, 2005). On the other, as an in-kind benefit or monetary transfer (voucher), in the short-run education shapes the way in which governments mold income distribution (Lustig and Higgins, 2022) (chapter 1 in Volume 1 of this Handbook). This explains the fiscal relevance of the sector all around the world. OECD countries spend on average more than 6 percent of their GDP on education services, and their global contribution to government expenditure has risen steadily during the last decades (4.9 percent in 2014, compared with 3.9 percent reported in 2000). The potential redistribution effects of these efforts are the result of a simple and general economic logic: governments collect revenues from taxes, which are then allocated to different spending categories including in kind-transfers such as education.

Conventional fiscal incidence analysis assesses the point-in-time impact of these actions. In particular, by comparing the pre- and post-fiscal income distributions, the longstanding literature in public economics has characterized the impacts of the fiscal system (Musgrave, 1959). For example, using this approach, Lustig (2015) documents the contribution of public spending on education (and health) to the reduction in inequality across countries in Africa, Asia, and Latin America. Likewise, Younger, Osei-Assibey, and Oppong (2017) show for Ghana that two-thirds of the reduction in the Gini from Consumable to Final Income, a comparison highlighting the effects of public expenditures, can be attributed to education benefits. And Acerenza, and Gandelman (2019) report large Gini coefficients for household private educational spending for 12 Latin American and Caribbean countries (2003–14). However, once public spending on education is considered, inequality declines significantly.

This chapter presents a general fiscal incidence analysis of public education spending. In doing so, it makes two contributions. First, it posits and implements two methodologies for the estimation of the economic impact of public spending on the income distribution: the cost of public provision approach and a new alternative allowing for behavioral responses to subsidies. Thus, the discussion goes beyond the static accounting exercise, which adds/subtracts to prefiscal income the transfers/taxes each individual or household receives/pays at a specific time, and investigates the potential long-term consequences of fiscal efforts in education. Second, it describes some of the critical real-world data limitations that characterize the evidence in this field. To this end, it implements both methods and presents new empirical evidence for Chile and Ghana.

The selection of Chile and Ghana is not incidental. While the South American country is the region's most successful case of economic and social development, the African nation has consolidated its democracy and become one of the most promising economies in its continent. Nonetheless, when it comes to continuing and extending socioeconomic progress, both countries face significant challenges. With a per capita GDP of US$22,707 (2016, purchasing power parity-adjusted, or PPP), a poverty headcount ratio at US$1.90 a day (2011 PPP) of 1.3 percent (as proportion of population), and gross enrollment rates in primary and secondary education reaching 100 percent, during the last decade Chile has been actively promoting access to higher education as a mechanism to reduce its high and stable income inequality (Gini coefficient in 2013 was 0.491). Meanwhile, with a per capita GDP of US$3,980 (2016), a poverty headcount of 13.60 percent (2012), a Gini coefficient of 0.42 (2012), enrollment rates in secondary and tertiary education of 60 percent and 16 percent, respectively, and gross enrollment rates in primary schooling in excess of 100 percent, Ghana has continued strengthening efforts toward improving schooling attainment starting with secondary schooling. Importantly, the cross-country comparison reveals how public education initiatives (in-kind subsidies) might shape income inequality given different levels of economic and social development. To preview, we note that the findings document positive but heterogeneous economic returns to educational attainment, yet limited long-term effects of public efforts on income inequality.

Despite the advantages of a general framework, this chapter does not circumvent the natural complexities of educational systems. They adjust and evolve with political and socioeconomic conditions as well as societal needs and thereby altering the impact of government spending. Consequently, understanding and quantifying the allocation of public resources within the education sector becomes critical. For instance, it has been generally argued that investing in early stages (i.e., preschool) pays off more in the long-run than, for example, expanding coverage of other levels of education

(Garcia et al., 2016). Indeed, the recent evidence regarding the association between education spending and individuals' long-term outcomes confirms this rationale (Chetty et al., 2011). In this context, the static fiscal incidence analysis must be extended to fully characterize the impacts of these efforts.

To shed light on this matter, this chapter investigates the potential economic impact of public investments on human capital formation, and in so doing, it takes into account three interconnected elements: the impact of fiscal spending in education on income redistribution, the relative efficiency in the use of resources across schooling levels, and the effects of different education policies on individuals' future income. These elements constitute the building blocks of the evidence presented herein, which exploits the responses of school enrollment/attainment to public spending and seeks to capture the resulting long-term impact on labor market outcomes (earnings).

On empirical grounds, the text explores the extent to which conventional sources of information provide a conducive landscape for carrying out fiscal incidence analysis of education spending. To this end, we exploit cross-sectional household surveys and aggregate-level official data for Chile and Ghana. The evidence generated is then examined in light of the data available.

When it comes to the methodologies, the cost of public provision approach mimics the conventional accounting framework. It utilizes the monetary value of education services (costs) at different schooling levels as inputs for estimating the redistributive effect of public spending. In the spirit of the literature, this approach abstracts from potential behavioral responses and long-term considerations. This limitation gives rise to the second approach, which incorporates the effect of public spending on enrollment rates at different schooling levels. Here, we introduce two empirical strategies designed to characterize how additional financial resources affect student progression through the education system. One relies on aggregate-level information, whereas the preferred alternative exploits individual-level data. Equipped with these kits and information on age-earning profiles by schooling levels, we capture the long-term effects of public policies aimed at increasing school attainment and expanding education coverage on inequality. This complements the evidence from the conventional fiscal incidence analysis.

The chapter is organized as follows. Section 1 introduces the conceptual framework and describes the empirical strategy and the sources of information. Section 2 discusses the empirical analysis. Section 3 highlights the differences and similarities between Chile and Ghana. Section 4 presents the main results, and section 5 concludes.

1 The Conceptual Framework

This section introduces the basic concepts behind the fiscal incidence analysis of education spending. Let's begin by assuming individuals can either study or work, but cannot do both activities at the same time. As a student, each individual receives non-labor income (Y_0), pays taxes (T), and receives monetary transfers from the government (B). To a large extent, students do not directly bear the private costs of education.

School supplies, books, co-payments, and tuition fees are commonly paid for with re-sources from working relatives. Thus, an individual's Disposable Income Y_D is defined as $Y_0 - T + B$, while his or her Final Income, Y_F, includes the monetary value of in-kind transfers from the government (E_G) or private sources (E_F).

For workers, on the other hand, Market Income Y_M combines net labor income $Y_L(1 - \tau)$, where τ denotes the social security contribution rate, and non–labor income Y_0.[1] In this case, Disposable Income is defined as Y_M plus monetary transfers B minus taxes T. Finally, assuming the absence of other in-kind transfers and abstracting from consumption subsidies and taxes, Final Income Y_F equals Disposable Income minus private contributions to education.

What are the redistributional benefits of in-kind publicly funded education? Lambert's fundamental equation of the redistributive effect comes in handy to address this question (Lambert, 1993). His formulation delivers a mathematical expression linking the changes in the distributions of income resulting from general fiscal efforts with the redistributive effects of taxes and transfers. In particular, using Lambert's original no-tation, we see that the net fiscal incidence progressivity (Π_N) arising from the com-parison of the distributions of market and final income can be expressed as

(3-1)
$$\Pi_N = \frac{(1-g)\Pi_T + (1+b)\rho_B}{(1+b-g)},$$

where Π_T and ρ_B measure the progressivity/regressivity for T and B when applied sep-arately to initial income, respectively; g is the total tax ratio (total taxes over original income); and b is the total benefit ratio (total benefits over original income). Thus, re-gardless of whether progressive or regressive taxes are in place to fund education, it is intuitive to think of E_G as a progressive transfer defining ρ_B. The monetary value of in-kind transfers from the government should benefit more low- and middle-income households, particularly when the alternative of "free" public education is available.[2]

This chapter explores this framework while taking into considerations the features that make public spending in education distinctive relative to other fiscal efforts. Indi-viduals invest in human capital to build a better future. The full economic and social impacts of one dollar spent on education are realized only in the future. This inter-temporal connection represents a challenge for the standard fiscal incidence analysis formulation as it is usually carried out at a point-in-time rather than over the lifecycle (Lustig and Higgins, 2022). We revisit this issue throughout the chapter.

---

[1] Consistent with the *CEQ Assessment*, s can include contributions to old-age pensions if con-tributory pensions are treated as transfers.

[2] This expression implies that, given the dominant role of ρ_B (its associated weight is greater than one), even with regressive taxes ($\Pi_T < 0$), we should expect that "the net system exhibits more progressivity than regressive benefits alone ($\Pi_N > \rho_B > 0$)" (Lambert, 1993, 259). This result high-lights the inherent association among redistribution, taxes, and benefits.

2 The Value of Public Education Spending to Its Beneficiaries

In general, two approaches can be pursued to assess the economic value of public subsidies assisting the consumption of in-kind services. The first one uses the market value (prices) to directly capture the individual's own valuation (Aaron and McGuire, 1970). The second alternative, known as "benefit incidence analysis," combines information on provision costs and utilization (Selowsky, 1979) to impute a monetary value to those receiving the service of interest (beneficiaries). Its final objective is to express the subsidy as share of household expenditures, a proxy for its economic impact. Castro-Leal et al. (1999) use this approach to provide insights into the historical problems faced by African governments in delivering essential social services, including education, to vulnerable households. Using data from Brazil, Soares (2018) compares the redistributive impact of education as captured by the cost of provision and market approaches and reports that both yield similar estimates. This approach is more closely connected to the analysis of this chapter.

Despite its practical advantages, the standard benefit incidence analysis needs further adjustments to fully characterize the impact of public education spending. Of course, identifying the precise monetary value of the transfer and discounting out-of-pocket fees and tuition expenses from the income of families contributing to the education of their children (beyond mandatory taxes for funding public education) are critical elements for understanding the static incidence of education spending. However, to capture the long-term impact of these public efforts on inequality, the analysis should incorporate their consequences on the overall human capital accumulation and the resulting income distribution. In what follows we develop such an analysis.

2.1 Cost of Provision as a Proxy for Benefits

The cost of public provision approach is the simplest method to approximate the monetary value of education services. Let Δ_s be the cost to the state of providing publicly funded education in school level s with $s = \{1, \ldots, S\}$. Information leading to the estimation of Δ_s is commonly available at different aggregate levels (e.g., municipality-level per student public expenditure).[3]

In the spirit of the static framework, total final income within the household becomes $Y_F = Y_D + \Sigma_s \delta_s \times n_s$, where n_s denotes the total number of students in level s. Thus, the direct comparison of distributional statistics obtained under Y_F and Y_D (e.g., the Gini coefficient) could be informative regarding the fiscal incidence of education.

As Soares (2018) discusses, despite its conceptual simplicity and modest data requirements, the cost of provision approach deflects some of the complexities associ-

---

[3] An alternative strategy for estimating Δ_s could exploit information on tuition costs from private schools. In this case, however, the analysis must control for potential differences in the production function of education services across provider types (Soares, 2018).

ated with standard welfare analysis. For instance, the obvious concerns regarding the distributional consequences of its sources of funding (taxes) are dismissed. In addition, it does not allow for the creation or destruction of welfare, behavioral responses, or general equilibrium effects. Moreover, whether Δ_s reflects marginal or average costs might be critical for the analysis. This comes as no surprise as this strategy does not aim at constructing the true counterfactual distribution of Final Income but instead is sought to provide a first-order static approximation to the incidence of in-kind transfers (Younger, 2022). However, as we show next, addressing the shortcomings of the cost of provision approach is not an easy task.

2.2 Incorporating Behavioral Responses

Governments promote school enrollment by increasing funding allocated to the education sector. Families, in turn, respond by sending more children to schools and keeping them enrolled in school for a longer time period. For individuals, the benefits of this efforts become apparent years later. This section introduces a strategy for a fiscal incidence analysis that allows for behavioral responses to in-kind education transfers. Conceptually, its two core ingredients are the elasticity of human capital investments with respect to the monetary value of the public transfer (the demand for education) and the long-term impact of education on labor market outcomes.

2.2.1 Public Subsidies and the Demand for Education

Let p_s be the probability of enrolling in schooling level s given that $s-1$ was completed, and E_s represents the value of publicly funded education directed to level s. Given the sequential nature of the human capital accumulation process, the probability of attending at least schooling level $s+1$ (or the survival function), ξ_{s+1}, and the probability of reaching $s+1$ (and stopping there), q_{s+1}, can be defined as

$$(3\text{-}2) \qquad \xi_{S+1} = \prod_{j=0}^{s+1} p_j,$$

$$(3\text{-}3) \qquad q_{s+1} = (1 - p_{s+1}) \prod_{j=0}^{S} p_j.$$

Using this definition, we can approximate the impact of public spending on the demand for education. Specifically, from the empirical assessment of these two probabilities, we can estimate the behavioral response to education spending.

Since behavioral responses drive the empirical association between enrollment levels and public expenditure over time, $\left\{ \dfrac{\partial p_j}{\partial E_j} \right\}_{j=0}^{s+1}$ can be identified from aggregate time series data. Fortunately, the microeconomic foundations of discrete decision models extend the empirical frontiers. To see this, let's assume schooling decisions are made by considering the relative benefits and costs of the different alternatives. Thus, if we let U_s be the associated indirect utility of schooling level s given that $s-1$ is completed, an individual should enroll/complete s as long as $U_s \geq 0$, which implies that $ps = \Pr[U_s \geq 0]$ for all s.

In general, a large set of observed and unobserved characteristics can determine I_s, including the value of the transfers E_s.[4] This would be consistent with an economic framework in which public education spending determines individual or collective budget sets (e.g., via direct monetary or in-kind transfers to families). And despite the fact that the functions U_s and $\Pr[\cdot]$ are ex-ante unknown, standard parametric specifications, in combination with individual-level information, can be imposed for practical purposes and lead to their estimation and construction of the expression

$$\frac{\partial q_{s+1}}{\partial E_{s'}} = \frac{\partial \left[(1 - \Pr[U_{s+1}(E_{s+1}) \geq 0]) \prod_{j=0}^{s} \Pr[U_j(E_j) \geq 0] \right]}{\partial E_{s'}},$$

where $s+1 \geq s^1$. This expression captures the strategic responses of individuals to educational spending, which can be linked to individual-level willingness to pay for education (as public spending increases). It can be easily extended to allow for heterogeneous responses to changes in E_s. This might be particularly important if, for example, the objective is to identify those who benefit the most from policy efforts in a specific schooling level.

2.2.2 Long-Term Impacts of Education

Higher levels of human capital produce better future labor market outcomes. This empirical regularity should direct parents toward seeking more and better education services today. However, if the supply of such services is not guaranteed, upward socioeconomic mobility could be limited and income distribution of future generations transformed. To the extent that public provision of education depends on taxes and transfers across generations, a comprehensive analysis of its incidence should move beyond static considerations.

Figure 3-1 illustrates the potential mechanism through which fiscal resources can affect the education system. In a nutshell, public funding allocated to schooling level s, E_s, can be conceptualized as one of the inputs determining investment levels, $I(s)$, which in turn affect the human capital that individuals attain and their future labor market opportunities. Thus, the association between human capital accumulation and

---

[4] The set of dimensions to be controlled for when modeling this probability should include variables characterizing individual's preferences for education (tastes) (Keane and Wolpin, 1997a) as well as controls capturing labor market prospects (Willis and Rosen, 1979) and financial constraints (Becker, 1962).

FIGURE 3-1

The Causal Chain of Resources Allocated to Education Systems

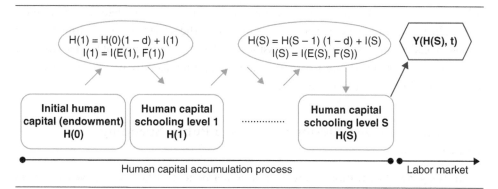

Notes: E(S) denotes the economic resources allocated to the schooling level *S*; *F* (*S*) denotes parental inputs; *I*(*S*) denotes investments levels in schooling level *S*; *H*(*S*) denotes human capital levels at the end of schooling level *S*; *d* denotes depreciation; *Y*(*H*(*S*), *t*) denotes period *t* income levels of an individual with human capital *H*(*S*).

labor income should lie at the core of the fiscal incidence of education spending. In what follows we discuss this long-term perspective.

Let labor income $Y_L(\cdot)$ be determined by the stock of human capital (e.g., years of education, or *s*) and labor market experience (*t*). The present value of an income stream (given *s*), $V(s)$, which encapsulates the sequence of earnings through retirement age (*T*), is a construct commonly used to approximate the monetary value associated with schooling level *s*. Formally,

$$(3\text{-}4) \qquad V(s) = \int_s^T Y_L(s, t-s)\,dt,$$

where $Y_L(s, t-s)$ includes the discount factor. From this expression we can define the economic benefits of an increase in education spending, which should operate through two interconnected channels: extra human capital investments and a boost to labor market productivity (see figure 3-1). Hence, from (3-4) we obtain

$$(3\text{-}5) \qquad \frac{\partial V(s)}{\partial E_s} = \int_s^T \frac{\partial Y_L(s, t-s)}{\partial s} \times \frac{\partial s}{\partial E_s}\,dt - Y_L(s, 0)\frac{\partial s}{\partial E_s},$$

where $\partial Y_L(s, t-s)/\partial s$ represents the effect of human capital on earnings (the return to education), $\partial s/\partial E_s$ captures how schooling decisions depend on public transfers, and the last term comes from the potential impact of E_s on the age at which individuals start their careers. In addition, the accumulation of human capital involves monetary and nonmonetary (psychological) costs, which must be considered when defining the demand for education. Importantly, some of these can be alleviated by public spending. Thus, if *C*(*s*) denotes the total costs, the net value of schooling level *s* is defined as

(3-6) $\tilde{V}(s) = V(s) - C(s),$

where $\partial C(s)/\partial E_s \neq 0$. The empirical assessment of $\tilde{V}(s)$ and its determinants represents a heavy burden to bear as it involves modeling the underlying schooling decision problem leading, for example, to expressions (3-2) and (3-3). In spite of the fact that the econometric tools for doing this exist, data limitations usually prevent it. Section 3 below describes a feasible alternative.

2.3 Long-Term Distributional Effects of Public Spending in Education

From the general definition of the economic net benefits attached to s we can assess the long-term distributional consequences of public spending in education.

Let $G\,[\cdot]$ be the inequality indicator of interest. Thus, for a given population of N individuals with idiosyncratic net values of education, $\{\tilde{V}_i(s)\}_{i=1}^N$, we can construct

$$G = G[\{\tilde{V}_i(s)\}_{i=1}^N].$$

By combining this expression and equation (3-5), we can quantify the intertemporal impact of changes in educational spending on income inequality from $\partial G/\partial E_s$. Notice this generalizes the static approach based on the study of $G[\{Y_{D,i}(s)\}_{i=1}^N]$.

This analysis, however, does not consider the fact that schooling decisions are made under uncertainty, and that, at any point in time, future labor market outcomes are unknown to the agent. To incorporate this into the framework, we define $\mathbb{E}[\tilde{V}]$ and $\mathbb{E}[\tilde{V}(s)|s]$ as the unconditional and conditional (on s) expectations of $\tilde{V}(s)$, respectively. Thus,

(3-7) $\mathbb{E}[\tilde{V}(s)] = \sum_{j=0}^{S} \mathbb{E}[\tilde{V}(j)\,|\,j \text{ is selected}] \times q_j,$

where q_j is defined in (3-3). Equipped with proper data, econometric models can deliver each of the elements of this expression. In that case, we could construct $G[\{\mathbb{E}[\tilde{V}_i(s)]\}_{i=1}^N]$ and its derivative with respect to E_s, which would now characterize the impact of public education spending on inequality under uncertainty.

Despite its theoretical simplicity, the empirical implementation of this framework involves multiple challenges. First, the setting implicitly assumes the availability of rich longitudinal information containing data on earnings (lifetime), schooling progression, and monetary and nonmonetary costs of education by schooling level, among other variables. Such data are rarely available.

Second, and now on econometric grounds, constructing (3-7) (and any of its special cases) would involve the estimation of earnings profiles that take into account the self-selection of individuals across different schooling levels. Although there is a long-standing literature dealing with the estimation of the hedonic models in education controlling for its endogeneity, the vast majority of those efforts comes from reduced-form strategies, which omit the dynamic nature of the schooling decision process.

The empirical approach described next overcomes some of these difficulties. It is designed for settings in which longitudinal information is not available, but the researcher has access to cross-sectional data from a population-based study. This information is complemented with information on monetary costs of education and taxes. The strategy to generate individual-level streams of future earnings uses flexible versions of the Mincer model (Mincer, 1974). The next sections describe this framework, which is applied to Chile and Ghana.

Conceptually, the analysis also omits two important dimensions. By focusing on private returns, it overlooks the role of collective/social benefits. This is particularly important if one considers the positive externalities emerging from education. The analysis also omits the role of quality in capturing the impact of public expenditure on education. In this context, the results presented in this chapter should be interpreted as lower bounds.

3 Chile and Ghana: Differences and Similarities

Africa and South America are at different levels of economic and social developments. As figure 3-2 shows, the average GDP per capita in Africa in 2014 was just above US$5,000 (PPP), which was the average for South America in 1990. However, despite the differences, both regions have heavily bet on human capital formation as a determinant of sustainable economic progress. This explains the upward trends in government expenditure on education observed during the last decades. According to UNESCO, from 1999 to 2013, government expenditure on education as a percentage of GDP increased from 3.4 percent to 4.5 percent in Sub-Saharan Africa (it reached 4.47 percent in Middle and East Africa), while in Latin America and the Caribbean it went from 3.84 percent to 5.21 percent during the same period. These efforts have significant effects on school enrollment. For instance, between 1999 and 2016, gross enrollment in primary education in Ghana increased from 81 percent to 108 percent, and from 35 percent to 62 percent in secondary education. Likewise, Chile's gross enrollment in secondary education during this period went from 83 percent to 100 percent, whereas enrollment in tertiary education increased from 37 percent to 88 percent. All in all, during the last two decades, public efforts in the education sector resulted in higher enrollment rates throughout the whole schooling system.[5]

---

[5]Government expenditure on education in Chile increased from 2.6 percent (1994) to 4.6 percent in 2013. For Ghana, it went from 4.1 percent (1999) to 6.1 percent in 2013. See UNESCO (n.d.).

FIGURE 3-2
GDP per Capita: Africa vs. Latin America and the Caribbean, 1990–2014

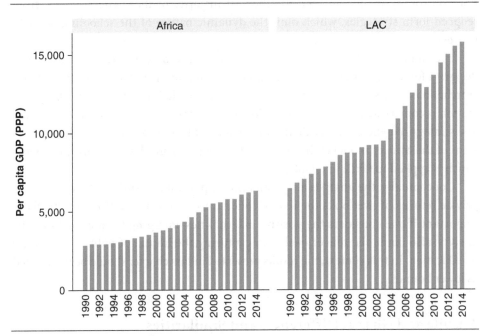

Source: World Bank Open Data. https://data.worldbank.org.

A strong positive correlation between labor income and years of education has played a key role supporting this social agenda. Figure 3-3 presents the Mincerian return to an extra year of education from African and Latin American countries during the period 1990–2012 as reported by Montenegro and Patrinos (2014). As is standard in the literature, these are obtained from linear regressions of (log) earnings on years of schooling (see section 4 for a description of Mincer model). In both cases the estimated returns are high, reaching averages of 10 percent and 13 percent per year of education over the period for Latin America and Africa, respectively. Interestingly, the average returns are relatively stable in both regions throughout the period.

But focusing on the average linear association between years of education and income puts out of sight potential nonlinearities describing the economic consequences of human capital formation on labor outcomes. Heterogeneity in the population (e.g., preferences or endowments), direct and indirect costs, human capital depreciation, the economics of skill formation, and signaling mechanisms are all factors that could explain why, for example, one extra year of education in primary, secondary, or tertiary school yields different labor market outcomes (Heckman, Lochner, and Todd, 2006). Figure 3-4 explores this idea. It decomposes the returns to education on labor income by schooling level (primary, secondary, and tertiary) for Africa and Latin America and

FIGURE 3-3

The Evolution of the Mincerian Returns to an Additional Year of Education: Africa vs. Latin America and the Caribbean, 1997–2012

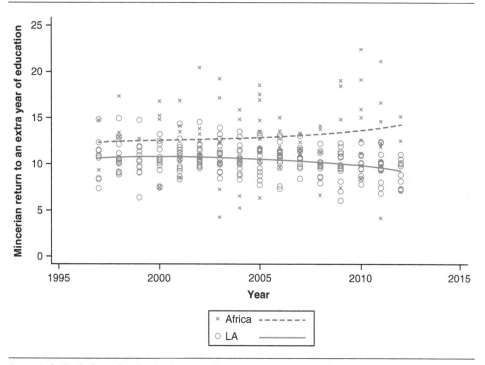

Source: Author's calculations based on Montenegro and Patrinos (2014).

Notes: This figure displays the Mincerian returns to education for Africa and Latin America (LA), which can be interpreted as the average rate of return to years of schooling with respect to earnings. These are obtained from linear regressions of (log) earnings on years of education, experience, and experience squared. Each "x" represents the estimated return for a specific African country and year. The dashed line captures the associated nonlinear trend. Likewise, each "o" represents the estimated return for a specific Latin American country and year, and the solid line captures the nonlinear trend.

the Caribbean (LAC). For both, the largest economic benefits are associated with tertiary education, whereas secondary and primary degrees "produce" relatively lower contributions. In Africa, the overall return to tertiary education reaches 50 percent (21.56 percent) relative to the alternative of no completing primary education (obtaining a high school diploma). In LAC, the figure is approximately 35 percent (17 percent). Interestingly, at any level the Mincerian returns in Africa are larger than those reported in LAC.[6]

---

[6] For an analysis of the factors explaining the evolution of the returns to education during the last two decades in Latin America and the Caribbean, see Ferreyra et al. (2017). For Africa, Montenegro and Patrinos (2014) report unstable returns to primary education and increasing returns to tertiary education.

FIGURE 3-4

Mincerian Returns to Education in Africa and Latin America by Schooling Level

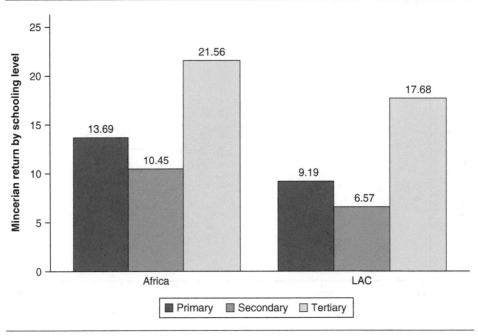

Source: Author's calculations based on Montenegro and Patrinos (2014).

Notes: This figure displays the Mincerian returns to education for Africa and Latin America (LA) at different schooling levels during the period 1997–2012. These are obtained from linear regressions of (log) earnings on a set of dummy variables characterizing the final schooling level of each individual in the sample. After fitting this (extended) earnings function (using the dummies instead of years of schooling function), the rate of return to another year of schooling across different levels of schooling can be derived taking into account the duration of each successive level.

Table 3-1 displays the Mincerian returns to education by schooling level in Chile and Ghana for 1991, 2005, and 2011. In the case of primary education, they decreased during the last decade in both countries. For secondary and tertiary education, the returns increased in Ghana, and, although they remained high in Chile, both decreased. Overall, these results could justify the notion that public efforts should largely concentrate on promoting access to tertiary education. This interpretation, however, provides only a narrow perspective. Perhaps in countries with already high enrollment rates in primary education, focusing on secondary and tertiary education might be economically appealing as they might yield large positive private returns. Nonetheless, it is not obvious that expanding access to schooling levels that exhibit lower enrollment is socially optimal. For example, a number of papers on developing economies have shown that the returns to tertiary education may be low, or even negative, if the expansion does not come along with proper quality standards or take into account the costs and dynamic consequences of the process (Urzua, 2012; Espinoza and Urzua, 2016; Gonzalez-Velosa et al., 2015). Although the analysis of this chapter does not deal with the issue of school quality, this is a critical point future research must address.

TABLE 3-1

Returns to Education by Schooling Level in Chile and Ghana, 1990–2012

Country	Year	Primary (%)	Secondary (%)	Tertiary (%)
Ghana	1991	1.4	7.9	12.2
	2005	4.7	7.8	23.2
	2012	2.7	8.8	28.7
Chile	1992	6.2	7.2	10.5
	2003	6.8	7.2	19.3
	2011	3	5.6	17.6

Source: Montenegro and Patrinos (2014).

Notes: The returns to education are obtained from linear regression models of (log) earnings on a series of dummy variables denoting the maximum schooling level achieved. Empirical analysis is carried out using household surveys.

The evidence described next sheds light on this reasoning. By comparing the cost of providing education with the earning trajectories of students who benefit from a higher spending, we assess the impact of public spending at different education levels. This analysis exploits the differences between Chile and Ghana, but we first describe the sources of information for each country.

3.1 Data Sources

The implementation of the conceptual frameworks introduced in section 2 requires micro-level information on multiple dimensions, ranging from variables characterizing individual schooling background to labor market outcomes. In addition, the information must be complemented with data on costs of public provision of education across different schooling levels.

Our main sources of information are household surveys in Chile and Ghana. We rely as much as possible on these sources in order to facilitate the replicability of the methodology in other countries where similar surveys are available.[7] More detailed information comes at the cost of replicability. Given the highly heterogeneous quality of data sources across countries, household surveys provide a more unified and consistent source to compare the results across different economies. We also use the UNESCO Database of Resources on Education (UNESCO, n.d.), which contains aggregated data on a number of education indicators, such as public spending in education, enrollment rates, and learning indicators.

3.1.1 Chile

The primary source of information is Chile's National Socioeconomic Characterization Survey of 2013 (Encuesta de Caracterizacion Socioeconomica Nacional, or CASEN).

---

[7] For Brazil, see Soares (2018).

CASEN is a nationally representative household survey run by the Chilean Ministry of Social Development. It covers 66,725 households. CASEN has been extensively used to monitor and evaluate the impact of social policies and to measure socioeconomic outcomes such as poverty rates and inequality as well as issues related to health and dwelling conditions. It contains education and labor modules providing information on the highest level of education attained, the type of institution attended (private or public), and labor market experience and earnings, among other variables. The survey is taken every two years. We use its 2013 version, which coincides with the year of the household survey for Ghana. We also gather data from the OECD (2013) on the average cost of attending primary, secondary, and tertiary education in Chile, as well as the fraction of the cost that is shared by the state and families.

3.1.2 Ghana

Our main data source is the Ghana Living Standards Survey (GLSS) 2012–13 (round 6). The GLSS is part of an international project, the Living Standard Measurement Study (LSMS), which was initiated in 1980 by the Policy Research Division of the World Bank. We use the sixth version of the GLSS, which was run by the Ghana Statistical Service agency and covers 18,000 households. This sample is the same utilized by Younger, Osei-Assibey, and Oppong (2017) in their investigation of the fiscal incidence in this country. The GLSS is nationally representative and provides household information on a number of relevant issues, including household consumption, educational attainment, access to financial services, economic activity, and migration, among others. The GLSS education module provides information on the educational history and final attainment of respondents, as well as on private expenditures in education, including fees and other expenses. We also use data on aggregate education statistics, such as number of schools and total enrollment across different levels from the Ministry of Education of Ghana.

3.2 Educational Attainment Levels

Optimally, the analysis should be carried out by year of additional education. This would make possible the estimation of the impact of public spending at each grade. However, given data limitations, it is impossible to construct comparable series across countries at that level of detail. Therefore, we instead implement the analysis according to the following taxonomy:

1. Primary education: In Chile, primary education comprises eight grades, and students are expected to first enroll at age six. Pre-primary education (before age six) was not mandatory in 2013. In Ghana, primary education lasts 11 years and students typically are enrolled from age four to 15. Primary education formally includes two years of pre-primary education, six years of primary school, and three years of junior secondary school. To secure the comparability of the results, we exclude pre-primary education when possible.

2. Secondary education: Secondary education lasts four and three years in Chile and Ghana, respectively.
3. Tertiary education: In both countries, we define tertiary education by any degree granted by a university. For the sake of comparison, we assume an average duration of four years. Post-graduate education, such as masters or doctoral programs, is excluded from the analysis.

Throughout most of the analysis we use "less than primary education" (no formal education) as the baseline. Each individual in our sample belongs to one of the above-defined levels based on his or her highest degree attained. For instance, a student that dropped out from primary school will belong to the "No Formal Education" group, whereas one who dropped out from secondary will belong to the "Primary Education" group.

It is worth noting that the human capital accumulation process involves a sequential decision process (completion of primary level is required to enroll in secondary school, and a secondary education is required to enroll in university). This explains why the return to schooling level s is defined as the economic benefits associated with the decision to complete s relative to a specific alternative, for example, $s-1$. This sequential ordering cannot be overlooked when estimating the economic value of education, and, as shown below, it has direct implication for the practical assessment of the long-term impact of public subsidies on the demand for education.

3.3 Costs of Education

We distinguish between the public and private costs of education. For Ghana, we use data from the GLSS to estimate the average cost at each schooling level. The education module of the GLSS contains information on actual household spending per person in each level. The data include information on tuition fees as well as other expenses, including transportation costs, materials, and lodging. By averaging the total expenditure across the population in the sample, we compute the average private costs of education at each level. For Chile, we use data from the OECD (2013) on the costs of education. OECD (2013) reports total spending by education level, as well an estimate of the fraction of the cost that is borne by families. For both countries, we complement the data on public spending using UNESCO Database of Resources on Education which contains information on public expenditure and enrollment rates for multiple countries and years.[8]

3.4 Summary Statistics

We present descriptive statistics in table 3-2. We find significant differences in government expenditure in primary education across both countries, with the Chilean government spending upwards of US$2,000 per pupil, and its Ghanian counterpart

---

[8] See UNESCO (n.d.).

TABLE 3-2
Education Systems in Chile and Ghana, 2013

	Chile	Ghana
A. Primary education		
Gross enrollment rate (%)	100.18	108.47
# of students	1,472,348	4,062,026
Compulsory	YES	YES
Length (years)	8	9
Gov. expenditure per student in constant US$	2,270.1	161.4
Annual tuition (avg. US$)	. . .	31.65
Other expenses (avg. US$)	. . .	69.71
Total private cost (avg. US$)	706.414	101.36
B. Secondary education		
Enrollment rate (%)	100.45	61.08
# of students	1,571,374	2,356,686
Compulsory	YES	YES
Length (years)	4	3
Gov. expenditure per student in constant US$	2,417.2	499.8
Annual tuition (avg. US$)	. . .	163.16
Other expenses (avg. US$)	. . .	133.85
Total private cost (avg. US$)	665.54	297.01
C. Tertiary education		
Enrollment rate (%)	83.81	14.3
# of students (ISCED 6)	755,508	201,536
Compulsory	NO	NO
Length (years)	4–7	4
Gov. expenditure per student in constant US $	2,755.7	1,390.8
Annual tuition (avg. US$)	. . .	558.52
Other expenses (avg. US$)	. . .	264.83
Total private cost (avg. US$)	5,531.68	823.35

Notes: Information on the costs of education for Chile (all levels) were obtained from OECD (2013). Costs of education in Ghana were obtained directly from household survey GLSS-6. Enrollment rates are reported by UNESCO Database of Resources on Education.

ISCED = International Standard Classification of Education; ". . ." = not available.

spending US$160 per student. While the Chilean government spends slightly more in secondary education, increasing its outlays to around US$2,400 per student, the government of Ghana almost triples its spending for its secondary students, reaching US$500. At the same time, while Chilean families bear an additional cost equivalent to one-third of government expenditures in these two levels, expenditures by Ghanian

Table 3-3

Schooling Transition Probabilities in Chile and Ghana

A. Ghana			
Increase in enrollment			
Attainment	Primary	Secondary	Tertiary
Primary	0.611	n.a.	n.a.
Secondary	0.344	0.810	n.a.
Tertiary	0.045	0.190	1.000

B. Chile			
Increase in enrollment			
Attainment	Primary	Secondary	Tertiary
Primary	0.352	n.a.	n.a.
Secondary	0.353	0.545	n.a.
Tertiary	0.295	0.455	1.000

Notes: The table presents how changes in enrollment levels affect final schooling attainment. In particular, each column shows the distribution of schooling levels associated with an increase in enrollment in primary, secondary, and tertiary education.

"n.a." = not applicable.

households account for at 35–40 percent of total spending in primary and secondary education. Finally, there is a significant change in the financing of tertiary education (panel C): while governmental expenditure on this level in Chile far exceeds that of Ghana's government, Chilean households account for two-thirds of total spending at this level, relative to less than 40 percent for their counterparts in Ghana.

We also examine how enrollment rates vary across educational levels in these two countries. Despite the large differences in educational expenditures in primary schooling, there are no observed differences in gross enrollment at this level. In fact, the gross enrollment rate in Ghana exceeds that of Chile, possibly reflecting a larger share of students who have fallen behind in their education.[9] Nonetheless, significant differences appear as early as secondary school. For instance, while the gross enrollment rate in secondary education in Chile is 100 percent, the corresponding value in Ghana is only 61 percent. Similarly, there are vast differences in tertiary education, such that upwards of 80 percent of Chilean students reach this level, compared to just 14 percent of students in Ghana. This comparative analysis suggests that there is a large scope for increasing access to both secondary and tertiary education in Ghana.

---

[9] The gross enrollment rate is defined as the ratio between the net enrollment and the total population in the age of being enrolled in a certain level of education. For this reason, the gross enrollment rate can take values greater than one.

TABLE 3-4

Value of In-Kind Transfer by Schooling Level in Chile and Ghana

	Schooling level	Ghana (1)	Chile (2)	Chile (3)
Value of one	Pre-primary	105	2,770	1,162–1,414
year of publicly	Primary	161	2,270	1,104–1,414
funded	Secondary	499	2,417	n.a.
schooling	Conventional	n.a.	n.a.	1,244–1,689
(annual US$)	Technical/Vocational	n.a.	n.a.	1,511–1,917
	Tertiary	1,390	2,755	2,755

Notes: Columns 1 and 2: The monetary value of an extra year of publicly funded schooling across schooling levels is obtained from UNESCO (undated). Column 3: The values correspond to per-student transfers reported by the Ministry of Education of Chile (2014). The smallest transfer values are associated with half-day schools. The largest transfer values are associated with full-day schools. Gini coefficients are computed using household level full income. Marginal and cumulative effects are computed after adding to total income the respective cost of one year of publicly funded education for each school-age child attending school.

"n.a." = not applicable.

The disparities in enrollment rates translate into contrasting patterns in schooling transition probabilities (q_s in section 2). Table 3-3 presents these results. The chances of completing a tertiary degree for a student attending primary education are almost 30 percent in Chile but just 4.5 percent in Ghana. Among those attending secondary school, the proportions increase significantly, up to 45.5 percent and 19 percent, respectively, yet large differences remain. As we show in Section 4.5, these differences are critical for understanding the differential effects of public spending on enrollment rates in each country.

4 Empirical Analysis

The objective of this section is two-fold. It first discusses the empirical implementation of the model of section 2, describing each of its components in detail. It then presents the main results. We begin by examining the static cost of provision account.

4.1 The Cost of Provision Approach

Table 3-4 displays the cost associated with the public provision of education services in Chile and Ghana across schooling levels. For Chile, it includes both the figures reported by UNESCO and those obtained from official sources (Ministry of Education), which take into account the value of the fiscal transfers to schools depending on their type (e.g., conventional or technical high schools) and shift (half- or full-day schools).

Using the empirical strategy described in section 2, table 3-5 presents the results obtained for the cost of provision approach. The outcome of interest in panel A is the Gini coefficient obtained using disposable per capita income within the household to

TABLE 3-5

Impact of Education Spending on Inequality in Chile and Ghana

		Ghana		Chile		
Gini	Original	0.423		0.530		
		(1)	(N)	(3)	(4)	(N)
A. Only those enrolled in publicly subsidized institutions						
Marginal effects	Pre-primary	0.419	(735,632)	0.524	0.527	(637,009)
	Primary	0.395	(4,260,708)	0.518	0.523	(1,312,752)
	Secondary	0.423	(392,061)	0.525	0.526	(549,088)
	Tertiary	0.427	(131,860)	0.529	0.528	(213,977)
Cumulative effects	Pre-primary	0.419		0.524	0.527	
	+Primary	0.392		0.512	0.519	
	+Secondary	0.392		0.507	0.516	
	+Tertiary	0.396		0.505	0.514	
B. All those enrolled						
Marginal effects	Pre-primary	0.420	(1,180,199)	0.523	0.526	(836,200)
	Primary	0.391	(5,956,728)	0.516	0.522	(1,967,008)
	Secondary	0.424	(500,235)	0.522	0.523	(995,207)
	Tertiary	0.431	(171,092)	0.527	0.525	(1,100,704)
Cumulative effects	Pre-primary			0.523	0.526	
	+Primary	0.386		0.509	0.518	
	+Secondary	0.387		0.502	0.513	
	+Tertiary	0.394		0.498	0.508	

Notes: The monetary values of an extra year of publicly funded schooling across schooling levels are reported in table 3-4. For Chile, the numbers under (3) are obtained using the values reported in UNESCO (n.d.). Column (4) uses the official public per-student transfers. These consider whether the individuals are enrolled in half- or full-day schools. Gini coefficients are computed using household level Disposable Income. Marginal and cumulative effects are computed after adding to total income the respective value of one year of publicly funded education for each school-age child. For both countries, column (N) reports the number of individuals for which the monetary value of the in-kind transfer is imposed.

which, depending on the number of students attending publicly subsidized institutions, the respective monetary value of the subsidy is added.

Column 1 contains the results for Ghana, whereas column *N* reports the number of individuals eligible to receive the in-kind transfer. The largest decline in inequality is reported for primary education (0.395 versus the original 0.423), where the number of beneficiaries reaches more than 4 million. For the other groups the simulated effects are negligible.

Columns 3 (UNESCO) and 4 (official figures) display the results for Chile. The impact is modest. As for Ghana, the largest decline in inequality comes from education services in primary education (0.527 versus 0.523). It is worth mentioning that for both countries, the marginal contribution of tertiary education implies a small increase in the Gini coefficients, which is the result of a regressive access to publicly funded higher education institutions.

Finally, panel B repeats the analysis but now assuming all students, regardless of whether they attend publicly subsidized institutions, internalize the monetary value associated with the provision of public education. As expected, the cumulative effects go in the same direction as those reported in panel A but are now larger in magnitude. For Ghana and Chile we report a modest decline in inequality.

4.2 Behavioral Responses in Practice

As discussed in section 2, two approaches can be used to estimate the behavioral responses of individuals to government spending in education. Both assume access to limited data. We first describe each approach separately and then discuss how to integrate age-earnings profiles into the analysis.

4.2.1 Approach 1: Aggregate Enrollment and Public Spending

In order to estimate the elasticity of enrollment with respect to educational spending, one can exploit comparable aggregate information. Thus, we supplement data from the household surveys for Chile and Ghana with enrollment rates and educational expenses for Latin American and African countries as reported by UNESCO Database of Resources on Education.

Consider the following empirical model:

$$(3\text{-}8) \qquad T_{l,t} = \alpha_l + \theta_l G_t + \varepsilon_{l,t}, \quad l = \{1, \ldots, L\} \text{ and } t = \{1, \ldots, T\},$$

where G_t defines government spending on education in year t, $T_{l,t}$ captures enrollment rates for educational level l, and θ_l embeds the correlation between public expenditure and the enrollment rate in education level l (for those eligible to attend). A positive θ_l implies that increases in G_t is associated with an increment in the probability that a student goes ahead and enrolls in level l. Moreover, a higher enrollment rate in level l gives the option to the cohort of students who have benefited from the policy to go on and enroll in higher levels. For instance, if government spending increases primary level enrollment, a fraction of these new students might also attend secondary schools, and some could pursue tertiary education. The estimation of (3-8) can help to account for this fact. In particular, equipped with the sequence of these parameters, $(\theta_2, \ldots, \theta_L)$, the analyst can evaluate the aggregate and long-term effects of changes in G_t on the overall distribution of final schooling levels in the population. Lastly, since different schooling levels exhibit different expected earning profiles, we can estimate the economic impact of public expenditure in education by calculating the change in labor market outcomes induced by an increase in public expenditure.

TABLE 3-6

Elasticities: Cross-Country Regressions in 48 Sub-Saharan African Countries, 1976–2016

Controls	Enrollment in:		
	Primary	Secondary	Tertiary
Expenditure primary	4.497***		
	(1.216)		
Expenditure secondary		18.208***	
		(2.255)	
Expenditure tertiary			−0.358
			(0.831)
Constant	92.965***	19.595***	7.797***
	(2.750)	(3.517)	(0.885)
R^2	0.05	0.25	0.00
N	263	202	182

Note: The table presents the estimated effects of gross enrollment rates on public expenditure; see equation (3-8).

"***" = Statistically different from zero ($p < 0.001$).

We estimate the regression model (3-8) separately for the two regions using data for the period 1976–2016. We impute the estimated correlation among Latin American countries to Chile and the corresponding coefficients for Africa to Ghana. Tables 3-6 and 3-7 report the estimated parameters for Africa and Latin America, respectively.

The results for Africa suggest a clear association between schooling spending and enrollment in primary and secondary education. These results fit in with those presented earlier, as governmental expenditures in Ghana across these two levels is small compared to private expenditures. Hence, a modest increase in public spending could go a long way toward increasing primary and, more critically, secondary schooling. The estimated elasticity for tertiary education, however, is small and statistically insignificant. This result may be explained by the low enrollment levels in tertiary education observed in the region during the period of analysis. The findings reported in table 3-6 indicate that enrolling an additional student in primary and secondary education requires approximately US$2,500 and US$1,100 of government financing per year, respectively.[10]

Table 3-7 reports positive and statistically significant enrollment-expenditure coefficients for secondary and tertiary education in Latin America. These results suggest that enrolling extra students in secondary and tertiary education would cost governments around US$30,000 and US$10,000 per year, respectively. However, in the case of primary education the estimated parameter is small and not significant. This may be explained by large baseline enrollment rates in primary schooling during 1976–2016, such that additional governmental funding would not further increase enrollment.

[10] We note that these estimates do not take into account capacity constraints.

TABLE 3-7

Cross-Country Regressions in 41 Latin American and Caribbean Countries, 1976–2016

Controls	Enrollment in:		
	Primary	Secondary	Tertiary
Expenditure primary	−0.958		
	(0.974)		
Expenditure secondary		8.207***	
		(1.193)	
Expenditure tertiary			22.106***
			(3.015)
Constant	113.118***	74.604***	19.238***
	(1.783)	(1.976)	(2.844)
R^2	0.00	0.16	0.24
N	245	244	169

Note: The table presents the estimated effects of gross enrollment rates on public expenditure; see equation (3-8).

"***" = Statistically different from zero ($p < 0.01$).

4.2.2 Approach 2: Individual-Level Analysis

Schooling decisions can be examined using a microeconomic setting and household survey data. Following the notation introduced in section 2, if we assume a linear and separable model for the net utility associated with schooling level s after completing schooling level $s-1$, $U_s^*(\cdot)$, we can use standard discrete choice models to characterize the sequence of schooling decisions. Formally, given a set of observed (Z) and unobserved (ε) characteristics, we define the transition probability across schooling levels as a function of the net utility ($U_s^*(Z, \varepsilon) = \varphi_s(Z_{s,i}) - \varepsilon_{s,i}$) as follows:

$$p_s = \Pr(\phi(Z_{s,i}) \geq \varepsilon_{s,i} \mid Z)$$
$$= F_{\varepsilon_s}(\phi_s(Z_i)),$$

where $\varepsilon_{s,i}$ is the error term, $F_{\varepsilon_s}(\cdot)$ is its cumulative density function, and $\varphi_s(\cdot)$ is a general function of $Z_{s,i}$.[11] Under the assumption of normally distributed error terms at each step of the decision process (i.e., $\varepsilon_s \sim N(0,1)$), and linear in parameters specifications for $\varphi_s(\cdot)$, we can estimate the sequence of probabilities using a sequence of probit models.[12]

Tables 3-8 and 3-9 present the results—point estimates as well as estimated marginal effects—for the discrete choice models characterizing the sequence of schooling

---

[11] Observed ($Z_{s,i}$) and unobserved ($\varepsilon_{s,i}$) are assumed to be independent. Furthermore, error terms are assumed independent across individuals and schooling levels.

[12] The structure mimics a dynamic decision model (Cameron and Heckman, 1998). The empirical caveats of implementing this framework using cross-sectional information are discussed below.

TABLE 3-8

Transition Probabilities for Chile: Results from Probit Models

	p3	p4	p5	p6	p7	p8	p9	p10	p11	p12	p13+
Income	0.0148***	0.1288***	0.0185***	0.0733***	0.0249***	0.1217***	0.0548***	0.0596***	0.0548***	0.0611***	0.0858***
	(0.0056)	(0.0082)	(0.0028)	(0.0052)	(0.0025)	(0.0046)	(0.0017)	(0.0023)	(0.0017)	(0.0021)	(0.0008)
	[0.0000]	[0.0001]	[0.0001]	[0.0002]	[0.0002]	[0.0005]	[0.0014]	[0.0009]	[0.0017]	[0.0014]	[0.0224]
	<0.0000>	<0.0000>	<0.0000>	<0.0000>	<0.0000>	<0.0000>	<0.0000>	<0.0000>	<0.0000>	<0.0000>	<0.0002>
Female	0.3837***	-0.0239*	0.0617***	0.4290***	0.3551***	0.2065***	0.5131***	0.5039***	0.5941***	0.5201***	0.5793***
	(0.0216)	(0.0145)	(0.0101)	(0.0135)	(0.0084)	(0.0093)	(0.0057)	(0.0073)	(0.0061)	(0.0077)	(0.0032)
	[0.0004]	[-0.0000]	[0.0004]	[0.0009]	[0.0031]	[0.0007]	[0.0123]	[0.0077]	[0.0180]	[0.0113]	[0.1446]
	<0.0000>	<0.0000>	<0.0001>	<0.0000>	<0.0001>	<0.0000>	<0.0001>	<0.0001>	<0.0002>	<0.0002>	<0.0008>
Rural	-0.0311	0.0607***	-0.2317***	0.1139***	-0.0037	0.0180*	-0.1585***	-0.0227***	0.0272***	0.1165***	-0.1650***
	(0.0194)	(0.0168)	(0.0114)	(0.0128)	(0.0088)	(0.0100)	(0.0056)	(0.0075)	(0.0066)	(0.0093)	(0.0047)
	[-0.0000]	[0.0001]	[-0.0017]	[0.0002]	[-0.0000]	[0.0001]	[-0.0046]	[-0.0004]	[0.0008]	[0.0024]	[-0.0456]
	<0.0000>	<0.0000>	<0.0001>	<0.0000>	<0.0001>	<0.0000>	<0.0002>	<0.0001>	<0.0002>	<0.0002>	<0.0014>
Father's ed.	0.0500***	0.0882***	0.0092***	0.0459***	0.0452***	0.0520***	0.0421***	0.0348***	0.0315***	0.0274***	0.0629***
	(0.0026)	(0.0021)	(0.0016)	(0.0016)	(0.0011)	(0.0013)	(0.0008)	(0.0010)	(0.0008)	(0.0010)	(0.0005)
	[0.0001]	[0.0001]	[0.0001]	[0.0001]	[0.0004]	[0.0002]	[0.0011]	[0.0006]	[0.0010]	[0.0006]	[0.0164]
	<0.0000>	<0.0000>	<0.0000>	<0.0000>	<0.0000>	<0.0000>	<0.0000>	<0.0000>	<0.0000>	<0.0000>	<0.0001>
Mother's ed.	0.0388***	0.0064***	0.0515***	0.0824***	0.0666***	0.0666***	0.0791***	0.0691***	0.0738***	0.0385***	0.0819***
	(0.0027)	(0.0022)	(0.0016)	(0.0017)	(0.0012)	(0.0014)	(0.0008)	(0.0010)	(0.0008)	(0.0011)	(0.0006)
	[0.0000]	[0.0000]	[0.0003]	[0.0002]	[0.0006]	[0.0003]	[0.0020]	[0.0011]	[0.0023]	[0.0009]	[0.0213]
	<0.0000>	<0.0000>	<0.0000>	<0.0000>	<0.0000>	<0.0000>	<0.0000>	<0.0000>	<0.0000>	<0.0000>	<0.0001>
p	0.988	0.977	0.973	0.980	0.946	0.980	0.911	0.967	0.944	0.967	0.668
N	1,806,780	1,805,345	1,803,183	1,798,347	1,793,526	1,771,659	1,740,845	1,591,351	1,403,423	1,224,055	977,926

Notes: Per capita family income in thousand US dollars; (standard errors); [associated marginal effect at the means]; <marginal effect's standard errors>; *** $p < 0.01$, ** $p < 0.05$, * $p < 0.1$.

TABLE 3-9

Transition Probabilities for Ghana: Results from Probit Models, Including Controls for Parent Education

	p3	p4	p5	p6	p7	p8	p9	p10	p11	p12	p13+
Income	0.1143	0.1810	0.0256	0.1590	0.0918	0.1965**	0.2117**	0.1366	0.0339	0.0790	0.1118
	(0.1680)	(0.1255)	(0.0521)	(0.1149)	(0.0629)	(0.0799)	(0.1024)	(0.0959)	(0.0508)	(0.1257)	(0.0991)
	[0.0018]	[0.0064]	[0.0014]	[0.0165]	[0.0153]	[0.0382]	[0.0359]	[0.0455]	[0.0066]	[0.0117]	[0.0441]
	<0.0026>	<0.0044>	<0.0028>	<0.0118>	<0.0105>	<0.0155>	<0.0171>	<0.0318>	<0.0098>	<0.0185>	<0.0391>
Female	−0.0228	0.0046	0.0660	0.0012	0.0587	−0.0899*	0.0774	−0.1186*	0.0564	0.1312	−0.1450
	(0.0994)	(0.0765)	(0.0697)	(0.0586)	(0.0533)	(0.0542)	(0.0619)	(0.0621)	(0.1085)	(0.1183)	(0.1192)
	[−0.0004]	[0.0002]	[0.0035]	[0.0001]	[0.0098]	[−0.0175]	[0.0131]	[−0.0395]	[0.0109]	[0.0194]	[−0.0572]
	<0.0016>	<0.0027>	<0.0037>	<0.0061>	<0.0089>	<0.0106>	<0.0105>	<0.0207>	<0.0209>	<0.0176>	<0.0470>
Rural	−0.2905**	−0.3397***	−0.3730***	−0.2577***	−0.3035***	−0.3028***	−0.2742***	−0.5515***	−0.2946***	−0.3600***	−0.3466***
	(0.1133)	(0.0889)	(0.0789)	(0.0649)	(0.0572)	(0.0577)	(0.0674)	(0.0653)	(0.1067)	(0.1166)	(0.1292)
	[−0.0047]	[−0.0125]	[−0.0208]	[−0.0272]	[−0.0519]	[−0.0606]	[−0.0484]	[−0.1894]	[−0.0616]	[−0.0602]	[−0.1374]
	<0.0020>	<0.0035>	<0.0050>	<0.0069>	<0.0097>	<0.0117>	<0.0120>	<0.0224>	<0.0224>	<0.0209>	<0.0509>
Father's ed.	0.0427***	0.0342***	0.0459***	0.0384***	0.0371***	0.0366***	0.0251***	0.0412***	0.0371***	0.0378***	0.0351***
	(0.0130)	(0.0080)	(0.0069)	(0.0072)	(0.0060)	(0.0061)	(0.0076)	(0.0066)	(0.0113)	(0.0146)	(0.0127)
	[0.0007]	[0.0012]	[0.0025]	[0.0040]	[0.0062]	[0.0071]	[0.0043]	[0.0137]	[0.0072]	[0.0056]	[0.0139]
	<0.0002>	<0.0003>	<0.0004>	<0.0008>	<0.0010>	<0.0012>	<0.0013>	<0.0022>	<0.0022>	<0.0021>	<0.0050>
Mother's ed.	0.0395**	0.0413***	0.0299***	0.0348***	0.0246***	0.0192***	0.0380***	0.0249***	0.0150	0.0188	0.0098
	(0.0161)	(0.0108)	(0.0090)	(0.0083)	(0.0072)	(0.0071)	(0.0087)	(0.0079)	(0.0117)	(0.0142)	(0.0128)
	[0.0006]	[0.0015]	[0.0016]	[0.0036]	[0.0041]	[0.0037]	[0.0065]	[0.0083]	[0.0029]	[0.0028]	[0.0039]
	<0.0003>	<0.0004>	<0.0004>	<0.0008>	<0.0012>	<0.0014>	<0.0015>	<0.0026>	<0.0023>	<0.0021>	<0.0051>
P	.9455	0.9263	0.9258	0.917	0.896	0.855	0.868	0.657	0.884	0.914	0.647
N	7,686	7,587	7,350	7,027	6,495	5,423	4,235	3,128	1,838	1,353	821

Notes: Income in thousand dollars; (standard errors); [associated marginal effect at the means]; <marginal effect's standard errors>; *** p < 0.01, ** p < 0.05, * p < 0.1.

decisions for Chile and Ghana, respectively. For both cases, the empirical analysis is carried out using household survey data and comparable sets of controls.

For Chile, we observe statistically significant positive effects across schooling levels for family income, gender (in favor of females), and parental education. This suggests a critical role for socioeconomic background as determinant of schooling choices, which is a well-known feature of the Latin American country. Only the dummy variable "Rural" in table 3-8 has ambiguous (and sometimes non-significant) effects across columns, which is not surprising given both the decline in the number of families living in rural areas and the efforts to secure school enrollments in K–12 throughout the country. Enrollment rates by level, reported under row p, confirm these efforts as they indicate that more than 95 percent of school-age individuals attend school in Chile, and approximately 70 percent pursue tertiary education.

The results from Ghana offer a somewhat different perspective, highlighting the contrasts between the two countries. As in Chile, the father's education emerges as a significant determinant of all transition probabilities, whereas mother's education does so only until tenth grade. This suggests a more prominent role of the father figure within Ghana's households, which is consistent with the loss of statistical power of some of the positive effects reported for family income. Gender, on the other hand, does not seem to determine schooling transition, whereas a rural residency reduces the probabilities of progressing throughout the system.

Despite the fact that monetary transfers are not directly accounted for in this model, we can use family income to simulate the impact of monetary transfers directed to households with school-age children. The positive coefficients associated with family income estimated for Chile and Ghana across the probit models facilitate this strategy. We develop this logic next, but first we need to integrate age-earnings profiles into the analysis.

4.3 Human Capital and Earnings Profiles

Regardless of the approach aimed at connecting public spending and enrollment, the second ingredient of our analysis has to do with the estimation of earnings profiles. To this end, we borrow from the long-standing literature in labor economics estimating earnings equations (Heckman, Lochner, and Todd, 2006; Card, 2001). Let s denote the schooling level attained, with $s = 1, \ldots, S$; Y be the outcome of interest (e.g., log annual earnings); and X be labor market experience. Thus, the Mincer model delivers the following regression equation:

$$(3\text{-}9) \qquad Y = \pi_0 + \pi_1 S + \beta_1 X + \beta_2 X^2 + \varepsilon,$$

where ε is an idiosyncratic error term and π_1 captures $\partial E[Y|S, X]/\partial S$, that is, the average difference in the expected value of Y between individuals with S and $S - 1$ year of education, after controlling for the effect of labor market experience. This model can be trivially extended to allow for level-specific returns. Let D_s be a dummy variable such that $D_s = 1$ if the individual reaches schooling level s, 0 otherwise. Thus, we can rewrite equation (3-9) as follows:

$$Y = \pi_0 + \sum_{s=1}^{S} \pi_s D_s + \beta_1 X + \beta_2 X^2 + \varepsilon.$$

The coefficient π_s is typically interpreted as the economic return to schooling level s, where the baseline category is no formal education. However, this expression still imposes linear separability between education and labor market experience. To relax this assumption, using the sample of individuals reporting each schooling level s, we can estimate that

(3-10) $$Y_s = \pi_s + \beta_{1,s} X + \beta_{2,s} X^2 + \varepsilon_s.$$

Notice that with the estimated coefficients in (3-10), we can construct a series of labor earnings until a given age of retirement for any given schooling level s.[13]

In what follows, we estimate earnings profiles following the Mincer regression specified in equation (3-10) using cross-section data from the household surveys. The left-hand side of (3-10) measures the natural logarithm of net annual earnings. Net earnings are calculated after subtracting the prevailing income tax rates in Chile and Ghana shown in table 3-10. Years of labor market experience are constructed subtracting the total number of years of formal education from the current worker's age. We limit the minimum working age to 15, which is the minimum legal age to work in both countries. Moreover, we include only workers who are not currently studying or pursuing any degree. As is well-known in this literature, educational attainment is endogenous to individual's unobserved characteristics, which affect both attainment and labor market outcomes. To address this endogeneity, we complement our Ordinary Least Squares (OLS) estimates with an instrumental variables approach, for which we

---

[13]Conventional estimates based on earnings regressions are subject to important qualifications (Heckman, Lochner, and Todd, 2006). The potential endogeneity of education, a result of its correlation with the unobserved component, ε_i, is a source of econometric concerns widely discussed in the literature (Card, 2001). The exact specification of the equation has been a subject of much debate as well (Heckman, Lochner, and Todd, 2006). Another important drawback of this approach is that it does not take into account the cost that students and their families face when investing in education. Educational attainment implies monetary and nonmonetary costs that affect the decision of investing in human capital. First, there is an opportunity cost of studying. People could join the labor market instead, and earnings foregone during the study period can be an important factor driving the education decision. Second, there are monetary expenses in acquiring education. In some cases, there is tuition to be paid to educational institutions. Even if education is tuition-free, there are often other expenses, such as transportation, lodging, or materials costs that people have to incur. Finally, there are nonpecuniary costs, such as psychological costs, of pursuing education. Despite these empirical difficulties, from expression (3-10) we can obtain a simple proxy for the value of education.

TABLE 3-10

Monthly Personal Income Tax Rate in Chile and Ghana

A. Chile (in pesos)		
From	To	Tax rate
0	$1,111.29	0.0%
$1,111.29	$2,469.53	4.0%
$2,469.53	$4,115.89	8.0%
$4,115.89	$5,762.25	13.5%
$5,762.25	$7,408.60	23.0%
$7,408.60	$9,878.13	30.4%
$9,878.13	$12,347.67	35.5%
$12,347.67	or more	40.0%

B. Ghana (in Ghanaian cedis)		
From	To	Tax rate
0	$216.00	0.0%
$216.00	$324.00	5.0%
$324.00	$475.00	10.0%
$475.00	$3,240.00	17.5%
$3,240.00	or more	25.0%

Sources: Chilean Tax Revenue Authority (2014) and Ghana Revenue Authority (2013).

use reported family income and parental education as instruments for educational attainment. The results are presented in table 3-A1.[14]

Table 3-11 displays the estimated coefficients from the Mincer regression for Chile (columns 1 and 2) and Ghana (3 and 4). The first OLS column in each country includes the full sample of respondents over 15, whereas in the second one, we restrict our attention to dependents who are 15–35 years old. This comparison informs the robustness of the results to different samples. The findings show significant returns to an additional year of education for students who have not gone beyond secondary school in both countries. For Chile, an extra year of education is associated with an increase in annual earnings in the range of 9–11 percent, which is in line with previous estimates by Montenegro (2001). Despite the difference in enrollment and financing patterns in Ghana, we also find large and significant returns in this country, in the range of 7–8 percent. These results

---

[14]Different empirical approaches have been proposed to account for the endogeneity of educational attainment (Card 2001, Carneiro et al. 2003, Heckman, Lochner, and Todd, 2006, among others). We note that data limitations in household surveys in both Chile and Ghana limit our ability to follow recent econometric approaches designed to address this issue. This topic remains a promising avenue for future research once better data become available.

TABLE 3-11
Results from Mincer Regressions for Chile and Ghana

Variable	Chile		Ghana	
	(1)	(2)	(3)	(4)
Years of education (≤12)	0.114***	0.091***	0.080***	0.072
	(0.004)	(0.009)	(0.008)	(0.029)
Tertiary	2.198***	1.800***	1.640***	1.452***
	(0.043)	(0.104)	(0.105)	(0.383)
Experience	0.050***	0.067***	0.078***	0.065*
	(0.002)	(0.007)	(0.006)	(0.035)
Experience^2	−0.001***	−0.001***	−0.001***	−0.001
	(0.000)	(0.000)	(0.000)	(0.001)
Education (≤12) × exp.	−0.002***	−0.002***	−0.002***	−0.002
	(0.000)	(0.000)	(0.000)	(0.002)
Tertiary × experience	−0.022***	−0.035***	−0.020***	−0.004
	(0.001)	(0.006)	(0.004)	(0.027)
Rural	−0.227***	−0.050**	−0.003	−0.328***
	(0.009)	(0.021)	(0.024)	(0.082)
Female	−0.500***	−0.167***	−0.446***	−0.268***
	(0.005)	(0.015)	(0.022)	(0.080)
R^2	0.30	0.22	0.19	0.22
N	90,339	11,689	16,073	1,354
Sample	Full	15–35 y/o	Full	15–35 y/o

Sources: Own calculations using data from CASEN 2013 (Chile) and GLSS-6 (Ghana) data.

Notes: We include only workers whose age is above 15 years and who are not currently studying or pursuing any degree. Parental education is used as source of instruments for both countries. *** $p < 0.01$, ** $p < 0.05$, * $p < 0.1$.

are largely in line with previous findings by Duflo, Dupas, and Kremer (2021), who find a return of 13 percent for secondary school students in Ghana enrolled in a vocational track, and Peet, Fink, and Fawzi (2015), who find an estimated return of 4.7 percent to an additional year of education in Ghana using LSMS data between 1982 and 2012.[15] At the same time, we find significantly larger and significant returns to completing tertiary education in both countries, exceeding 140 log points in all specifications.

The Mincerian regression also allows us to examine the returns to experience. The results in columns 1 and 3 indicate that the returns to experience tend to be higher in Ghana than in Chile, reaching 8 percent in the former compared to just 5 percent in the latter. They become larger in columns 2 and 4. In addition, we find that in both countries

[15] For a review of estimated Mincerian returns by level of education in Africa, see Barouni and Broecke (2014).

and across all levels of education, earnings profiles are concave. Figures 3-5 and 3-6 show the post-tax age-earning profiles for different levels of education in Chile and Ghana, respectively. These profiles are estimated using the estimated coefficients reported in table 3-11 and illustrate the significant differences between the age-earnings profiles associated with tertiary versus other levels of educations. In Chile, the concave pattern is starker for students who have attained a tertiary degree, where a clear peak is observed at around 27 years of experience, which corresponds to adults in their early fifties. While there is a concave pattern for Chileans with lower levels of attainment, the relationship is less clear. Nonetheless, we note that the earnings peak occurs at a higher level of experience, which corresponds with the fact that less educated individuals enter the labor force at earlier ages.

We find similar patterns in Ghana: there are concave earnings patterns across all educational levels, though the pattern is starker for the highest achieving individuals, whose earnings peak at 23–25 years of experience. Finally, we note that table 3-11 shows larger returns to experience for less educated students, as the coefficient on the education and experience interaction is negative across all specifications (although not significant in a few of them). Consistent with the literature (Heckman, Lochner, and Todd, 2006), the evidence confirms the importance of allowing for interactions in the context of the Mincer model. However, these results do not account for the costs of education or its dynamic benefits. The next section extends the analysis along these lines.

4.4 Benefits versus Costs

In order to assess the impact of public spending, it is important to first put in context the amount of resources involved in the provision of educational services and the benefits obtained from them. To this end, we define two constructs that serve as proxies for the economic value of education and take into account its costs: internal rate of returns (IRR) and net present values (NPV). In brief, using the notation introduced in section 2.2, we can define the NPV associated with schooling level s as

$$(3\text{-}11) \qquad \tilde{V}_r(s) = \sum_{t=s+1}^{T} \frac{Y_L(s,t)}{(1+r)^t} - \sum_{t=1}^{s} \frac{C(s,t)}{(1+r)^t},$$

where $Y_L(s, t)$ denotes the annual income of someone reporting s years of education and t years of labor market experience, $C(s, t)$ is the annual private cost associated with s, r is the discount rate, and T is the retirement age. Expression (3-11) is the discrete version of (3-6). Notice that $\tilde{V}_r(s)$ at least partially embeds "social gains" from achieving level of education s, as $Y_L(s, t)$ is pretax income, and hence, NPV includes taxes that will be collected by the government. On the other hand, the IRR between school levels s and $s+1$, with associated $\tilde{V}_r(s)$ and $\tilde{V}_r(s+1)$, is the rate $\tilde{r}$ such that $\tilde{V}_r(s) = \tilde{V}_r(s+1)$. The estimation of NPV and IRR in both countries can be used to understand the magnitudes and potential effects of increased educational spending.

In principle, the sources of information commonly exploited by researchers (e.g., household surveys) do not suffice to bear the empirical challenges associated with

FIGURE 3-5
Earnings Profiles in Chile, 2013

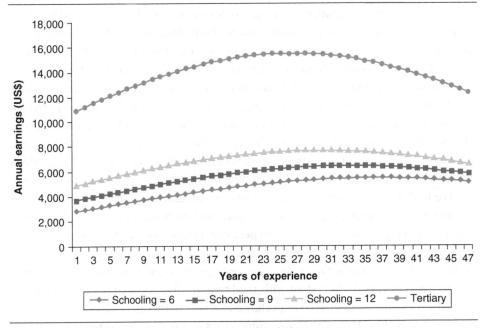

Source: Author's calculations using data from the CASEN 2013 and results from earnings regressions.

FIGURE 3-6
Earnings Profiles in Ghana, 2013

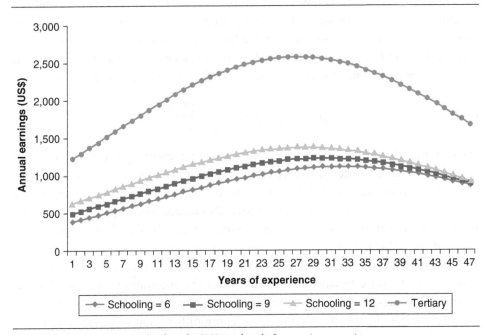

Source: Author's calculations using data from the GLSS-6 and results from earnings regressions.

the estimation of NPVs and IRRs. This lack of longitudinal data constitutes a major limitation. Nonetheless, we can exploit cross-sectional data to generate sequences of $Y_L(s, t)$ for different s. To see how, first notice that equation (3-10) defines the average growth rate of earnings at each experience level. Then, for a given schooling level s, we can combine the estimands reported in table 3-11 and average earnings after, for example, five years of working experience to predict average earnings for any s and t. Formally, given $Y_L(s, \bar{t})$ in the data, we can use the estimated values for $\beta_{1,s}$ and $\beta_{2,s}$ to generate $\hat{Y}(t, s)$ for any s and t.[16] Of course, this exercise is subject to the qualifications emerging from multiple assumptions (e.g., no cohort effects and functional forms), but it enables a simple strategy for later examining the incidence of public spending by exploiting cross-sectional information that is typically available.

To illustrate its potential, we implement this approach using household survey data from Chile and Ghana. The resulting sequences of $\hat{Y}(t, s)$ are then used in estimating IRRs across schooling levels. In this way, we show how to overcome the data limitations usually faced by researchers when estimating the economic returns of achieving further education, while taking into account the direct costs and benefits of investing in human capital, the opportunity costs (foregone earnings), and the option value of reaching a higher education level (Heckman, Urzua, and Yates, 2007). For example, increasing schooling attainment from primary to secondary education not only delivers a direct benefit through higher wages, but also provides individuals with the opportunity of reaching a higher schooling level. Thus, students who have completed secondary schooling are able to further enroll in tertiary education and capture its corresponding benefits. This is not the case for secondary school dropouts. We carry out this analysis using baseline enrollment rates at each education level along with the estimated transition probabilities from one level to the next. In other words, we estimate the probability of reaching a higher schooling level by computing the unconditional probability that can be inferred from enrollment rates.

Table 3-12 presents the IRRs for the different pairwise comparisons of schooling levels constructed using the reported cost of education (section 4.2) and the estimated age-earnings profiles. Within this simple framework, the IRR of completing a secondary degree for someone who has already completed the primary level is large in Chile, reaching upwards of 7 percent. And despite larger costs, the result is similar when comparing tertiary and secondary education.

In Ghana the estimated IRRs are significantly smaller, remaining below 1 percent for the two schooling levels considered, with the rate associated with completing a tertiary degree below that of a secondary degree. At first glance this might appear surprising, but in light of our analysis three distinctive features of the country can explain these negligible values: (1) a large opportunity cost resulting from the small wage premia; (2) the small

---

[16] To control for the fact the dependent variable in (3-10) is log earnings, from $\beta_{1,s}$, $\beta_{2,s}$ and σ_s^2 (the variance of ε), we compute $\hat{Y}(s, t) = \hat{Y}(s, t-1)e^{\beta_{1,s} + 2\beta_{2,s}(t-1) + 0.5\sigma_{\varepsilon_s}^2}$, where $\hat{Y}(s, t)$ denotes the estimated average annual earnings (in levels) for a worker with education s and t years of labor market experience.

TABLE 3-12
Internal Rate of Returns (IRRs) across Schooling
Levels in Chile and Ghana

Level vs.	Baseline	Chile	Ghana
Secondary vs.	Primary	7.67%	0.454%
Tertiary vs.	Secondary	7.12%	0.101%

Note: IRRs are measured with respect to the previous level of education.

chance of progressing throughout the schooling system after completing elementary education (see transition matrix in table 3-3); and (3) the nation's considerable direct costs of education per students (US$499 for secondary and US$1,390 for tertiary).

All in all, these results lead us to question the idea of positive and large private returns to education, particularly after factoring in its costs. We next carry out simulation exercises to analyze how an increase in public spending in both countries would affect the income distribution in future generations. This analysis highlights one of the key points from our conceptual framework: the difference in the fiscal incidence of educational spending when viewed through a static versus a dynamic lens.

4.5 Assessing the Long-Term Impact of Public Spending on Inequality

The conceptual framework presented above indicates that public spending on education affects long-term outcomes, including income inequality, through its effect on educational transitions and final schooling attainment. To estimate the impact of public spending in education, we consider three different exercises: a public subsidy equivalent to 10 percent, 30 percent, and 80 percent of the annual average costs per schooling level. The 10 percent increase corresponds to a per-student increase in financing of US$1,894 in Chile and of US$163 in Ghana—corresponding to 2.2 percent and 1.8 percent of GDP, respectively. We assume that these resources are transferred directly to each school-age individual as a permanent annual subsidy and explore the long-term impact on a cross-sectional sample of 12 different generations of students (each attending a different grade at the time the policy is implemented). In this way, the analysis takes into account the intensity of public spending as first grade students will experience 12 years of subsidies, whereas those in the last year of high school will experience only one. Within each cohort, we also control for the current quintile of family income. We report the impact of the subsidies on transition probabilities and then the resulting future income distribution.[17]

---

[17] In the context of our economic setting, when the government increases public expenditure, say in primary education (s_1), $E(s_1)$, enrollment will increase at a per-student cost equal to κ_1. Given the cumulative effect of education, a new enrollee will achieve complete primary education with probability $p(s_1, s_0)$, where s_0 represents the alternative of no formal education, will pursue and

Table 3-13 displays the effects of each scenario on the transition probabilities for Chile (panel A) and Ghana (panel B) for the generation of individuals attending second, sixth, and twelfth grades. Across both countries, we find limited impacts of the 10 percent increase in spending on educational attainment, though the effects are larger in Chile than in Ghana. This result holds for the three cohorts, as well as across quantiles of family income. This policy would increase the probability of attaining tertiary education for a low-income child in Chile by 2 percentage points, yet the equivalent effect for a child in Ghana would be 0.4 percentage points. An 80 percent increase in spending, on the other hand, would deliver sizable effects on tertiary enrollment in both countries, with larger effects in Chile than in Ghana. For instance, enrollment rates in tertiary education for a middle-income twelfth-grader in Chile would increase from 74.2 to 83.7 percent under the simulated policy. Meanwhile, enrollment rates would increase from 49.8 to 52.9 percent for the equivalent child in Ghana. Interestingly, panel B shows that the size of the subsidy produces nonlinear effects on enrollment. For instance, panel B.3 shows that while neither the 10 percent nor the 30 percent increase in spending would affect tertiary school enrollment, the largest policy would have a sizable impact for all levels of family income.

Table 3-14 reports the estimated effects of the education subsidies on individuals' NPV. Recall that equations (3-6) and (3-11) indicate that this figure depends on the costs of education, a new schooling history, and resulting earnings. Panel A shows the results for Chile. We find that each of the three simulated increases in educational spending would result in significant increases in the NPV associated with education. For instance, a 10 percent increase in spending would yield a US$776 increase in this expected value measure for a second grade student. A similar reform in Ghana, presented in panel B, would increase the expected value by only US$10. These results hold across the three cohorts and for all simulated policies: the increase in the NPV would be significantly larger in Chile than in Ghana. These results are in line with our previous findings presented in table 3-13, which shows that increases in educational spending would have smaller impacts on tertiary enrollment in Ghana than in Chile.

---

complete secondary education with probability $p(s_2, s_1)$, and will complete tertiary education with probability $p(s_3, s_2)$. Since each of these paths is associated with a corresponding earnings stream (or NPV at a given discount rate r), $\tilde{V}_r(s_1), \tilde{V}_r(s_2), \tilde{V}_r(s_3)$, we define the return to educational spending for an individual selecting schooling level s^* as

$$(3\text{-}12) \qquad \frac{\partial \Delta_{s^*, s^*-1}}{\partial E(s_1)} = \frac{\partial [V_{s^*, s^*-1} - V(s^*-1, r)]}{\partial E(s_1)}.$$

The effect of educational spending on educational attainment depends directly on an individual's value associated with education levels s and $s-1$. Furthermore, the implicit costs Cs^*, s^*-1 now include the additional obligations associated with κ_s. This measure can be complemented with the estimation of internal rate of return, which is defined as the discount rate that would equate the net present values of the baseline (no extra funding for primary education) and resulting (extra funding) schooling levels.

TABLE 3-13

Effects of Public Spending in Education on the Probability of Attaining Tertiary Education, by Family Income, in Chile and Ghana

Scenario	Quintiles of family income				
	(1)	(2)	(3)	(4)	(5)

Chile

A.1 Generation of second-graders

Baseline—No Intervention	0.542	0.596	0.673	0.770	0.925
10% increase	0.562	0.614	0.689	0.783	0.931
30% increase	0.599	0.650	0.722	0.809	0.941
80% increase	0.688	0.732	0.793	0.864	0.961

A2. Generation of sixth-graders

Baseline—no intervention	0.564	0.625	0.685	0.766	0.917
10% increase	0.583	0.643	0.701	0.780	0.923
30% increase	0.619	0.677	0.732	0.805	0.934
80% increase	0.704	0.754	0.801	0.861	0.956

A3. Generation of twelfth-graders

Baseline—no intervention	0.633	0.701	0.742	0.802	0.937
10% Increase	0.648	0.715	0.755	0.814	0.941
30% Increase	0.678	0.742	0.780	0.835	0.950
80% Increase	0.748	0.804	0.837	0.881	0.967

Ghana

B.1 Generation of second-graders

Baseline—no intervention	0.139	0.155	0.200	0.238	0.318
10% increase	0.143	0.160	0.205	0.244	0.324
30% increase	0.152	0.170	0.216	0.255	0.335
80% increase	0.175	0.194	0.243	0.285	0.361

B2. Generation of sixth-graders

Baseline—no intervention	0.146	0.173	0.212	0.247	0.325
10% increase	0.149	0.178	0.217	0.252	0.330
30% increase	0.157	0.187	0.228	0.264	0.341
80% increase	0.178	0.212	0.256	0.294	0.368

TABLE 3-13   (continued)

Scenario	Quintiles of family income				
	(1)	(2)	(3)	(4)	(5)
B3. Generation of twelfth-graders					
Baseline—no intervention	0.470	0.501	0.498	0.512	0.581
10% increase	0.470	0.502	0.500	0.515	0.586
30% increase	0.472	0.507	0.507	0.523	0.596
80% increase	0.485	0.527	0.529	0.548	0.621

Sources: Information on the costs of education for Chile (all levels) comes from OECD (2013). Costs of education in Ghana were obtained directly from Household Survey GLSS-6.

Notes: The subsidy is defined as a percentage of the costs of education. Categories of family income are constructed using household income at the time of the survey. The table reports the probabilities of reporting "tertiary education" under three different exercises. Each one adds a different amount (10 percent, 30 percent or 80 percent of costs of education) to family income and uses the schooling choice model to compute the long-term impact.

While increasing spending would still promote enrollment, we note that this policy may not necessarily be efficient. In the second column of table 3-14, it is clear that the investment associated with the increased public expenditures would far exceed the gain in individuals' expected value of tertiary schooling. As a result, policymakers may be interested in analyzing whether alternative policy designs could deliver the same effects on tertiary school enrollment through other channels.

Figure 3-7 displays the predicted distribution of adult earnings for the current generations of second-, sixth-, and twelfth-graders in Chile and Ghana. But it reports them by quintile of (family) income at the time of the intervention (school-age period). In this way, we seek to examine the intergenerational impact of education spending.

To make the results comparable, the distributions are obtained after simulating salaries 30 years since the last year of formal education. As expected, the patterns suggest larger responses associated with larger increases in spending. However, the responses by the number of years during which the individuals received the subsidies, say second versus twelfth grades, are less clear. The small differences between second- (panel A.2) and twelfth- (panel C.2) graders in Ghana illustrate this point. This, of course, comes as no surprise as transition probabilities were less sensitive to family income; hence, the intervention was expected to be less effective in this country. In turn, this explains why among those who already reached twelfth grade the subsidy produces a more pronounced impact (panel C.2).

The key result of this exercise, however, comes from the comparisons across quintiles (x-axis). Regardless of the cohort, Chilean students at the bottom of the distribution of family income benefit the most from the intervention in the long run. Their income distribution shifts right (up in the box plot) as the size of the subsidy increases. Something similar is observed among sixth- (panel B.2 in figure 3-7) and twelfth- (C.2) graders in Ghana. Figure 3-8 further extends these results by showing the distribution

TABLE 3-14
Long-Term Effects of Public Spending in Education by Generation in Chile and
Ghana, Net Present Value (NPV, US$)

Scenario	NPV (1)	Investment (2)	Δ NPV (3)
Chile			
A.1 Generation of second-graders			
Baseline - No Intervention	80,317.7	—	—
10% increase	81,095.3	1,476.0	777.6
30% increase	82,563.1	4,449.8	2,245.4
80% increase	85,735.2	11,979.3	5,417.5
A.2 Generation of sixth-graders			
Baseline—no intervention	107,861.9	—	—
10% increase	108,814.0	1,088.3	952.1
30% increase	110,778.1	3,288.7	2,916.2
80% increase	115,015.6	8,901.1	7,153.7
A.3 Generation of twelfth-graders			
Baseline—no intervention	137,934.0	—	—
10% increase	140,050.5	308.2	2,116.5
30% increase	144,314.7	936.3	6,380.7
80% increase	154,132.0	2,568.6	16,198.0
Ghana			
B.1 Generation of second-graders			
Baseline—no intervention	8,248.4	—	—
10% increase	8,258.8	105.5	10.5
30% increase	8,284.1	317.6	35.8
80% increase	8,340.5	853.8	92.1
B.2 Generation of sixth-graders			
Baseline—no intervention	11,533.5	—	—
10% increase	11,547.7	69.1	14.2
30% increase	11,575.0	208.2	41.6
80% increase	11,645.9	561.5	112.4

TABLE 3-14   (continued)

Scenario	NPV (1)	Investment (2)	Δ NPV (3)
B.3 Generation of twelfth-graders			
Baseline—no intervention	13,930.5	—	—
10% increase	13,985.1	25.4	54.6
30% increase	14,045.8	76.4	115.3
80% increase	14,268.1	204.7	337.5

Sources: Information on the costs of education for Chile (all levels) comes from OECD (2013). Costs of education in Ghana were obtained directly from Household Survey GLSS-6.

Note: The subsidy is defined as a percentage of the costs of education.

of labor income during adulthood (also 30 years after the reform) for individuals who belong to the bottom 20 percent of the distribution of family income (while in school). For Chile we document a marked decline in inequality. Unfortunately, despite the documented impact on NPV, the distribution remains almost unchanged in Ghana. This sheds light on the difficulties of reducing long-term inequality.

5 Conclusions

The quantification of the net benefits of education has fueled economic research for decades (Becker, 1962; Card, 2001; Heckman, Humphries, and Veramendi, 2018). A greater stock of human capital should lead to better labor market prospects, including more stable occupations and higher future earnings (Heckman et al., 2014). But, of course, accumulating human capital also involves costs (Rodriguez, Urzua, and Reyes, 2015). Uncertainty and the intrinsic dynamic learning value of schooling must also be factored in (Levhari and Weiss, 1974; Keane and Wolpin, 1997; Weisbrod, 1962; Altonji, 1993; Arcidiacono, 2004). In this context, rational individuals should weigh the expected long-term costs and benefits when deciding whether or not to invest in education (Willis and Rosen, 1979). This illustrates why estimating the impact of public education spending on any outcome is a complex task.

When governments subsidize the provision of education services, prices cannot be used to yield measures of benefit incidence as they do not necessarily reflect the marginal willingness to pay across consumers (Castro-Leal et al., 1999).[18] This chapter

---

[18]Experimental evidence exists (Muralidharan and Sundararaman, 2011), but it is rare and hard to extrapolate to different settings, making comparative policy analysis within and across countries difficult. Observational studies (quasi-experimental designs) are similarly affected by data limitations and natural difficulties in establishing proper identification strategies (Rosenbaum, 2002, 2010). Nevertheless, despite these issues, carefully implemented observational studies can offer insights into the mechanisms through which public spending in education could alter income inequality and promote poverty reduction in the long run.

FIGURE 3-7
Annual Earnings during Adulthood after Increasing Average Annual Expenditure in Education per Student during School-Age Years, by Cohort and Quintile of Family Income at the Time of the Intervention

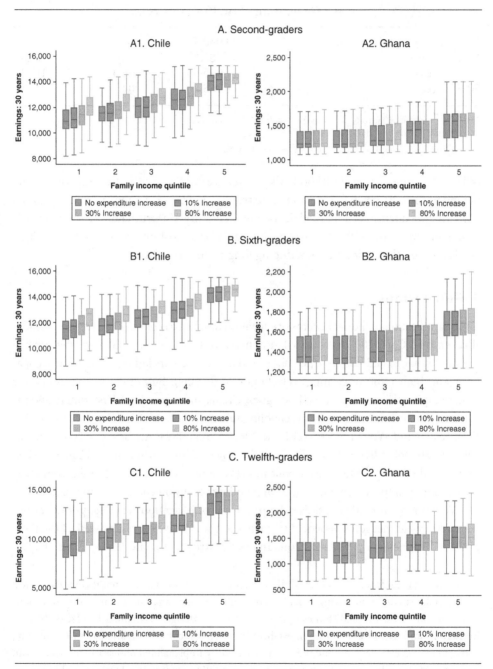

Notes: Implicit rate of return to education is 3.9%. Results obtained under the assumption of 30 years of labor market experience.

FIGURE 3-8

Distribution of Labor Income during Adulthood (30 Years Later) for Those Individuals with Family Income at the Bottom 20% While in School: Baseline vs. Transfers (10%, 30%, and 80% of Public Expenditure per Student)

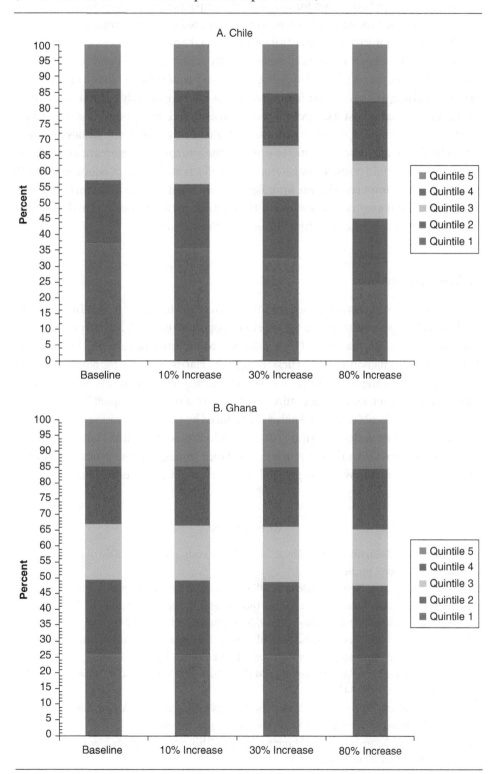

Notes: Both panels are simulated using the results from the models of labor market income as a function of years of education and the empirical framework examining the association between transition probabilities and family income. Public transfers are assumed to increase per capita family income when the individual was deciding whether or not to continue his or her education.

introduces two methodologies for assessing the impact of public spending in the education sector when the researcher has access to limited data. The empirical analysis is carried out using micro-level data from Chile and Ghana.

Our results suggest substantial heterogeneity across countries and schooling levels. For example, the returns to investing in primary education in Ghana are low. This is not surprising as gross enrollment rates in this level are already high, so the expansion comes at a large cost. However, when it comes to secondary education, Ghana exhibits large returns. For Chile, the results indicate positive economic values to education. Finally, we use these estimates to simulate the returns to government expenditure in education. We find positive but heterogeneous effects at all levels of education in both countries. More importantly, our findings not only highlight the differences between the methods, but empirically document the contrast between conventional estimates and the returns to public spending in the education sector.

Acknowledgments

This research project was conducted for the Commitment to Equity (CEQ) Institute. The study was made possible thanks to the generous support of the Bill & Melinda Gates Foundation. For more information on CEQ, visit www.commitmentoequity.org. I am grateful to Francois Bourguignon, Gary Burtless, Douglas N. Harris, Nora Lustig, Norbert Schady. Sergei Soares, and Stephen Younger for their comments on earlier drafts of this chapter. I also thank the contributions of seminar participants at the workshop on "Methodological Advances in Fiscal Incidence Analysis" organized by the CEQ Institute and Universidad de San Andres in Buenos Aires (2017). Ricardo Espinoza, Camila Galindo and Fernando Saltiel provided valuable research assistance throughout the project. All errors and omissions remain my sole responsibility. E-mail: urzua@econ.umd.edu.

References

Aaron, Henry, and Martin C. McGuire. 1970. "Public Goods and Income Distribution." *Econometrica* 38, no. 6, pp. 907–20.

Acerenza, Santiago, and Nestor Gandelman. 2019. "Household Education Spending in Latin America and the Caribbean: Evidence from Income and Expenditure Surveys." *Education Finance and Policy* 14 (1): 61–87. doi: https://doi.org/10.1162/edfp_a_00241.

Altonji, Joseph G. 1993. "The Demand for and Return to Education When Education Outcomes Are Uncertain." *Journal of Labor Economics* 11, no. 1, part 1, pp. 48–83.

Arcidiacono, Peter. 2004. "Ability Sorting and the Returns to College Major." *Journal of Econometrics* 121, no. 1, pp. 343–75.

Barouni, Mahdi, and Stijn Broecke. 2014. "The Returns to Education in Africa: Some New Estimates." *Journal of Development Studies* 50, no. 12, pp. 1593–1613.

Becker, Gary S. 1962. "Investment in Human Capital: A Theoretical Analysis." *Journal of Political Economy* 70, no. 5, pp. 9–49.

Cameron, Stephen V., and James J. Heckman. 1998. "Life Cycle Schooling and Dynamic Selection Bias: Models and Evidence for Five Cohorts of American Males." *Journal of Political Economy* 106, no. 2, pp. 262–333.

Card, David. 2001. "Estimating the Return to Schooling: Progress on Some Persistent Econometric Problems." *Econometrica* 69, no. 5, pp. 1127–60.

Carneiro, Pedro, Karsten T. Hansen and James J. Heckman. 2003. "2001 Lawrence R. Klein Lecture: Estimating Distributions of Treatment Effects with and Application to the Return to Schooling and Measurement of the Effects of Uncertainty on College Choice." *International Economic Review* 44, no. 2 (May), pp. 631–422.

Castro-Leal, Florencia, Julia Dayton, Lionel Demery, and Kalpana Mehra. 1999. "Public Social Spending in Africa: Do the Poor Benefit?" *World Bank Research Observer* 14, no. 1, pp. 49–72.

Chetty, Raj, John N. Friedman, Nathaniel Hilger, Emmanuel Saez, Diane Whitmore Schanzenbach, and Danny Yagan. 2011. "How Does Your Kindergarten Classroom Affect Your Earnings? Evidence from Project Star." *Quarterly Journal of Economics* 126, no. 4, pp. 1593–1660.

Chilean Tax Revenue Authority. 2014. "Tabla de Impuesto Global Complementario." Servicio de Impuestos Internos, Chile. https://www.sii.cl/pagina/valores/global/igc2014.htm.

Duflo, Esther, Pascaline Dupas, and Michael Kremer. 2021. "The Impact of Free Secondary Education: Experimental Evidence from Ghana." NBER Working Paper 28937. Cambridge, MA: National Bureau of Economic Research. http://www.nber.org/papers/w28937.

Espinoza, Ricardo, and Sergio Urzua. 2016. "The Economic Returns to Higher Education: Funding, Coverage and Quality in Latin America." Background paper for the study of higher education in Latin America of the World Bank. https://conference.iza.org/conference_files/EcoEdu_2016/espinoza_r24401.pdf.

Ferreyra, María M., Ciro Avitabile, Javier Botero, Francisco Haimovich, and Sergio Urzua. 2017. *At a Crossroads: Higher Education in Latin America and the Caribbean.* Washington, DC: World Bank.

García, Jorge Luis, James J. Heckman, Duncan Ermini Leaf, and Mara Jose Prados. 2016. "The Life-Cycle Benefits of an Influential Early Childhood Program," NBER Working Paper 22993, December. Cambridge, MA: National Bureau of Economic Research.

Ghana Revenue Authority. 2013. "Pay As You Earn." Domestic Tax Revenue Division Department. https://gra.gov.gh/domestic-tax/tax-types/paye/.

Gonzalez-Velosa, Carolina, Graciana Rucci, Miguel Sarzosa, and Sergio Urzua. 2015. "Returns to Higher Education in Chile and Colombia." IDB Working Paper Series No. IDB-WP-587, March. Washington, DC: Inter-American Development Bank.

Heckman, James J., John Eric Humphries, and Gregory Veramendi. 2018. "The Nonmarket Benefits of Education and Ability." *Journal of Human Capital* 12, no.2, pp. 282–304.

Heckman, James J. John E. Humphries, Gregory Veramendi, and Sergio Urzua. 2014. "Education, Health and Wages." NBER Working Paper W19971. Cambridge, MA: National Bureau of Economic Research.

Heckman, James J., and Alan B. Krueger. 2005. *Inequality in America: What Role for Human Capital Policies?* Edited and with an introduction by Benjamin M. Friedman. Cambridge, MA: MIT Press.

Heckman, James J., Lance J. Lochner, and Petra E. Todd. 2006. "Earnings Functions, Rates of Return and Treatment Effects: The Mincer Equation and Beyond." In *Handbook of the Economics of*

Education, vol. 1, edited by Eric A. Hanushek and Finis Welch, pp. 307–458. Amsterdam: Elsevier.

Heckman, James J., Sergio Urzua, and George Yates. 2007. "The Identification and Estimation of Option Values in a Model with Recurrent States." Unpublished manuscript, University of Chicago, Department of Economics.

Keane, Michael P., and Kenneth I. Wolpin. 1997. "The Career Decisions of Young Men." *Journal of Political Economy* 105, no. 3, pp. 473–522.

Lambert, P. J. 1993. *The Distribution and Redistribution of Income: A Mathematical Analysis*. Manchester: Manchester University Press.

Levhari, David, and Yoram Weiss. 1974. "The Effect of Risk on the Investment in Human Capital." *American Economic Review* 64, no. 6, pp. 950–63.

Lustig, Nora. 2015. "The Redistributive Impact of Government Spending on Education and Health: Evidence from 13 Developing Countries in the Commitment to Equity Project." CEQ Working Paper 30, Commitment to Equity Institute, Tulane University.

Lustig, Nora, and Sean Higgins. 2022. "The *CEQ Assessment*: Measuring the Impact of Fiscal Policy on Inequality and Poverty," chap. 1 in *Commitment to Equity Handbook: Estimating the Impact of Fiscal Policy on Inequality and Poverty*, 2nd. ed., Vol. 1, edited by Nora Lustig. Brookings Institution Press and CEQ Institute, Tulane University. Free online version available at www.commitmentoequity.org.

Mincer, Jacob. 1958. "Investment in Human Capital and Personal Income Distribution." *Journal of Political Economy* 66, no. 4, pp. 281–302.

———. 1974. *Schooling, Experience and Earnings*. New York: National Bureau of Economic Research; distributed by Columbia University Press.

———. 1993. *Investment in U.S. Education and Training*. New York: Columbia University, Department of Economics.

Ministry of Education of Chile. 2014. "Subvención Escolar Preferencial: Orientaciones de Apoyo a la Gestión." Technical Report n. 162. https://bibliotecadigital.mineduc.cl/handle/20.500 .12365/2169.

Montenegro, Claudio E. 2001. "Wage Distribution in Chile: Does Gender Matter? A Quantile Regression Approach." World Bank Working Paper Series No. 20, Development Research Group/Poverty Reduction and Economic Management Network, December. Washington, DC: World Bank.

Montenegro, Claudio E., and Harry A. Patrinos. 2014. "Comparable Estimates of Returns to Schooling Around the World." Policy Research Working Paper Series 720, September. Washington, DC: World Bank.

Muralidharan, Karthik, and Venkatesh Sundararaman. 2011. "Teacher Performance Pay: Experimental Evidence from India." *Journal of Political Economy* 119, no. 1, pp. 39–77.

Musgrave, Richard. 1959. *The Theory of Public Finance: A Study in Public Economy*. New York: McGraw-Hill.

OECD. 2013. "Education at a Glance: Chile." Technical Report. Paris: OECD Publishing.

Peet, Evan, Gunther Fink, and Wafaie Fawzi. 2015. "Returns to Education in Developing Countries: Evidence from the Living Standards and Measurement Study Surveys." *Economics of Education Review* 49, pp. 69–90.

Rodriguez, Jorge, Sergio Urzua, and Loreto Reyes. 2015. "Heterogeneous Economic Returns to Postsecondary Degrees: Evidence from Chile." *Journal of Human Resources* 51, no.2, pp. 416–60.

Rosenbaum, Paul R. 2002. *Observational Studies.* New York: Springer.

———. 2010. *Design of Observational Studies.* New York: Springer.

Selowsky, Marcelo. 1979. *Who Benefits from Government Expenditure?* New York: Oxford University Press.

Soares, Sergei. 2019. "The Market Value of Public Education: A Comparison of Three Valuation Methods," CEQ Working Paper 71 (revised June), Commitment to Equity Institute, Tulane University.

UNESCO. n.d. UIS.Stat home page. http://data.uis.unesco.org.

Urzua, Sergio. 2012. "La rentabilidad de la educación superior en Chile." *Estudios Públicos* 125, pp. 1–52.

Weisbrod, Burton A. 1962. "Education and Investment in Human Capital." *Journal of Political Economy* 70, no. 5 (part 2), pp. 106–23.

Willis, Robert, and Sherwin Rosen. 1979. "Education and Self-Selection." *Journal of Political Economy* 87, no. 5, pp. S7–36.

Younger, Stephen. 2022. "Ghana and Tanzania: The Impact of Reforming Energy Subsidies, Cash Transfers, and Taxes on Inequality and Poverty," chap. 16 in *Commitment to Equity Handbook: Estimating the Impact of Fiscal Policy on Inequality and Poverty*, 2nd ed., Vol. 1, edited by Nora Lustig. Brookings Institution Press and CEQ Institute, Tulane University. Free online version available at www.commitmentoequity.org.

Younger, Stephen, Eric Osei-Assibey, and Felix Oppong. 2017. "Fiscal Incidence in Ghana." *Review of Development Economics* 21, no. 4, pp. e47–e66.

Appendix 3A

Dynamic Fiscal Incidence of Public Spending in Education

This appendix extends the conceptual framework of section 2 to a general dynamic economic setting with uncertainty.

1 The Recursive Problem

By its very nature, and as illustrated by expressions (3-2) and (3-3), the accumulation of human capital throughout the schooling system involves sequential decision processes. Enrollment in schooling level s requires the completion of schooling level $s-1$, with $s=\{1, \ldots, S\}$. As before, let p_{s+1} be the probability of attending schooling $s+1$, given that level s is completed. The provision of education services is costly. Let $C(s+1)$ be the cost associated with schooling level s. Thus, the expected private net benefit of attending level $s+1$ as perceived by an individual reporting s, $V_{s+1,s}$, can be written as

(3A-1) $V_{s+1,s} = p_{s+2} \times [V_{s+2,s+1}] + (1 - p_{s+2}) \times V(s+1) - C(s+1)$ for $s = \{0, \ldots, S-1\}$,

where $V(s+1)$ represents the economic value associated with the alternative of reaching schooling level $s+1$ and not continuing the accumulation of human capital after that. This recursive system captures the dynamic effects of investing in education, which must be taken into account when defining its returns. In particular, for an individual who has completed schooling level s, the decision to continue (or not) his or her formal education process might depend on whether $V_{s+1,s}$ is larger (or smaller) than $V(s)$.[19]

Thus, the relevant economic indicator of the value associated with schooling level $s+1$ becomes

(3A.2) $$\Delta_{s+1,s} = V_{s+1,s} - V(s),$$

with associated expected overall costs, $C_{s+1,s}$, equal to

(3A-3) $C_{s+1,s} = p_{s+2} \times C_{s+2,s+1} + C(s+1)$ for $s = \{0, \ldots, S-1\}$.

This last expression highlights the fact that effective public efforts promoting the accumulation of human capital throughout formal education must alleviate more than the contemporaneous costs of the process, as educational attainment depends on the

---

[19] This approach provides us with a mechanism to evaluate the decision of pursuing higher levels of education. For example, we can rationalize the decision of a student with a secondary degree deciding whether or not to pursue a tertiary education degree. We can also estimate the economic benefits associated with pursuing secondary education versus remaining with primary education. Thus, for any two final schooling levels $s-1$ and s, e.g., secondary and tertiary education, $r_{s,s-1} = V(s) - V(s-1)$ represents the extra (discounted) net dollars an individual would obtain in the event of completing schooling level s (and not pursuing additional education) versus $s-1$. In particular, Willis and Rosen (1979) study to what extent individuals compare $V(s)$ and $V(s-1)$ when deciding whether to pursue a college degree after graduating from high school. The economic consequences of this decision can be rationalized in at least two different ways. One is by directly comparing $V(s)$ with $V(s-1)$. For a given discount rate r, the difference between the two discounted net present values can be interpreted as the differential benefit of pursuing s. Thus, we can define the returns to s relative to $s-1$ as $\rho_s = \dfrac{V(s) - V(s-1)}{V(s-1)}$. A main drawback of this approach is that we need to specify a discount rate, which may differ across individuals, and may not be easy to define. Instead, one could use an alternative approach based on the estimation of the IRR of pursuing schooling level s. Specifically, IRR_s is defined as the discount rate that makes the two streams equal in present value, $V(s, IRR_s) = V(s-1, IRR_{s-1})$. Therefore, at any discount rate r, if $r < IRR_s$, pursuing s will be a better financial investment.

sum of costs across all decisions. The empirical applications discussed below consider this insight. As a result, in order for an increase in spending $E(s)$ to affect final attainment, enough resources are required to modify at least some of the probabilities in the set $\{p_{s+1}\}_{s=1}^{S}$. The identification of the parameter of interest, $\dfrac{\partial \Delta_{s+1,s}}{\partial E(s)}$, critically depends on how the sequence of probabilities $\{p_{s+1}\}_{s=1}^{S}$ is affected by the change in public spending. In what follows we propose two simple empirical methods to estimate the private returns to education in a dynamic setting with uncertainty, each with a distinctive logic and interpretation. One approach follows aggregate level information, whereas the other one exploits individual-level data.

2 Intertemporal Fiscal Incidence Analysis

Conceptually, the provision of public education services must be understood as an in-kind transfer, but also as a particular one. It shares the obvious complexities associated with the valuation of any benefit of its type, but since its goal is to boost the skills and abilities of the "beneficiaries," one cannot abstract from its middle- and long-term consequences even when carrying out a static fiscal incidence of public spending in the sector. To see this, we must first acknowledge the economic forces linking past public efforts in education and present income (Mincer, 1993). In particular, there is a long-standing literature documenting the causal association between investment in human capital and labor market outcomes (Mincer, 1958, 1974). Thus, if we denote by $Y_{M}'(t)$ the contemporaneous labor income of workers and by $E_{F}(t-1)$ the monetary value of education-related transfers in-kind for the previous generation, any past public action generating the incentives for yesterday's children (today's adults) to attend and/or stay in school, should lead to a structural association from $E_{F}(t-1)$ to $Y_{M}'(t)$. In other words, transfers in one period affect the distribution of next-period original income. Importantly, this association is not deterministic as investments in education involve uncertainty about their future effects.

Understanding the implications of the intertemporal association between transfers and Market Income impels the static fiscal incidence analysis beyond the conventional framework. And this is not because public spending in education might re-rank households according to per capita income once the taxes to pay for or benefits associated with it are taken into account; rather, it is due to the time dependence now affecting Π_{N}. In particular, by adding a time dimension t to the terms in expression (3-1) and assuming stable total tax and benefit ratios, we can use Lambert's equations over two time periods to write

$$\Pi_{N}(t) - \Pi_{N}(t-1) = \frac{(1-g)[\Pi_{T}(t) - \Pi_{T}(t-1)] + (1+b)[\rho_{B}(t) - \rho_{B}(t-1)]}{(1+b-g)},$$

where $\Pi_{T}(t)$ depends on $\rho_{B}(t-1)$ as taxes and benefits are connected throughout the effects of education. Two interesting results emerge from this expression. First, the progress in redistribution can be faster than the advances in regressive benefits (i.e., $\Pi_N(t) - \Pi_N(t-1) > \rho_B(t) - \rho_B(t-1) > 0$) even under a deterioration of the progressivity of taxes $(0 > \Pi_T(t-1) > \Pi_T(t))$.[20] Second, even if the redistributive effects of benefits when applied to the original income are constant over time, i.e., $\rho_B(t) = \rho_B(t-1)$, the net fiscal system can increase its progressivity as education can lead to $\Pi_N(t) - \Pi_N(t-1) > 0$ even if $\Pi_N(t) < 0$.

The precise identification of these dynamics goes beyond the scope of this chapter. However, they illustrate how by studying not only the long-term economic returns to education but also the individuals' responses to human capital investments throughout the lifetime, one could provide new insights into the challenges of the fiscal incidence analysis of public spending in education.

Appendix 3B

Instrumental Variable

The IV results presented in columns 3 and 6 of table 3B-1 deliver significantly lower, and non-significant, point estimates. The discrepancy between our Ordinary Least Squares (OLS) and Instrumental Variable (IV) estimates may be due to the lack of an appropriate instrument, so we note further work is needed in this area. At the same time, we find significantly larger estimates to completing tertiary education in both countries, and these results are significant in both OLS and IV specifications, exceeding 150 percent in the two OLS regressions and 200 percent in instrumental variable estimations.

---

[20] The condition is $\dfrac{(g-1)}{g}[\Pi_T(t) - \Pi_T(t-1)] < [\rho_B(t) - \rho_B(t-1)]$.

TABLE 3B.1
Results from Mincer Regressions: Ordinary Least Squares (OLS) vs. Instrumental Variables (IV)

Variable	Chile				Ghana	
	OLS (1)	OLS (2)	IV (3)	OLS (4)	OLS (5)	IV (6)
Years of education (≤12)	0.114***	0.091***	0.092	0.080***	0.072**	0.209
	(0.004)	(0.009)	(0.089)	(0.008)	(0.029)	(0.167)
Tertiary	2.198***	1.800***	2.703**	1.640***	1.452***	3.811*
	(0.104)	(0.104)	(1.066)	(0.105)	(0.383)	(2.062)
Experience	0.050***	0.067***	0.124	0.078***	0.065*	0.237
	(0.002)	(0.007)	(0.081)	(0.006)	(0.035)	(0.195)
Experience^2	-0.001***	-0.001***	-0.003**	-0.001***	-0.001	-0.004
	(0.000)	(0.000)	(0.001)	(0.000)	(0.001)	(0.004)
Education (≤12) × exp.	-0.002***	-0.002***	-0.002	-0.002***	-0.002	-0.011
	(0.000)	(0.000)	(0.005)	(0.000)	(0.002)	(0.012)
Tertiary × experience	-0.022***	-0.035***	-0.110*	-0.020***	-0.004	-0.139
	(0.001)	(0.006)	(0.065)	(0.004)	(0.027)	(0.185)
Rural	-0.227***	-0.050**	-0.003	-0.351***	-0.328***	-0.221**
	(0.009)	(0.021)	(0.029)	(0.024)	(0.082)	(0.095)
Female	-0.500***	-0.167***	-0.281***	-0.446***	-0.268***	-0.282***
	(0.005)	(0.015)	(0.023)	(0.022)	(0.080)	(0.084)
R^2	0.30	0.22	0.11	0.19	0.22	0.16
N	90,339	11,689	7,163	16,073	1,354	1,354
Sample	Full	15–35 y/o	15–35 y/o	Full	15–35 y/o	15–35 y/o

Sources: Own calculations using CASEN 2013 (Chile) and GLSS 2012-13 (Ghana) data.

Notes: We include only workers whose age is above 15 years and who are not currently studying or pursuing any degree. Parental education is used as source of instruments for both countries.

Chapter 4

THE MARKET VALUE OF OWNER-OCCUPIED HOUSING AND PUBLIC INFRASTRUCTURE SERVICES

Sergei Soares

Introduction

The value of owner-occupied housing is relevant in the income distribution. It is the only form of capital earnings that is important for most households, often including those in the lower half of the income distribution. It is usually included in national accounts, but many analysts of household income and its distribution leave it out. One reason for doing so is that it is not trivial to decide how much owner-occupied housing services are worth for each household.

Likewise, access to public infrastructure services such as water or electricity is also relevant for the distribution of income. A roof over one's head is unquestioningly important, but anyone who has had to deal with water or power shortages for extended periods of time knows that access to public infrastructure services is also quite important.

The market value of both owner-occupied housing and public infrastructure can be estimated using hedonic price equations. The approach followed here is to use the market value of housing services to estimate what families would have to pay for their housing if they did not own it. The basic idea is to use the rental market and then apply the values paid by renters to owners of similar houses. It is a typical hedonic price approach, which will be detailed below.

This chapter begins with a brief overview of the literature on using a hedonic process to value owner-occupied housing rental services. Section 2 details the methodology and the data to be used. Section 3 applies the methodology to 2015, while section 4 applies it to 2005 and 1995 to understand changes over time. Section 5 concludes.

1 Literature

Estimating housing value via hedonic prices was pioneered by Rosen (1974). While he is very clear as to the limits of the hedonic price approach to a market characterized by non-divisibility and discontinuities in tied packages (one cannot sell only the bathroom of a house), he shows that the "the economic content of the relationship between observed prices and observed characteristics becomes evident once price differences among goods are recognized as equalizing differences for the alternative packages they embody" (p. 54). In other words, while one cannot sell only the bathroom of a house, the price difference between otherwise identical houses that differ only by a single bathroom is the value of that bathroom. This notion has laid the basis for a large body of work on the determinants of rental and property values.

Using hedonic prices to analyze demand and supply of housing or other aspects of rental markets in Brazil is nothing new, but the literature is mostly in the area of urban studies, with scant distributive considerations. Dantas and Cordeiro (1988) use hedonic prices to estimate housing values in Recife. Gonzalez and Formoso (1994) study the dynamics of the rental market in Porto Alegre using hedonic prices. Aguirre and Macedo (1996) and Paixão (2015) study the Belo Horizonte housing market. Favero et al. (2008) do the same for São Paulo. The most complete study is that of Morais and Cruz (2015), who analyze all of urban Brazil using the Pesquisa National por Amostra de Domicilios (PNAD). These studies, however, are not concerned with the distributive impacts of owner-occupied housing but are rather analysis, in lesser or greater depth, of the housing market itself.

There are studies with a distributive slant, but they are fewer. Figueroa (1993) uses hedonic prices to evaluate low-income housing policy in Paraguay. Nascimento et al. (2000) study how property is distributed according to income in Brazil, but do not impute incomes for owner-occupied housing. They do not even calculate concentration coefficients for housing so their distributive analysis is incomplete. Ferreira, Lanjouw, and Neri (2003) use hedonic prices to impute rents and in order to calculate poverty, but they, too, limit their analysis to the bottom of the distribution. Smeeding et al. (1993) value owner-occupied housing and impute these values in their distributive analysis of seven countries. However, instead of using rents, the authors use the actual property values as the basis for imputing owner-occupied rents into the income distribution. They multiply property values by 2 percent and consider that this is the rental value of owner-occupied housing.

There are few studies that use hedonic prices to impute values for owner-occupied housing and calculate standard income distribution statistics. Yates (1994) finds that in Australia imputed rent increases the incomes of homeowners by about 10 percent and makes the Gini coefficient fall from 0.39 to 0.38 (one Gini point). Frick and Grabka (2003) show that imputed rent reduces the Gini coefficient by about 0.2 Gini point in the United States, by less than 0.1 Gini point in West Germany, and slightly increases inequality in Great Britain. They also show that there is an important age dimension in these three countries since the elderly have both lower incomes and higher home ownership. The effects on inequality are small (and negative in Great Britain) because, absent the age dimension, renters are relatively poor in all three countries. The results in this chapter show much larger impacts in Brazil because renters are relatively rich.

What I did not find in the literature is an estimate of which part of this imputed income is due to public infrastructure services. It is not obvious that this makes any sense. Public infrastructure services such as piped water or connections to the electric grid are paid for every month (or bimonthly in some cases), and if you do not pay for your water it usually gets cut off. The argument I make here is that water, electricity, or garbage collection are not pure private goods. A pure private good can be bought or sold in any quantity, and the price will depend on supply and demand. They are, of course, not public goods either; the water I drink cannot be drunk by anyone else. The argument in favor of estimating their values using hedonic equations is that while they are paid for, their price is determined by the public sector, by laws or a regulating agency, and will often have scant relation to how much they are actually worth. What this chapter provides is a welfare value for access to these services. This welfare value is important and has particularly relevant distributional consequences when access is still unequal and subject to early capture by the rich (or richer) population, which is often the case in developing countries.

2 Methodology

Valuation of public infrastructure such as water or sewage connections, trash collection, or access to electricity is not particularly difficult. All that is needed is a household survey that contains questions both on rents paid by those who do not own their houses and on the existence and quality of these public infrastructure services. Furthermore, most surveys also identify houses that are in the same census tract, which will indicate whether the house is in a rich neighborhood or a poor one. Today, the usual housing price model is multiplicative so that the existence of a sewage connection in a wealthy neighborhood will have a larger impact on rental price than in a poor one.[1] In this model, rent will be

(4-1) $$R_{h,n} = C_n \prod_l e^{\beta_l x^l_{h,n}},$$

where $R_{h,n}$ represents the rent paid in house h in neighborhood n, C_n represents the rent of the standard house in neighborhood n, and $x^l_{h,n}$ represents the l-th characteristic of house h in neighborhood n. This means that having an extra bathroom will increase rental values more in Ipanema than in a forgotten rural area of the Northeast. Taking logs, we have

---

[1]See Maclennan (1982) or Morais and Cruz (2015), for example.

(4-2) $$r_{h,n} = c_n \sum_l \beta_l x_{h,n}^l.$$

Estimation is straightforward: both the $c_n s$ and the vector β_l can be estimated using a fixed-effects model, which usually consists of a dummy for each neighborhood n. The neighborhood can be proxied by the census tract in which house h can be found. The β_l coefficients are the hedonic prices themselves, which are needed only to make sure they are not unusual in any sense and conform to the literature.

Estimation of a fixed-effects model is possible either by using a dummy for each census tract or by estimating a model in which the census tract average is subtracted from all variables in that census tract:

(4-3) $$r_{h,n}^l = (r_{h,n} - \bar{r}_n) \text{ and } x_{h,n}^l = (x_{h,n} - \bar{x}_n).$$

While equation (4-2) is estimated using only those individuals who pay rent, the value of the owner-occupied housing is then imputed to the income of the those who own their houses. This creates a new income distribution, whose parameters can then be calculated and compared to the non-imputed distribution. These parameters can be income means, Gini coefficients, and Lorenz curves. The terminology used here to distinguish the two distributions are "ex ante" and "ex post." "Ex-ante" refers to the distribution with no imputed rents for owner-occupied housing, and "ex-post" refers to the distribution with imputed rents.

Once imputed rents are available, calculating the value of public infrastructure services is also simple. Suppose the service whose value is to be calculated is piped water. To calculate its value, take the predicted rental value for a given owner-occupied house with access to water, calculated using the observed vector of public infrastructure services, $R_{hn}(\beta_1 x_{hn}^1, \beta_2 x_{hn}^2, \beta_3 x_{hn}^3 \dots \beta_{water}(water = 1) \dots \beta_1 x_{hn}^1)$, and subtract from it the predicted rental value for the same owner-occupied house with no water: $R_{hn}(\beta_1 x_{hn}^1, \beta_2 x_{hn}^2, \beta_3 x_{hn}^3 \dots \beta_{water}(water = 0) \dots \beta_1 x_{hn}^1)$. This means that the value of water supply for house h in neighborhood n is

(4-4) $$Water\ value = R_{hn}(\beta_1 x_{hn}^1 \dots \beta_{water}(water = 1) \dots \beta_1 x_{hn}^1)$$
$$- R_{hn}(\beta_1 x_{hn}^1 \dots \beta_{water}(water = 0) \dots \beta_1 x_{hn}^1).$$

Aggregate over all H houses in all N neighborhoods, and the market value of the water supply will be given. The same approach can be used for sewage, garbage collection, electricity, or even piped gas. Once the distribution is known, means, concentration coefficients, and concentration curves can be calculated.

The Pesquisa National por Amostra de Domicilios (PNAD) has always been a large survey, with over 100,000 households and close to 400,000 individuals. This large sample is necessary because it covers the entirety of the country (bar the rural north until 2004), and the results need to be statistically significant for each of the 27 states in the federation. It is carried out once per year, except during census years, and goes to the field in the third quarter of the year. I use the years 1995, 2005, and 2015, which have very similar questionnaires.

The income used in the PNAD is Gross Income (pretax, post transfer), at least theoretically. The PNAD takes into account both labor and transfer incomes, and although property incomes are notoriously underestimated, they are also included, in theory. The definition of income used by the PNAD is pretax income. Interviewers are instructed to look at paychecks if these are available and copy this information to the questionnaire. There is some evidence reported in Rocha (2002), such a small net minimum wage spike, that some people report post-tax (or post–direct tax) income, but most wage earners report Gross Incomes. Self-employed incomes are harder to define, but the PNAD asks for incomes net of taxes paid by the business but including taxes paid by individuals (the concept is known as *retirada*), but it is unlikely that reporting is exact.

What problems can be anticipated?

The first is that there may be no households paying rent in a given census tract. This is not particularly troubling if census tracts can be aggregated at the level of municipality; c_n can be substituted for the average rent of the municipality as a whole. Countries in which rental markets are so thin that even at the provincial level there are few rented houses (this may well occur in rural areas) create a limitation to this method. If there are significant populations in areas in which there are no rental markets, hedonic housing prices simply cannot be estimated, and this method cannot be used.

A less serious problem is when almost everyone has access to a certain infrastructure service. For example, access to electricity in 2015 Brazil was close to 99 percent. There is certainly not be enough variation to find hedonic prices. I can see no easy solution to this problem, and a market value for access to electricity in 2015 cannot be calculated using hedonic prices. The solution is to exclude the variable.

An in-between problem is when few of the households that have access to an infrastructure service pay rent. Piped water in 2015 Brazil, for example, was provided to approximately 80 percent of Brazilian households, which left about 20 percent without it. However, among rented houses, only 5 percent did not have piped water. Once again, I can find no easy solution to the problem, other than hope that there is a common support.

3 Imputing Rents and Public Infrastructure Services for 2015

Following the approach highlighted above, the first step is to estimate a fixed-effects model for rents. This is relatively easy, using the grouping variable v0102, which identifies census tracts. There are 9,146 census tracts in the 2015 PNAD but only 2,170 of these have any renters. This means no information from the remaining 6,976 tracts are used in the estimation. This lack of information is because most of the PNAD's census tracts are in rural areas with few people and even fewer renters. The 2,170 census tracts that do have renters account for 80 percent of all residences in the PNAD.

TABLE 4.1

Fixed Effects Estimation of Log(Rents)

R2		Observations per group	
Within	0.388	Minimum	1
Between	0.505	Mean	2.9
Overall	0.454	Maximum	15

Other statistics		Observations	
corr(u_i, Xb)	0.3005	No observations	19,936
F(15,13708)	550.49	No groups	6901

ln(rent)	Coefficient	p-value
Dwelling characteristics		
House	−0.071	0.00
Brick walls	0.338	0.00
Wooden walls	0.113	0.07
Tiled roof	0.013	0.73
Cement roof	0.078	0.04
Zinc roof	0.024	0.63
No. of rooms	0.094	0.00
No. of bedrooms	0.086	0.00
No. of bathrooms	0.084	0.00
Infrastructure		
Piped water	0.027	0.07
Sewage	0.031	0.00
Garbage collection	0.069	0.00
Fixed phone line	0.060	0.00
Piped gas	0.109	0.00
Log per capita income	0.096	0.00

Source: PNAD, 2015.

The dependent variable is the natural logarithm of the rent, and the explanatory variables can be grouped into two categories. The first are characteristics of the dwelling itself, such as the materials of the walls, the number of rooms and bathrooms, and so on. The second are the public infrastructure services: piped water, sewage, garbage collection, fixed phone lines, and piped gas. Noticeably absent in 2015 is electricity. There were almost no residences without electricity in 2015, which makes it impossible to estimate a hedonic price for this service. The logarithm of per capita income is used as a control variable. The results of the estimation can be found in table 4-1.

The results more or less conform to what is expected and to what is found in works such as Morais and Cruz (2015). Apartments are more valued than houses, brick walls more than wooden ones, and each additional room, bedroom, and bathroom increases the rent by about 8–9 percent. Regarding infrastructure, sewage, piped gas, and a fixed phone line increase the rent by about 6 percent and piped water and garbage collection by about 3 percent. While there are no comparisons for these values in the literature, they are not unexpected.

These coefficients refer to people living in rented houses. With these coefficients and average rents by census tract, it is possible to predict what the 83 percent of Brazilians who owned their houses in 2015 would pay if they had to rent. This unpaid rent can be construed as an income that can be added to per capita incomes, thereby changing the income distribution. Table 4-2 shows by how much.

There are two types of concentration coefficients in table 4-2. The one labeled "Ex-ante concentration refers to the concentration of whatever is being measured (income, imputed rent, or public infrastructure) relative to the income distribution with no imputed rents. The one labeled "Ex-post concentration" refers to the concentration of whatever is being measured relative to the income distribution with imputed rents included as income.

The two columns labeled "Gini" and "Theil T" are Gini and Theil T coefficients for various income distributions. For the line called "Per capita income" they are merely the observed inequality indices for the non-adjusted income distribution. For the line called "PC income with imputed rent," they are the Gini and Theil indices for the income distribution with imputed rents (and imputed infrastructure income that comes with the imputed rents). The entries on the lines for water, sewage, garbage, fixed phone, and gas refer to Ginis and Theils for the income distribution with only the imputed income from that one type of infrastructure. For example, the value of 0.5112 for the column Gini in the water line means that the Gini of per capita income would fall from 0.5142 to 0.5112 if the imputed income that comes from having a water connection were to be included.

Finally, the "All infrastructure" line refers to the sum of all infrastructure (water, sewage, garbage, fixed phone, and gas) but not including the imputed income from the house itself. Infrastructure accounts for about 16 percent of the value of owner-occupied housing.

The most impressive result is that owner-occupied housing in Brazil is quite progressive. While no Bolsa Familia (whose concentration coefficient is close to −0.5), the figures for imputed rent on these dwelling are 0.280 (ex ante) and 0.298 (ex post). When the market value of owner-occupied housing is included in family incomes, the Gini coefficient falls from 0.5142 to 0.4820, and household incomes increase by about 14 percent. The reduction in inequality is much larger than that estimated by Frick and Grabka (2003). The largest reduction in equality that they find is 0.24 Gini point for the United States in 1994, which is about one-tenth the reduction of 3.2 Gini points found here. This is entirely due to the large proportion of homeowners among the poor in Brazil.

TABLE 4.2
Means, Concentrations, and Gini and Theil Coefficients, 2015

Distribution	Population in millions	Mean	Ex-ante concentration	Ex-post concentration	Gini coefficient	Theil T
Per capita income	198.2	1,056.63	0.514		0.5142	0.5310
Per capita income with imputed rent	197.5	1,209.58		0.482	0.4820	0.4612
Water	197.3	4.19	0.280	0.298	0.5112	0.5223
Sewage	197.3	3.92	0.346	0.362	0.5115	0.5229
Garbage	197.3	10.36	0.282	0.299	0.5099	0.5194
Fixed phone	197.3	4.68	0.500	0.523	0.5121	0.5239
Gas	197.3	1.29	0.795	0.808	0.5125	0.5252
All infrastructure	197.3	24.43	0.361	0.379	0.5088	0.5166
Per capita imputed rent	197.5	149.45	0.240	0.285	n.c.	n.c.
Avg. census tract per capita rent	198.2	180.56	0.280	0.298	n.c.	n.c.
Per capita rent	33.2	211.15	0.334	0.334	n.c.	n.c.
Rents	198.2	16.8%	0.016	−0.116	n.c.	n.c.

Source: PNAD, 2015.

"n.c." = not calculated.

Just to make sure this progressivity is no quirk of the estimation method, I calculated the concentration coefficient of average rents by census tract.[2] The concentration coefficient was close at 0.280. This means that rents go up less than proportionately with income. While the percentage of renter family income eaten by rent for top decile families was 13 percent, it was 24 percent for the fifth decile, and a huge 65 percent for the bottom decile (luckily few people at the bottom are renters). This also holds true for imputed rents. The relation between imputed rents and incomes in the lowest decile is 26 percent, but in the top decile it is only 7 percent.

So owner-occupied housing is an important reducer of inequality. What about public infrastructure services?

The concentration coefficients for infrastructure range from 0.280 to 0.795 (ex ante). All but gas are less than the Gini coefficient, which would suggest that gas connections increase inequality when monetized. However, in an example of Lambert's conundrum, the Gini coefficient of the income distribution actually falls 0.2 Gini points when the value of having a gas connection is imputed to per capita income. Water, sewage, and fixed phone connections also reduce inequality, as do garbage collection services.

Figure 4-1 shows more or less the same results as the fourth column in table 4-2 (ex-ante concentration coefficient). Apart from piped gas and fixed phone, all other infrastructure services are progressively distributed relative to the income distribution. As mentioned above, rents are the most progressively distributed income source in figure 4-1. Garbage collection and piped water are also highly progressive (and very close to each other), followed by sewage.

When the changes brought to the income distribution with the inclusion of imputed rents are taken into consideration, the result is the ex-post concentration curves, shown in figure 4-2. While real (as can be seen comparing the last two columns of table 4-2), the changes between ex-ante and ex-post are modest. Imputed rent remains inequality-reducing, as are garbage collection and piped water. The concentration curve of fixed phone services crosses the Lorenz curve, and piped gas remains regressive, although only in a very small way.

The main conclusion that can be drawn from this discussion regards the progressivity of owner-occupied housing services and public infrastructures services. Has this long been so? A look at 2005 and 1995 will attempt to provide an answer.

4 Comparisons with 2005 and 1995

The same procedure, with some very minor changes, was applied to 2005 and 1995. One of the changes is that electricity was used in 2005 and 1995 but piped gas was not. This

---

[2] This means taking the average per capita rent in fact paid by renters and assigning it to everyone in the census tract. Census tracts without averages get the municipal average.

FIGURE 4-1

Concentration Curves for Income, Rents, and Infrastructure Services (Ex Ante)

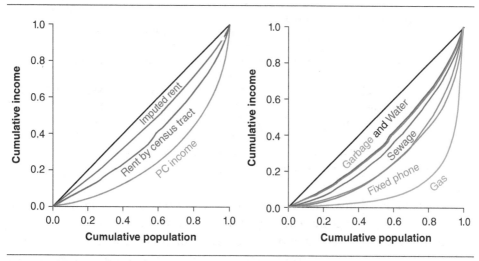

Source: PNAD, 2015.

FIGURE 4-2

Concentration Curves for Income, Rents, and Infrastructure Services (Ex Post)

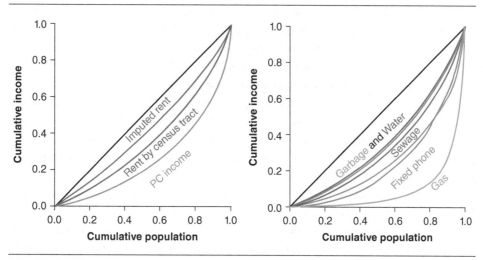

Source: PNAD, 2015.

is because access to an electric current was at 96 percent in 2005, which is high but low enough to use in a hedonic regression with a significant *p*-value. Piped gas, on the other hand, falls to less than 2 percent of households.

Tables containing the regression coefficients for 2005 and 1995 are omitted from this chapter. They are more or less in line with those for 2015, and the objective here is

TABLE 4.3

Percentage Increases in Public Infrastructure, 1995–2015

Public infrastructure service	1995	2005	2015
Water	69.50	77.72	83.58
Sewage	45.00	53.14	63.14
Electricity	90.90	96.58	99.73
Garbage	69.50	83.59	82.49
Fixed phone	20.30	46.40	34.58
Gas	1.40	1.63	3.32

Sources: PNAD, 1995, 2005, and 2015.

to understand their impact upon the income distribution, which means that concentration curves and their coefficients are the most important consideration.

The imputation proceeded in the same way as for 2015. Most of the census tract had no rents, but three-quarters of the population lived in census tracts that did have rents. There are two important differences between 2015 and the earlier years.

The first is that inequality has been falling over the whole period. The Gini coefficient as measured by the PNAD household questionnaire fell from 59.2 in 1995 to 56.3 in 2005 and to 51.4 in 2015.[3]

The second is that access to public infrastructure services has expanded over the period, as table 4-3 shows. With the exception of fixed phones, which declined from 2005 to 2015 due to the onslaught of cell phones, all other types of public infrastructure in the PNAD have increased, sometimes considerably.

Noteworthy is the almost complete universalization of electricity and large improvements in garbage collection, sewage, and piped water. If public infrastructure expansion begins with the wealthier households through early capture and then proceeds down the income distribution, the result should be a decrease of its concentration coefficients. Table 4-4 shows that this was indeed the case between 2005 and 2015.

Imputed rents made the Gini coefficient fall by 2.6 points in 2005 as opposed to 3.0 for 2015. Average incomes increased by 12.1 percent in 2005, as opposed to 11.9 percent in 2015. Public infrastructure was slightly more concentrated in 2005 than in 2015. The ex-ante concentration coefficient for water fell from 0.36 to 0.28 during the ten years from 2005 to 2015. Trash collection mirrored piped water quite closely. For sewage, the improvement was from 0.45 to 0.35. Even fixed phone availability became more equally distributed, and its concentration coefficient fell from 0.53 to 0.50.

---

[3] Other surveys and other definitions of income show different values for the Gini coefficient but all show the same fall.

TABLE 4.4
Means, Concentrations, and Gini and Theil Coefficients, 2005

Distribution	Population in millions	Mean	Ex-ante concentration	Ex-post concentration	Gini coefficient	Theil T
Per capita income	178.6	436.07	0.563		0.5631	0.6432
Per capita income with imputed rent	178.6	487.97		0.537	0.5372	0.5803
Water	178.4	3.24	0.364	0.380	0.5611	0.6372
Sewage	178.4	2.73	0.448	0.333	0.5618	0.6388
Electricity	178.4	11.80	0.317	0.462	0.5561	0.6252
Garbage	178.4	8.87	0.354	0.370	0.5584	0.6304
Fixed phone	178.4	3.81	0.525	0.542	0.5622	0.6392
All infrastructure	178.4	30.45	0.371	0.386	0.5505	0.6092
Per capita imputed rent	178.6	51.90	0.302	0.335	n.c.	n.c.
Avg. census tract per capita rent	178.6	62.75	0.305	0.316	n.c.	n.c.
Per capita rent	25.9	78.87	0.362	0.362	n.c.	n.c.
Rents	178.6	14.5	0.093	−0.008	n.c.	n.c.

Source: PNAD, 2005.
"n.c." = not calculated.

FIGURE 4-3

Difference in Concentration Curves

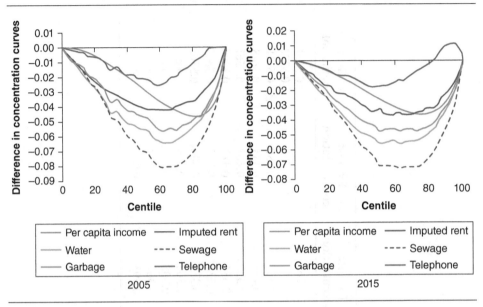

Sources: PNAD, 2005 and 2015.

Figure 4-3 shows the differences in detail across the distribution.

The ex-ante and ex-post differences (i.e., the right and left panels in figure 4-3) between 2005 and 2015 are similar. The highest progressive change in the value of a public infrastructure service was in sewage, indicated by the dotted red lines. This was followed by piped water and garbage collection. The behavior of fixed phones was more erratic as both higher- and lower-income households decided to forgo land lines and rely entirely on cell phones.

Of more consequence is that imputed rent as a whole has also become more progressive; hence the fact that the reduction in the Gini coefficient due to its inclusion in income increases from 2.6 to 3.2 Gini points.

Table 4-5 shows the same statistics for 1995.

The same trends that can be seen from 2005 to 2015 are visible from 1995 to 2005. The concentration coefficient for imputed rent fell another five points, from about 0.35 to about 0.33. The concentration coefficients for public infrastructure also fell from 1995 to 2005. Imputed rents increased incomes by about 14 percent in 1995.

5 Conclusions

The main conclusion is that owner-occupied housing is highly progressive in Brazil, with a concentration coefficient of close to 0.24. Its inclusion in per capita income reduces the Gini coefficient by 0.32 Gini points. This suggests that programs to expand

TABLE 4.5
Means and Concentration Coefficients, 1995

Distribution	Population in millions	Mean	Ex-ante concentration	Ex-post concentration	Gini coefficient	Theil T
Per capita income	146.2	205.52	0.592	n.a.	0.5917	0.7074
Per capita income with imputed rent	146.2	234.99	n.a.	0.564	0.5643	0.6372
Water	145.9	4.52	0.453	0.475	0.5881	0.6956
Sewage	145.9	1.84	0.539	0.414	0.5905	0.7023
Electricity	145.9	4.25	0.393	0.560	0.5870	0.6936
Garbage	145.9	3.61	0.462	0.482	0.5888	0.6975
Fixed phone	145.9	1.71	0.729	0.753	0.5921	0.7064
All infrastructure	145.9	15.94	0.479	0.500	0.5836	0.6811
Per capita imputed rent	146.2	29.47	0.353	0.390	n.c.	n.c.
Per capita rent	18.8	52.48	0.240	0.240	n.c.	n.c.
Rents	146.2	0.13	0.179	0.072	n.c.	n.c.

Source: PNAD, 1995.

"n.a." = not applicable. "n.c." = not calculated.

ownership of housing could have a significant impact on inequality in countries in which housing is less progressive.

Another conclusion is that public infrastructure services have become more progressive over time. This is a consequence of the fact that their provision begins with the wealthier households and gradually finds its way to the bottom of the income distribution. As Lanjouw and Ravallion (1999) eloquently state, for "public programs with relatively large start-up costs, early capture by the nonpoor may be the only politically feasible option" (p. 260). So early capture by the rich should surprise no one. Newer services, such as broadband internet, are almost certainly still regressive.

Future work points in two directions. The first is checking whether these findings also hold for other countries. Perhaps in very poor countries such as Honduras or Haiti, even services such as water or sanitation may still be regressive.

The second is looking for alternative ways to value housing and public infrastructure services so as to ascertain whether the results are not methodology-dependent. One possibility is to ask individuals what their willingness to pay for these services is. Another is to see in expenditures surveys how much they effectively pay. Yet another is to calculate the value of housing services from housing values à la Smeeding et al. (1993).

Acknowledgments

The author gratefully acknowledges support by the Commitment to Equity Institute.

References

Aguirre, Antonio, and Paolo Macedo. 1996. "Estimativas de preços hedônicos para o mercado imobilliario de Belo Horizonte." Anais do XVIII Congresso da Sociedade Brasileira de Econometria, Belo Horizonte, Brasil.

Dantas, Rubens Alves, and Gauss Moutinho Cordeiro. 1988. "Uma nova metodolgoia para avaliação de imóveis utilizando modelos lineares generalizados." Revista Brasileira de Estatística 49, no. 191, pp. 27–46.

Favero, Luiz Paulo Lopes, Patrícia Prado Belfiore, and Gerlando A. S. Franco de Lima. 2008. "Modelos de Precificação Hedônica de imóveis residenciais na Região Metropolitana de São Paulo: Uma abordagem sob as perspectivas da demanda e da oferta." Estudos Econômicos (São Paulo) 38, no. 1, pp. 73–96.

Ferreira, Francisco H. G., Peter Lanjouw, and Marcelo Neri. 2003. "A Robust Poverty Profile for Brazil Using Multiple Data." Revista Brasileira de Economia (Rio de Janeiro) 57, no. 1, pp. 59–92.

Figueroa, B. Eugenio. 1993. "Estimaciones hedónicas del valor de mercado de los programas de vivienda social en la América Latina." El Trimestre Económico 60, no. 240, pp. 779–805.

Frick, Joachim R., and Markus M. Grabka. 2003. Imputed Rent and Income Inequailty: A Decomposition Analysis for Great Britain, West Germany and the United States. Berlin: DIW Berlin.

Gonzalez, Marco Aurelio Stumpf, and Carlos Torres Formoso. 1994. "Especificação de modelos de preços hedônicos para locação residencial em Porto Alegre." Cadernos IPPUR/UFRJ 8, no 1, pp. 59–72.

Lanjouw, Peter, and Martin Ravallion. 1999. "Benefit Incidence, Public Spending Reforms, and the Timing of Program Capture." *World Bank Economic Review* 13, no. 2, pp. 257–73.

Maclennan, Duncan. 1982. *Housing Economics*. London: Longmans.

Morais, Maria da Piedade, and Bruno de Oliveira Cruz. 2015. "Demand for Housing and Urban Service in Brazil: A Hedonic Approach." IPEA Discussion Paper 120, January.

Nascimento, Mabel, Marcelo Cortes Neri, Alexandre Pinto de Carvalho, and Edward Joaquim Amadeo. 2000. "Assets, Markets and Poverty in Brazil." *Ensaios Econômicos* no. 374.

Paixão, Luiz Andrés Ribeiro. 2015. "Índice de preços hedônicos para imóveis: Uma análise para o Município de Belo Horizonte." *Economia Aplicada* 19, no. 1. doi.org/10.1590/1413-8050/ea36708.

Rocha, Sonia. 2002. "A Investigação do rendimento na PNAD—Comentario e sugestões à pesquisa nos anos 2000." IPEA Discussion Paper 899, August, Rio de Janeiro.

Rosen, Sherwin. "Hedonic Prices and Implicit Markets: Product Differentiation in Pure Competition." *Journal of Political Economy* 82, no. 1, pp. 34–55.

Smeeding, Timothy M., Peter Saunders, John Coder, Stephen Jenkins, Johan Fritzell, Aldi J. Hagenaars, Richard Hauser, and Michael Wolfson. 1993. "Poverty, Inequality, and Family Living Standards Impacts across Seven Nations: The Effect of Noncash Subsidies for Health, Education and Housing." *Review of Income and Wealth* 39, no. 3, pp. 229–56.

Yates, Judith. 1994. "Imputed Rent and Income Distribution." *Review of Income and Wealth* 40, no. 1, pp. 43–66.

Fiscal Incidence of
Corporate Taxes

Chapter 5

TAXES, TRANSFERS, AND INCOME DISTRIBUTION IN CHILE
Incorporating Undistributed Profits

Bernardo Candia and Eduardo Engel

Introduction

Distributive issues have been at the center of public debate since the 2000s, due to increasing inequality in various developed countries, among other reasons. Chile was no exception to this trend. During the presidential campaign in 2013, an ambitious tax reform, which was the central element of the program of the winning candidate Michelle Bachelet, was approved by Congress in 2014. This reform changed the tax regime for companies in order to establish a more progressive tax and increase tax revenue from 19 percent to 22 percent of GDP. Additional resources were allocated, mostly to finance educational reform.

Measuring the distributive impact of a tax structure and of transfers financed by tax revenues proves to be a methodological challenge, especially because it is desirable to have a standard methodology that allows for comparison across countries. Developing such a methodology, which includes a range of sources of income, taxes, and transfers and is applicable in a growing number of countries has been an important initiative of the Commitment to Equity (CEQ) Institute.

This chapter contributes to the CEQ project by proposing a methodology for incorporation of capital income into the calculations of distributive impact of fiscal interventions.[1] With that aim, we have applied the methodology used by Engel, Galetovic, and Raddatz (1999) to combine the information from the National Survey of Socioeconomic Characterization (CASEN for its name in Spanish: Encuesta de Caracterizacion Socioeconomica Nacional) with the administrative data of the Internal

---

[1] The taxes and transfers, both monetary and non-monetary, are specific cases of fiscal interventions.

Revenue Service (SII for its name in Spanish: Servicio de Impuestos Internos) to pair individuals from both sources of information.

Unlike Engel, Galetovic, and Raddatz (1999), we have had access to information about the accrued income of high-income Chilean taxpayers through their firms and companies. The income accrued, but not received, by high-income individuals is particularly important in the case of Chile, at least before the 2014 reform of the tax regime because the integrated character of the tax regime facilitated indefinite deferment of income tax payments through the creation of investment companies. Therefore, taking into account the income of firms and companies as the income of their owners, even though they are not withdrawn or paid out in dividends, leads to a more accurate measurement of inequality.[2]

The difference between the distribution of accrued and received income turns out to be significant. Taking data for the year 2013, the Gini coefficient is calculated for five income distributions, from that of the market, passing through the one immediately after tax collection, and also considering the one after the transfers (monetary and nonmonetary) financed by the state with its income (we call it Final Income). In all the cases, the Gini coefficient is higher when working with accrued income, with a rather stable difference, by about 6 Gini percentage points.

We have also concluded that going from the Market Income distribution to the Final Income distribution (after taxes and transfers), the distribution of the income improves by almost 7 Gini percentage points. This finding leads to another topic of this chapter: how to assign this improvement in the distribution between different fiscal interventions.

This chapter considers 16 different possible fiscal interventions—among them, direct taxes, indirect taxes, and different types of spending on education and health—and evaluates the distributive impact of each of them. One logical step is to compare the Gini coefficient for the income distribution before and after the application of a particular intervention that we are evaluating. The problem is that there are a great number of possible referenced income distributions—the distribution before the intervention—to consider when calculating the redistributive impact of the intervention. In effect, the referenced income distribution could be after any subset of the other 15 that are not being considered. This is to say that there are $2^{15} = 32,768$ possible income distributions to which we can apply the intervention of interest so we can later calculate and observe how the Gini coefficient varies. Which of these distributions do we work with?

A secondary contribution of this work, following Sastre and Trannoy (2002), is to apply the Shapley value to assign the change in the income distribution to the fiscal interventions that originated it. This focus gives a simple and reasonable criterion to average the large number of changes in the Gini coefficient just described. We first applied this methodology to the 2013 income distribution and concluded that half of the

---

[2] Fairfield and Jorrat (2014) emphasize this point.

improvement was due to transfers in education. Direct taxes explained only a 20 percent decline in the Gini coefficient. Here, we consider an impact simulation of the 2014 tax reform conducted by the World Bank (2016). According to this estimation, the reform would result in an additional reduction of 2 points of the Gini if switched from Market Income to Final Income. Upon using the Shapley value to distribute this additional improvement among the 16 fiscal interventions considered, we conclude that two-thirds are explained by an increase in education spending that is financed by the reform.

This chapter is organized as follows: section 1 gives a brief description of the Chilean tax regime. Section 2 describes our proposal to incorporate capital income into the CEQ methodology. This proposal is applied using Chilean data from 2013 in section 3, where we compare the distribution of Market Income with Final Income (and several stages in between), taking capital income into consideration in two possible scenarios: accrued and received. Section 4 explains how to use the Shapley value to measure the distributive impact of a particular fiscal intervention. The methodology has an additive property: the sum of the values assigned to individual interventions is equal to the impact of all the interventions combined. Section 5 applies the findings from previous sections to estimate expected distributive impact of the 2014 tax reform. Section 7 concludes.

1 Tax Regime and Social Spending in Chile

1.1 Tax Regime

In the Chilean tax system, two types of taxes are observed: direct taxes and indirect taxes. Direct taxes are applied to income and equity, while indirect taxes affect wealth, encumbering acts, and/or contracts.

1.1.1 Direct Taxes

The most important direct tax in Chile is income tax, which, in 2013, consisted of three different taxes: a flat rate of 20 percent on company profits (First Category Tax), a tax on dependent work incomes (Second Category Tax), and a general tax encumbering all income generated by a natural person (Complementary Global Tax). The work tax and general tax shared the same structure of progressive rates, with eight different brackets, starting with the exempt bracket and ending with the highest bracket, which was subject to a marginal rate of 40 percent. The only difference between these taxes was that the Second Category Tax was retained and deposited into state coffers by the employer on a monthly basis, while the Global Tax was paid once a year.

The main characteristic of income tax in 2013 was that it represented an integrated regime in which the subject of taxation had to be a natural person. In order to assure the integration of the regime, the tax paid for concept of First Category Tax acts as an income tax credit, which is recognized at the moment of withdrawing profit or receiving company dividends. The essential difference between the maximum marginal rate

TABLE 5-1
Chilean Tax System, 2013

	% of total revenue	% of GDP
Direct taxes		
Business taxes	22.1	3.7
Personal taxes	7.9	1.3
Additional tax	6.8	1.1
Others	2.8	0.5
Total	**39.6**	**6.6**
Indirect taxes		
VAT	47.5	7.9
Alcoholic/nonalcoholic beverages	1.1	0.2
Additional others	0.1	0.0
Excise taxes	8.7	1.4
Import tariffs	1.4	0.2
Total	**58.7**	**9.8**
Others	1.9	0.3
Total	**100**	**16.7**

Source: Author's calculations based on 2009–4 annual tax revenue, SII.

of the complementary tax and the rate of First Category Tax is 20 percentage points, which generates incentives to defer the payment of tax on capital income.

Table 5-1 shows the proportion of tax revenues and the percentage of GDP that each direct tax represents for 2013. It shows that direct taxes amounted to 39.6 percent of total tax collection (6.6 percent of GDP). This table considers personal taxes as well as corporate taxes.

1.1.2 Indirect Taxes

The most important indirect tax in Chile is value added tax (VAT), which generates the largest quantity of tax income (47.5 percent of total tax collection). In 2013 the majority of transactions were encumbered with a fixed rate of 19 percent, which was applied to the sales price in the case of internal sales and to the cost, insurance, and freight (CIF) value, plus tariff, in the case of imports. VAT has relatively few exemptions, the most important being those that benefit exportations and services related to health, education, and transportation. As shown in table 5-1, indirect taxes represent 58.7 percent of total tax collection (9.8 percent of GDP). Indirect taxes considered in this chapter are VAT, taxes on luxury products, taxes on alcoholic and nonalcoholic beverages and similar products, tobacco tax, fuel taxes, and import tariffs.

TABLE 5-2
Social Spending in Chile, 2013

	% of social spending	% of GDP
Social security	43.0	6.1
Education	30.0	4.3
Health	27.0	3.8
Total	**100**	**14.2**

Source: Authors' calculations based on the 2013 executed budget, DIPRES.

1.2 Social Spending

As shown in table 5-2, the social spending for Chile in 2013 was 14.2 percent of GDP, and it was mainly disaggregated as an expense for social protection, education, and health. In this section, the most important components of this spending are briefly described.

1.2.1 Social Protection System

The social protection system in Chile is based on two subsystems: Ethical Family Income and the Family Benefit System.

Ethical Family Income, which aims to eradicate extreme poverty, is the sum of benefits given by the state to the most vulnerable persons and families. In 2013, 170,000 families received these benefits, which include access to personalized social support programs and delivery of bonuses. Among the main beneficiaries are elderly people who are living in dire conditions, homeless people, and minors whose legal guardians are incarcerated. The program seeks to provide individuals with tools for facilitating entry into the labor market and improving the self-sufficiency of households. The bonuses are given after certain achievements and upon fulfilment of duties in the area of health, education, and employment.

The Family Benefit System is a set of subsidies that aims to complement family income for the most vulnerable part of the population. This study considers all bonuses and subsidies related to these programs.[3]

1.2.2 Pension System

In the Chilean pension system all persons save in one individual capitalization account that will later finance their pensions and whose amount depends on the number, amount, and temporary ordering of the contributions, of their salary profile, retirement

---

[3] They include household allowance, single family subsidy, mental disability subsidy, family protection bonus, family base bonus, bonus for medical control for children, school attendance bonus, school achievement bonus, and working woman bonus.

age, and the profitability of the funds. The pension system is based on three basic pillars: a contributive pillar of a mandatory nature, a poverty prevention pillar (solidarity pillar), and a voluntary savings pillar.

The solidarity pillar is oriented to provide a minimum pension to those people who are not part of the pension system, such as informal workers, and to those whose level of savings is very low, either because their working life was interrupted or because they joined the pension system late in life. The resources to finance these types of pensions are obtained from Fiscal Income—thus the name "Solidarity."

1.2.3 Education System

In brief, there are three key features of the Chilean education system: the market model (competition and free election), state subsidiaries, and territorial decentralization. This system is made up of four levels of teaching: preschool, primary, secondary, and superior. The administrative dependency may be municipal, subsidized (on behalf of people or institutions called "holders"), or private. The subsidy per student that the state provides to educational establishments, whether municipal or subsidized, is the same, and 93 percent of students attend these kinds of educational institutions,[4] which makes education a large public spending item. As shown in table 5-2, 30 percent of social spending in 2013 went to education, which represented 4.3 percent of GDP.

1.2.4 Health System

The Chilean health system is made up of two subsystems: one public and one private. The public system includes all organizations that form the National System of Health Services (SNSS for its name in Spanish: Sistema Nacional de Servicios de Salud)— namely, the Ministry of Health and its dependent bodies (Undersecretariat of Public Health and Undersecretariat of Welfare Networks), the Institute of Public Health, and the Central Supply and Superintendence of Health. The National Health Fund (FONASA for its name in Spanish: El Fondo Nacional de Salud) is a public organization in charge of providing health coverage to its beneficiaries, which in 2013 reached approximately 76.3 percent of the country's population. FONASA is financed mostly with the fiscal contributions established by the Law on Budgets (58.4 percent) and with health contributions from affiliates (36.4 percent).[5] As table 5-2 shows, the spending on health corresponds to 27 percent of social spending, which represents 3.8 percent of GDP.

The private system is in the hands of so-called Private Health Institutions (ISAPRE for the name in Spanish: Instituciones de Salud Previsional), which are in charge of financing healthcare and benefits in accordance with plans agreed upon

---

[4] This figure was calculated based on information concerning enrollments provided by the Ministry of Education for preschool, primary, secondary, adult, and special education.

[5] The pension and healthcare system of armed forces (CAPRADENA) and police force (DIPRECA) also are part of the public system and are financed mostly by fiscal income.

with its affiliates. The beneficiary population of these types of institutions reached 17.8 percent of the population in 2013.

2 Data, Methodology, and Assumptions

We apply the *CEQ Assessment* (Lustig and Higgins, 2022) to estimate the incidence of social spending, subsidies, and taxes in Chile. The objective is to measure the degree of redistribution resulting from social spending, subsidies, and taxes, quantify the progressivity of the tax regime and government spending, and determine what changes in social spending and taxes can achieve a better distribution of wealth and a greater reduction in poverty within the context of fiscal responsibility.

The CEQ methodology defines main concepts of income in order to measure the redistributive effect and the impact on poverty of fiscal interventions. Prefiscal income is defined in terms of Market Income. Post-fiscal incomes reflect income obtained after a set of fiscal interventions is applied and consist of Net Market Income, Disposable Income, Consumable Income, and Final Income. The analysis unit is the household.

The analysis developed in this chapter involves two innovations intended to improve CEQ methodology: first, we use tax administrative information in order to develop a methodology that will allow incorporation of capital income, and second, we include corporative taxes into the analysis.

Figure 5-1 explains the construction of the main concepts of income analyzed in this study. Two initial scenarios defining Market Income are established. The first scenario corresponds to received Market Income, which considers dependent and independent work income, pensions, rent, interest, private money transfer, consumption of own production, imputed rent, capital gains, dividends, and withdrawals.[6] The second scenario corresponds to accrued Market Income that, as a part of personal income, includes income not distributed by companies.[7] This definition of income is very close to the Haig-Simmons definition, which defines income as consumption expenditure plus the change in equity.[8] The second scenario is better for doing distributional analysis because retained profits correspond to a fundamental component of high-income households given the particularities of the Chilean tax system described in

---

[6] This corresponds to the definition of Market Income plus Pensions as defined in chapter 6 by Ali Enami, Sean Higgins, and Nora Lustig in Volume 1 of this Handbook (Enami, Higgins, and Lustig, 2022).

[7] The received income scenario considers dividends and withdrawals, while the accrued income scenario considers financial profit according to the participation in a given property.

[8] The main difference in the definition of accrued income in this study and Heig-Simmons income is that the latter does not include pensions as part of income but considers them a dissaving.

FIGURE 5-1
Definitions of the Main Concepts of Income

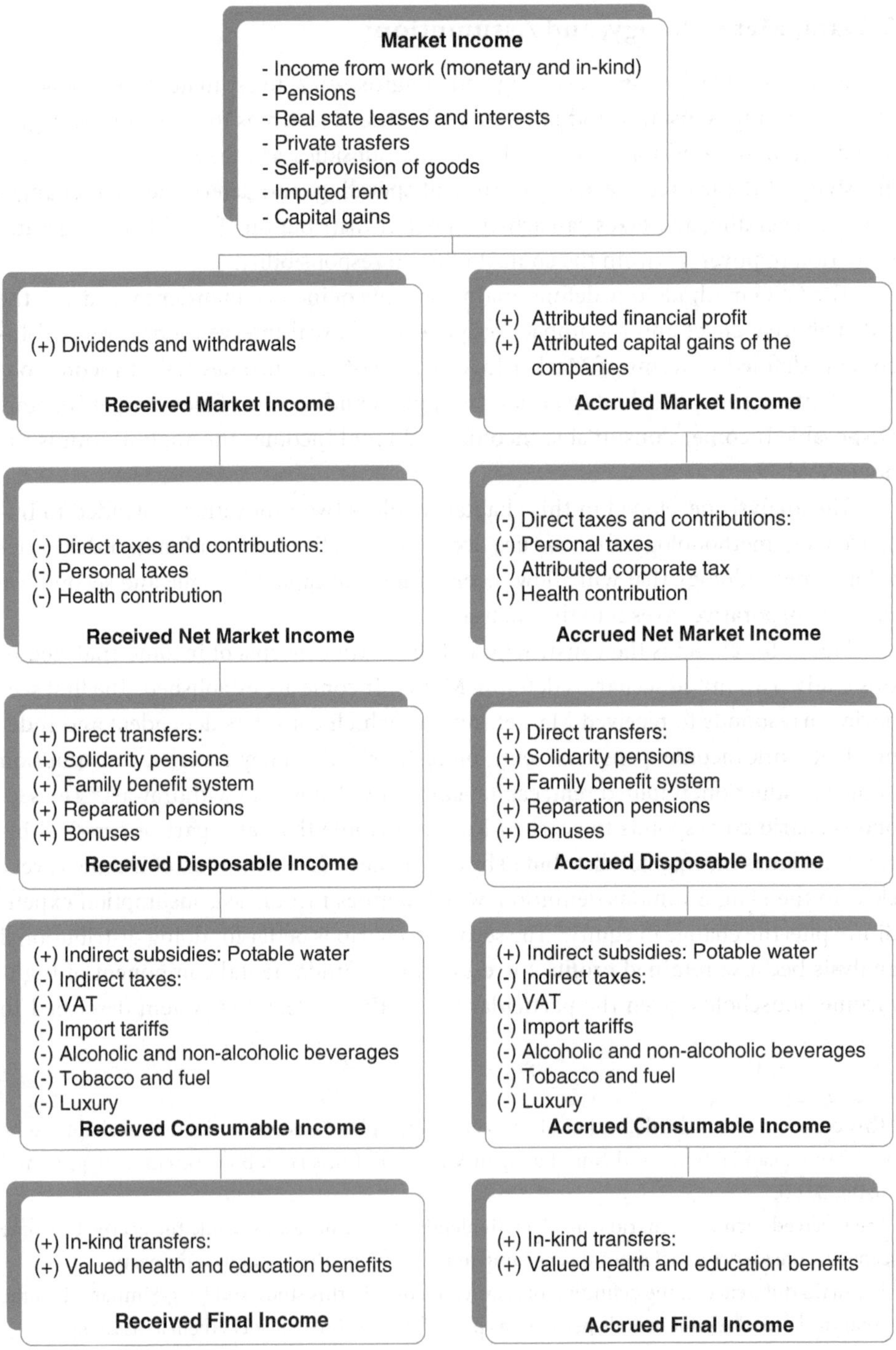

Market Income
- Income from work (monetary and in-kind)
- Pensions
- Real state leases and interests
- Private trasfers
- Self-provision of goods
- Imputed rent
- Capital gains

(+) Dividends and withdrawals **Received Market Income**	(+) Attributed financial profit (+) Attributed capital gains of the companies **Accrued Market Income**
(-) Direct taxes and contributions: (-) Personal taxes (-) Health contribution **Received Net Market Income**	(-) Direct taxes and contributions: (-) Personal taxes (-) Attributed corporate tax (-) Health contribution **Accrued Net Market Income**
(+) Direct transfers: (+) Solidarity pensions (+) Family benefit system (+) Reparation pensions (+) Bonuses **Received Disposable Income**	(+) Direct transfers: (+) Solidarity pensions (+) Family benefit system (+) Reparation pensions (+) Bonuses **Accrued Disposable Income**
(+) Indirect subsidies: Potable water (-) Indirect taxes: (-) VAT (-) Import tariffs (-) Alcoholic and non-alcoholic beverages (-) Tobacco and fuel (-) Luxury **Received Consumable Income**	(+) Indirect subsidies: Potable water (-) Indirect taxes: (-) VAT (-) Import tariffs (-) Alcoholic and non-alcoholic beverages (-) Tobacco and fuel (-) Luxury **Accrued Consumable Income**
(+) In-kind transfers: (+) Valued health and education benefits **Received Final Income**	(+) In-kind transfers: (+) Valued health and education benefits **Accrued Final Income**

Source: Higgins and Lustig (2022).

section 1.[9] However, it is possible to incorporate corporate taxes into the analysis as part of the direct taxes.[10]

2.1 Data

The main source of information related to income is the 2013 National Survey of Socioeconomic Characterization (CASEN). The Ministry of Social Development conducts this survey every two years in order to collect data related to social and economic characteristics of a representative sample of the population. The survey includes 218,401 individuals from 66,725 households. We use data from the 2013 survey and a traditional methodology that adjusts for non-declaration and under-declaration of income in such a way that the income in different categories is the same as the one observed in the national account.[11]

The database of the SII was used as a complementary source of income information and to determine the direct tax payment of households. This database contains information on income and tax payments of 9,064,803 taxpayers for the year 2013 and corresponds to the database used in World Bank (2016).

The consumption pattern of households was estimated based on the 2011–12 Family Budget Survey (EPF for its name in Spanish: Encuesta de Presupuesto Familiar). This survey was conducted by the National Statistics Institute and provides information on the spending structure and consumption patterns in every regional capital of the country. It is conducted every five years, and its main objective is to identify goods and services on the basis of which the institute can calculate the inflation rate.

The 2012 Input-Output Matrix (IOM) constructed by the Central Bank of Chile makes it possible to determine the fraction of household spending that corresponds to imported and tradable goods, both in final goods and supplies used in national production, and thus allows the estimation of the tariff payments for households.

---

[9] Agostini, Martínez, and Flores (2012) and Fairfield and Jorrat (2014) are examples of recent studies of income distribution in which accrued profits have been incorporated.

[10] Even though the definition of accrued income is better for doing distribution analysis, we chose to present the results under both definitions of income with the aim of providing a better comparison.

[11] The Economic Commission for Latin America and the Caribbean (CEPAL) carried out this procedure. The proportional difference between CASEN and the data from national accounts is imputed uniformly for each category of income (wages and salaries, independent work income, social security provisions, and imputed rent). The adjustment coefficients are estimated for national accounts on the basis of the year 2008. For property incomes, the difference between CASEN and national accounts is attributed to 20 percent of the highest income individual receivers in a manner proportional to independent income. This corresponds to the database used by the SII to measure evasion. In the year 2013, CASEN published the results with and without adjustment for national accounts.

It also enables us to determine how fuel taxes affect the price of supplies.[12] We combine EPF 2011–12 and IOM 2012 to estimate the effect of the payment of indirect taxes on the consumption of households.

Finally, valuable data was provided by the Ministry of Finance, Ministry of Education, Ministry of Social Development, National Institute of Statistics, FONASA, and the Budget Office.

2.2 Construction of the Main Concepts of Income

The following explains how the main concepts of income were constructed.[13]

2.2.1 Market Income

The main idea is to assign to CASEN individuals variables not reported in the CASEN survey such as financial profit, capital gains, and taxes through a cross-reference with the database provided by the SII. The strategy consists in matching both sources of information through a variable that is contained in both databases.[14]

The SII database provided contains a variable of income received from the individual that is defined as the sum of income from dependent and independent work, capital gains, interest income, income from real estate leases, withdrawals, dividends, and pensions.[15] The same variable of received income is constructed for CASEN individuals.[16]

Then CASEN individuals are identified with a received income higher than the minimum amount of taxable liquid income from which individuals must pay taxes; these amount to a total of 3,282,402 individuals.[17] The same procedure is carried out in the SII database, where a total of 2,286,190 individuals exceed the income tax payment threshold.[18] Thus, there is a difference of 996,212 individuals between both sources of information.

These individuals are considered as non-declarants, either because they receive income in the informal sector of the economy, because they evade taxes, or because they receive exempt income that should not be declared, such as the income received from

---

[12] Only the payment of the specific tax is considered as an input of transportation services since the fuel used in the production process is exempt from the tax payment.

[13] The technical detail of the construction of the concepts of income is contained in a methodological appendix, available upon request from the authors.

[14] The CASEN survey is anonymous so it is not possible to make a direct cross.

[15] This corresponds to the variable y_1 in World Bank (2016).

[16] The non-declaration and under-declaration of dividend income and interest income in CASEN were corrected using the methodology of Engel, Galetovic, and Raddatz (1999).

[17] In 2013, the tax payment threshold corresponded to $6,605,304 per year.

[18] For this procedure, the capital gains of the individuals in the SII database were not considered, since CASEN does not report capital gains.

the rental of housing associated with the Law Decree 2 of 1968 (DFL2).[19] The rest of CASEN individuals are considered potential contributors. CASEN individuals classified as non-declarants have an annual income exceeding the tax payment threshold and less than $21,000,000.[20] It is assumed that it is not possible for an individual with an annual income exceeding $21,000,000 to not pay any kind of tax and that the probability of not paying taxes decreases linearly with income. The probability distribution used to select the non-declarants was parameterized in such a way that the probability of an individual not declaring an annual income higher than $21,000,000 is zero, and the expected value of the number of non-declarants is equal to the actual number of non-declarants.

Once the number of potential taxpayers in CASEN is equal to the number of individuals who exceed the tax payment threshold according to information on received income from the SII database, the individuals in both databases are ordered by centiles of received income. It is assumed that the individuals that make up the nth centile in CASEN are the same as those who make up the nth centile in the SII database. Then the variables that are contained only in the SII database are imputed to the CASEN individuals. These variables correspond to the attributed financial profit,[21] capital gains, attributed capital gains of the companies,[22] tax base, and total direct taxes paid by the individual.[23] The imputation is made proportionally to the received income of the CASEN individual.

Once the procedure described above is carried out, it is possible to construct received Market Income and accrued Market Income (see figure 5-1). It should be remembered that received Market Income considers only the income obtained by taxpayers who are natural persons, while accrued Market Income also considers the income generated at the company level and attributed to individuals according to their ownership

---

[19] The DFL2 is a regulation that governs properties for residential use, which have a built area of less than 140 square meters and are intended for natural persons. Among the main advantages of this decree is the reduction in taxes for owners.

[20] A person with an annual income exceeding $21,000,000 is among the richest 7.2 percent of individuals over 20 years old with positive income.

[21] For a detailed description of the process of attribution of financial profits in the income of individuals, see methodological annex 2 of World Bank (2016). Only the positive financial profits generated by the companies (corporations and partnerships) were attributed.

[22] It considers only the capital gains (of individuals and companies) taxed. These correspond to the operations described in Article 17, Number 8, of the Law No. 824, Diciembre 31, 1974, Diario Oficial [D.O] (Chile). The amount recorded generally corresponds to the difference between the acquisition value and the sale value of the share.

[23] The tax base corresponds to the income base on which the payment of Second Category Tax and Complementary Global Tax is calculated. The total payment of direct taxes corresponds to the amount of First Category Tax attributed, First Category Single Tax of persons and company attributed (this tax applies to certain capital gains), Second Category Tax, and Complementary Global Tax, less reductions for First and Second Category credits.

participation. As CASEN reports the liquid income of the individuals—that is, net of taxes and contributions—market income is constructed by adding health contributions and tax payments. For received income, the payment of taxes is obtained by applying the tax regulations on the tax base variable, which allows personal taxes to be calculated.

2.2.2 Net Market Income

Net Market Income is obtained by subtracting the payment of direct taxes and health contributions from Market Income.[24] The payment of direct taxes considered under the definition of received income and accrued income is different. For the received income scenario, only personal taxes are considered—that is, the payment of Second Category Tax and the Global Complementary Tax. For the accrued income scenario, personal taxes and business taxes attributed to individuals are considered.

2.2.3 Disposable Income

Disposable Income is constructed by adding money transfers from the government to the Net Market Income. CASEN contains information about beneficiaries of social programs and the amount of money received, so it is possible to make the allocation directly. The analysis includes the benefits related to the Family Benefit System (Single Family Subsidy, Family Allowance, and Subsidy for Mental Disability), Solidarity Pensions, bonuses related to the Ethical Family Income program (school attendance bonus, healthy child control bonus, family base bonus, school achievement bonus, women's work bonus, and family protection and discharge bonus), Pensions of Special Reparation Laws, and other government bonuses (Golden Anniversary bonus, Winter bonus, March bonus). The coverage and the average amount of the benefits were adjusted in such a way that they coincide with the coverage and average amount contained in the administrative records of the different social programs according to information from the Ministry of Social Development (MDS for its name in Spanish: Ministerio de Desarrollo Social).[25]

2.2.4 Consumable Income

Consumable Income is obtained by adding the subsidies to Disposable Income and subtracting the payment of indirect taxes. The only subsidy considered in the analysis is

---

[24] Pension contributions are not considered, since pensions are part of Market Income; that is, a pension is understood as deferred income independent of the pension system from which it comes.

[25] To correct for under-reporting of beneficiaries of the Family Allowance, Single Family Subsidy, Family Base Bonus, March Bonus, Winter Bonus, and School Achievement Bonus programs, the Souza, Osorio, and Soares (2011) method was applied. The method of correction for under-reporting for the rest of the social programs (if possible) is explained in detail in the methodological appendix.

the potable water subsidy, which is reported in CASEN.[26] To calculate the payment of indirect taxes it is necessary to know what fraction of Disposable Income received from a household corresponds to the payment of indirect taxes. For this, the methodology of Engel, Galetovic, and Raddatz (1999) was employed to measure the burden of these types of taxes, for which it was necessary to combine information provided by the EPF 2011–12 and IOM 2012 constructed by the Central Bank.[27]

Indirect taxes produce an increase in the price of goods (price effect) and an increase in the cost of inputs (input effect). The EPF gives us the consumption patterns of households and allows us to determine the price effect, while the IOM describes the production relationships between different sectors or economic activities and allows us to determine the input effect. Among the indirect taxes considered are VAT and tariffs, as well as taxes on alcoholic and nonalcoholic beverages and similar products, luxury products, tobacco, and fuels (diesel oil and gasoline).

We order the households contained in the EPF by deciles of Disposable Income, and we calculate the fraction of Disposable Income that corresponds to the payment of indirect taxes. Then, we order the households contained in the CASEN by deciles of Disposable Income, and we assume that all CASEN households belonging to the same decile have the same consumption pattern as the household representative of each decile in the EPF survey. For the analysis of incidence, we assume that the burden of indirect taxes falls entirely on consumers and that the fraction of household income allocated to the consumption of each good and service is independent of the tax structure.

2.2.5 Final Income

Final Income is constructed by adding the value of health and education benefits to Consumable Income. In the case of the value of benefits in education, information was requested from the Ministry of Education about the cost of education and the number of enrollments, differentiated by educational level and administrative unit of the educational institution, with which it was possible to calculate the average expenditure per type of student. The method of allocating the average expenditure on education is imputation, since CASEN contains information to identify who in the household attends an educational institution, the administrative unit (public, subsidized, or private) and the educational level (preschool, primary, secondary, tertiary, adult, and special).[28]

To determine the average expenditure on health, we use Benavides, Castro, and Jones (2013) as the main source of information. It estimates the per capita public expenditure depending on the sex, age, and income level of the beneficiary for the year 2011. Health expenditure is determined by type of care modality and by the characteristics

---

[26] Corrected for under-reporting using the Souza, Osorio, and Soares (2011) method.

[27] The methodology is explained in detail in the methodological appendix.

[28] We thank Sandra Martinez-Aguilar who provided relevant information to allocate the average expenditure in tertiary education. These data were used in Martinez-Aguilar et al. (2017).

FIGURE 5-2

Effect of Fiscal Interventions on Income Inequality

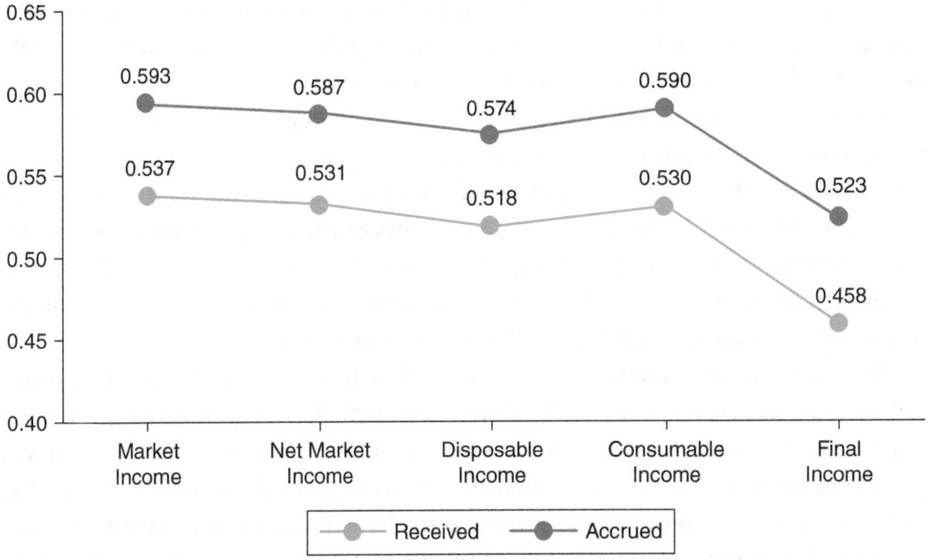

Sources: Authors' calculations based on CASEN, SII, and official government data.

of the beneficiary. FONASA's health expenditure is divided into two broad categories: medical benefits and other services. Within the medical benefits is the Institutional Care Modality (MAI for its name in Spanish: Modalidad de Atención Institucional), to which all insured persons are entitled, and the Free Choice Modality (MLE for its name in Spanish: Modalidad de Libre Elección), to which only people who contribute 7 percent to healthcare are entitled (groups "B," "C" and "D"). Other services include medical loans, subsidies for work disability, and other types of expenses. Since CASEN contains information about the age, sex, and FONASA group to which the individual belongs, it was possible to impute the average expenditure.[29]

3 Results

Figure 5-2 shows the Gini coefficient for the main concepts of income. The Gini coefficient of accrued Market Income (0.593) is considerably higher than the Gini coefficient of received Market Income (0.537), because the definition of accrued income cap-

---

[29] The average expenditure per capita was adjusted in proportion to the real growth in the FONASA budget between 2011 and 2013. For the individuals belonging to CAPREDENA and DIPRECA, the average expenditure charged was calculated from the official budget execution data published by the Budgets Office. For more details see the methodological appendix.

TABLE 5-3
Income Shares

Income	Top 1 %	Top 5 %	Top 10%
Received			
Market	13.2	31.5	44.1
Net Market	12.4	30.6	43.3
Disposable	12.2	30.1	42.6
Consumable	12.4	30.7	43.5
Final	11.0	27.5	39.2
Accrued			
Market	18.7	38.7	50.8
Net Market	17.7	37.6	49.9
Disposable	17.4	37.0	49.2
Consumable	18.2	38.3	50.6
Final	16.5	34.8	46.3

Source: Authors' calculations based on CASEN, SII, and official government data.

tures the income of high-income individuals better. It is observed that the set of fiscal interventions (all taxes and transfers) has an equalizing effect on the distribution of income measured by the Gini coefficient. When going from Market Income to Net Market Income, the Gini coefficient is slightly reduced under both definitions of income, so the joint effect of direct taxes and health contributions is equalizing.[30] On the other hand, when going from Disposable Income to Consumable Income, inequality increases in both scenarios, reflecting the unequalizing effect of indirect taxes in Chile.

Table 5-3 shows the income shares of the top 10 percent, 5 percent, and 1 percent for the main concepts of income. The share in accrued Market Income from the top 1 percent is 18.7 percent, while the share in received Market Income from the top 1 percent is 13.2 percent. For the accrued income scenario, the share of the top 1 percent is reduced by 2.2 percentage points (from 18.7 percent to 16.5 percent) when going from Market Income to Final Income, while the share of the top 10 percent is reduced by 4.5 percentage points (from 50.8 percent to 46.3 percent). A similar reduction is observed for the scenario of received income.

The Kakwani index of the tax system in the received income scenario and in the accrued income scenario is −0.006 and −0.022, respectively.[31] That is to say, under both

---

[30] It should be remembered that in the received income scenario, only personal taxes are considered, while in the accrued income scenario, personal taxes and corporate taxes attributed to individuals are considered.

[31] The Kakwani index (Kakwani, 1977) is a measure of the progressivity of fiscal interventions. Values can vary between −1 to 1; with positive values indicating an equalizing effect and negative values an unequalizing effect. The higher the index, the greater the progressivity of the fiscal

definitions of income (and direct taxes) the tax system is slightly regressive, which is consistent with previous studies of tax incidence in Chile.[32] When analyzing the received income scenario, separating by type of tax, we find that the Kakwani index is 0.40 for direct taxes and −0.12 for indirect taxes. On the other hand, for the accrued income scenario, the Kakwani index is 0.34 for direct taxes and −0.18 for indirect taxes; that is, direct taxes are less progressive and indirect taxes are more regressive compared to the scenario of received income. The Kakwani index for direct transfers in both definitions of income is higher than 0.85, which reflects the good targeting of social spending in Chile.

In a system with multiple taxes and transfers, Kakwani's progressivity index of a given fiscal intervention does not provide direct information as to whether the intervention has an equalizing or unequalizing effect.[33] To determine the effect on the income distribution of a given fiscal intervention, it is more appropriate to observe its marginal contribution, which is defined as the difference between the Gini coefficient of some end concept of income without the intervention and the Gini coefficient of the end concept of income with the intervention. In this way, if the marginal contribution is positive, the intervention helps to reduce inequality.

Figure 5-3 shows the marginal contribution of a series of fiscal interventions for both definitions of income. Panel A considers disposable income as the end concept of income, while panel B considers consumable income as the end concept of income. There are no qualitative differences in the marginal contribution of the different fiscal interventions under both definitions of income. It is observed that direct transfers and direct taxes contribute to improving the distribution of income, while health, VAT, and other indirect taxes contribute to increasing inequality.[34] In particular, when moving from Disposable Income to Consumable Income, the Gini coefficient increases from 0.518 to 0.530 under the received income scenario and from 0.574 to 0.590 under the accrued income scenario.[35] Moreover, as shown in the next section, the marginal contribution of indirect taxes is negative, independent of the end concept of income used.

---

intervention. The Kakwani index for a tax is defined as the difference between the coefficient of concentration of the tax and the Gini coefficient of the prefiscal income (Market Income), while for a transfer it is defined as the difference between the Gini coefficient of the prefiscal income and the concentration coefficient of the transfer.

[32] See Engel et al. (1999) and Cantallopts, Jorrat, and Sherman (2007).

[33] Enami, Lustig, and Aranda (2022) (chapter 2 in Volume 1 of this Handbook) carry out a detailed study of the conditions that taxes and transfers must meet to determine whether they are equalizing, neutral, or unequalizing.

[34] Other indirect taxes correspond to the sum of import tariffs, taxes on jewelry, alcoholic and nonalcoholic beverages and similar items, tobacco, gasoline, diesel oil, and luxury goods.

[35] Martinez-Aguilar et al. (2017) find that the Gini coefficient decreases when going from Disposable Income to Consumable Income, where the main intervention between both incomes is VAT.

FIGURE 5-3

Marginal Contribution of Fiscal Interventions to Income Inequality (Gini Points)

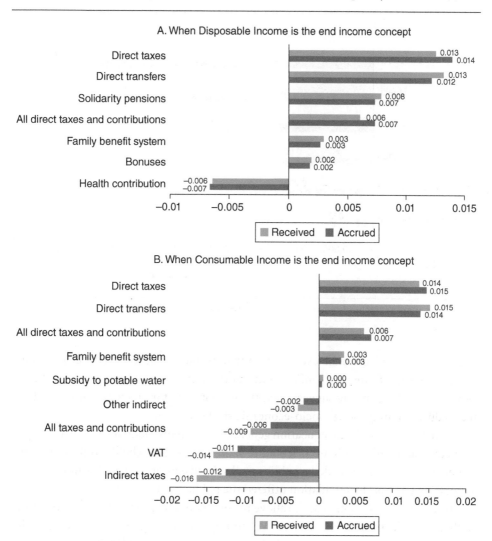

A. When Disposable Income is the end income concept

B. When Consumable Income is the end income concept

Sources: Authors' calculations based on CASEN, SII, and official government data.

In-kind transfers of education and health services have a significant equalizing effect. When passing from Consumable Income to Final Income, the Gini coefficient goes from 0.530 to 0.458 in the received income scenario and from 0.590 to 0.523 in the accrued income scenario. Figure 5-4 shows the marginal contribution of transfers in kind to income inequality when the end concept of income is final income. The marginal contribution of benefits valued in education and health is 0.040 and 0.029 Gini points, respectively, for the received income scenario. When disaggregating transfers

FIGURE 5-4

Marginal Contribution of Transfers in Kind to Income Inequality (Gini Points)

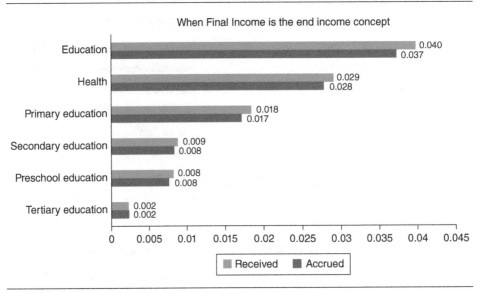

When Final Income is the end income concept

Sources: Authors' calculations based on CASEN, SII, and official government data.

in education by educational level, we find that primary education reduces inequality in the most significant way, while the marginal contribution of tertiary education is close to zero. This finding suggests that the proportion of individuals who attend tertiary education in the lower socio-economic strata is lower.

Transfers in health and education generate a high redistributive effect because private education and health are oriented to high-income households. Indeed, in 2013, 93 percent of students attended a public or subsidized educational establishment,[36] and about 85 percent of the population utilized the public health system.

It is important to note that the above results should be viewed with caution, especially the results related to education. When imputing average expenses, services delivered are not corrected for quality, but more importantly, the administration of educational establishments is carried out by the municipalities, which often divert the resources allocated for education to other activities, so that the effective spending on education should be less than what is observed in budget line items.[37] The same can happen with the holders of subsidized educational establishments.

[36] This percentage does not consider tertiary education.

[37] The Chilean Educational Reform aims to end municipalization with the goal of eliminating this distortion.

FIGURE 5-5
Effect of Fiscal Interventions on Poverty (Percentage of Vulnerable Population, by Concept of Income)

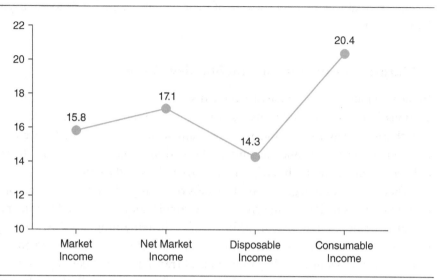

Sources: Authors' calculations based on CASEN, SII, and official government data.

Fiscal interventions also have an impact on poverty.[38] Figure 5-5 shows the percentage of the population vulnerable by way of income under the received income scenario.[39] We use the vulnerability threshold for middle-income countries—as in the case of Chile—defined in Lopez-Calva and Ortiz-Juarez (2014).[40] When going from Market Income to Net Market Income, the percentage of the vulnerable population increases from 15.8 to 17.1 percent. This increase is explained by the health contributions that dependent workers have to pay more than for the direct taxes they pay, since the payment of this type of taxes is only made by 20 percent of the higher income individuals.

When going from the net market income to the disposable income, the fraction of the vulnerable population falls from 17.1 to 14.3 percent. This fall is explained by direct transfers, whose main objective is to provide social protection. Finally, when going from

---

[38] For a discussion of the effect of fiscal interventions on poverty, see Higgins and Lustig (2016). Higgins and Lustig (2016) shows that a significant fraction of the population becomes impoverished despite the fact that the tax-transfer system is progressive. The implication is that some individuals receive fewer transfers than they have to pay in taxes.

[39] Results are not shown under accrued income because they are almost identical to the results of received income.

[40] The threshold corresponds to US$10/day, at constant international prices from 2005.

disposable income to consumable income, the percentage of the vulnerable population increases by one-third, from 14.3 to 20.4 percent. This increase reflects the negative impact of indirect taxes on poverty. The poorest quintile consumes practically all their income, so that a significant fraction of their income corresponds to the payment of indirect taxes.[41]

4 Marginal Contribution and Shapley Value

In the previous section we measured the distributive impact of a series of fiscal interventions (various taxes and transfers) setting the measure of income to be considered in each case (see figures 5-3 and 5-4). For example, we saw that, whether we work with received or accrued income, the impact of spending on education on the distribution of Final Income is approximately 4 percentage points of the Gini.

There is a certain degree of arbitrariness regarding which income concept should be used for the previous comparisons. For example, for a tax, should pre-intervention income consider Market Income before or after the remaining taxes? And for a particular transfer, should the pre-intervention income be before or after the remaining transfers? Nor is it obvious that the evaluations of transfers must take as pre-intervention income the one that includes the collection of all taxes. After all, the budgetary logic of governments works simultaneously with expected incomes and expenditure items.

That arbitrariness means that the distributive impact of particular fiscal interventions will depend on which of the remaining interventions is included in the income that is used to make the comparison. This leads us to consider the impact of measures that average over all possible income options. In this section we apply the Shapley value (Shapley, 1953) to calculate this average.[42]

The Shapley value is a concept in game theory that corresponds to the criterion of distribution of income among n players in a competitive game that complies with certain properties (axioms). In our application of the Shapley value, the income to be distributed is the reduction in the Gini coefficient when going from Market Income to Final Income, and the players are all the interventions under consideration, which include various taxes and transfers.

We assume that the total number of interventions is n and that they are applied sequentially, so that there are $n!$ possible sequences for the order in which resources are collected and spent. Then, to measure the contribution of a particular intervention, we calculate its contribution to the Gini for each of the previous sequences, taking as a measure of income that which results from applying the interventions that appear before the one of interest, and then we calculate the average of these differences. As we

---

[41]For a more detailed analysis of the incidence of different fiscal interventions on poverty for Chile, see Martinez-Aguilar et al. (2022) (chapter 13 in Volume 1 of this Handbook).

[42]Sastre and Trannoy (2002) are the first to apply the Shapley value to assess the distributive impact of interventions on income distribution.

shall see below, the difference between the Gini coefficient of Final Income and the Gini coefficient of Market Income will be equal to the sum of the individual Shapley values of the interventions considered.

4.1 Formalization

Consider a society composed of m individuals indexed by the set $M = \{1, \ldots, m\}$. Within this society, each individual $i \in M$ has a Market Income M_i and also receives n interventions, indexed by the set $N := \{1, \ldots, n\}$ and summarized in the field $I_i = (I_{1i}, \ldots, I_{ni})$, where the taxes have a negative sign, and transfers a positive sign. Thus, the income of any individual $i \in M$ after applying a set of interventions $S \subseteq N$ will be given by

$$(5\text{-}1) \qquad Y_i(S) = M_i + \sum_{k \in S} I_{ki}.$$

Given $S \subseteq N$, we assume without loss of generality that $Y_1(S) \leq \ldots \leq Y_m(S) \ \forall S \subseteq N$. Then, the Gini coefficient after the set of interventions S will be

$$(5\text{-}2) \qquad G(S) = \frac{2}{m} \frac{\sum_{i \in M} i Y_i(S)}{\sum_{j \in M} Y_j(S)} - 1 - \frac{1}{m}.$$

For example, $G(\{1, 2, 3, \ldots, n\})$ is the Gini coefficient once all fiscal interventions have been applied to Market Income; that is, it is the Gini coefficient of Final Income, and $G(\{1\})$ is the Gini coefficient when only fiscal intervention 1 has been applied to Market Income. There are many ways to measure the impact of incorporating a fiscal intervention k into the income distribution. For example $G(\{2\}) - G(\{1, 2\})$ and $G(\{2, 3, 4\}) - G(\{1, 2, 3, 4\})$ are two different ways of measuring the impact of the fiscal intervention 1.[43]

With Market Income as the starting point, there are $n!$ ways to incorporate each fiscal intervention until reaching the Final Income. The Shapley value of fiscal intervention k corresponds to the weighted average of all possible ways to measure the impact on the Gini coefficient.

Suppose you want to calculate how many of the possible trajectories the impact of the reduction in the Gini due to the application of fiscal intervention 1 correspond to $G(\{2, 3, 4\}) - (G\{1, 2, 3, 4\})$. In other words, we want to calculate the number of trajectories where fiscal intervention 1 is incorporated, when fiscal interventions 2, 3, and 4 have already been incorporated, and fiscal interventions 5 to n have not. There are 3! ways to order interventions 2, 3, and 4, then fiscal intervention 1 is added, and there are $[n - (3+1)]!$ ways to order the remaining interventions. Therefore the weighting of $G(\{2, 3, 4\}) - (G\{1, 2, 3, 4\})$ corresponds to $3! \times [n-(3+1)]!/n!$, since the number of N permutations that 2, 3, and 4 have before 1 and the remaining interventions after 1 is $3!(n-4)!$.

---

[43] We subtract the Gini with the interest intervention to the Gini without the intervention so that improvements in the Gini are associated with positive values.

Given the above, the Shapley value of the fiscal intervention $k \in N$ is defined as

$$(5\text{-}3) \qquad \Phi_k = \sum_{S \subseteq N \setminus \{k\}} \frac{\# S!(n - \# S - 1)!}{n!} \{G(S) - G(S \cup \{k\})\},$$

where $\# S$ denotes the number of elements of S. We also note that the empty set ϕ is a subset of $N \setminus \{k\}$, where $G(\phi)$ corresponds to the Gini coefficient of the market income.

An important result for the Shapley values is that

$$(5\text{-}4) \qquad \sum_{k=1}^{n} \Phi_k = G(N) - G(\phi).$$

That is, the sum of the Shapley value of all the interventions is equal to the difference between the Gini coefficient of Final Income and the Gini coefficient of Market Income, of which this difference measures the total redistributive effect. The percentage contribution of the intervention $i \in N$ will then be

$$(5\text{-}5) \qquad \frac{\Phi_i}{G(N) - G(\phi)} = \frac{\Phi_i}{\sum_{k=1}^{n} \Phi_k}.$$

The application of the Shapley value to measure the redistributive impact assigned to each tax and transfer assumes that there is no particular order in which the different fiscal interventions must be applied and that there is no hierarchy of aggregation of the fiscal interventions.[44] This assumption is reasonable because in practice the different tax interventions are applied simultaneously.

4.2 Application

Table 5-4 shows the percentage of the Gini reduction attributed to each fiscal intervention calculated from the Shapley value for both income scenarios. On average, health contributions, VAT, and other indirect taxes increase inequality while direct taxes, subsidies, and direct transfers and benefits valued in health and education reduce inequality.

The percentage of total redistributive effect attributed to direct taxes is 20.1 percent when considering accrued income and 16.2 percent when considering received income. Consequently, under the accrued income scenario, direct taxes contribute more to the Gini reduction.

The interventions that contribute the most to reducing the Gini coefficient are transfers (in-kind) in education. These interventions explain, as a whole, approximately

---

[44] In the case of an existing aggregation scheme, the Shapley value must be applied hierarchically, since the "simple" Shapley value does not comply with the principle of independence at the level of aggregation. See Sastre and Trannoy (2002) and Shorrocks (2013).

TABLE 5-4
Percentage of Decrease in Gini Coefficient Attributed
to Each Fiscal Intervention

Fiscal intervention	Received	Accrued
Bonuses	2.3	2.4
Direct taxes	16.2	20.1
Adult education	0.3	0.3
Preschool education	10.5	10.9
Primary education	22.8	23.5
Secondary education	11.2	11.7
Special education	0.9	0.9
Tertiary education	3.2	3.6
Family benefit system	3.5	3.5
Health	35.6	37.7
Health contribution	−6.9	−8.2
Other indirect	−1.4	−2.7
Potable water	0.5	0.6
Reparation pensions	0.6	0.6
Solidarity pensions	10.0	10.4
VAT	−9.3	−15.1

Source: Authors' calculations based on CASEN, SII, and official government data.

half of the Gini reduction (48.9 percent with received income, 50.9 percent with accrued income). Primary education accounts for almost half of this contribution, followed by preschool and secondary education, each of which accounts for around 10 percent. Expenditure on tertiary education, on the other hand, contributes very little to improving the Gini, as explained in section 1.

It is interesting to visualize the distribution of all the marginal contributions for each one of the interventions—that is, the distributions whose averages we report in table 5-4. This is what is done in figure 5-6 for received income and in figure 5-7 for accrued income. For each intervention, the smallest and largest marginal contribution is indicated as a percentage of the total redistributive effect and the histogram is plotted with the relative frequencies.[45] The red line corresponds to the Shapley value. The marginal contribution ranges are particularly large for VAT (12.3 percent), health (11.9 percent), and primary education (8.1 percent). By contrast, direct taxes always have a positive marginal contribution—that is, they always contribute to reducing inequality—and their variance is much smaller.

---

[45] The distance between the highest marginal contribution and the lowest marginal contribution was divided into 20 equal tranches, and the fraction was calculated for all possible orders where the marginal contribution was within each tranche.

FIGURE 5-6
Received Income

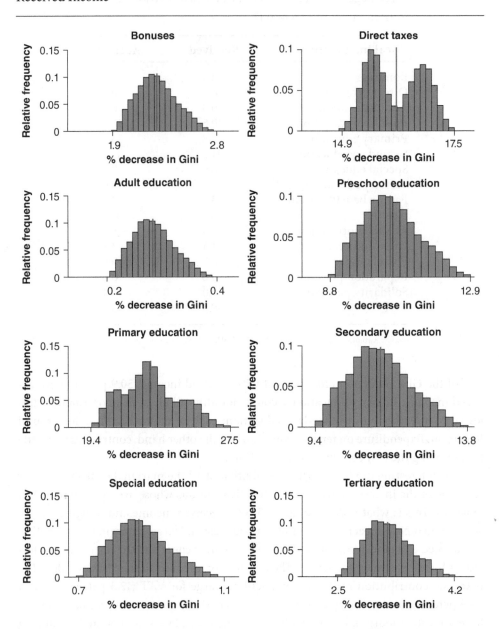

Next, we will see what the magnitude and sign of the marginal contribution of a particular intervention depends on. From equation (7) in Lambert (1985) the change in the Gini coefficient of applying a tax to a "pre" distribution corresponds to

$$(5\text{-}6) \qquad G^{\text{Pre}} - G^{\text{Post}} = [t/(1-t)](C^{\text{Tax}} - G^{\text{Pre}}),$$

FIGURE 5-6   (continued)

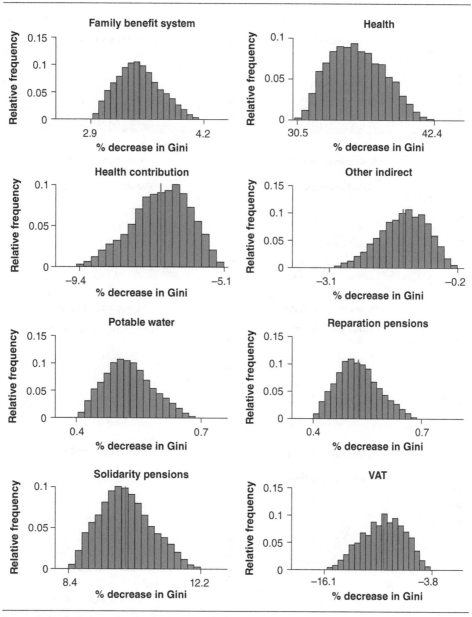

Sources: Authors' calculations based on CASEN, SII, and official government data.

where G^{Pre} is the Gini coefficient before applying the intervention, G^{Post} is the Gini coefficient after applying the intervention, C^{Tax} is the concentration coefficient of the tax, and t is the fraction of the total income (prior to the intervention) paid in the tax. On the other hand, the change in the Gini coefficient of applying a transfer to a "Pre" distribution corresponds to

FIGURE 5-7
Accrued Income

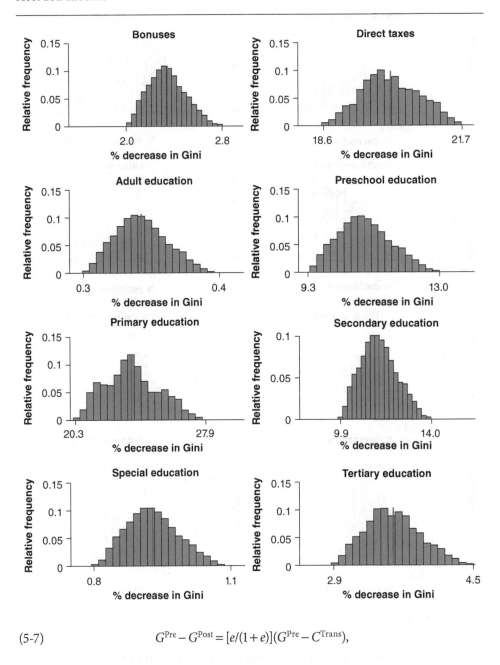

$$(5\text{-}7) \qquad\qquad G^{\text{Pre}} - G^{\text{Post}} = [e/(1+e)](G^{\text{Pre}} - C^{\text{Trans}}),$$

where C^{Trans} is the concentration coefficient of the transfer and e is the fraction of the total income (prior to the intervention) received in the transfer.[46] The expressions above show

---

[46] Note that $C^{\text{Tax}} - G^{\text{Pre}}$ corresponds to the Kakwani progressivity index of the tax with respect to the income distribution before applying the tax and $G^{\text{Pre}} - C^{\text{Trans}}$ corresponds to the Kakwani

FIGURE 5-7 (continued)

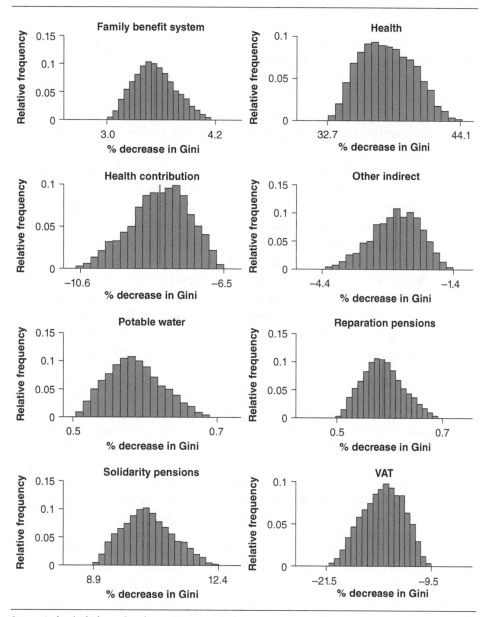

Sources: Authors' calculations based on CASEN, SII, and official government data.

that the magnitude of the marginal contribution depends on the fraction of the total income represented by the intervention and its progressivity index. On the other hand,

progressivity index of the transfer with respect to the distribution of the tax income before applying the transfer. When using concentration curves, we ignore the possibility of changes in the ranking of individuals when applying a tax or a transfer.

whether the marginal contribution is unequalizing, equalizing, or neutral with respect to the "Pre" distribution depends on whether the intervention is regressive, progressive, or neutral with respect to the reference distribution, not the intervention burden.[47]

The greater the progressivity of the intervention with respect to the "pre-" distribution, the greater its marginal contribution will tend to be.[48] If the intervention is progressive, a greater burden of the intervention will tend to increase its marginal contribution, while if the intervention is regressive, a greater burden of the intervention will tend to decrease its marginal contribution.[49]

If an intervention is progressive with respect to all the reference distributions, the marginal contribution will tend to be greater the more progressive the intervention is, and the greater the burden of the intervention on the reference distribution. In contrast, if an intervention is regressive with respect to all reference distributions, the marginal contribution will tend to be greater, while the intervention is less regressive and the intervention's burden on the reference distribution is smaller.

It could be that an intervention is progressive for some reference distributions and not for others. The marginal contribution will tend to be higher the greater the burden is and the more progressive the intervention with respect to the reference distribution, while the marginal contribution will tend to be lower the greater the burden is and the more regressive the intervention with respect to the reference distribution.[50]

To visualize the above, let's take health spending as an example of transfer and VAT as an example of tax in the accrued income scenario. Health spending is always pro-

---

[47] C^{Tax} and C^{Trans} depend only on the distribution of the intervention, so they are independent of the order of application of the intervention. The mean of the correlation between the intervention burden (t or e) and the Gini coefficient of the reference distribution (G^{Pre}) for the 16 fiscal interventions is 0.539 (standard deviation of 0.071). The moderate positive correlation between the intervention burden and the Gini coefficient of the reference distribution is explained because, in the case of Chile, the transfers are progressive, so that when applied, the Gini coefficient decreases, and as total income increases, the burden of the intervention decreases. On the other hand, taxes are regressive, so when applied, the Gini coefficient increases, and, as total income decreases, the burden of the intervention also increases. The only exception is direct taxes, which are progressive. This also explains why the correlation between the intervention burden and the Gini coefficient of the reference distribution for direct taxes is the highest among the 16 fiscal interventions (0.793).

[48] The lower is G^{Pre}, more progressive is the tax with respect to the reference distribution. The greater is G^{Pre}, more progressive is the transfer with respect to the reference distribution.

[49] The largest marginal contribution of an intervention is obtained when the improvement in the distribution of income is the greatest—that is, when $G^{Pre} - G^{Post}$ is at the maximum. Note that for the case of an intervention that is regressive with respect to all reference distributions, the largest marginal contribution is obtained when the distribution of income worsens the least.

[50] The 16 interventions analyzed in this study comply with being progressive or regressive with respect to all reference distributions. This can be seen in the histograms of figures 5-6 and 5-7, where there is no intervention where the histogram passes through 0. For example, direct taxes are progressive for all reference distributions, whereas VAT is regressive for all distributions of reference.

TABLE 5-5
Maximum and Minimum Marginal Contribution

Marginal contribution	Burden	Progressivity	$G^{Pre} - G^{Post}$	$\dfrac{G^{Pre} - G^{Post}}{G(N) - G(\phi)}$
Health	$e/(1+e)$	$G^{Pre} - C^{Trans}$		
Maximum	0.0461(1)	0.7003(609)	0.0323(1)	44.1
Minimum	0.0374(32768)	0.6411(31453)	0.0239(32768)	32.7
First intervention	0.0397(25536)	0.6893(2956)	0.0273(17813)	37.3
Last intervention	0.0431(7233)	0.6437(30890)	0.0277(15282)	37.8
VAT	$t/(1-t)$	$C^{Tax} - G^{Pre}$		
Maximum	0.0733(30369)	−0.0964(1)	−0.0070(1)	−9.6
Minimum	0.0817(2400)	−0.1928(32768)	−0.0157(32768)	−21.5
First intervention	0.0786(10688)	−0.1834(32485)	−0.0144(32107)	−19.7
Last intervention	0.0760(22081)	−0.1023(218)	−0.0077(312)	−10.6

Source: Authors' calculations based on CASEN, SII, and official government data.

Notes: The figures in parentheses correspond to the ranking occupied by the burden, the progressivity, and the marginal contribution when ordered from highest to lowest, in $2^{15} = 32,768$ possible income distributions to which the intervention can be applied. The first intervention refers to the marginal contribution of the intervention when applied to Market Income, while the last intervention refers to the marginal contribution of the intervention once the rest of the fiscal interventions have been applied to Market Income.

gressive, whereas VAT is always regressive. As table 5-5 shows, the largest marginal contribution of health expenditure is 44.1 percent and the lowest marginal contribution is 32.7 percent of the reduction in the Gini coefficient. The largest marginal contribution of health expenditure is obtained when all taxes on Market Income have been applied. In this case, the fraction that represents health expenditure over total income is the maximum possible. In addition, the application of VAT, health contributions, and other indirect taxes contributes to increasing inequality, increasing the progressivity of health spending (higher G^{Pre}). On the other hand, the lowest marginal contribution of health expenditure is obtained once the rest of the transfers have been applied to Market Income. The fraction that represents health expenditure over total income is the minimum possible once all transfers have been applied to Market Income. In addition, transfers help to reduce inequality, thereby reducing the progressivity of health spending (lower G^{Pre}).

As table 5-5 shows, the largest marginal contribution of VAT is −9.6 percent, and the lowest marginal contribution of VAT is −21.5 percent of the reduction in the Gini coefficient. The largest marginal contribution of VAT is obtained when all transfers and direct taxes on Market Income have been applied. When applying transfers and direct taxes to Market Income, the VAT regressivity is the minimum possible. In contrast, the VAT burden is lower once the transfers have been added to the Market Income since the total income increases. However, the lowest marginal contribution of VAT is obtained once health contributions and other indirect taxes have been applied to Market

TABLE 5-6
Decomposition of Decrease in Gini Coefficient

	Received		Accrued	
Tax	% of collection	% of change in Gini	% of collection	% of change in Gini
Direct taxes	19.2	35.6	26.4	48.1
Health contribution	13.6	6.9	12.4	4.9
Other indirect	12.4	11.2	11.3	9.2
VAT	54.9	46.4	50.0	37.9
Total	**100**	**100**	**100**	**100**

Source: Authors' calculations based on CASEN, SII and official government data.

Income. The implication is that both health contributions and other indirect taxes are regressive, so G^{Pre} increases and consequently increases the regressivity of VAT when applied to Market Income. On the other hand, since health contributions and other indirect taxes generate a decrease in total income once they are applied to Market Income, the VAT burden is higher on this distribution.

A problem with the previous analysis is that it does not take into account the fact that taxes are what finance social spending, so a good idea would be to calculate the net redistributive effect by type of tax. Table 5-6 breaks down the improvement in income distribution, measured through the Gini coefficient, in the contribution of direct taxes, health contributions, and VAT and other indirect taxes.[51] For the received income scenario, 46.4 percent of the improvement in the distribution of income is due to VAT, while 35.6 percent to direct taxes. Although VAT is a regressive tax, it is assigned a high value in the reduction of the Gini coefficient, since it generates a high tax collection (54.9 percent).

For the accrued income scenario, 48.1 percent of the reduction in the Gini coefficient is due to direct taxes, while 37.9 percent to VAT. The surprising thing about this result is that, although the participation in the tax collection of direct taxes (26.4 percent) is approximately half of the participation in the tax collection of VAT (50 percent), the net redistributive effect of direct taxes is greater, which reflects the high progressivity of this type of tax.

5 Distributive Effects of the 2014 Tax Reform

In 2014, the government of President Michelle Bachelet approved a tax reform that made a series of important changes to income taxation of companies. The reform had four

---

[51]To obtain the decomposition in the reduction of the Gini coefficient among the four taxes, the Shapley value was applied, where it was assumed that the share of each tax in social expenditure is proportional to its participation in the collection.

main objectives: (1) to increase tax collection by 3 GDP points to finance educational reform, increase health spending, and reduce the structural balance deficit; (2) to advance tax equity by improving the distribution of income; (3) to introduce new and more efficient savings incentives for investment; and (4) to incorporate new measures to combat tax evasion and avoidance.

Within the main modifications implemented by the reform, the most relevant are the profound changes in the income tax: taxation on the profits of companies on an attributed basis, the increase in the First Category Tax rate from 20 percent to 25 percent in the integrated system and 27 percent in the semi-integrated system, the partial integration (and not total) of taxes on individuals and businesses, and the reduction of the higher marginal rate of the Second Category Tax. In addition, changes in the tax structure of companies reduce the incentive for the unlimited deferral of the income tax applicable at the time of the distribution of profits. In this way, these changes were intended to improve the neutrality of the system insofar as the previous mechanism disproportionately benefited the income from capital.[52] The implementation of the tax reform has been gradual and was completed in 2018.

The objective of this section is to measure the impact of the tax reform on distribution of income using the main income concepts of the CEQ methodology. The World Bank micro-simulation model (World Bank, 2016) simulated the total direct tax payment in 2013 of the taxpayers under the taxation rules on the income established by the tax reform.[53] To correctly measure the impact of the tax reform on the distribution of income, it is necessary to make a comparison based on accrued income, since an important part of the reform was aimed at reducing the gap between accrued and received income from capital. In particular, it is not possible to measure the direct effect of the changes introduced in the First Category Tax under the definition of received income.

Although the changes introduced in the payment of indirect taxes are of a smaller size, they are still included in the analysis. Changes in tax rates for tobacco and alcoholic and nonalcoholic beverages and similar products are considered. Given that one of the main objectives of the tax reform is to increase public spending on education and health, it was assumed that the average state expenditure on these services would increase in proportion to the expected increase in the budget allocated to education and health.[54] Figure 5-8 shows the effect of fiscal interventions on income inequality in the pre-reform and post-reform scenarios.

---

[52] The methodological appendix contains a detailed comparison of the pre-reform and post-reform tax system.

[53] This variable was attributed to CASEN individuals using the same method of construction of market income. The detail of the methodology used by SII can be found in World Bank (2016).

[54] Based on information provided by the Ministry of Finance in 2014, 1.5 GDP points would be allocated to education and 0.5 GDP points to health. It is assumed that spending on education of

FIGURE 5-8

Effect of Fiscal Interventions on Income Inequality

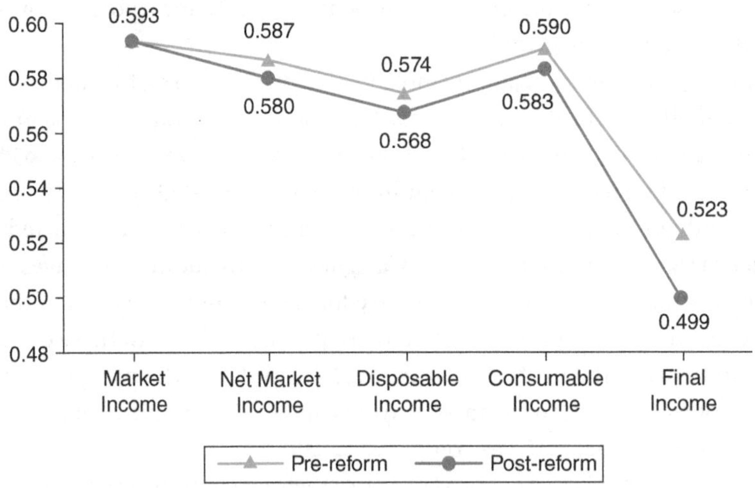

Sources: Authors' calculations based on CASEN, SII, and official government data.

The Gini coefficient of net Market Income passes from 0.587 to 0.580, which represents a reduction of 0.007 Gini points.[55] The reduction in the Gini coefficient is modest, because the tax reform affects mainly high-income individuals, so there is no considerable change in the area between the line of perfect equality and the Lorenz curve. The Kakwani index of the tax system in the pre-reform scenario is −0.022, while the Kakwani index of the post-reform scenario is 0.033—that is, the tax system stops being slightly regressive to become slightly progressive. By looking independently by type of tax, we see that direct taxes increase their progressivity and indirect taxes remain the same. The main redistributive effect of the tax reform can be observed in Final Income. The Gini coefficient goes from 0.523 to 0.499, which represents a reduction of 4.6 percent.

Figure 5-9 shows the marginal contribution of fiscal interventions in income inequality in the Pre-reform and Post-reform scenarios when Disposable Income is the end concept of income. Direct taxes become more equalizing, increasing their marginal contribution from 0.015 to 0.022 Gini points, which represent a percentage increase of 46.6 percent. When considering the joint effect of all taxes and contributions,

---

the different educational levels rises in the same proportion. The adjustment factor for transfers in education is 1.43, and the adjustment factor for transfers in health is 1.11.

[55] While this is exactly the same redistributive effect found in the World Bank (2016) study, it is not entirely comparable, since in this study the unit of analysis is the per capita income of the household while in the study of the World Bank it is the individual. Moreover, the method of data crossing between CASEN and SII is different.

FIGURE 5-9

Marginal Contribution of Fiscal Interventions to Income Inequality (Gini Points)

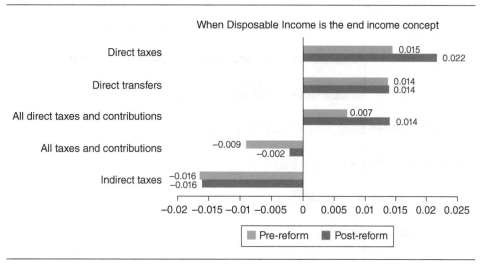

When Disposable Income is the end income concept

Direct taxes: 0.015, 0.022

Direct transfers: 0.014, 0.014

All direct taxes and contributions: 0.007, 0.014

All taxes and contributions: −0.009, −0.002

Indirect taxes: −0.016, −0.016

Legend: Pre-reform, Post-reform

Sources: Authors' calculations based on CASEN, SII, and official governmental data.

the marginal contribution remains negative, but is less unequal than in the pre-reform scenario. The marginal contribution of indirect taxes does not change significantly.

Figure 5-10 shows the marginal contribution of benefits valued in education and health when the end concept of income is Final Income. The tax reform increases the marginal contribution of transfers in education from 0.037 to 0.051 Gini points, which represents an increase of 37.8 percent and explains approximately two-thirds of the Gini improvement going from the distribution of Market Incomes to the distribution of Final Incomes. When disaggregated by different educational levels, the marginal contribution of primary education increases by 35.2 percent, secondary education by 37.5 percent, and preschool education by 25 percent. The marginal contribution of tertiary education remains slightly equalizing. Health transfers increase their contribution by only 3.5 percent.

Table 5-7, which considers accrued income, applies Shapley values to give a more robust support to the previous conclusions. Column 2 shows the increase of the Gini from Market Income to Final Income, which corresponds to each intervention, as a result of the 2014 tax reform.[56] This column can be compared to column 1, which includes the contributions of each intervention with the tax structure of 2013. Column 3 reports the difference between columns 2 and 1 as a fraction of the improvement of the Gini due to the tax reform. We see that direct taxes account for almost 30 percent of the Gini reduction, showing that the reform had some success in making the tax

---

[56] It must be remembered that we work with data that simulates the impact of the reform, based on World Bank (2016).

FIGURE 5-10

Marginal Contribution of Transfers in Kind to Income Inequality (Gini Points)

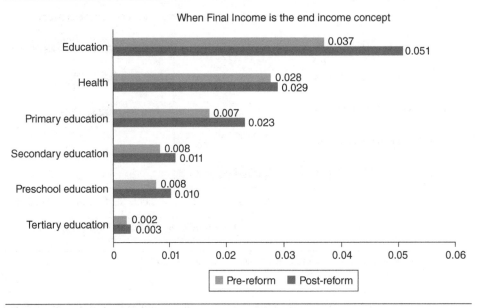

Sources: Authors' calculations based on CASEN, SII, and official government data.

TABLE 5-7

Shapley Value (Accrued Income)

Fiscal intervention	Pre-reform (1)	Post-reform (2)	Tax reform (%) (3)
Bonuses	0.00165	0.00160	−0.2
Direct taxes	0.01410	0.02093	28.5
Adult education	0.00022	0.00030	0.4
Preschool education	0.00761	0.01061	12.5
Primary education	0.01648	0.02298	27.1
Secondary education	0.00817	0.01137	13.4
Special education	0.00062	0.00087	1.0
Tertiary education	0.0025	0.00343	3.9
Family benefit system	0.00247	0.00240	−0.3
Health	0.02637	0.02838	8.4
Health contribution	−0.00577	−0.00547	1.3
Other indirect	−0.00191	−0.00181	0.4
Potable water	0.00039	0.00037	0.0
Reparation pensions	0.00042	0.00040	−0.1
Solidarity pensions	0.00727	0.00707	−0.9
VAT	−0.01057	−0.00945	4.7

Source: Authors' calculations based on CASEN, SII, and official government data.

structure more progressive. On the other hand, the various interventions in education, which is where spending increased significantly with the reform, explain 58.3 percent of the fall of the Gini. Finally, figure 5-11 shows the marginal contribution of fiscal interventions in the post-reform scenario for all possible orders that are considered when calculating the Shapley decomposition.

6 Conclusions

Our main findings are as follows:

1. The difference between the distribution of accrued income and received income turns out to be important in Chile. For each of the main concepts of income of the CEQ methodology, the Gini coefficient is higher when working with accrued income, with a fairly stable difference, of around 6 Gini percentage points.
2. Moving from the distribution of Market Income to the distribution of Final Income (after taxes and transfers), the income distribution improves by almost 7 Gini percentage points, which reflects the good targeting of social spending in Chile. Under the accrued income scenario, the Gini coefficient falls from 0.593 to 0.523, while for the received income scenario, the Gini coefficient falls from 0.537 to 0.458.
3. The Shapley value was applied to assign the improvement in the distribution of income among a set of 16 fiscal interventions. For both definitions of income, approximately half of the improvement is due to transfers in education, followed by transfers in health (around 35 percent). Direct taxes, on the other hand, explain only 20 percent of the decrease in the Gini coefficient. The ability to improve the distribution of income through a progressive tax, as is the case of direct taxes in Chile, is limited and will be lower the more unequal the market distribution.
4. The Chilean tax system is slightly regressive. Direct taxes are highly progressive and represent a smaller fraction of collection, while indirect taxes are regressive and represent a larger fraction of collection. When considering the net redistributive impact by type of tax, we find that 46.4 percent of the improvement in the distribution of income is due to VAT and 35.6 percent to direct taxes in the scenario of received income. However, under the accrued income scenario, which considers the tax paid by the companies, 48.1 percent of the reduction in the Gini coefficient is due to direct taxes, while 37.9 percent is due to VAT.
5. Based on the simulation of the impact of the 2014 tax reform (World Bank, 2016), we estimated that the reform would have led to an additional reduction of 2.4 Gini percentage points when going from Market Income to Final Income. When using the Shapley value to distribute this additional improvement among the 16 fiscal interventions considered, we found that two-thirds are explained by the higher

FIGURE 5-11
Accrued Income Post-Reform

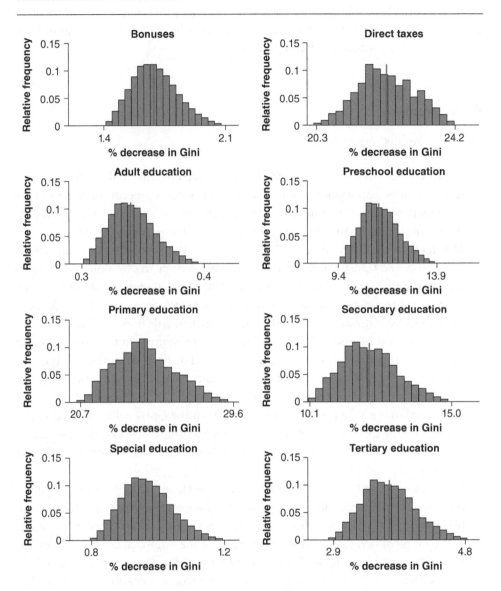

spending on education that is financed by the reform. Direct taxes account for al-most 30 percent of the Gini reduction, which suggests that the reform was intended to make the tax structure more progressive.

Acknowledgments

We thank the Coordination of Economic Studies at the Ministry of Finance of Chile and the Department of Economic and Tax Studies at the Internal Revenue Service of

FIGURE 5-11   (continued)

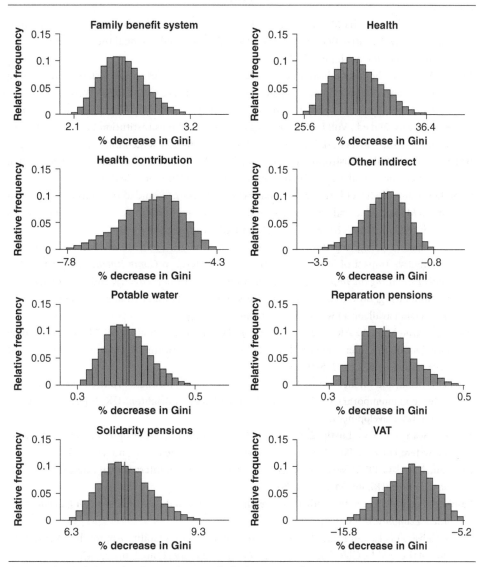

Sources: Authors' calculations based on CASEN, SII, and official government data.

Chile for providing the data to carry out this research. We are especially grateful to Hector Monsalve and Francisco Henríquez. We also thank Paula Benavides, Ivan Gutierrez, Jelena Laketic, Alejandro Micco, Nora Lustig, Francisca Pacheco, and the participants of the CEQ-Universidad de San Andrés Workshop (Buenos Aires, 2017) for valuable comments and suggestions. Financial support from the CEQ Institute is gratefully acknowledged. This study is part of the global CEQ project and is based on Bernardo Candia's master's thesis in economics, at the University of Chile, written under the supervision of Eduardo Engel.

References

Agostini, Claudio, Claudia Martinez, and Barbara Flores. 2012. "Distributional Effects of Eliminating the Differential Tax Treatment between Business and Personal Income Tax in Chile." *Cepal Review* 108, no. 1, pp. 175–201.

Enami, Ali, Sean Higgins, and Nora Lustig. 2022. "Allocating Taxes and Transfers, Constructing Income Concepts, and Completing Sections A, B, and C of *CEQ Master Workbook*," chapter 6 in *Commitment to Equity Handbook: Estimating the Impact of Fiscal Policy on Inequality and Poverty*, 2nd ed., Vol. 1, edited by Nora Lustig (Brookings Institution Press and CEQ Institute, Tulane University). Free online version available at www.commitmentoequity.org.

Benavides, Paula, Ruben Castro, and Ingrid Jones. 2013. "Sistema Público de Salud, Situación Actual y Proyecciones Fiscales 2013–2050." Santiago de Chile: Direccion de Presupuestos.

Cantallopts, Jorge, Michel Jorrat, and Danae Scherman. 2007. "Equidad triburaria en Chile: Un Nuevo Modelo para Evaluar Alternativas de Reforma" [online]. https://coyunturapolitica.files.wordpress.com/2011/12/reforma-tributaria-chile-world-bank.pdf.

Enami, Ali, Nora Lustig, and Rodrigo Aranda. 2022. "Analytic Foundations: Measuring the Redistributive Impact of Taxes and Transfers," chapter 2 in *Commitment to Equity Handbook: Estimating the Impact of Fiscal Policy on Inequality and Poverty*, 2nd ed., Vol. 1, edited by Nora Lustig. Brookings Institution Press and CEQ Institute, Tulane University. Free online version available at www.commitmentoequity.org.

Engel, Eduardo M. R. A., Alexander Galetovic, and Claudio E. Raddatz. 1999. "Taxes and Income Distribution in Chile: Some Unpleasant Redistributive Arithmetic." *Journal of Development Economics* 59, no. 1, pp. 155–92.

Fairfield, Tasha, and Michel Jorrat. 2014. "Top Income Shares, Business Profits, and Effective Tax Rates in Contemporary Chile." ICTD Working Paper 17. Brighton, UK: International Centre for Tax Development.

Higgins, Sean, and Nora Lustig. 2016. "Can a Poverty-Reducing and Progressive Tax and Transfer System Hurt the Poor?" *Journal of Development Economics* 122, no. 1, pp. 63–75.

Kakwani, Nanak C. 1977. "Measurement of Tax Progressivity: An International Comparison." *Economic Journal* 87, no. 345, pp. 71–80.

Lambert, Peter. 1985. "On the Redistributive Effect of Taxes and Benefits." *Scottish Journal of Political Economy* 32, no. 1, pp. 39–54.

Lopez-Calva, Luis F., and Eduardo Ortiz-Juarez. 2014. "A Vulnerability Approach to the Definition of the Middle Class." *Journal of Economic Inequality* 12, no. 1, pp. 23–47.

Lustig, Nora, and Sean Higgins. 2022. "The *CEQ Assessment*: Measuring the Impact of Fiscal Policy on Inequality and Poverty," chap. 1 in *Commitment to Equity Handbook: Estimating the Impact of Fiscal Policy on Inequality and Poverty*, 2nd ed., Vol. 1, edited by Nora Lustig. Brookings Institution Press and CEQ Institute, Tulane University. Free online version available at www.commitmentoequity.org.

Martinez-Aguilar, Sandra, Alan Fuchs, Eduardo Ortiz-Juarez, and Giselle Del Carmen. 2017. "The Impact of Fiscal Policy on Inequality and Poverty in Chile." Policy Research Working Paper 7939. Washington, DC: World Bank.

———. 2022. "Chile: The Impact of Fiscal Policy on Inequality and Poverty," chap. 13 in *Commitment to Equity Handbook: Estimating the Impact of Fiscal Policy on Inequality and Poverty*,

2nd ed., Vol. 1, edited by Nora Lustig. Brookings Institution Press and CEQ Institute, Tulane University. Free online version available at www.commitmentoequity.org.

Sastre, Mercedes, and Alain Trannoy. 2002. "Shapley Inequality Decomposition by Factors Components: Some Methodological Issues." *Journal of Economics* 9, no. 1, pp. 51–89.

Shapley, Lloyd S. 1953. "A Value for N-Person Games." *Contributions to the Theory of Games* 2, no. 28, pp. 307–17.

Shorrocks, Anthony F. 2013. "Decomposition Procedures for Distributional Analysis: A Unified Framework Based on the Shapley Value." *Journal of Economic Inequality* 11, no. 1, pp. 99–126.

Souza, Pedro H. G. F., Rafael G. Osorio, and Sergei Soares. 2011. "Uma metodologia para simular o Programa Bolsa Familia." Instituto de Pesquisa Economica Working Paper, Brasilia.

World Bank. 2016. "Chile-Efectos Distributivos de la Reforma Tributaria 2014." Working Paper 104099. https://documents1.worldbank.org/curated/en/496131468228282235/pdf/Chile-Efectos-distributivos-de-la-reforma-tributaria-2014.pdf.

Redistributive Impact of Contributory Pensions

Chapter 6

THE WITHIN-SYSTEM REDISTRIBUTION OF CONTRIBUTORY PENSION SYSTEMS
A Conceptual Framework and Empirical Method of Estimation

Carlos Grushka

Introduction

This chapter presents a conceptual framework to estimate within-system redistribution, analyzes in detail the case of Argentina, and proposes a viable empirical approach to estimate the extent of redistribution in different countries and periods. Although the distinction is framed in terms of the distinction between deferred wage and tax-transfers social security (SS) systems, we recognize that the boundary is not simple given that pension systems have multiple objectives: at a minimum, consumption smoothing, insurance, and poverty relief.[1] We do not ignore the complex distinction between risk-sharing (i.e., insurance) and redistribution.

In principle, if SS pensions are considered deferred wages, the redistributive effects should be analyzed as an income redistribution within the lifecycle (from a younger to an older self) and not among individuals (such as from the richer to the poorer). Thus, pension benefits are strictly actuarial and are usually considered neutral, depending on

---

[1] As discussed in chapter 1 by Nora Lustig and Sean Higgins in Volume 1 of this Handbook, treating pensions as deferred income or as government transfers has very important consequences for the distributional impact of pensions (Lustig and Higgins, 2022). This Handbook recommends conducting the fiscal incidence analysis under both scenarios, which we call Pensions as Deferred Income (PDI) and Pensions as Government Transfer (PGT). Also see how the prefiscal income is calculated for each scenario in Volume 1's chapter 6 by Ali Enami, Sean Higgins, and Nora Lustig (Enami, Higgins, and Lustig, 2022). In particular, see Table 6-5.

(a) the size of the worker's pension accumulation, (b) the remaining life expectancy at pension age of his or her birth cohort, and (c) the return to pension saving over retirement. However, in the simplest case, this rule is violated in significant ways. With uniform annuity pricing there is redistribution from men to women, from less to more healthy (for smokers to nonsmokers), and from poorer people (with shorter life expectancies on average) to richer people. Separately priced annuities for each of these groups might be considered, but these are difficult to implement (treating men and women separately is ruled out in the European Union and the United States, among other countries, by law as well as custom). A lower bound on redistribution is group insurance with individuals' remaining life varying from the average.

The way that benefits are determined plays a significant role in determining within-system redistribution. SS coverage is crucial for incorporating the effects of the labor market performance on the elderly and providing some sort of compensation to those who lacked opportunities during active ages. The financing of the benefits under payment is crucial to evaluate the overall effective redistribution: SS "selectivity" and distribution are not independent from its funding.

It is also important to distinguish between a pension system and the different elements of the system, which Barr and Diamond (2009) refer to as "pension plans." Since pensions have multiple objectives, a well-designed system generally comprises multiple plans. In the Netherlands, for example, the mandatory system includes a tax-financed noncontributory pension and fully funded industry plans. In Chile, the system comprises competing fully funded individual accounts run by private pension managers (AFPs) and the solidarity pension. In both countries, a holistic view of the system would also include income-tested social assistance. The analysis on redistribution should cover the system, not only a plan. In the case of Argentina, the mature and almost universal "pay-as-you-go" (PAYG) SS system encompasses different plans and special treatments for specific groups of workers and pensioners, and the overall redistributive effect of this defined benefit system is very controversial (Moncarz, 2015).

In section 1, we discuss the way SS pensions are commonly considered, as tax-transfers or as deferred wages. In the second section, we analyze how SS pensions and levels of redistribution are basically a question of definition, which then leads us to review concepts such as neutrality and actuarial fairness. In section 3, we present how SS works in Argentina, detailing its fragmentation and heterogeneity. In section 4, we analyze different means of redistribution within SS pensions in Argentina, and finally, in section 5, we provide an alternative methodological framework, introducing a simple redistribution index based on cross-sectional data.

1 Are Pension Systems Tax-Transfers or Deferred Wages Schemes?

This section discusses the underlying rationale for considering pension systems as tax-transfer schemes (where government collects taxes and spends as in any other area or public policy) or as deferred wage schemes (where the role of the public sector is neutral, and pensions should be considered part of the wages earned by workers but paid later at an actuarially fair value). The difference between these two approaches is critical when discussing the distributional impacts of pension systems. If the first approach is to be adopted, then all taxes and benefits should be considered in the same way as other taxes and payments are. In the second approach, supposing pensions are deferred wages, the distribution impact would depend on whether benefits are an actuarially fair payment of previously withheld wages, and, if not, the difference between actual payments and fair estimations should be considered a transfer and accounted for distributional analysis purposes.

Pension systems are relatively modern public policies that aim to provide income support to the elderly once they retire from the labor force and become unable to finance their consumption with wages or other income sources. These policies originated in industrial economies in the late 1800s, as salaried work expanded to many areas of activity, in a context where traditional family arrangements to support the elderly were declining. The basic design principles of these programs are built from two alternative models, usually referred to by the name of its creators, Bismarck and Beveridge.

As the first modern program was created in Germany in the 1880s, Chancellor Otto von Bismarck has been credited as being the founder of modern SS. He introduced the concept of contributory pensions, which aim at replacing preretirement income by requiring contributions that are proportional to earnings while active and then provide a proportional benefit after retirement. In the early years of the twentieth century, most continental European countries, as well as several in Latin America, adopted similar models, which focus on the "formal" labor force (that is, workers who were formally registered and made their contributions accordingly). SS systems were designed as PAYG schemes, such that revenues are used to pay benefits immediately, or as "funded" schemes, where contributions were accumulated and invested and then assets were used to pay benefits in the form of annuities.

The rationale of PAYG schemes provided two clear advantages that were important to gain support among policymakers: First, the programs can be self-sufficient in financial terms, as contributions can finance benefits, eliminating the need to find other fiscal resources to protect the elderly's income. Also, by linking rights to previous contributions, the program has an implicit self-targeting mechanism. Given the goal of replacing labor income after retirement, if the program requires workers to contribute a part of their salaries, these contributions not only finance current benefits, but also identify the contributors as salaried workers who will need benefits in the future. By the same logic, those who do not contribute are excluded from the system, because their lack of contributions indicate that they do not have salaries, and thus there is no need to replace them after retirement.

Such contributory schemes have some risks and disadvantages. First, restricting coverage to those who contributed excludes several groups that, in many cases, may represent a large proportion of the population. This includes, for example, the self-employed, informal workers, or housekeepers. Moreover, if the programs become financially unbalanced and require funding from other fiscal sources, inequities and undesired distributional impacts may arise, as those excluded from the systems may end up financing part of the benefits of participants.

At the end of World War II, the United Kingdom implemented a different model, inspired in a report prepared by Lord William Beveridge, which aimed at providing a basic income protection to all workers. In a clear difference from what was already common in other countries, the Beveridge approach focused on redistribution. The system still required contributions from active workers, but the size of the pension was not linked to those contributions. This approach solves the issue of poverty relief, but it creates a new challenge, as benefits cannot truly replace previous income (or a fixed proportion of it), so individuals need to rely on other income sources (either savings or additional pension plans) in order to maintain an income flow consistent with their preretirement earnings.

The differences in objectives and design between these two models have resulted in two very different approaches to the analysis of the fiscal (i.e., on the overall tax burden, fiscal deficit, and public debt) and distributional impacts on pension systems. On the one hand, if pension schemes are assumed to be contributory schemes where each and every participant pays for his or her own future benefits, then the programs can be thought of as a deferred wage or a compulsory savings scheme. If this is the case, it would be reasonable to argue that there are no fiscal impacts (as the public institutions involved in managing the programs are only collecting the deferred salaries and then paying them) and of course no distributional effects (as each individual finances his or her own pension, so the lifetime income is not affected). As Barr (2012) noted, whether workers perceive benefits to be actuarial poses an issue: future benefits "are payable only in certain contingencies, can be changed by legislation, and will depend on marital status; and it is not possible to borrow against future benefits, which must therefore be weighted by the probability that each benefit will be received at some given future date. The weighted benefits must then be discounted to present value using the market rate of interest or, for people who cannot borrow as much as they wish, at a personal rate of time preference" (p. 42).

On the other hand, a pure Beveridge-style program can be considered in the same way as any other public policy, such as education, defense, or utility subsidies, where the state collects some revenues (in this case, taxes on wages) and uses them (or other resources) to finance the provision of transfers or services to a certain part of the population. According to this approach, all contributions should be considered part of fiscal revenues, all benefits are part of public expenditures, and both taxes and trans-fers will have some impact on income distribution.[2]

As policies evolved and real-world restrictions and demands were confronted, pen-sion systems in most countries have mixed components from the two original models. In most modern economies, there are pension systems that pay benefits linked to pre-vious contributions, but with some internal distributive provisions, such as the use of minimum and maximum pensions, as well as progressive benefit formulas and differ-ent pooling mechanisms. In addition, noncontributory pensions, also known as social pensions or universal basic pensions, are offered in most countries to those who, for various reasons, do not qualify for the contributory schemes. Both contributory and noncontributory schemes are usually financed by a mix of earmarked wage and non-wage taxes, as well as general revenue by the governments.

In this context, measuring distributional impacts of a pension system is a serious conceptual and methodological challenge. If we take a "pure" tax transfer approach, the situation appears to be rather simple: all contributions should be considered in a similar way as other taxes (hence, their distributional impact will depend on the distribution of those contributing), and benefits are transfers from the public sector to families. How-ever, a significant challenge remains, and that is the treatment of privately managed pension funds (usually, complementary to public schemes) with compulsory participa-tion. In principle, if the objective is to understand the distributive impact of the pension system, then the whole system should be considered, regardless of whether management is public or private, given that participation is required as part of a public policy.

In practical terms, the question is to determine the boundary between a public in-tervention (which should be considered) and private initiative. Is this limit defined by the institutional character of the agency in charge of managing the system (i.e., public or private)? Or should this limit depend on whether authorities register contributions and payments as part of the fiscal accounts? These boundaries are blurred, and almost identical programs can fall on one side of the classification or the other in different countries for reasons that should not be relevant in this analysis. An alternative test should be whether participation is voluntary or compulsory.

If the analysis starts from a deferred wages viewpoint, the analysis becomes more complex. In a first look, the approach should consider what is the actuarially fair ben-efit level and then consider a transfer (or a tax) all payments in excess (or defect) of this level. However, several questions immediately arise. For example, when an excess

---

[2] While the alternative designs maybe associated to the alternative analytical approaches, this is not a prerequisite. In fact, there is no reason for somebody studying distributional impacts of pension systems to adopt a full tax-transfer approach even if the system under analysis is a con-tributory one, and vice-versa. The analytical criteria should not be defined by the stated princi-ples that were used to originally design the pension systems, but by the conceptual approach of the analyst, including his or her main concerns when discussing income distribution.

payment should be considered a transfer or how heterogeneity should be treated are two critical questions:

A. Timing: Distributional analysis is usually based on period data. Unless the assessment considers the lifetime of all individuals, the excess or deficit income must be assigned to a certain period. In this regard, there are four possible approaches:
  1. Estimate a "fair" annual benefit based on the accumulated contributions, and categorize any excess (or defect) from this level as a transfer for each year. This requires knowledge (or assumptions) about a number of variables, such as contribution history, mortality rates, implicit interest rates, marital status (if survivors' benefits are available), as well as benefit history and expected trends in benefit levels.
  2. Estimate a "fair" annual contribution, based on the expected benefits, and categorize any excess (or deficit) from this level as a transfer for each year. This option is similar to the previous one, except that it assigns the transfer to the active years instead of the retirement period.
  3. Apply a similar approach as in case 1, but instead of assigning the excess (or deficit) proportionally to each year of benefits, estimate the number of years the beneficiary would receive a benefit at the current level if actuarially fair rules were applied and then consider a transfer all additional years of benefits.
  4. Follow a procedure similar to 3, but applied on the contribution side of the process.
B. Intra-cohort transfers: Defining an actuarially fair benefit requires considering actual flows of contributions and expected benefits for each individual. A reasonable approach to this would be to consider all individuals to be average, assuming similar contributory histories, mortality risks, and marital status, as well as some level of stability in the system's rules. However, if a simplified assumption of no heterogeneity in the population is adopted, then by definition there will be no distributional impacts, as everyone will contribute and receive the same. In fact, the interesting aspect of this analysis is that we know that populations are not homogeneous, and we expect that those differences will have an impact. Hence, it is critical to define what dimensions should be considered in this analysis. Among them are
  1. Income: This is clearly a critical variable, as it reflects the objective of the analysis (income distribution) and is a critical element that defines differences in treatment in most pension systems. As discussed before, most pension systems have income-related rules, such as minimum and maximum pensions and nonlinear formulas that are designed to have a distributional impact. Income is also a strong determinant of other relevant variables, such as employment, whether employed in the formal or informal sector, and mortality, producing an indirect impact that should be measured.

2. Sex: Data around the world show that income and mortality are consistently different by sex. Women tend to have lower income (for a number of reasons linked to labor market performance, individual choices, and, of course, discrimination), but they also tend to have a lower mortality.

3. Economic sector: Pension systems usually have differential regimes with conditions more generous for specific groups of workers, who either are exposed to higher risks for which society tries to compensate them or have found a way to receive an advantageous treatment thanks to effective lobbying of policymakers. As a result, these groups receive a higher benefit (and, consequently, a higher transfer) than others.

Thus, there are several approaches to measure the distributional impacts of pension systems that might be reasonable, but not necessarily consistent across countries. Hence, we suggest adopting a two-stage approach to improve comparability across countries. First, all pension system distributive impact analysis should be conducted under two alternative assumption sets. On the one hand, the analysis should be prepared assuming that pensions are a tax-transfer scheme, which includes a privately managed component with publicly mandated participation. This would imply that all contributions should be considered part of Gross Income (and, consequently, taxes), while benefits should be considered government transfers that contribute to after-Market Income. On the other hand, a specific analysis considering the systems as deferred labor income schemes should be prepared. In this case, for the sake of simplicity, pension contributions should be considered part of labor income (which is compulsory "saved"); meanwhile, actuarially fair pension benefits should be considered a reduction in savings, and any excess (or deficit) benefits beyond those actuarially fair would be transfers (or taxes).

2 Redistribution, Neutrality, and Actuarial Fairness

Social security (SS) pensions and the levels of redistribution are basically a question of definition. According to William Beveridge (1942), SS is first and foremost a method to redistribute income, in order to put the most urgent needs first. However, there are many ways to look at redistribution. What should we call "neutrality"? There are different categories of people in SS pensions, organized by sex, race, education, occupation, and income. The analysis might be based on period or cohorts; cohorts' behavior might be considered ex ante or ex post. Neutrality depends on individuals over time ("actuarial fairness"), or is neutrality a couple's (household) decision at different periods?

Further, there are different channels of redistribution. A more direct (and more well-known) one is from "rich" to "poor" through the establishment of minimum pensions, fixed sums and/or differentiated scales (formula to determine benefits). However, on a more subtle level, there are other mechanisms based on social cuts that might be regressive: on the one hand, differential mortality (life expectancy at retirement age) and, on the other, labor market characteristics that determine participation (entry and stability) and/or access to coverage (requirements).

There are many variables affected by pension systems design that have an impact of the prevailing levels of redistribution: retirement age (IAA, 2016), contribution rates, required years of contribution, determination of the benefit, benefit adjustment, replacement rates, and duration of benefits (life expectancy at retirement). This chapter will attempt to analyze most of the variables involved, and propose a simplified model based on available data in Argentina and the experience during the 2010s.

SS pensions in Argentina are characterized as relatively low contribution in active ages (Bertranou et al., 2011, 2012, 2015; CEPAL, 2018; Rofman and Oliveri, 2011), and thus, despite high requirements, the elderly (ages 65 and over) average few years of contribution, and so the analysis includes differentials by sex and education.

Moreover, elderly SS coverage may be estimated from different data sources, for all types of benefits (old-age, survivorship, "moratoria," provinces, noncontributive), varying from 91 to 98 percent, circa 2015 (Grushka, Gaiada, and Calabria, 2016). Differential regimes for "unhealthy" activities allow specific groups to retire with less effective years of service and age than required. Additionally, there are a few "Special Regimes" with different legal frameworks, requirements and benefits that deserve separate analyses. While the demography of contributors and benefits in the National Pension System (Sistema Integrado Previsional Argentino, SIPA) and Special Regimes affects financial (dis)equilibrium, the way that income increases by age, how pension benefits are established (and distributed by quintile), and differential adjustments should also be considered (Grushka, Gaiada, and Calabria, 2016).

Regarding differential mortality by pension income, Bramajo and Grushka (2019) analyzed the odds of dying and their differentials according to age, sex, and pension income in Argentina in 2015–16. They also estimated life expectancy at age 65 (e_{65}), by sex and pension income. "Doubling the income" results in average gains of close to one year for males and females. This also means that those who earn larger pension amounts tend to enjoy their benefit longer, which, in turn, implies a regressive redistribution.

A challenge ahead for Argentina is to attempt to integrate empirically observed differences in an "actuarial" model that determines contributions and wages by age, based on educational levels, and separate estimates for self-employed, "waged-general," and "special regimes" to be applied proportionally.

For individuals, a pension system is usually considered "fair" or "actuarially fair" as long as benefits are established proportionally to the contributions as in the classical formula

(6-1)
$$B(R,t) = \frac{K(R,t)}{a(R;t)} = \frac{\sum_{x=15}^{R-1} c(t)\, w(x,t)(1+i)^{(R-x)}}{\sum_{x=R}^{w} p(R;x-R)\left(\dfrac{1}{(1+i)}\right)^{(x-R)}},$$

where: B = benefit, R = age of retirement; t = time/period; K = accumulated capital; c = contribution rate; w = wage or salary; i = interest rate; $p(R; x - R)$ = survivorship probability from age R to age $x > R$.

Thus, the pension system as a whole is considered "neutral" and sometimes is wrongly considered "sustainable" just because of the ways that benefits are determined. However, there are many caveats, and the roles of the different variables involved are not that clear.

Obviously, the accumulated capital is a function of (1) contribution rate (varying across time, although usually supposed to be constant); (2) wage (varying across age and time); (3) interest rate (usually supposed to be constant although it varies across time); (4) survivorship by age (varying across time). Each one of these variables has a different impact on the individual level of benefit and also affects the averages for each cohort.[3]

In PAYG regimes, the way benefits are established implies different "winners" and "losers": benefits might be a function of last (or best) salary, average of (few) last years, or lifetime average. With the exception of the last alternative, those with earnings increasing at higher rates tend to benefit more than those with almost constant (minimum) salaries. In addition, the way that nominal salaries are indexed becomes especially relevant for countries with high inflation rates.

Another relevant point is that wages have to be earned (and contributions paid). Unemployment and informality are two key variables that play significant roles determining individual and average contribution "densities" (proportion of years with effective contributions in terms of the total years in active ages). In PAYG regimes, there is usually a required minimum years of contributions, and thus, the probability of not receiving a benefit is highly associated with being part of the less favored groups (women and less-educated and less-skilled workers, who become unemployed or are employed in the informal sector), as shown for Argentina by Moncarz (2015).

Barnay (2007) posits that differential mortality responds to social heterogeneities and inequalities based in socioeconomic position. In the context of the French PAYG Defined Benefit SS system, and taking into account the concept of actuarial fairness, the author suggests that in order to avoid an anti-redistributive impact, different retirement ages should be considered for different social categories (similar to different annuity prices as discussed above). He concludes that the most favored groups (executives and intermediate professions) benefit the most from because of their higher life expectancy in comparison to less favored groups (manual workers). That means that there is a lack of equality in flows between contributions and pensions due to differential mortality. Thus, a possible way to achieve actuarial equilibrium is to allow unskilled workers to leave the labor force market earlier. In the future, if life expectancy differences among different groups tend to narrow, probably a single retirement age will be adequate.

---

[3] See simulations in ISSA (2007).

Caselli et al. (2003) express a similar concern regarding the Italian system. The unprecedented growth in elderly populations stimulated an effort to rethink and redesign the traditional pension systems. Considering that Italy had one of the highest life expectancies in the globe and by extent, one of the lowest old-age dependency rates, a change from a PAYG system with a defined benefit to a notional defined contribution scheme was gradually adopted (Barr and Diamond, 2015).

While Barnay (2007) was more concerned with differences among social groups based on occupation, the Italian researchers, after analyzing life expectancy at age 60 by gender and region, establish how gender-based and regional conversion factors differed from the legislated values at the time. The author found that those conversion factors were very sensitive to even slight variations in mortality, which was particularly important due to the rapidly increasing survival rates of old-age adults. Ultimately, Caselli et al. (2003) reach a similar conclusion as Barnay (2007): actuarial fairness (with uniform annuity pricing) is not enough as a mechanism to guarantee neutrality; due to differential mortality, there is a substantial degree of redistribution from high mortality groups to low mortality groups.

3 Social Security Pensions in Argentina

As previously established, SS pension systems allow to reassign funds from active to inactive ages. Comelatto (2014) showed how consumption and labor income per capita differed by age in Argentina during 2010 (figure 6-1). Although there are three ways to reassign surplus to deficit, in this case SS (public transfers) clearly play a more significant role than family support and other income (own savings).

SS in Argentina has a relatively low participation during active ages, a topic that is not developed in this study but is highly relevant for a global perspective, especially due to its differential impact.[4] During the 1990s the proportion of active age population contributing to SS fell from 38 percent to 26 percent, and several years were needed to recover up to the initial levels (see figure 6-2).

In the same way, the proportion of waged workers contributing to SS ("formal employment") fell from more than 60 percent to less than 50 percent between 2001 and 2004 and recovered only in 2008. A significant point is the different impact that these proportions have had on the different quintiles (based on income from the main occupation): while the first quintiles fell from 30 percent to less than 10 percent and recovered up to 20 percent, the fifth quintile maintained over 80 percent during the whole period (figure 6-3).

Unfortunately, there are very few surveys or data sources that allow for a longitudinal approach. Retrospective reports on years of work and contribution based on 2015 Protection and Social Security Survey (Encuesta de Proteccion y Seguridad Social,

---

[4] See Bertranou et al. (2011, 2012, 2015); CEPAL (2018); Rofman and Oliveri (2011).

FIGURE 6-1
Life cycle Deficit: Consumption and Labor Income per Capita in Argentina, 2010

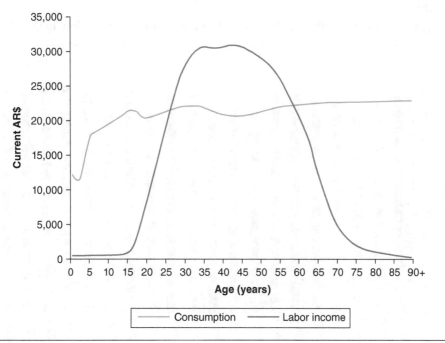

Source: Comelatto (2014).

FIGURE 6-2
Proportion of Active Age Population Contributing to Social Security (%), 1991–2015

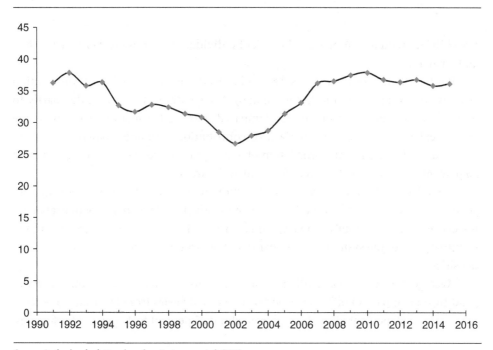

Source: Author's calculations based on Bertranou et al. (2011).

FIGURE 6-3

Employees Who Contribute to SS (%), by Income Quintile of Main Job, 1995–2015

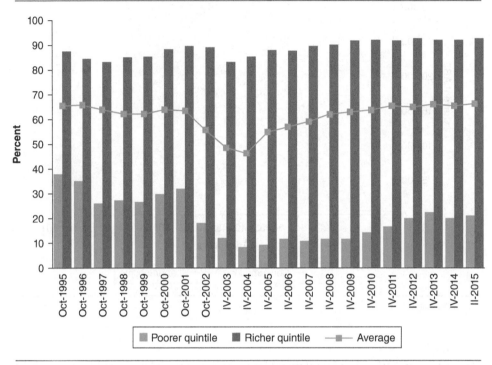

Source: Author's calculations based on 1995–2015 household surveys EPH-INDEC (Encuesta Permanente de Hogares).

ENAPROSS) tend to compensate the lack of individual histories (as there are in Chile and Uruguay).

For the elderly population (aged 65 and over) the average number of contribution years is 20 (26 for males and 15 for females). The gender differential is due partly to fewer years of work for women (23, compared with 32 for men) and partly to the greater extent of informal labor (lack of contributions) among women. Density of contribution (defined as the proportion of active years since age 20) averages around 50 percent for men and 30 percent for women (figure 6-4).

The relation of low density to redistribution arises when people with low density get no benefit at all (distribution becoming regressive), and where low actuarial benefits cause concerns about adequacy, which in turn lead to other, progressive redistributive parts of the system being larger than they would be with higher contribution densities.

Average density is clearly different according to sex and levels of education: depending on completion of high (secondary) school, it varies from less than 50 percent to more than 60 percent for males and from about 25 percent to 45 percent for females.

FIGURE 6-4

Density of Contribution Years by Age and Sex, Based on Retrospective Reports

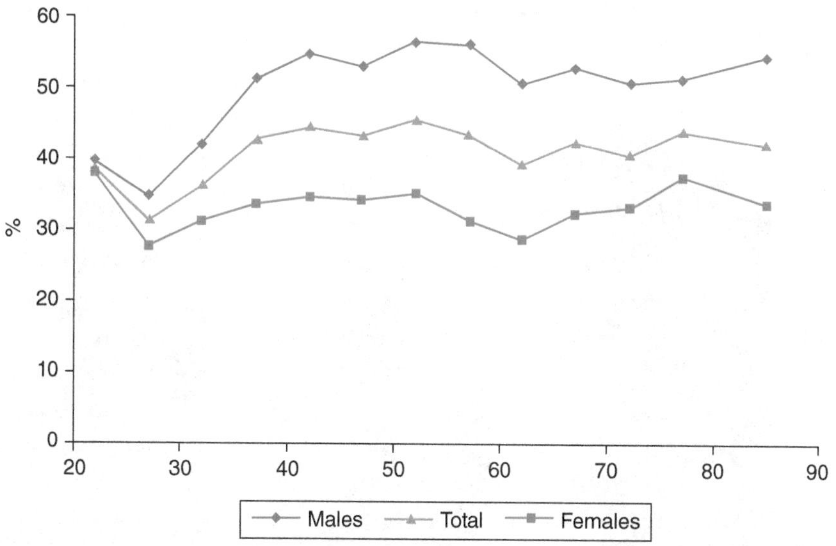

Source: Author's calculations based on 2015 Protection and Social Security Survey (ENAPROSS).

Similarly, the average number of contribution years varies from less than 20 to more than 26, especially for women (from 14 to 24) (see Figure 6-5, next page).

SS coverage for the elderly (ages 65 and above) has become almost universal during the last decade, through different type of benefits: old age, survivorship, "moratoria," provincial regimes, and noncontributive pensions (see table 6-1).[5]

A significant characteristic of SS in Argentina is the level of fragmentation due to many different rules applying to special groups. The General Regime (Law 24241) requires 30 years of service and 65 years of age for males (60 for females) and establishes the defined benefit as a flat sum (around 15 percent of the average salary) plus 1.5 percent per every year of contribution applied to the average wage earned during the last ten years of service.

One of those groups, called "Differential Regimes," which involve mostly hard and undesirable work, requires fewer effective years of service and age. During 2015, there were 48,000 new cases (30 percent of old age pensions), averaging 59 years of age and 27.5 of service. There are also special norms for workers in given public enterprises and additional payments for beneficiaries living in the Austral Zone (Law 19485 and Decree 1472/08).

---

[5] See Bertranou et al. (2011) for a detailed explanation.

FIGURE 6-5

Average Contribution Years by Sex and Level of Education (ages 65+), Based on Retrospective Reports

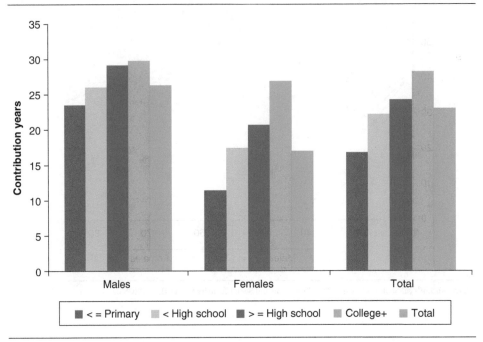

Source: Author's calculations based on 2015 Protection and Social Security Survey (ENAPROSS).

TABLE 6-1

Elderly Social Security Coverage: Different Data Sources, All Types of Benefits, Ages 65+, circa 2015

National census Oct-2010	93.0%
Household survey EPH 2Q2015	90.8%
Urban annual survey EAHU 2014	90.6%
Social protection survey ENAPROSS 2015	93.5%
ANSES Registries 2015	97.5%

Source: Grushka, Gaiada, and Calabria (2016).

The most favored groups, called "Special Regimes," have specific legal frameworks, different requirements, and better benefits than the General Regime. There are five Special Regimes that correspond to teachers (Law 24016, Decree 137/05), university professors (Law 26508), scientific researchers (Law 22929, Decree 160/05), judiciary power (Law 24018), and foreign service (Law 22731). Many times, they are considered together with electricians (*luz y fuerza*), who have only a better benefit. They amount to half a million contributors, or 5 percent of the total.[6]

Employees of the Special Regimes take advantage not only of a higher income but also of a higher growth rate with age during their career (3.8 percent per year, compared to 1.8 percent for other employees, 1.6 percent for contributing self-employed, and 0.1 percent for domestic service). In addition, their pension is established around 82 percent of the final salary. Special Regimes have .2 million beneficiaries (3 percent of the total),[7] although they take 9 percent of the total expenditure.

In figure 6-6, we summarize the level of fragmentation already mentioned, showing differences in inter- and intra- groups of beneficiaries. Note that Special Regimes

FIGURE 6-6

Distribution of Pension Benefits: Average Benefit by Quintile, and Regime, July 2017

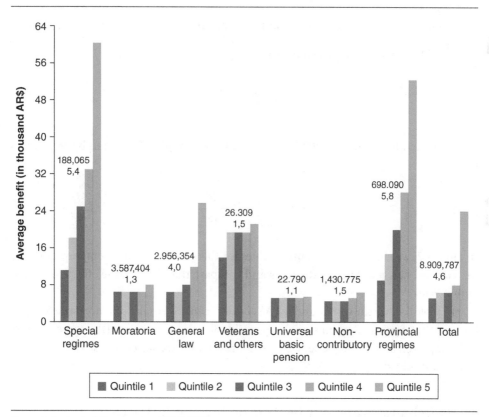

Source: Author's calculations based on ANSES (2018).

Note: For each regime, the number of beneficiaries and the ratio between extreme quintiles are included.

---

[6] See table 6A-1 in the Appendix.

[7] See table 6A-2 in the Appendix.

also have also different rules to adjust their benefits, but during the last decade, they tended to converge with SIPA, averaging 30 percent a year, about 2 percent over annual inflation.

4 How Redistribution Works for Social Security Pensions in Argentina

Equilibrium in a pure PAYG Model, based on Iyer (1999), is determined by the equation

(6-2) $$A^t \times W^t \times c^t = B^t \times P^t;$$

that is, in a given period of time (t), the product of active contributors (A), salaries (W), and the contribution rate (c) equal the product of beneficiaries (B) and pension amounts (P).

Then, the "equilibrium" contribution rate depends on a demographic ratio $\left(\dfrac{B^t}{A^t}\right)$ and the effective replacement rate $\left(\dfrac{P^t}{W^t}\right)$:

(6-3) $$c^t = \frac{B^t}{A^t} \times \frac{P^t}{W^t}.$$

Also, taking into account the demographic impact through differentials by age (x) and sex (s),

(6-4) $$c^t = \frac{\sum_{x;s} B^t_{x;s} \times P^t_{x;s}}{\sum_{x;s} A^t_{x;s} \times W^t_{x;s}}.$$

In table 6-2, we show the differential values for these ratios for SIPA employees under the General Law and Special Regimes and compare the "fair" to the effective contribution rates.

In table 6-3, we show that under PAYG rules "general employees" are close to equilibrium, but Special Regimes are responsible for the deficit of SIPA wage-earners (self-employed and domestic service are not taken into account because they receive a significant subsidy).

4.1 Differential Mortality by Pension Income, 2015–16

While differential mortality by sex is well known and documented for most of the countries in the world, and especially for Argentina (Grushka, 2014; United Nations, 2017), there are few studies showing differentials by income. Bramajo and Grushka (2019) analyzed the odds of dying and their differentials according to age, sex, and pension income in 2015–16. They also estimated life expectancy at age 65 -e(65)- by sex

TABLE 6-2

Argentine Pension System (SIPA) and Special Regimes Ratios, July 2017

Pension Regime	Demography (A/B)	Replacement rate (W/S)(%)	"Fair" contribution rate (%)	Effective contribution rate (%)
Teachers	2.5	125	50	22
University professors	13.8	157	11	22
Scientific researchers	4.5	90	20	25
Electricity	0.3	60	178	22
Judiciary power	2.5	91	37	27
Foreign service	1.8	86	49	27
Total Special Regimes	**2.4**	**111**	**46**	**23**
General Law—employees	2.3	50	22	22
Total SIPA employees	**2.3**	**54**	**24**	**22**

Source: Author's calculations based on ANSES (2018).

Note: University professors have significant participation of part-time employees, combining their contributions and benefits with other income.

TABLE 6-3

Argentine Pension System (SIPA) and Special Regimes Financial (Dis)Equilibrium, in Millions of Pesos (AR$), July 2017

Pension Regime	Revenue	Expenditure	Result	Result / Revenue
Teachers	1,466	3,272	−1,805	−123%
University professors	349	182	167	48%
Scientific researchers	398	325	72	18%
Electricity	138	1,108	−,970	−702%
Judiciary power	418	576	−158	−38%
Foreign service	53	97	−44	−82%
Total Special Regimes	**2,822**	**5,561**	**−2,738**	**−97%**
General Law—employees	34,048	34,634	−587	−2%
Total SIPA employees	**36,870**	**40,195**	**−3,325**	**−9%**

Source: Author's calculations based on ANSES (2018).

and pension income, taking advantage of near 4.7 million SS records from pensioners (SIPA, Non-Contributive Pensions, and Non-Transferred Provinces) for July 2015. They use a maximum likelihood logit model in order to establish the incidence of sex, age, and pension income in the probabilities of death in the pensioner population (see table 6-4).

Estimates of e(65) for selected values of pension income, derived from the established coefficients, are shown in table 6-5. e(65) for those pensioners with an

TABLE 6-4

Logit Model of Mortality by Age, Sex, and
Pension Income

Variable	Coefficients	
	β	Exp (β)
Age	.091	1.095
Sex	−2.185	.122
Age * sex	.022	1.022
Income (ln)	−.157	.855
Intercept	−8.336	n.c.

Source: Bramajo and Grushka (2019).

Age * sex = age is multiplied by sex to take into account the impact of
the interaction between the two variables; ln = natural log. β = estimated
coefficients of the logit regression; n.c. = not calculated.

TABLE 6-5

Life Expectancy at Age 65 by Sex and Selected Amounts of Pension Income (in
Terms of Minimum Pension Benefits [MPBs]), Argentina, 2015–16

e(65) by sex	Pension Income				Diff. 8–1 MPB
	MPB	2 MPB	4 MPB	8 MPB	
Male	15.1	15.9	16.7	17.6	2.5
Female	18.9	19.7	20.5	21.3	2.4
Difference	3.8	3.8	3.8	3.7	—

Source: Bramajo and Grushka (2019).

income of eight minimum pension benefits (MPB) is 2.5 years higher than those
who earn only the MPB, so each income duplication implies a gain of 0.8 years.
When income doubles, the differences by sex will be the same, due to the model
specification.

As expected, inequalities based in different socioeconomic positions persist even
in old age: people with higher pension incomes tend to have a higher e(65) compared
with those who earn a minimum pension benefit.

Despite important improvements in regard to pension coverage, SS pensions in Argentina still have a regressive feature since those with higher benefits have lower risks
of dying and thereby enjoy them for longer durations.

4.2 Preliminary Estimates of Redistribution

Following Barnay (2007), it is possible to estimate the impact of the different variables analyzed through representative agents, modifying values one at a time.

In a simplified model where workers contribute 20 percent of their salary, with a 70 percent density between ages 20 and 65, salaries growing annually 1 percent, and a real interest rate of 1 percent, the accumulated capital is equivalent to pay during 15 years of about 63 percent of the last salary (or 60 percent of the average during the last ten years). Just by chance, this is quite close to the simulated PAYG defined benefit (around 58 percent).

However, while high-earning employees (under "general" rules) meet declining replacement rates (from 90 percent at the minimum to 50 percent at the top) due to the flat sum, participants in Special Regimes have many advantages:

- The lack of solidarity expressed in their proportionally high 82 percent represents larger earnings (a difference from 90 percent to 415 percent).
- The higher growth rate of their salaries (3 percent a year instead of 1 percent) while basing the benefit on the last salary enable them to earn up to 14 percent more.
- The fact that those with higher educational levels and higher earnings live longer represents about a 10 percent differential.
- Adding the three previous elements, benefits more than double "actuarially fair" values.

The political path dependency of Special Regimes is understandable, but these regimes imply a highly inefficient pension design, as the empirical analysis shows. The general theoretical balance in terms of redistribution still needs to find the proper weights to apply proportionally for self-employed, employees, and Special Regimes. The continuing changes in rules and practices and the need to estimate the effective contribution rate (which is not publicly available) pose very difficult challenges ahead.

5 An Alternative Methodological Framework

Given the lack of detailed data, an alternative approach to assess redistributive effects in different countries and periods consists in trying to determine their levels from only cross-sectional data. Thus, we compare two or three groups of the population based on their level of education. The idea is that level of education works as a proxy of lifetime income, and its use allows comparisons of different cohorts, assuming there are no significant changes in schooling during the last three decades.

Taking into account that many of the rules present in any SS pension system may have different impacts on the general level of redistributions, we will compare only a "gross" substitution rate (GSR) estimated as the ratio between average pension income (PI, ages 65+) and average work income from main job (WI, ages 20–64):

$$GSR^t = PI^t / WI^t.$$

Using this approach, we estimate the general balance, in terms of redistribution, as the difference in the GSR by (extreme) education levels. This measure is denominated *redistribution index* (RI).

When the SS pension system is neutral we might expect no difference between GSR at different levels of education (RI = 0). When the SS system is extended (universal) and progressive, we might expect a declining GSR at increasing levels of education (RI > 0). When the SS system is segmented (not universal) and/or regressive, we might expect an increasing GSR as education increases (RI < 0).[8]

Let us illustrate the case of SS pensions in Argentina to approach levels of redistributions (table 6-6). In 2003, RI was negative (−.08) mainly due to the lack of coverage at low levels of education. By 2006, after some exceptional increases for minimum pensions were applied, the system was less regressive (RI = −.01). By 2009, the program to expand coverage began to play a significant role in equalizing the GSR at higher levels (RI = −.01). From 2009 to 2017 pensions were indexed not only to wages but also to general revenue (benefited from economic growth) and grew more than general wages

TABLE 6-6

Gross Substitution Rates (GSRs) by Level of Education and Selected Quarters, Argentine Urban Agglomerates, 2003–2018

Level of education	IV 2003	IV 2006	IV 2009	IV 2012	II 2015	IV 2018
< High school	53.8%	53.5%	56.6%	63.9%	72.6%	74.7%
High school	62.5%	58.9%	57.4%	64.4%	68.6%	74.9%
College +	61.4%	54.7%	57.7%	60.6%	60.5%	64.7%
Total	47.0%	47.6%	48.7%	56.5%	62.1%	63.5%
RI = GSR(< HS) — GSR (College)	−0.08	−0.01	−0.01	0.03	0.12	0.10

Source: Author's calculations based on 2003–2018 household surveys EPH-INDEC (Encuesta Permanente de Hogares).

---

[8] It is important to note that the average pension income is estimated including those without pensions (PI = 0).

(although not that much for the well-educated).[9] Redistribution improved as RI reached values larger than .10.

Note that the GSR for the total population increases significantly during the period (due to increasing coverage and specific policies), but with lower levels than the three groups considered. This is possible only due to the different (and changing) distribution by level of education at active and advanced ages: College+ represents around 22 percent among workers and only 11 percent among the elderly.

The RI is useful to offer an idea on how the SS pension system works, but also provides information for the debate on tax-transfers (when $RI > 0$) or deferred wages (when $RI <= 0$).[10] Note however, that additional knowledge for three related variables is always necessary: the rules for determining benefits, the level of SS coverage, and the level of funding from general revenue.[11]

6 Conclusion

As stated at the beginning of this chapter, the way that benefits are determined (usually with decreasing replacement rates by income level) plays a significant role in determining the within-system redistribution of contributory pensions systems. However, to evaluate the overall effective redistribution it is crucial to incorporate the effects of SS coverage, or "selectivity," and the funding or financing of the benefits under payment.

The within-system redistribution is highly affected by the changes in rules over time, the specific ways that they apply in each country, the different approaches available for data on SS revenue and expenditure, and the lack of up-to-date estimates for SS coverage. The proposed redistribution index can be estimated from cross-sectional income surveys and works as an excellent complement to or as a reasonable proxy for SS redistribution in a given period.

A final remark, without any intention to be original: more research is needed; the challenge is ahead.

Acknowledgments

The author is especially thankful to Nicholas Barr (peer reviewer) for his detailed thought-provoking remarks, and to Nora Lustig and Rafael Rofman for their

---

[9] Many widowhood pensioners had the chance to increase their income by obtaining their own old-age pension.

[10] For example, the RI for Paraguay (Encuesta Permanente de Hogares Continua) was −0.1, due to the low SS coverage for the elderly.

[11] The extent of redistribution that derives from general government revenue depends not only on who gets the pension benefits, but also on who pays the taxes: redistributive pensions financed from a progressive tax on high earners will be more redistributive than one financed from a regressive sales tax.

insightful comments. Rafael Rofman is jointly responsible for the contents of the second section. Emanuel Agú and Octavio Bramajo were very helpful for the final editing.

References

ANSES (Administracion Nacional de Seguridad Social). 2018. Unpublished presentation for the Social Security Secretariat. Buenos Aires.

Barnay, Thomas. 2007. "Redistributive Impact of Differential Mortality in the French Pay-as-You-Go System." *Geneva Papers* 32, pp. 570–82. https://link.springer.com/content/pdf/10.1057/palgrave.gpp.2510145.pdf.

Barr, Nicholas. 2012. *The Economics of the Welfare State*, 5th ed. Oxford: Oxford University Press.

Barr, Nicholas, and Peter Diamond. 2009. "Reforming Pensions: Principles, Analytical Errors and Policy Directions." *International Social Security Review* 62, no. 2, pp. 5–29. http://economics.mit.edu/files/4025.

——. 2015. "Italy's Pension Reforms: Facing the Facts." *Italy 24* op-ed, May 15. http://www.italy24.ilsole24ore.com/print/ABPf2NgD/0.

Bertranou, F., O. Cetrangolo, C. Grushka, and L. Casanova. 2011. *Encrucijadas en la Seguridad Social Argentina: Reformas, Cobertura y Desafíos Para el Sistema de Pensiones*. Buenos Aires: CEPAL-OIT. http://www.ilo.org/buenosaires/publicaciones/WCMS_BAI_PUB_94/lang—es/index.htm.

Bertranou, F., O. Cetrangolo, C. Grushka, and L. Casanova. 2012. "Mas alla de la privatizacion y reestatizacion del sistema previsional de Argentina: Cobertura, fragmentacion y sostenibilidad." *Desarrollo Economico, Revista de Ciencias Sociales* 52, no. 205, pp. 3–30.

Bertranou, F., O. Cetrangolo, L. Casanova, A. Beccaria, and J. Folgar. 2015. *Desempeño y Financiamiento de la Proteccion Social en Argentina*. Buenos Aires: OIT. http://www.ilo.org/wcmsp5/groups/public/—americas/—ro-lima/—ilo-buenos_aires/documents/publication/wcms_427607.pdf.

Beveridge, William. 1942. *Social Insurance and Allied Services. Report by Sir William Beveridge*. London: HMSO. https://ia801604.us.archive.org/2/items/in.ernet.dli.2015.275849/2015.275849.The-Beveridge.pdf.

Bramajo, O., and C. Grushka. 2019. "Mortalidad diferencial de adultos mayores en Argentina, 2015–2016. El rol del ingreso previsional." *Revista Latinoamericana de Poblacion* 14, no. 26, pp. 46–69. https://doi.org/10.31406/relap2020.v14.i1.n26.3.

Caselli, G., F. Peracchi, E. Barbi, and R. M. Lipsi. 2003. "Differential Mortality and the Design of the Italian System of Public Pensions." *Labour* 17, Special Issue, pp. 45–78.

CEPAL (Comision Economica para America Latina y el Caribe). 2018. *Panorama Social de America Latina, 2017*. LC/PUB.2018/1-P, Santiago. https://repositorio.cepal.org/bitstream/handle/11362/42716/4/S1800002_es.pdf.

Comelatto, Pablo. 2014. "Cuentas nacionales de transferencias en Argentina." In *Los Años no Vienen Solos. Oportunidades y Desafios Economicos de la Transicion Demografica en Argentina*, edited by M. Gragnolati, R. Rofman, I. Apella, and S. Troiano. Buenos Aires: World Bank. http://documents.worldbank.org/curated/en/419121468002092154/pdf/880550WP0P13310o0vienen0solos0FINAL.pdf.

Enami, Ali, Sean Higgins, and Nora Lustig. 2022. "The *CEQ Assessment*: Measuring the Impact of Fiscal Policy on Inequality and Poverty," chapter 6 in *Commitment to Equity Handbook: Estimating the Impact of Fiscal Policy on Inequality and Poverty*, 2nd ed., Vol. 1, edited by Nora Lustig. Brookings Institution Press and CEQ Institute, Tulane University. Free online version available at www.commitmentoequity.org.

Grushka, Carlos. 2014. "Casi un siglo y medio de mortalidad en la Argentina..." *Revista Latinoamericana de Poblacion* 8, no. 15, pp. 93–118. https://doi.org/10.31406/relap2014.v8 .i2.n15.4.

———. 2016. *Perspectivas del Sistema Integrado Previsional Argentino y de ANSES, Años 2015–2050*. Buenos Aires: ANSES. http://observatorio.anses.gob.ar/archivos/publicaciones /Perspectivas%20del%20Sistema%20Integrado%20Previsional%20Argentino%20y%20 de%20ANSES%20anios%202015-2050.pdf.

Grushka, C., J. Gaiada, and A. Calabria. 2016. *Sistema(s) Previsional(es) en la Argentina y Cobertura: Analisis de las Diversas Fuentes de Datos y de los Diferenciales por Edad, Sexo y Jurisdiccion*. Buenos Aires: ANSES. http://observatorio.anses.gob.ar/archivos/documentos/DT _1601_Cobertura%20Previsional.pdf.

IAA (International Actuarial Association). 2016. "Determination of Retirement and Eligibility Ages: Actuarial, Social and Economic Impacts." Population Issues Working Group (PIWG) of the Scientific Committee of the International Actuarial Association. http://www .actuaries.org/LIBRARY/Papers/PIWG_Retirement_and_Eligibility_Ages_Paper_final _11March2016.pdf.

ISSA (International Social Security Association). 2007. *Developments and Trends: Supporting Dynamic Social Security*. World Social Security Forum, 10–15 September 2007, Moscow. https://ww1.issa.int/sites/default/files/documents/publications/2DT07_en-24381.pdf.

Iyer, Subramaniam. 1999. *Actuarial Mathematics of Social Security Pensions*. Geneva: International Labour Office/International Social Security Association.

Lustig, Nora and Sean Higgins. 2022. "The CEQ Assessment: Measuring the Impact of Fiscal Policy on Inequality and Poverty," chapter 1 in *Commitment to Equity Handbook: Estimating the Impact of Fiscal Policy on Inequality and Poverty*, 2nd ed., Vol. 1, edited by Nora Lustig. Brookings Institution Press and CEQ Institute, Tulane University. Free online version available at www.commitmentoequity.org.

Moncarz, Pedro E. 2015. "Implicit Redistribution within Argentina's Social Security System: A Micro-Simulation Exercise." *Latin American Economic Review* 24, no. 2, pp. 1–35. doi 10.1007/ s40503-015-0016-8.

Rofman, Rafael and Maria Laura Oliveri. 2011. "La cobertura de los sistemas previsionales en America Latina: conceptos e indicadores." Serie de Documentos de Trabajo sobre Politicas Sociales No. 7. Buenos Aires: World Bank.

United Nations. 2017. *World Mortality Report 2015*. New York: Department of Economic and Social Affairs, Population Division (ST/ESA/SER.A/381).

Appendix 6A

TABLE 6A-1
Distribution of Contributors to Argentine Pension System (SIPA) and
Special Regimes, July 2017

Type of contributors	Cases	
TOTAL Employees	**7,174,186**	**76.7%**
Employees—General Regime	**6,715,993**	**71.8%**
Special Regimes TOTAL	**458,193**	**4.9%**
Teachers	332,833	3.6%
University professors	69,908	0.7%
Scientific researchers	29,364	0.3%
Electricity	13,300	0.1%
Judiciary power	11,688	0.1%
Foreign service	1,100	0.0%
Self-employed	**2,177,096**	**23.3%**
Registered professionals	357,460	3.8%
Simplified program "Monotributo"	1,392,670	14.9%
Domestic service	426,966	4.6%
Total	**9,351,282**	**100.0%**

Source: Author's calculations based on ANSES (2018).

TABLE 6A-2
Distribution of Argentine Pension System (SIPA) and
Special Regimes Benefits, July 2017

SS Regime	Cases	
Teachers	131,996	1.9%
University professors	5,060	0.1%
Scientific researchers	**6,579**	0.1%
Electricity	39,154	0.6%
Judiciary power	4,709	0.1%
Foreign service	624	0.0%
Total Special Regimes	**188,122**	**2.8%**
Moratorium	3,589,003	52.9%
General Law	2,974,778	43.9%
Malvinas veterans	22,112	0.3%
Political prisoners	4,198	0.1%
Total SIPA	**6,778,213**	**100.0%**

Source: Author's calculations based on ANSES (2018).

Fiscal Redistribution
and Sustainability

Chapter 7

INTERTEMPORAL SUSTAINABILITY OF FISCAL REDISTRIBUTION
A Methodological Framework

Jose Maria Fanelli

Introduction

Fiscal redistributions can have important consequences for both the allocation of wealth—including natural capital—across generations and fiscal sustainability.[1] In turn, when fiscal sustainability is under scrutiny, the ability of the state to improve income distribution and protect the poor might be affected for long periods. The following points will help to show the relevance of the issue.

First, taxes and transfers that seek to bring about changes in income distribution typically modify the intertemporal allocation of fiscal revenues, expenses, and the primary balance, implying that fiscal sustainability might be at stake and, hence, could limit the public sector's ability to access credit markets. This suggests that sustainability tests should be part and parcel of the design of redistribution policies in order to check for intertemporal stability and reduce the probability of disorderly fiscal adjustments.

Second, the existing structure of fiscal redistributions or changes in it must be financed, and some financial strategies may have undesirable consequences for future generations. If the redistribution is financed with debt to avoid increasing prevailing taxes, the financial burden will be shifted toward future generations, and the way in which the shift impacts on each of the future generations will not be independent of

---

[1] In this chapter we call "fiscal redistributions" the difference between households' Final Income and households' Market Income that results from the incidence of taxes, expenditures, and transfers that are primarily intended to produce changes in income distribution. We utilize the definitions corresponding to the CEQ (Commitment to Equity Institute) methodology; see section 1 and Lustig and Higgins (2022) (chapter 1 in Volume 1 of this Handbook).

the stage of the demographic transition that the economy is experiencing. In this regard, policymakers should take into account that children and unborn generations cannot participate in the markets and may have a weak or no voice in the political arena.

Third, fiscal redistributions may affect natural capital. In particular, if redistribution initiatives are financed with rents from natural resources, they may ultimately deplete natural capital, leaving no accumulation of reproducible capital to compensate for such depletion as required, for example, by the criterion of weak sustainability (Hartwick, 1977; Hamilton, 2008). In addition, when positive but transitory shocks occur, such as improvements in the terms of trade in natural resource–rich economies, the short-run political economy equilibrium may result in fiscal redistributions that are progressive and favor the poor but cannot be maintained under normal circumstances once the positive shock has passed. To avoid reducing progressive expenditures when rents are falling, state-owned firms frequently increase the level of oil and other natural resource extraction beyond the optimum. A closely related problem has to do with nontargeted subsidies embodied in the prices of energy in oil-rich countries, which may lead not only to regressive results but also to negative effects on the stock of natural capital when lower prices provide stronger incentives for the excessive consumption of energy.[2] In all these cases fiscal redistributions would be financed by depleting future generations' natural resources, and, under such circumstances, fiscal sustainability might appear to be ensured when, in fact, it would not be. These factors are highly relevant in low- and middle-income countries where natural capital represents a much higher proportion of total wealth (World Bank, 2011), and, consequently, it is highly probable that the state finances public policies based on natural resources rents.

The main purpose of this chapter is to present a set of methodological tools to address these types of problems. We focus on the linkages between fiscal redistributions, fiscal sustainability, and the government's wealth constraint. To this end, we will use concepts developed in four sources: fiscal incidence (Lustig and Higgins, 2022) (chapter 1 in Volume 1 of this Handbook), fiscal sustainability (Escolano, 2010), sustainable development (Dasgupta, 2009; Neumeyer, 2010; United Nations, 2015), and the demographic transition (Mason and Lee, 2011). Two additional objectives are to identify new research questions and new data requirements.

The structure of the chapter is as follows. The next section elaborates on three central concepts of our analysis—fiscal redistributions, public wealth, and fiscal sustainability—and the linkages between them. We use the set of income concepts developed by the Commitment to Equity Institute (CEQ) to define the components of fiscal redistributions,[3] present the concept of public wealth, and show what the fiscal sustainability conditions are for a given set of fiscal redistributions. The section addresses two additional issues: the connections between fiscal sustainability and public

---

[2] See for example De la Torre, Fajnzylber, and Nash (2009) and Fanelli, Jiménez, and López Azcúnaga (2015).

[3] See Lustig and Higgins (2022).

wealth; and the relation between this latter wealth, natural resources, and (weak) development sustainability, when the government owns the natural resources. We also examine the consequences on the distribution of wealth between the public and the private sectors when capital gains are considered, in line with Vincent, Panayotou, and Hartwick (1997). Section 2 addresses the demographic dimension. We first present a set of concepts developed by the National Transfer Accounts project (NTA) to conceptualize and measure the economic consequences of the demographic transition.[4] Based on such concepts, we study the cross-cohort distribution of income and wealth, on the one hand, and the relationship between sustainability and fiscal redistributions, on the other. Section 3 introduces disaggregation by income strata and investigates the relations with cohorts and aggregate wealth. This is necessary to study the consequences of changes in taxes or transfers whose primary purpose is to ensure fiscal sustainability. Section 4 comments on a set of policy implications that follow from our methodological framework. The chapter has two appendixes. Appendix 7A modifies the framework to analyze the consequences of assuming that the contributions to social security are forced savings rather than a tax and, hence, the associated transfers constitute the perception of deferred income. Appendix 7B presents a list of the framework's variables.

1 Income Concepts, Fiscal Redistributions, and Sustainability

In this section we first present the income concepts utilized by CEQ Institute researchers—that is, Market Income, Disposable Income, Consumable Income, and Final Income. Second, we define the government's intertemporal budget constraint in terms of such concepts and include natural resources in the government's balance sheet. Third we discuss the relation of our approach to the notion of fiscal sustainability commonly used in policymaking analyses—for example, in the case of the IMF's sustainability exercises (Escolano, 2010)—and identify assumptions that are frequently made concerning government wealth constraints. Finally, we analyze the linkages between rents from natural resources, wealth distribution, and fiscal redistributions.

1.1 CEQ Income Concepts

We begin by defining *Market Income* (Y_t^M) as the sum of market labor income (Y_t^L) and the Market Income stemming from accumulated assets (Y_t^A) before taxes. Income from assets includes private transfers such as private pensions and remittances. Hence, Market Income can be written as

$$(7\text{-}1) \qquad\qquad Y_t^M = Y_t^L + Y_t^A.$$

---

[4] On the NTA methodology, see Mason and Lee (2011).

In addition to Market Income, *Disposable Income* (Y_t^D) takes into account direct cash and near cash transfers—the sum of pension transfers (G_t^A) and other transfers (G_t^O)—net of employee contributions to social security (T_t^A) and personal taxes (T_t^Y). Examples of other transfers are conditional and unconditional cash transfers, school feeding programs, and free food transfers. Hence,

$$(7\text{-}2) \qquad Y_t^D = Y_t^L + Y_t^A + G_t^O + G_t^A - T_t^A - T_t^Y.$$

Consumable Income (Y_t^C) is obtained by adding indirect subsidies (G_t^I) to energy, food, and other general targeted subsidies and subtracting indirect taxes (T_t^I) from Disposable Income. So, Consumable Income (Y_t^C) is

$$(7\text{-}3) \qquad Y_t^C = Y_t^L + Y_t^A + G_t^O + G_t^A + G_t^I - T_t^A - T_t^Y - T_t^I.$$

Final Income (Y_t^F) is calculated by adding expenditures in kind related to education (G_t^E) and health (G_t^H) and subtracting fees (T_t^F) from the previous income concepts:

$$(7\text{-}4) \qquad Y_t^F = Y_t^L + Y_t^A + G_t^O + G_t^A + G_t^I + G_t^E + G_t^H - T_t^A - T_t^Y - T_t^I - T_t^F.$$

Based on these income concepts, we define (net) *fiscal redistributions* (N_t^D) as the difference between Market Income and Final Income—that is,

$$(7\text{-}5) \qquad N_t^D = Y_t^F - Y_t^M.$$

The variable N_t^D can be interpreted as the net overall costs that the public sector must incur to implement a specific set of fiscal redistributions aimed at achieving a given target concerning income redistribution. This variable connects two central aspects of fiscal policies: redistributions and sustainability. To examine specific issues concerning the effects of public policies on income distribution, fiscal redistributions can be defined more narrowly. More specifically, N_t^D can be defined in two alternative ways: as a difference between Market Income and Disposable Income or as the difference between Market Income and Consumable Income. However, in the case of our analysis, it is the variable N_t^D that will play the central role in showing the linkages between redistributive initiatives, fiscal sustainability, and demography. This is so because it is the ampler definition of fiscal redistributions and is thus more suitable for examining the consequences at the macroeconomic level. But, in any case, the methodological framework that we develop can be easily adapted to any of the above definitions of fiscal redistributions.

Our next step is to define the fiscal deficit in terms of N_t^D. The primary fiscal deficit (D_t^{PG}) is the government net borrowing, excluding interest payments on consolidated government liabilities, which equals the difference between primary expenditures and taxes and other revenues. In addition to the items that we have already presented, primary expenditures include government investment (I_t^G) and a variety of other items associated with the provision of public goods, which we call G_t^R. Taxes, in turn, usually comprise a number of miscellaneous revenues (including corporate taxes) besides the set of taxes that we have introduced above; we call them T_t^R. If the capital accumulated on the basis of public investment generates an income (for example, highway tolls or hospital fees), it is included in T_t^R. In other parts of this chapter, when it is necessary to discuss specific problems, we change the assumptions concerning the returns of public investment. We also introduce a variable that stands for the net incidence of the miscellaneous components of the budget that are not part of what we have called fiscal redistributions:

$$(7\text{-}6) \qquad\qquad N_t^R = G_t^R - T_t^R.$$

The primary fiscal deficit can then be expressed as

$$(7\text{-}7) \qquad\qquad D_t^{PG} = N_t^D + N_t^R + I_t^G - E_t^G,$$

where E_t^G are rents from natural resources, which can take the form of dividends from government-owned natural resource firms or royalties and may account for a significant share of fiscal revenues in natural resource–rich countries. E_t^G is equal to the variation in the quantity of natural resources ($\Delta Q_t^G < 0$) times the value of the rents of natural resources p_t (the price net of marginal costs).[5] Hence, $E_t^G = -p_t \Delta Q_t^G$.

1.2 Public Wealth Constraint

The assets that make up public wealth are reproducible capital (K_t^G) and nonrenewable natural resources (Q_t^G). If B_t^G is the stock of government debt net of financial assets held by the government, the government's net worth, W_t^G, can be defined as

$$(7\text{-}8) \qquad\qquad W_t^G = K_t^G + p_t Q_t^G - B_t^G.$$

When the stock of natural resources is included in the government's balance sheet, a number of particularities have to be considered. The two most relevant to our analysis are the definition of net, "adjusted" savings to take into account the depletion of natural resources and the capital gains originating in changes in the value of rents.

To calculate net, adjusted savings (S_t^G), we have to deduct both the depreciation of capital (ςK_t^G) and resource depletion ($\overline{E}_t^G$) from gross savings. Hence, if r is the interest rate—which we simplify by assuming constant—we can write

$$(7\text{-}9) \qquad\qquad S_t^G = E_t^G + rK_{t-1}^G - rB_{t-1}^G - N_t^D - N_t^R - \varsigma K_{t-1}^G - \overline{E}_t^G.$$

---

[5] Of course, ΔQ_t^G can be positive as a consequence of discoveries, but we simplify by not including discoveries.

Gross savings, in turn, provide the funds to finance the accumulation of capital and to repay public debt:

$$(7\text{-}10) \qquad S_t^G + \overline{E}_t^G + \varsigma K_{t-1}^G = I_t^G - \Delta B_t^G.$$

These definitions of gross and net savings are consistent with the sustainable approach to development.[6] However, this definition of adjusted savings is less restrictive than that of the World Bank (2011), which excludes additional items from gross savings. We ignore those items, as well as the capital depreciation term (ςK_t^G), because they play no particular role in our analysis—and can easily be included if necessary. We focus on the way in which rent revenues and the depletion of nonrenewable resources can influence fiscal redistribution policies. Note, nonetheless, that different approaches exist concerning the adjustment of savings to account for depletion.[7] To reflect this fact, we define $\overline{E}_t^G = -m_t p_t \Delta Q_t^G$, where: $0 \le m_t \le 1$; $\forall t$. In the case of the Hartwick (1977) rule, $m_t = 1$ and $S_t^G \ge 0$, which implies that fiscal redistributions are subject to the restriction $N_t^D \le r(K_{t-1}^G - B_{t-1}^G) - N_t^R$. If, instead, we followed the El Serafy (1989) approach, then $0 < m_t < 1$. In the usual NTA calculations $m_t = 0$. In the two latter cases it is easier to comply with $S_t^G \ge 0$, and, consequently, there is more room to expand fiscal redistributions: $N_t^D \le (1 - m_t)E_t^G + r(K_{t-1}^G - B_{t-1}^G) - N_t^R$. In what follows, we assume $m_t = 1$ in line with the World Bank's measurement of adjusted savings.

The increase in the value of the portion of wealth held in natural resources can be decomposed as follows:

$$(7\text{-}11) \qquad p_t Q_t^G - p_{t-1} Q_{t-1}^G = \Delta p_t Q_{t-1}^G + p_t \Delta Q_t^G = \hat{p}_t p_{t-1} Q_{t-1}^G + p_t \Delta Q_t^G.$$

Capital gains stem from changes in the value of rents. In each period, capital gains amount to $\Delta p_t Q_{t-1}^G = \hat{p}_t p_{t-1} Q_{t-1}^G$. If these gains are different from zero, the increase in wealth (ΔW_t^G) differs from savings. Since natural capital is not usually, or only partially, recorded in public sector balance sheets, capital gains associated with the stock of natural resources are mostly ignored when stating fiscal sustainability conditions. When capital gains are considered, government wealth (W_t^G) evolves according to

$$(7\text{-}12) \qquad W_t^G = W_{t-1}^G + S_t^G + \hat{p}_t p_{t-1} Q_{t-1}^G = K_{t-1}^G - B_{t-1}^G + I_t^G - \Delta B_t^G + p_t Q_t^G,$$

where $I_t^G = \Delta K_t^G$ stands for government investment. If, additionally, we assume—in line with the Hotelling (1931) rule—that $r = \hat{p}_t$, capital gains can be expressed as $r p_{t-1} Q_{t-1}^G$. Whenever $r \ne \hat{p}_t$ as a consequence of a shock, the activity of speculators will induce a rapid "jump" in stock prices so as to restore the parity, giving rise to a once-and-for-all variation in the value of under-the-ground resources and, consequently, of public

---

[6] See Hamilton (2008).

[7] See Neumayer (2010).

wealth. So, if natural resources were owned by the government, it would be the treasury and not the private sector that would be favored by capital gains. In fact, in a closed economy where the public sector owns a natural resource that is used as an input for production or for consumption—such as oil—when $r = \hat{p}_t > 0$, the private sector will become relatively less rich than the public sector because of capital gains. On the other hand, if the country were a net oil exporter, part of the capital gains would be at the cost of the rest of the world. These gains represent the capitalized value of the increase in national income induced by the increase in p_t.[8]

In addition, in countries where natural resources account for a relevant share of exports, when sizable unexpected positive terms-of-trade shocks occur (p_t jumps), the fiscal space typically widens substantially because of the increase in the value of the flow of rents E_t^G. Fiscal sustainability might also improve for two reasons. First, since the value of domestic assets that can be used as collateral is higher, the public debt ratio that market participants perceive as sustainable might increase. Second, the improvement in the agents' perception of the treasury's ability to pay might reduce the interest rate and thus, as we will see, have a direct positive impact on fiscal sustainability. Under these circumstances, as we mentioned above, the political pressures on the government to implement bolder fiscal redistributions will be typically stronger, and the consequences of mistaking a transitory shock for a permanent one can be very damaging to the stability of fiscal redistributions and, hence, fiscal sustainability. The consequences of these simultaneous distributional and financial changes on the macroeconomic and political economy dimensions can give rise to symptoms of the natural resource course.

Under many circumstances—especially when studying the demographic dimension—we conduct the analysis in per capita terms. Therefore, to simplify the notation, we use lowercase letters to express the value of the variables in per capita terms. Hence, for example, per capita income is $y_t = \dfrac{Y_t}{X_t}$, where X_t stands for the total population. In addition, we use Greek letters when we express a per capita variable as a ratio of per capita income. Therefore, fiscal redistributions, for instance, are $\eta_t^D = \dfrac{n_t^D}{y_t}$. Note, however, that in the case of financial variables, we use a tilde instead of a Greek letter to express the per capita variable as a ratio of per capita income. In this way, $\tilde{b}_t^G = \dfrac{b_t^G}{y_t}$ is the stock of net government debt per capita as a ratio of per capita income. Using these conventions, we can express (7-12) as a ratio of GDP in the following way:

$$(7\text{-}13) \qquad \omega_t^G = \frac{\omega_{t-1}^G}{1+g} + \sigma_t^G + \hat{p}_t p_{t-1} \frac{\xi_{t-1}^G}{1+g},$$

---

[8] See Vincent, Panayotou, and Hartwick (1997).

where $\omega_t^G = \dfrac{W_t^G}{Y_t}$; $\sigma_t^G = \dfrac{S_t^G}{Y_t}$; $\xi_t^G = \dfrac{Q_t^G}{Y_t}$; $\hat{p}_t = \dfrac{\Delta p_t}{p_{t-1}}$, and g is the GDP growth rate. Since we have assumed that $E_t^G = \bar{E}_t^G$, the expression for the public wealth can also be written as

$$\omega_t^G = (1+\lambda)(\kappa_{t-1}^G - \tilde{b}_{t-1}^G) - (\eta_t^D + \eta_t^R) + (1+\lambda_t^*)p_{t-1}\xi_{t-1}^G,$$

where we defined $\kappa_t^G = \dfrac{K_t^G}{Y_t}$; $\eta_t^R = \dfrac{N_t^R}{Y_t}$; $1+\lambda = \dfrac{1+r}{1+g}$ and $1+\lambda_1^* = \dfrac{1+\hat{p}_t}{1+g}$. Under the Hotelling (1931) rule, $1+\lambda_t^* = 1+\lambda$, and, therefore, in period N, the government's net worth as a ratio of GDP will be

(7-14)
$$\omega_N^G = \kappa_N^G - \tilde{b}_N^G + p_N\xi_N^G = (1+\lambda)^N(\kappa_0^G + p_0\xi_0^G - \tilde{b}_0^G)$$
$$- \sum_{t=1}^N (1+\lambda)^{N-t}(\eta_t^D + \eta_t^R).$$

Expressing (7-14) at present value we obtain

(7-15)
$$\omega_N^G(1+\lambda)^{-N} = (\kappa_0^G + p_0\xi_0^G - \tilde{b}_0^G) - \sum_{t=1}^N (1+\lambda)^{-t}(\eta_t^D + \eta_t^R).$$

Assuming that the no-Ponzi game condition holds, that $r > g$, and taking into account that nonrenewable resources, by definition, have a finite duration, if we let $N \to \infty$, it follows that the intertemporal budget constraint that fiscal redistributions have to abide by is

(7-16)
$$\sum_{t=1}^\infty (1+\lambda)^{-t}\,\eta_t^D = (\kappa_0^G - \tilde{b}_0^G p_0 + \xi_0^G) - \sum_{t=1}^\infty (1+\lambda)^{-t}\eta_t^R.$$

Our definition of adjusted public savings, with $\bar{\varepsilon}_t^G = \varepsilon_t^G$, ensures that the full amount of rents received will be saved and used either to accumulate capital or to reduce public debt. If, instead, the authorities followed the El Serafy (1989) approach and only part of ε_t^G were allocated to finance depletion, there would be more fiscal space available to finance η_t^D. In the remainder of the chapter we use the wealth constraint (7-13) as our frame of reference and make different simplifying assumptions either to focus on specific issues or to adapt to the approach that is customarily applied in economic policymaking. We will now show the relationship between (7-13) and the usual approach to fiscal sustainability.

1.3 Fiscal Sustainability

Policymakers assessing fiscal sustainability emphasize debt sustainability. Neither reproducible capital nor the stocks of natural resources and their depletion are fully taken into consideration.[9] The budget constraint, however, does consider the rents that the government receives from natural resources in the form of dividends from public firms or royalty payments. In turn, public investment is an expenditure with no counterpart in the accumulation of capital in the government balance sheet. The investment in financial assets is, nonetheless, taken into account to the extent that the stock of debt is net of the financial assets that the government holds. Therefore, we can express the recursive equation governing the dynamics of the public debt to income ratio as[10]

$$(7\text{-}17) \qquad \tilde{b}_t^G = (1+\lambda)\tilde{b}_{t-1}^G + \eta_t^D + \eta_t^R + \iota_t^G - \varepsilon_t^g.$$

Liquidity considerations are probably an important reason to exclude capital gains associated with future dividends or royalty payments from equation (7-17), while including rents received, $\varepsilon_t^G = \dfrac{E_t^G}{Y_t}$. Capital markets are far from perfect, and, consequently, capitalized gains might be very difficult to realize over a short period. Liquidity may also be one of the reasons why $\overline{\varepsilon}_t^G = \dfrac{\overline{E}_t^G}{Y_t}$ is not included in the budget, missing the opportunity to make policy decisions based on adjusted rather than gross government savings. When access to credit markets becomes difficult, rents are a source of liquidity and will be available to the extent that they are not invested in reproducible capital to compensate for depletion. In addition, investment in reproducible capital $\left(\iota_t = \dfrac{I_t^G}{X_t}\right)$ may not be politically palatable to the extent that it represents an increment in public expenditures. In short, liquidity squeezes and capital market imperfections undoubtedly hinder the policymaker's ability to strike an appropriate balance between efficiency, intra- and intergenerational equity, and fiscal sustainability

The solution of the difference equation (7-17) is

$$(7\text{-}18) \qquad \tilde{b}_N = (1+\lambda)^N \tilde{b}_0 + \sum_{t=1}^{N}(1+\lambda)^{N-t}(\eta_t^D + \eta_t^R + \iota_t^G - \varepsilon_t^G).$$

This implies that policies that contribute to determining the allocation of resources between η_t^D, η_t^R, and ι_t^G over time, as well as the rents from state-owned assets ε_t^G, will have a bearing on the trajectory of the debt/per capita income ratio.

---

[9] See Escolano (2010).

[10] This follows from: $\dfrac{B_t}{Y_t} = \dfrac{(1+r)\,B_{t-1}}{Y_{t-1}}\dfrac{Y_{t-1}}{Y_t} + \dfrac{N_t^D}{Y_t} + \dfrac{N_t^R}{Y_t} + \dfrac{I_t^G}{Y_t} - \dfrac{E_t^G}{Y_t}$

$$\Rightarrow \tilde{b}_t = \frac{1+r}{1+g}\tilde{b}_{t-1} + \eta_t^D + \eta_t^R + \iota_t^G - \varepsilon_t^G.$$

It also shows, as is well known, that the evolution of the interest rate-growth differential (λ, which we call the "effective" interest rate) has an effect on the path of public sector liabilities.[11] We can write the previous equation in present-value terms as

(7-19) $$(1+\lambda)^{-N}\tilde{b}_N = \tilde{b}_0 + \sum_{t=1}^{N}(1+\lambda)^{-t}(\eta_t^D + \eta_t^R + \iota_t^G - \varepsilon_t^G).$$

This is the intertemporal version of the government budget constraint in the "debt sustainability" approach. Consequently, for the level of public indebtedness to be sustainable, it is necessary to impose the no-Ponzi-game condition, which means that the government cannot service the interest and principal on its debt on a regular basis. This implies that the fiscal authorities must respect the following constraint:

(7-20) $$\lim_{N \to \infty}(1+\lambda)^{-N}\tilde{b}_N = 0.$$

The government budget constraint then becomes

(7-21) $$\tilde{b}_0 = \sum_{t=1}^{\infty}(1+\lambda)^{-t}(\varepsilon_t^G - \eta_t^D - \eta_t^R - \iota_t^G) = -\sum_{t=1}^{\infty}(1+\lambda)^{-t}\tilde{d}_t^{PG},$$

where $\tilde{d}_t^{PG} = \dfrac{D_t^{PG}}{Y_t}$. This means that the surpluses that the government plans to run in the future must be equal to the value of the current stock of debt, and, consequently, the intertemporal restriction that the sequence of fiscal redistributions must respect over time will be

(7-22) $$\sum_{t=1}^{\infty}(1+\lambda)^{-t}\eta_t^D = \sum_{t=1}^{\infty}(1+\lambda)^{-t}(\varepsilon_t^G - \eta_t^R - \iota_t^G) - \tilde{b}_0.$$

Since this expression ignores some government-owned assets, it differs from (7-16), which does include $\kappa_0^G + \xi_0^G$. The restriction on the fiscal redistributions would be softer if the stocks of natural resources and natural capital were taken into account in (7-22). For the sake of simplicity, we are omitting the role of human capital, although this kind of capital would play a role similar to that of physical capital: as in the case of physical capital, equation (7-22) includes expenditures on education and health in calculating the primary deficit but excludes the accumulation of human capital as a source of social benefits. In addition, (7-22) implicitly assumes $\bar{\varepsilon}_t^G = 0$, and, consequently, restriction (7-22) does not exclude the possibility of fiscal sustainability

---

[11]If λ is not constant and equal to λ_t at time t, the solution is

$$\tilde{b}_N = \tilde{b}_0 \prod_{t=1}^{N}(1+\lambda_t) + \sum_{t=1}^{N}\prod_{i=t+1}^{N}(1+\lambda_i)(\eta_t^D + \eta_t^R + \iota_t^G - \varepsilon_t^G),$$

being achieved at the cost of sacrificing the (weak) sustainability of the development process.

If, in order to meet constraint (7-22), the government were to implement a fiscal rule to maintain the ratio between the primary deficit and overall income constant, such a primary deficit would have to be $\tilde{d}^{PG^*} = -\lambda \tilde{b}_0$, because $\sum_{t=1}^{\infty}(1+\lambda)^{-t} = \dfrac{1}{\lambda}$. This implies that the government should run a surplus if it were a net debtor. Under these conditions, at each point in time, fiscal redistributions would face the restriction

$$(7\text{-}23) \qquad \eta_t^D = \varepsilon_t^G - \eta_t^R - \iota_t^G - \lambda\,\tilde{b}_0.$$

At each point in time, then, fiscal redistributions (η_t^D) would compete with other items in the budget (η_t^R and ι_t^G). If the economy grew faster, the trade-off would be softer because the effective interest rate λ would be lower; the opposite would happen if there were an increase in the interest rate. This is why the "lost decades" situations are so disruptive to fiscal redistribution policies: they combine high interest rates—because of the increment in risk aversion—and low growth for long periods, making sustainability harder to achieve and constraining the government's ability to implement fiscal redistributions that aim to improve equity. Obviously, an improvement in the terms of trade that elevated ε_t^G via state-owned firms' profits would increase the fiscal space, making the implementation of fiscal redistributions easier. However, if the shock is transitory and the fiscal redistribution permanent, an inconsistency could arise once the shock disappears because the sustainability restriction must be respected throughout all periods. If the level of fiscal redistribution is maintained, the natural resources could be exhausted.

For political economy reasons and market failures, the planning horizon is, in practice, short of infinite and fiscal rules that set a maximum public debt/per capita income value are, instead, frequent. If the fiscal authority sets $\tilde{b}_t = \tilde{b}^*$ as a sustainability rule, it follows that

$$\lambda \tilde{b}^* = \varepsilon_t^G - \eta_t^D - \eta_t^R - \iota_t^G = \tilde{d}^{PG^*}.$$

And the constraint on the costs of fiscal redistributions that holds at each time becomes

$$(7\text{-}24) \qquad \eta_t^{D^*} = \varepsilon_t^G - \eta_t^R - \iota_t^G - \lambda \tilde{b}^*.$$

If $\eta_t^D \neq \eta_t^{D^*}$, we can call $(\eta_t^D - \eta_t^{D^*})$ the "fiscal sustainability gap." It represents the fiscal effort that would be necessary to meet the sustainability constraint expressed in terms of existing fiscal redistributions.

Two clarifications are in order. First, if the cause of the gap is that $\tilde{b}^* < \tilde{b}_t$, the treasury will have to make an additional effort to follow the rule because the surplus will probably have to be higher than $\lambda\tilde{b}^*$ for a number of periods until the stock of public debt achieves the target $\tilde{b}^*$. Once this target is achieved, the public debt/income ratio can be maintained on the basis of a primary surplus equal to $\lambda\tilde{b}^*$. Second, the rationale for a fiscal rule that sets a constant primary surplus equal to $\lambda\tilde{b}^*$ has mainly to do with political economy and financial factors, because, strictly speaking, the rule will maintain $\tilde{b}^* = \tilde{b}_0$ in the long run only if $\tilde{b}_t$ is already equal to $\tilde{b}^*$. The debt-stabilizing rule should, in fact, be set in terms of the overall deficit, $\tilde{d}^G$. The rule that makes $\tilde{b}_t$ asymptotically converge to $\tilde{b}^*$ is $\tilde{d}^{G^*} = -\dfrac{g^n}{1+g^n}\tilde{b}^*$, where g^n is the nominal growth rate of income.[12] With this caveat in mind, we will discuss the linkages between fiscal sustainability and redistributions in terms of the primary deficit because such deficit shows the stock and flow constraints in a clearer way and because the reference to the primary deficit is the norm rather the exception in policymaking analysis. This makes sense because, concerning the market sentiment and political economy constraints, what usually matters the most in the short to medium run is the stabilization of the public debt ratio at a "reasonable" level.

1.4 Natural Resource Rents, Wealth, and Fiscal Redistributions

Fiscal sustainability restrictions give rise to complex issues in resource-rich countries, and, consequently, fiscal redistributions should be carefully designed. But the issue is also relevant to resource-poor economies because of the effects of changes on international prices of imported resources, which reduce national income and could impinge on fiscal redistributions. To clarify this point, we now further explore the relationship between natural resources, fiscal redistributions, and public wealth. We focus on two factors: the pattern of depletion over time and the effects of capital gains associated with changes in the value of scarcity rents. We assume that the public sector owns all natural resources.

We use the expressions for the stocks of capital net of public debt (7-25) and natural resources (7-26) corresponding to period N to organize the analysis. These expressions are

$$(7\text{-}25) \qquad \kappa_N^G - \tilde{b}_N^G = (1+\lambda)^N(\kappa_0^G - \tilde{b}_0^G) + \sum_{t=1}^{N}(1+\lambda)^{N-t}\varepsilon_t^G$$
$$-\sum_{t=1}^{N}(1+\lambda)^{N-t}(\eta_t^D + \eta_t^R);$$

---

[12] See Escolano (2010).

(7-26) $$p_N \xi_N^G = (1+\lambda)^N p_0 \xi_0^G - \sum_{t=1}^{N}(1+\lambda)^{N-t}\varepsilon_t^G.$$

To highlight the problems facing fiscal authorities in a resource-rich developing country, we assume that r and p_t are exogenously determined by international markets and that the economy is a net exporter of renewable resources. We also make the simplifying assumption that the Hotelling (1931) rule holds and continue to assume $\varepsilon_t^G = \overline{\varepsilon}_t^G$.

Let us begin with the depletion pattern. Up to period N, the total amount of rents received will be $\sum_{t=0}^{N}(1+\lambda)^{-t}\varepsilon_t^G$. If natural resources are depleted in N periods ($p_N \xi_N^G = 0$), it follows from (7-26) that the total amount of rents received will be equal to the stock of resources at the beginning of the period $p_0 \xi_0^G = \sum_{t=1}^{N}(1+\lambda)^{-t}\varepsilon_t^G$. Since we have imposed the condition that $\varepsilon_t^G = \overline{\varepsilon}_t^G$, the term $\sum_{t=0}^{N}(1+\lambda)^{-t}\varepsilon_t^G$ appears in equations (7-25) and (7-26), but with opposite signs. The term appears twice because capital accumulation fully offsets the depletion of natural resources over time. If we add (7-25) and (7-26), we obtain (7-14), that is, total wealth at the end of the period. Consequently, the distribution of rents and depletion over time is irrelevant to the value of $\kappa_N^G - \tilde{b}_N^G + p_N \xi_N^G$, the stock of wealth at period N.

In the real world, where market imperfections and political economy matter, the ΔQ_t^G sequence will not be optimally determined on the basis of a dynamic optimization model or, less ambitiously, trying to maintain the value of wealth for future generations.[13] To begin with, as we have mentioned, the fiscal authority does not often take into consideration the depletion of natural resources, and adjusted savings may become negative (World Bank, 2011). Hence, in the real world, depletion policy matters, particularly for intergenerational equity. If the government sets a low N and, consequently, sets high absolute values for the $\Delta Q_t^G < 0$ sequence, fewer generations will benefit from rents. For example, the government might easily finance both η_t^D and i_t^D when $t \leq N$, but, afterward, the treasury might face a strong trade-off between fiscal redistributions and capital accumulation.

In order to avoid the need for marked fiscal adjustments after period N—and seek intergenerational equity—ensuring that $\overline{\varepsilon}_t^G - \varepsilon_t^G = 0$ and $\sigma_t^G \geq 0$ appears to be a sensible strategy. However, this may not be the case. If public savings are positive but the accumulation of reproducible capital takes the form of, say, investment in infrastructure—or education—with no or partial user charge, the treasury might not recover the funds invested. And, if fiscal sustainability were in jeopardy, the fiscal authority would have to implement undesired changes in fiscal redistributions. The government might, of course, utilize rents to repay debt instead of investing them, and, eventually, $\tilde{b}_t^G$ might even become negative. This would be the case of a country that accumulated

---

[13] See the discussion in Neumayer (2010), pp. 137–41.

a sovereign wealth fund.[14] Such a policy would reinforce sustainability, but it could be at the cost of weakening capital accumulation, which could have a higher rate of social return.[15] Furthermore, when resources remain under the ground, it is as if the fiscal authority were systematically reinvesting the capital gains, and, consequently, natural resource reserves grow at the rate r. But if the resources are extracted and converted into productive capital, the rents, ε_t^G, may or may not be reinvested in productive capital, and the same is true of the future proceeds ($r\varepsilon_t^G$). Therefore, because of political economy constraints, the government may decide not to extract the resource to prevent it from being squandered.

The expected and unexpected changes in the value of scarcity rents give rise to capital gains that may be partially or totally overlooked when planning fiscal redistributions. To illustrate the point, let us assume the limiting case of no depletion ($\varepsilon_t^G = 0, \forall t$). The value of the stock of resources (ξ_t^G) will increase at the effective rate λ. In period N, the value of natural resource wealth will be $p_N \xi_N^G = (1+\lambda)^N p_0 \xi_0^G$. However, if the resources are not appropriately recorded in the government's balance sheet, the increase in government wealth will not always be correctly considered.

Capital gains are not neutral for wealth and income distribution because those who buy the resources—domestic consumers or the rest of the world—face systematically increasing prices. At the domestic level, if natural resources are owned by the government, public wealth increases compared to private wealth, while national wealth augments in relation to the rest of the world. For example, assume that the government seeks to maintain the present value of its wealth, reinvesting all the rents and the returns from the capital invested. Taking into account capital gains, the total value of wealth at period N would be $\kappa_N^G - \tilde{b}_N^G + p_N \xi_N^G = (1+\lambda)^N (\kappa_0^G - \tilde{b}_0^G + p_0 \xi_0^G)$, and fiscal redistributions would be subject to the restriction $\sum_{t=1}^N (1+\lambda)^{N-t} \eta_t^D = \sum_{t=1}^N (1+\lambda)^{N-t} \eta_t^R$. Under the conditions of this policy, the state would become increasingly rich while simultaneously facing a tight constraint on fiscal redistributions. Furthermore, note that if $r > g$, the government income share will also grow systematically, creating a situation akin to that highlighted by Piketty (2014) with regard to capitalists. Obviously, the public sector can use the returns from capital and capital gains stemming from natural resources to finance fiscal redistributions. This fact creates a natural link between capital gains and fiscal redistributions because capital gains create fiscal space and the government has to decide whether to become richer than the private sector or to transfer the capital gains to that sector via fiscal redistributions. It would be wise,

---

[14] To be sure, human capital expenditures could compensate for the depletion, but for the sake of simplicity we do not discuss this possibility here. See Hamilton (2008); World Bank (2011).

[15] If the natural capital under analysis does not have a market price—as in the case of many ecosystems that provide valuable productive services—or if market prices do not reflect social values because of the presence of externalities, the sustainability restriction becomes much more difficult to identify.

therefore, not to separate the design of fiscal accumulation and fiscal redistribution policies.

For example, the government could use not only the returns from capital but also the capital gains stemming from natural resources to finance $\eta_t^D + \eta_t^R$, which would imply the following restriction:

$$(7\text{-}27) \quad \sum_{t=1}^{N}(1+\lambda)^{N-t}(\eta_t^D + \eta_t^R) = (1+\lambda)^N(\kappa_0^G - \tilde{b}_0^G + p_0\xi_0^G) - (\kappa_0^G - \tilde{b}_0^G + p_0\xi_0^G).$$

This policy would maintain the value of wealth at the beginning of period. That is, $\kappa_N^G - \tilde{b}_N^G + p_N\xi_N^G - (\kappa_0^G - \tilde{b}_0^G + p_0\xi_0^G) = 0$.

Note that in debt sustainability studies, the variables are typically expressed as GDP ratios, while the sustainable development literature emphasizes welfare, per capita consumption, and the role of total wealth. In terms of these latter indicators, satisfying the public capital accumulation requirements of a young society going through the first stages of the demographic transition could be particularly hard. In a young society, the demand for public goods such as those that are complementary to private accumulation and urbanization will be high. Consequently, in young resource-rich countries, it is particularly relevant to consider how to spend the proceeds from natural resources. Public investment is an important determinant of the evolution of labor productivity—and, therefore, of the real wages of future workers who will have to provide for their children and retirees in the future. At the same time, a fall in public investment could easily result in a de facto accelerated reduction of public capital.

If the government's goal were to ensure the condition $\Delta w_t^G \geq 0$, so as to maintain at least per capita wealth $\left(w_t^G = \dfrac{W_t^G}{X_t} \right)$ rather than the wealth/GDP ratio, ω_t^G, the resulting restriction for each period would be $s_t^G + \hat{p}_t p_{t-1} \dfrac{q_{t-1}^G}{1+x} \geq x\, w_{t-1}^G$, where x is the rate of growth of the population. The increase in wealth is explained by both genuine savings and capital gains. The term on the right-hand side reminds us that wealth accumulation must satisfy population growth.

For the government wealth to be constant, part of the total wealth should be "consumed" to finance $\eta_t^D + \eta_t^R$. If we call such a part z, the per capita government wealth will remain constant at the level w^{G*} if

$$(7\text{-}28) \quad z = \frac{r-x}{1+x} w^{G*}.$$

This indicates that, if $r > x$, the government could allocate each year the sum z to fiscal redistribution and still respect the wealth constraint. In principle, this is independent of the path of extraction, provided that $\bar{\varepsilon}_t^G = \varepsilon_t^G$ and Hotelling (1931) rules hold. The returns from capital in the period $t+1$ will increase by re_t^G, while capital gains on the existing stock of natural wealth will decrease by the same amount. Note that this differs from the usual recommendation to follow a policy such that $s_t^G \geq 0$; under such a policy government wealth would grow systematically.

As we have already noted, the canonical approach to fiscal sustainability, which ignores government assets and natural resource depletion and pivots on equation (7-17), may be too restrictive to analyze some important linkages between fiscal sustainability and redistributions in developing countries that are going through the first stages of the demographic transition and/or are natural resource–rich. For example, when the deficit of the social security system increases because of the aging process, there will be less space for other distributional policies unless other items of the budget adjust accordingly. Furthermore, the consequences of aging can be regressive if those covered by the social security system are richer than those that suffer the expenditure cuts or bear the increase in the tax burden. A natural resource–rich country could finance the increase in η_t^D induced by aging with rents. But, if this led to the depletion of natural resources, the policy would be unsustainable. One additional complication is that deviations from the sustainability restrictions are difficult to detect when the budget is balanced in the short run. To avoid these difficulties, the fiscal authorities should take into account the consequences of the demographic transition. We next discuss the role of demography in more detail.

2 Fiscal Redistributions, Demography, and Wealth Constraints

This section introduces the demographic dimension and identifies the channels through which the demographic transition interacts with fiscal redistributions, sustainability, and wealth.

We use the sub-index a to identify the different cohorts. The age of the oldest cohort will be $\bar{a}$. The net effect of fiscal redistributions in the case of cohort a will then be

$$(7\text{-}29) \qquad N_{a,t}^D = G_{a,t}^O + G_{a,t}^A + G_{a,t}^I + G_{a,t}^E + G_{a,t}^H - T_{a,t}^A - T_{a,t}^Y - T_{a,t}^I - T_{a,t}^F.$$

Taking this equation and the notion of lifecycle deficit as points of departure, we show the linkages between the concepts utilized in the CEQ and NTA databases. To this end, we first introduce the notion of aggregate lifecycle deficit, and, based on the lifecycle deficit and the government deficit—which are flow variables—we subsequently study the linkages between these variables and the evolution of stocks to obtain a better grasp of the intertemporal restrictions. The notion of lifecycle wealth is central in this regard.

2.1 The Lifecycle Deficit

We define the lifecycle deficit using the concepts of *effective consumers* and *effective workers*, which play a pivotal role in the NTA database. We also use these two concepts to define the *support ratio*. This indicator is utilized in the NTA literature instead of the well-known dependency ratio because it better reflects the economic consequences of the demographic transition.

To define effective consumers, the NTA approach uses the concept of a cohort's consumption ($C_{a,t}$), which includes the public provision of health, education, and other public goods. We define the ratio between cohort a's per capita consumption and per capita income as $\varphi_{a,t} = \dfrac{c_{a,t}}{y_t}$, and the participation of cohort a in the total population at time t as $u_{a,t} = \dfrac{X_{a,t}}{X_t}$, where $X_{a,t}$ is total population of cohort a. We are now prepared to define the number of effective consumers in cohort a ($C_{a,t}^E$) as follows:

$$(7\text{-}30) \qquad C_{a,t}^E = \varphi_{a,t}\, X_{a,t}.$$

This means that the effective consumers belonging to cohort a will increase when the cohort's propensity to consume is higher. For example, because of healthcare expenditures, the elderly's consumption tends to be higher than average consumption. Based on this, the aggregate propensity to consume at time t (ϕ_t) can be disaggregated to reflect the behavior of the different cohorts. If $\bar{a}$ stands for the oldest cohort, we can write

$$(7\text{-}31) \qquad \varphi_t = \sum_{a=0}^{\bar{a}} \varphi_{a,t}\, u_{a,t}.$$

The pattern of $u_{a,t}$ will depend on the stage of the demographic transition that society is experiencing. For example, $u_{a,t}$ for $a \leq 15$ is higher in "young" societies while the portion of the population that meets the condition $15 < a < 65$ reaches a maximum during the "demographic bonus" stage.

$Y_{a,t}^L$ stands for the labor income of cohort a at time t, and the share of cohort a in total per capita labor income ($\gamma_{a,t}$) is $\gamma_{a,t} = \dfrac{y_{a,t}^L}{y_t}$. Based on the labor share of each cohort, the number of effective workers ($L_{a,t}$) is defined as

$$(7\text{-}32) \qquad L_{a,t} = \gamma_{a,t}\, X_{a,t}.$$

The overall participation of workers in aggregate income will consequently be

$$(7\text{-}33) \qquad \gamma_t = \sum_{a=0}^{\bar{a}} \gamma_{a,t}\, u_{a,t}.$$

As in the case of the propensity to consume, the overall labor share in income will be a function of the demographic structure via $u_{a,t}$.

In applied work, the time index of the ϕ and γ coefficients is usually dropped because of data limitations, and the two parameters are measured only for the base year.

The nonlabor income part of Market Income is also influenced by demographic factors. Since $Y_t^A = \sum_{a=0}^{\bar{a}} Y_{a,t}^A$, the private sector nonlabor income share can be written as

$$(7\text{-}34) \qquad \varepsilon_t^p = \frac{y_t^A}{y_t} = \sum_{a=0}^{\bar{a}} \varepsilon_{a,t}^p u_{a,t},$$

with $\varepsilon_{a,t}^p = \frac{y_{a,t}^A}{y_t}$. We can state Market Income as

$$(7\text{-}35) \qquad Y_t^M = \varepsilon_t^p \, Y_t + \gamma_t Y_t = Y_t \left(\sum_{a=0}^{\bar{a}} \varepsilon_{a,t}^p + \gamma_{a,t} \right) u_{a,t}.$$

This expression shows that via $u_{a,t}$ the demographic transition is a determinant of the labor and nonlabor shares in total income.

The support ratio corresponding to cohort a is defined as the ratio between effective workers and effective consumers:

$$(7\text{-}36) \qquad SR_{a,t} = \frac{L_{a,t}}{C_{a,t}^E}.$$

The support ratio is lower when the effective consumers that make up the a cohort depend more heavily on the labor income of others to finance their own consumption. If we aggregate over cohorts, society's aggregate support ratio is

$$(7\text{-}37) \qquad SR_t = \frac{L_t}{C_t^E} = \frac{\gamma_t}{\varphi_t} = \frac{Y_t^L}{C_t}.$$

This implies that the economy's support ratio increases with the participation of labor income in aggregate income and decreases with the overall propensity to consume. The expression indicates that the evolution of these two variables over time depends on behavioral and demographic factors. In young societies the support ratio is lower because of the high proportion of young individuals in the family, and in old societies the support ratio is lower because of the larger share of retirees in the population. The maximum of the SR_t indicator occurs during the so-called demographic bonus stage of the demographic transition, when the conditions for growing faster improve because the proportion of the working age population in the total population reaches a maximum (Mason, Abrigo, and Lee, 2017).

Finally, the lifecycle deficit of the a cohort is the difference between the cohort's consumption and its labor income; expressed in per capita terms it is

$$(7\text{-}38) \qquad lcd_{a,t} = (\phi_{a,t} - \gamma_{a,t}) \, y_t.$$

We can then define $\delta_{a,t} = \dfrac{lcd_{a,t}}{y_t}$. In accordance with the lifecycle theory we expect this indicator to be high when a corresponds to young effective consumers or to workers who are retired, typically 60 years and older. Using the support ratio, the per capita value of the lifecycle of the cohort can be written as $\delta_{a,t} = \phi_{a,t}(1 - SR_{a,t})$.

The lower the cohort's support ratio is, the higher the cohort's lifecycle deficit will be. The aggregate life-cycle can be written as $LCD_t = y_t C_t^E(1 - SR_t)$, and, consequently,

$$(7\text{-}39) \qquad \delta_t = \sum_{a=0}^{\bar{a}} \varphi_{a,t}(1 - SR_{a,t}) u_{a,t}.$$

As can be seen, the lifecycle deficit depends on demographic factors and the behavior of each cohort concerning consumption and the capacity to generate labor income. If $\dfrac{\gamma_{a,t}}{\varphi_{a,t}}$ tends to be low and $u_{a,t}$ high for young cohorts, as is the case, for example, in young societies, the aggregate lifecycle deficit will be high and will weaken the economy's ability to sustain growth. In addition, there is likely to be a strong demand for the government to finance the lifecycle deficit, and this will, in turn, increase the fiscal deficit and public debt, thereby opening the way to sustainability problems. We next analyze the fiscal dimension of the demographic transition to show the connection between fiscal redistributions and demography.

2.2 Fiscal Redistributions and Cohorts

In order to introduce the fiscal dimension into the analysis so as to be consistent with the NTA methodology, it is necessary to define profiles for the "tax burden" ($\beta_{a,t}$) and for the "benefits received" ($\alpha_{a,t}$) by the groups. The parameter $\beta_{a,t}$ stands for per capita taxes corresponding to a given cohort normalized by per capita income and $\alpha_{a,t}$ are the transfers received by the group normalized in the same way. Hence,

$$(7\text{-}40) \qquad \beta_{a,t} = \frac{T_{a,t}^A + T_{a,t}^Y + T_{a,t}^I + T_{a,t}^F + T_{a,t}^R}{X_{a,t} y_t};$$

$$(7\text{-}41) \qquad \alpha_{a,t} = \frac{G_{a,t}^O + G_{a,t}^A + G_{a,t}^I + G_{a,t}^E + G_{a,t}^H + G_{a,t}^R}{X_{a,t} y_t}.$$

As in the case of the consumption and labor income profiles, we frequently assume that these parameters do not change because of data limitations, and, hence, we drop the t subscript and use the information corresponding to the base year. Based on the previous definitions, the aggregate tax burden and benefits as ratios of aggregate income are

(7-42)
$$\beta_t = \sum_{a=0}^{\bar{a}} \beta_{a,t} u_{a,t};$$

(7-43)
$$\alpha_t = \sum_{a=0}^{\bar{a}} \alpha_{a,t} u_{a,d,t}.$$

We are now prepared to study the linkages between demography and fiscal redistributions. The first step is to decompose the overall tax burden and benefits to identify fiscal redistributions. Using the superscripts D and R as we did previously,

(7-44)
$$\beta_t^D = \frac{T_t^A + T_t^Y + T_t^I + T_t^F}{Y_t};$$

(7-45)
$$\beta_t^R = \frac{T_t^R}{Y_t};$$

(7-46)
$$\alpha_t^D = \frac{G_t^O + G_t^A + G_t^I + G_t^E + G_t^H}{Y_t};$$

(7-47)
$$\alpha_t^R = \frac{G_t^R}{Y_t}.$$

We can then write $\beta_t^D + \beta_t^R = \beta_t$ and $\alpha_t^D + \alpha_t^R = \alpha_t$, and, consequently,

(7-48)
$$\eta_t^D = \alpha_t^D - \beta_t^D;$$

(7-49)
$$\eta_t^R = \alpha_t^R - \beta_t^R.$$

Thus, the relationship between Final Income and aggregate income $\left(\psi_t^F = \dfrac{y_t^F}{y_t} \right)$ will be

(7-50)
$$\psi_t^F = \psi_t^M + \eta_t^D = \psi_t^M + \sum_{a=0}^{\bar{a}} \alpha_{a,t}^D u_{a,t} - \sum_{a=0}^{\bar{a}} \beta_{a,t}^D u_{a,t}.$$

This means that the effects of fiscal redistributions on Final Income will depend on the demographic profile of the economy because of the influence of $u_{a,t}$.

The ratio of the primary fiscal deficit to income ($\tilde{d}_t^{PG}$) will also be closely related to the demographic structure because, from (7-7) $\tilde{d}_t^{PG} = (\alpha_t^D - \beta_t^D) + (\alpha_t^R - \beta_t^R) + \iota_t^G - \varepsilon_t^G$, and consequently

(7-51) $\tilde{d}_t^{PG} = \left(\sum_{a=0}^{\bar{a}} \alpha_{a,t}^D u_{a,t} - \sum_{a=0}^{\bar{a}} \beta_{a,t}^D u_{a,t} \right) + \left(\sum_{a=0}^{\bar{a}} \alpha_{a,t}^R u_{a,t} - \sum_{a=0}^{\bar{a}} \beta_{a,t}^R u_{a,t} \right) + \iota_t^G - \varepsilon_t^G.$

From (7-21), the debt sustainability constraint can be expressed as

(7-52)
$$\tilde{b}_0 = \sum_{t=1}^{\infty}(1+\lambda)^{-t}(\varepsilon_t^G - \alpha_t^D - \beta_t^D - \alpha_t^R - \beta_t^R - \iota_t^G),$$

or

(7-53)
$$\tilde{b}_0 = -\sum_{t=1}^{\infty}(1+\lambda)^{-t}\left[\left(\sum_{a=0}^{\bar{a}}\alpha_{a,t}^D u_{a,t} - \sum_{a=0}^{\bar{a}}\beta_{a,t}^D u_{a,t}\right)\right.$$
$$\left. +\left(\sum_{a=0}^{\bar{a}}\alpha_{a,t}^R u_{a,t} - \sum_{a=0}^{\bar{a}}\beta_{a,t}^R u_{a,t}\right) + \iota_t^G - \varepsilon_t^G\right].$$

If we interpret sustainability as a fiscal rule that sets $\tilde{b}^* = \tilde{b}_t$, at each point in time the treasury will have to respect the following restriction:

(7-54)
$$\lambda\tilde{b}^* = \tilde{b}^*\frac{r-g}{1+g} = \varepsilon_t^G - \left(\sum_{a=0}^{\bar{a}}\alpha_{a,t}^D u_{a,t} - \sum_{a=0}^{\bar{a}}\beta_{a,t}^D u_{a,t}\right)$$
$$-\left(\sum_{a=0}^{\bar{a}}\alpha_{a,t}^R u_{a,t} - \sum_{a=0}^{\bar{a}}\beta_{a,t}^R u_{a,t}\right) - \iota_t^G.$$

And, if alternatively, the rule sets $\tilde{d}_t^{PG^*} = \lambda b_0$, the constraint will be

(7-55)
$$\lambda b_0 = b_0\frac{r-g}{1+g} = \varepsilon_t^G - \left(\sum_{a=0}^{\bar{a}}\alpha_{a,t}^D u_{a,t} - \sum_{a=0}^{\bar{a}}\beta_{a,t}^D u_{a,t}\right)$$
$$-\left(\sum_{a=0}^{\bar{a}}\alpha_{a,t}^R u_{a,t} - \sum_{a=0}^{\bar{a}}\beta_{a,t}^R u_{a,t}\right) - \iota_t^G.$$

Given that these sustainability equations are, by definition, restrictions that must be respected over a long period, the demographic transition will exert its influence through the $u_{a,t}$ channel.

2.3 Wealth Constraints and Lifecycle Wealth

Let us now analyze the way in which the demographic transition influences the evolution of the intertemporal budget constraint of the cohorts, becoming a determinant of the path of the private and public sectors' stocks of wealth. We begin by defining the savings and wealth of the cohorts. We then aggregate those variables to obtain aggregate private savings and aggregate private wealth, and, finally, we show the linkages with the public sector's wealth constraint. In appendix 7A we illustrate the linkage between demography and wealth distribution in the case in which pensions are assumed to be deferred income.

2.3.1 Cohorts' Savings and Wealth

The a cohort's savings $(S_{a,t})$ is the difference between its Final Income and its consumption:

$$(7\text{-}56) \qquad S_{a,t} = Y_{a,t}^L + Y_{a,t}^A + G_{a,t}^O + G_{a,t}^A + G_{a,t}^E + G_{a,t}^H + G_{a,t}^I + G_{a,t}^R + N_{a,t}$$
$$- T_{a,t}^A - T_{a,t}^Y - T_{a,t}^I - T_{a,t}^R - T_{a,t}^F - C_{a,t}.$$

This can also be written as

$$(7\text{-}57) \qquad S_{a,t} = Y_{a,t}^F + N_{a,t}^R + N_{a,t}^P - C_{a,t}.$$

We added the variable $N_{a,t}^P$, which stands for the net transfers received by cohort a from other cohorts at time t. These transfers can obviously be negative and include bequests, which cannot be negative. At each point in time, private transfers have to meet the constraint $\sum_{a=0}^{a=\bar{a}} N_{a,t}^P = 0$.

The cohort savings does not change with the inclusion of consumption in kind in overall consumption because the amount $G_{a,t}^E + G_{a,t}^H + G_{a,t}^R$ is simultaneously added to both private income and private consumption. These public expenditures items, nonetheless, reduce public savings. Taking into account fiscal redistributions and the life-cycle deficit (LCD),

$$(7\text{-}58) \qquad S_{a,t} = Y_{a,t}^A + N_{a,t}^D + N_{a,t}^R + N_{a,t}^P - LCD_{a,t}.$$

Nonlabor income equals the sum of returns from capital and net financial assets in the cohorts' portfolio. That is,

$$(7\text{-}59) \qquad Y_{a,t}^A = r K_{a,t-1} + r B_{a,t-1} = r W_{a,t-1}^P,$$

where $W_{a,t}^P$ stands for the stock of the a cohort's wealth and $K_{a,t}$ and $B_{a,t}$ are the cohort holdings of capital and bonds issued by the government, respectively. To simplify, we assume a constant and equal rate of return for both assets. The "savings ratio" of the a cohort can then be defined as $\sigma_{a,t} = \dfrac{S_{a,t}}{X_{a,t}y_t} = \dfrac{s_{a,t}}{y_t}$, or

$$(7\text{-}60) \qquad \sigma_{a,t} = r\, \omega_{a,t-1}^P \frac{(1+x_t)}{(1+g)(1+x_{a,t})} + \eta_{a,t}^D + \eta_{a,t}^R + \eta_{a,t}^P - \delta_{a,t},$$

where $\omega_{a,t}^P = \dfrac{W_{a,t}^P}{X_{a,t}y_t} = \dfrac{w_{a,t}^P}{y_t}$ is the a cohort's "wealth ratio"; the ratio between the a cohort's per capita wealth and aggregate per capita income and x_t and $x_{a,t}$ are the rates of growth of the total population and the population of age a, respectively. Note that $\frac{(1+x_t)}{(1+x_{a,t})} = \frac{u_{a,t-1}}{u_{a,t}}$. Consequently, if cohort $a*$'s population is growing faster than the total population, *ceteris paribus*, it will be necessary to increase the cohort savings ratio to maintain the cohort's wealth ratio, and this might have consequences in terms of demands for fiscal redistributions—that is, in terms of demands for changing $\eta^D_{a,t}$ in favor of cohort $a*$.

In order to calculate the evolution of the stock of wealth of each cohort over time, it is useful to identify the cohorts. We do so according to its age at $t=0$. Therefore, $a_{0,t}$ will be the cohort of age a at $t=0$. The age of cohort a_0 at time t is equal to $a_0 + t$. The wealth at time t of the cohort that was a_0 years old at time $t=0$ will then be denoted as $W^P_{a_0,t}$. It increases on the basis of savings: $W^P_{a_0,t} = W^P_{a_0,t-1} + S_{a_0,t}$. Given that the maximum age is $\bar{a}$, $W^P_{a_0,t} = 0$ for $a_0 + t \geq \bar{a}$. This is also true for all the budget variables corresponding to those cohorts that meet this condition.[16] If we scale per capita wealth by per capita income, the cohort's wealth evolves according to

$$(7\text{-}61) \qquad \omega^P_{a_0,t} = \omega^P_{a_0,t-1} \frac{(1+x_t)}{(1+g)(1+x_{a,t})} + \sigma_{a_0,t}$$

$$= \omega^P_{a_0,t-1}(1+\lambda^a_t) + \eta^D_{a_0,t} + \eta^R_{a_0,t} + \eta^P_{a_0,t} - \delta_{a_0,t},$$

where

$$(7\text{-}62) \qquad (1+\lambda^a_t) = \frac{(1+r)(1+x_t)}{(1+g)(1+x_{a,t})}.$$

Note that the higher $x_{a,t}$ is, the lower the growth rate of the a cohort's per capita wealth will be. This introduces a bias against social strata with higher birth rates, which are usually the poor. It follows that to maintain the wealth ratio of these strata, fiscal redistributions should be biased in their favor. That said, to focus on the linkages between wealth dynamics and fiscal redistributions, for the moment we make the simplifying assumption that $x_{a,t} = x_t$. Consequently, at point $t = N$, the a_0 cohort's wealth will be

$$(7\text{-}63) \qquad \omega^P_{a_0,N} = \left((1+\lambda)^N \omega^P_{a_0,0} + \sum_{t=1}^{N}(1+\lambda)^{N-t}(\eta^D_{a_0,t} + \eta^R_{a_0,t} + \eta^P_{a_0,t} - \delta_{a_0,t}) \right).$$

---

[16] We establish the convention that $a_0 < 0$ for the cohorts that are unborn at $t=0$. So, for example, for those who are born two years after $t=0$, the "age" at $t=0$ will be $a_0 = -2$. In this way, $\omega^P_{40,9}$ is the aggregate wealth of those who are 49 years old at period 9, while $\omega^P_{-2,9}$ is the wealth of those who are 7 years old at $t=9$.

Expressed in present value terms,

(7-64) $\omega_{a_0,N}^p (1+\lambda)^{-N} = \omega_{a_0,0}^p + \sum_{t=1}^{N}(1+\lambda)^{-t}(\eta_{a_0,t}^D + \eta_{a_0,t}^R + \eta_{a_0,t}^P - \delta_{a_0,t})$.

Assuming that it is not possible to leave unpaid debts and that the members of each cohort consume or transfer to the members of other cohorts all their wealth before dying, we can write $\omega_{a_0,N}^p = 0$ for $N \geq \bar{a} - a_0$. It follows that $\omega_{a_0,\bar{a}-a_0}^p = 0$ and, consequently,[17]

(7-65) $(1+\lambda)^{\bar{a}-a_0}\, \omega_{a_0,0}^p = -\sum_{t=1}^{\bar{a}-a_0}(1+\lambda)^{\bar{a}-a_0-t}(\eta_{a_0,t}^D + \eta_{a_0,t}^R + \eta_{a_0,t}^P - \delta_{a_0,t})$.

This expression in present value is $\omega_{a_0,0}^p = -\sum_{t=1}^{\bar{a}-a_0}(1+\lambda)^{-t}(\eta_{a_0,t}^D + \eta_{a_0,t}^R + \eta_{a_0,t}^P - \delta_{a_0,t})$.

This implies that at time $t = 0$, given the planned bequest, the higher the value of the expected stream of fiscal redistributions is, the higher the planned value of the life-cycle deficit can be. For this reason, the generosity of the social security system could negatively affect the incentives for saving. However, given the planned value for $\delta_{a_0,t}$, the value of the fiscal redistributions and of other fiscal transfers directly contribute to determining the value of the bequests that each generation will leave, which are included in $\sum_{t=1}^{\bar{a}-a_0}(1+\lambda)^{\bar{a}-a_0-t}\,\eta_{a_0,t}^P$.

In sum, if any kind of transfer favors generation a_0^*, this generation will be able to run a higher lifecycle deficit and/or leave larger bequests. But we must take into account that private wealth may be unequally distributed within the a_0^* cohort. In the case of the members of the a_0 cohort who are wealthy, it is expected that both $\omega_{a_0,0}$ and bequests (in the form of $\eta_{a_0,t}^P$) will be large. If, as Piketty (2014) argues for the case of various developed countries, $r > g$ (and therefore $\lambda > 0$), we would expect the wealth ratio ($\omega_{a_0,0}^p$) of the wealthy to grow faster even if they run an elevated lifecycle deficit. We discuss this point further in the next section.

Following NTA terminology, we define the present value of cohort a's "lifecycle demand for wealth" (π) at time $t = 1$ as

(7-66) $\pi_{a_0,0} = \sum_{t=1}^{\bar{a}-a_0}(1+\lambda)^{-t}\delta_{a_0,t}$,

and consequently, using (7-65) in present value terms,

(7-67) $\pi_{a_0,0} = \omega_{a_0,0}^p + \sum_{t=1}^{\bar{a}-a_0}(1+\lambda)^{-t}(\eta_{a_0,t}^D + \eta_{a_0,t}^R + \eta_{a_0,t}^P)$.

This means that the a_0 cohort's demand for lifecycle wealth will be satisfied with the cohort's own wealth, fiscal redistributions, and other public or private transfers, which of course could be either positive or negative. For example, in the case of the

---

[17] We assume that the unborn do not own assets, so wealth is also zero for $N + a_0 < 0$.

wealthy we expect bequests to be large and to take the form not only of physical and financial assets but also of transfers to finance the accumulation of human capital.

2.3.2 Aggregation and the Macroeconomy

The evolution of the stock of wealth and of the demand for lifecycle wealth of each a_0 cohort is central to the analysis of the effects of fiscal redistributions on the allocation of wealth across generations. However, to study the consequences of the interactions between fiscal redistributions and the cohorts' behavior for macroeconomic equilibrium and the fiscal accounts, it is necessary to know the total amount of savings generated by all cohorts at each point in time and the stock of private wealth as well. We examine this macroeconomic dimension next.

The first step will be to obtain an expression for the overall propensity to save (σ_t^P). To that end, we have to aggregate the savings of all cohorts. Considering that the sum of private transfers adds up to zero, we can write

$$(7\text{-}68) \qquad \sigma_t^P = \frac{S_t^P}{Y_t} = \sum_{a=0}^{\bar{a}} \left(r\omega_{a,t-1}^P \frac{(1+x_t)}{(1+g)(1+x_{a,t})} + \eta_{a,t}^D + \eta_{a,t}^R - \delta_{a,t} \right) u_{a,t};$$

$$(7\text{-}69) \qquad \sigma_t^P = \frac{r\omega_{t-1}^P}{1+g} + \eta_t^D + \eta_t^R - \delta_t.$$

According to (7-68), the overall propensity to save is a function of fiscal redistributions and the demographic transition. Demography operates through three channels. The first is the private sector's behavioral profiles associated with nonlabor income ($r\omega_{a,t}^P$) and the life-cycle deficit ($\delta_{a,t}$). These variables are a function of the cohort's age, the behavior concerning bequests, and the features of the social security system. These two latter factors influence the incentives to accumulate wealth. The second has to do with fiscal redistributions, which also change according to age and the features of social protection policies, taxes, and the social security system. The third is the weight of each cohort's population in the total population, which is expected to change as the economy goes through the different stages of the demographic transition.

The overall private sector wealth constraint at time t results from the aggregation of the individual wealth of all cohorts:

$$(7\text{-}70) \qquad \omega_t^P = \frac{W_t^P}{Y_t} = \sum_{a=0}^{\bar{a}} \left(\frac{\omega_{a,t-1}^P}{(1+g)} u_{a,t-1} + \sigma_{a,t} u_{a,t} \right) = \frac{\omega_{t-1}^P}{1+g} + \sigma_t^P.$$

Using this expression and taking into account that we assume that the private sector does not own natural resources, we can state the aggregate savings ratio as

$$(7\text{-}71) \qquad \sigma_t^P = \frac{r\kappa_{t-1}^P + r\tilde{b}_{t-1}^P}{(1+g)} + \eta_t^D + \eta_t^R - \delta_t,$$

where kappa, the private "capital/output ratio," is defined as $\kappa_t^P = \dfrac{k_t^P}{y_t}$, and $\tilde{b}_t^P = \dfrac{b_t^P}{y_t}$ are the public bonds held by all cohorts in relation to GDP. We can see the way in which fiscal redistributions enter the picture if we write the aggregate wealth ratio in terms of savings components:

$$(7\text{-}72) \qquad \omega_t^P = \sum_{a=0}^{\bar{a}} [(1+\lambda)\omega_{a,t-1}^P u_{a,t-1} + (\eta_{a,t}^D + \eta_{a,t}^R - \delta_{a,t})u_{a,t}].$$

As was mentioned above, $u_{a,t}$ is expected to change substantially over the demographic transition, changing the group's wealth ratios. The aggregate private sector's wealth ratio can be written more synthetically as

$$(7\text{-}73) \qquad \omega_t^P = \frac{(1+r)}{1+g}\omega_{t-1}^P + \eta_t^D + \eta_t^R - \delta_t,$$

and

$$\kappa_t^P + \tilde{b}_t^P = (1+\lambda)(\kappa_{t-1}^P + \tilde{b}_{t-1}^P) + \eta_t^D + \eta_t^R - \delta_t$$

Solving this difference equation, we have

$$(7\text{-}74) \qquad \kappa_N^P + \tilde{b}_N^P = (\kappa_0^P + \tilde{b}_0^P)(1+\lambda)^N + \sum_{t=1}^{N}(1+\lambda)^{N-t}(\eta_t^D + \eta_t^R - \delta_t).$$

In present value terms

$$(7\text{-}75) \qquad (\kappa_N^P + \tilde{b}_N^P)(1+\lambda)^{-N} = \kappa_0^P + \tilde{b}_0^P + \sum_{t=1}^{N}(1+\lambda)^{-t}(\eta_t^D + \eta_t^R - \delta_t).$$

Assuming rationality and the no-Ponzi game condition, and taking $lim_{N\to\infty}$, we have

$$(7\text{-}76) \qquad \kappa_0^P + \tilde{b}_0^P = \sum_{t=1}^{\infty}(1+\lambda)^{-t}(\delta_t - \eta_t^D - \eta_t^R)$$

The aggregate wealth of the private sector must equal the present value of the lifecycle deficit net of public interventions.

And in terms of the aggregate private sector's lifecycle wealth (π),

$$(7\text{-}77) \qquad \pi_0 = \kappa_0^P + \tilde{b}_0^P + \sum_{t=1}^{\infty}(1+\lambda)^{-t}(\eta_t^D + \eta_t^R).$$

Given $\omega_0^P = \kappa_0^P + \tilde{b}_0^P$, the greater π_0 is, the higher the cohort's demand for public transfers and the provision of public goods will be. In particular, in an aging society we expect π_0 to be higher than in a young one. Consequently, if accumulated private wealth is low and the society is aging, there will be an increasing pressure on η_t^D via the social security system, and a substantial trade-off between η_t^D and η_t^R might arise. In any case, there is likely to be pressure on public primary expenditures and the primary deficit. However, beyond the financial difficulties associated with a higher deficit, it will not be possible to satisfy the private sector's demands if accumulated wealth is insufficient. In order to analyze this point we have to introduce the government's wealth constraint.

If the markets for bonds ensure that

$$(7\text{-}78) \qquad\qquad \tilde{b}_t = \tilde{b}_t^P,$$

we can state the national aggregate wealth ratio for the case of the closed economy (ω) as

$$(7\text{-}79) \qquad \omega_0 = \kappa_0^P + \kappa_0^G + p_0\varsigma_0^G = \sum_{t=1}^{\infty}(1+\lambda)^{-t}\delta_t = \pi_0.$$

That is, beyond public redistributions, existing national wealth should suffice to cover the present value of the stream of future lifecycle deficits. Note that $\kappa_0^G + p_0\varsigma_0^G = \pi_0 - \kappa_0^P$, which means that public wealth is used to finance the portion of the demand for lifecycle wealth that cannot be covered by private wealth. Hence, when publicly owned enterprises exploit natural resources, such resources can easily be consumed in a nonoptimal and/or inequitable way if the social security system is ill-designed. Note that if $\hat{p}_t > 0$ ($\hat{p}_t < 0$), the public sector will have a net gain (loss) of wealth, which will be symmetrical to the loss (gain) of the private sector. Since there is no wealth creation, the overall restriction (7-79) still holds. If we included the rest of the world, however, there would be a net gain (loss) for the national economy.

3 Fiscal Redistributions and Income Strata

So far, we have analyzed the budgetary consequences of fiscal redistributions without distinguishing between income strata. The main purpose of this section is to include the income strata in the methodological framework. We identify the strata with the subscript d, which can be interpreted, for example, as deciles or quintiles, or low income and high income. The effect of fiscal redistributions for the case of income group d at time t ($N_{d,t}^D$) will be

$$(7\text{-}80) \qquad N_{d,t}^D = G_{d,t}^O + G_{dt}^A + G_{d,t}^I + G_{d,t}^E + G_{d,t}^H - T_{d,t}^A - T_{d,t}^Y - T_{d,t}^I - T_{d,t}^F.$$

Whether the sign of $N_{d,t}^D$ is positive or negative for a specific stratum is central to assessing the overall impact of redistributions. If $N_{d^*,t}^D < 0$, the stratum d^* will be contributing to finance aggregate fiscal redistributions. This means that the Final Income will be higher for those income groups that benefit from fiscal redistributions and lower for the groups that contribute to financing such policies because $Y_{d,t}^F = Y_{d,t}^M + N_{d,t}^D$. In order to assess the impact of specific fiscal redistributions, a common strategy is to compare the value of the Gini coefficient before the intervention (i.e., calculated on the basis of $Y_{d,t}^M$) with the value of that coefficient after the intervention (i.e., calculated on the basis of $Y_{d,t}^F$). If the former is higher, we can say that the public redistribution is progressive.

If the total number of strata is $\bar{d}$, it is possible to implement a policy for which $N_{d,t}^D \geq 0; \forall d$ and, therefore, $\sum_{d=1}^{\bar{d}} N_{d,t}^D > 0$. One would expect that this type of redistribution would face less resistance, but it could have negative effects on fiscal sustainability or distortionary effects on the allocation of the fiscal space, as we have already discussed. Additionally, it is important to evaluate the incidence of all the components included in $N_{d,t}^D$, especially when the policy seeks to protect the poor or can impinge differently on distinct cohorts. For example, protection policies that are targeted to curb poverty could be judged to be satisfactory because in the case of those below the poverty line, $G_{d,t}^O + G_{dt}^A + G_{d,t}^I + G_{d,t}^E + G_{d,t}^H > 0$. But when the incidence of indirect taxes is high on the poor (particularly consumption taxes), $N_{d,t}^D$ might become negative for those individuals with an income that falls below the poverty line, which means that the poor will contribute to financing fiscal redistributions in net terms.[18] And this may occur even if the fiscal intervention is progressive in the sense that $N_{d,t}^D < 0$ for the highest income levels.

We maintain the convention of using lowercase letters for variables expressed in per capita terms ($X_{d,t}$ will stand for the number of people in the group under consideration) and Greek letters for ratios with respect to aggregate income. Therefore, for example, $\psi_{d,t}^M$ is the pretax share of group d's per capita income in aggregate per capita income, which is equal to the sum of the participation of the group's per capita labor income ($\gamma_{d,t}$) and nonlabor income ($\varepsilon_{d,t}^p$) in aggregate per capita income—that is,

$$\psi_{d,t}^M = \frac{y_{d,t}^M}{y_t} = \frac{y_{d,t}^L + y_{d,t}^A}{y_t} = \gamma_{d,t} + \varepsilon_{d,t}^p.$$

A straightforward way to compare the effects of the set of existing fiscal redistributions on the Market Incomes of two specific groups is to calculate the ratio of the income shares of the two groups before and after fiscal redistributions. More specifically, consider two groups: high income ($d=h$) and low income ($d=l$). We can say that the existing fiscal redistributions favor group l over group h if $\dfrac{\psi_{h,t}^M}{\psi_{l,t}^M} > \dfrac{\gamma_{h,t} + \varepsilon_{h,t}^p + \eta_{h,t}^D}{\gamma_{l,t} + \varepsilon_{l,t}^p + \eta_{l,t}^D}$.

This means that both the labor share and the asset owners' share corresponding to the groups involved are likely to be affected by fiscal redistributions. Of course, the consequences in terms of incentives to invest and work will be different depending on the

---

[18] On this issue see Lustig et al. (2014).

effects of fiscal redistributions on the workers' or the capital owners' shares. Note that income distribution could worsen even though fiscal redistributions are very effective. This could happen if the income share of group h is increasing in relation to group l. Indeed, Stiglitz (2015) identifies a set of new stylized facts that requires explanation, and one of them is that the labor share is worsening. This is also compatible with the facts raised by Piketty (2014).

If $u_{d,t}$ is the share of the total population accounted for by group d, $\left(\dfrac{X_{d,t}}{X_t}\right)$, and $\eta_{d,t} = \dfrac{n_{d,t}^D}{y_t}$ is the ratio between per capita fiscal redistributions and per capita income corresponding to group d, we can write

$$(7\text{-}81) \qquad \eta_t^D = \frac{N_t^D}{Y_t} = \sum_{d=1}^{\bar{d}} \eta_{d,t}^D u_{d,t}.$$

Once we calculate the aggregate value η_t^D, using (7-7) we can obtain the value of the fiscal deficit ($\tilde{d}_t^G$) and show the linkages with income distribution:

$$(7\text{-}82) \qquad \tilde{d}_t^G = r\tilde{b}_{t-1} + \sum_{d=1}^{\bar{d}} \eta_{d,t}^R u_{d,t} + \sum_{d=1}^{\bar{d}} \eta_{d,t}^D u_{d,t} + \iota_t^G - \varepsilon_t^G.$$

And it is possible to assess the macroeconomic consequences in terms of fiscal sustainability using (7-21):

$$(7\text{-}83) \quad \tilde{b}_0 = \sum_{t=1}^{\infty}(1+\lambda)^{-t}\left(\sum_{d=1}^{\bar{d}} \eta_{d,t}^R u_{d,t} + \sum_{d=1}^{\bar{d}} \eta_{d,t}^D u_{d,t} + \iota_t^G - \varepsilon_t^G\right) = -\sum_{t=1}^{\infty}(1+\lambda)^{-t}\tilde{d}_t^{PG}.$$

These expressions show that the overall incidence of the fiscal redistributions as a share of per capita income (η_t^D) depends on both the incidence on the per capita income and the size of each group. For example, the case may be that $\eta_t^D > 0$ is sizable—which means that overall fiscal redistributions use a significant part of the fiscal space—while for the lowest income strata $\eta_{l,t}^D > 0$ but the size of the per capita transfer is meager because $u_{l,t}$ is large, which is the case in young societies. This could be a difficult situation if the tax base is reduced because evasion or elusion is pervasive, or because tax revenues are falling due to aging. Under such circumstances, the tax pressure on those who pay taxes will be too high while the benefits per capita received will be too low. Fiscal sustainability, in turn, could be at risk if initiatives to increase $\eta_{l,t}^D$ were implemented in circumstances in which access to credit is becoming difficult.

However, similar situations can occur because of perverse interactions between demographic factors and the features of the social security system—or when volatile rents of natural resources have an important role in generating fiscal resources to finance $\Delta\eta_t^D > 0$. For example, suppose that during the boom $\Delta\eta_t^D = \Delta\varepsilon_t^G$. If the positive shock is permanent, fiscal sustainability will not be affected. But if it is transitory, to meet the sustainability condition $\lambda b_0 = -\tilde{d}_t^{GP}$, fiscal redistributions should return to their previous values and the burden of the adjustment could be distributed in a more regressive way among the groups because of the urgencies of fiscal adjustment.

If the change in the structure of fiscal redistributions is not large, we can state

$$(7\text{-}84) \qquad \Delta\eta_t^D = \sum_{d=1}^{\bar{d}} \Delta(\eta_{d,t}^D u_{d,t}) \cong \sum_{d=1}^{\bar{d}} (\Delta\eta_{d,t}^D u_{d,t} + \Delta u_{d,t} \eta_{d,t}^D).$$

Note that demographic dynamics enter naturally into the analysis through the variable $\Delta u_{d,t}$. Even if the fiscal authorities established $\Delta\eta_{d,t}^D = 0$ in order to maintain the distributional status quo, $\Delta\eta_t^D$ would not be zero if the participation of each group in total population were changing. For example, this is the case for a state that experiences a mounting fiscal deficit and faces sustainability risks as a consequence of aging, as we have mentioned above. On the other hand, if the condition to be met were $\Delta\eta_t^D = 0$ in order to avoid budgetary imbalances, the changes in $\eta_{d,t}^D$ would have to compensate each other to offset the effects of budgetary changes: $\sum_{d=1}^{\bar{d}} \Delta\eta_{d,t}^D u_{d,t} \cong \sum_{d=1}^{\bar{d}} \Delta u_{d,t} \eta_{d,t}^D$. In this case, if the adjusting variable is, say, the VAT rate, the impact on the poor could be disproportionate.

The disaggregation of fiscal redistributions according to strata may help detect "perverse" distributional effects associated with the existing structure of fiscal redistributions. Consider an economy with a significant presence of informal labor markets. The pension system may also be a source of regressive fiscal redistributions. For example, this might easily happen if the main "redistributive mechanisms" are pension transfers that cover those retired workers who worked in the formal sector in a society that is undergoing the earlier stages of the demographic transition in which poverty is particularly high among the youngest.

3.1 Integrating Distribution and Demography

We now consider simultaneously the linkages between fiscal redistributions, on the one hand, and cohorts and income strata, on the other. We provide some examples that are relevant to the processes of structural change that usually accompany development and demographic transitions. The purpose is to highlight the relevance of having a greater availability of data that consider demography and income strata simultaneously.

We can identify the groups under analysis on the basis of the subscripts that we were using for cohorts and income strata—that is, a and d. Indeed, the main limitation in this regard is not methodological but rather data availability. Nevertheless, it is possible to use the methodology to perform simulation exercises based on partial information and educated guesses.

The net effect of the fiscal redistribution on the Market Income of the group of income level d and age a will be

$$(7\text{-}85) \quad N^D_{a,d,t} = G^O_{a,d,t} + G^A_{a,d,t} + G^I_{a,d,t} + G^E_{a,d,t} + G^H_{a,d,t} - T^A_{a,d,t} - T^Y_{a,d,t} - T^I_{a,d,t} - T^F_{a,d,t},$$

and, consequently, $\eta^D_{a,d,t} = \dfrac{n^D_{a,d,t}}{y_t}$ will stand for the ratio of per capita fiscal redistributions to per capita income corresponding to group of age a and stratum d.

The behavioral parameters that we need for the basic demographic notions must be redefined accordingly. Therefore, ϕ_t, for example, will have to be disaggregated to reflect the behavioral profiles of the different a,d groups: $\varphi_{a,d,t} = \dfrac{c^p_{a,d,t}}{y_t}$; therefore,[19]

$$(7\text{-}86) \qquad\qquad \varphi_t = \frac{C^P_t}{Y_t} = \sum_{a=0}^{\bar{a}} \sum_{d=1}^{\bar{d}} \varphi_{a,d,t}\, u_{a,d,t}.$$

The parameter $\phi_{a,d,t}$ is the share of the economy's overall propensity to consume corresponding to the group a, d at time t. Under these conditions, the overall propensity to consume at time t will be a function of both the demographic structure and the distribution of consumption among income strata because it depends on $u_{a,d,t}$ and $\phi_{a,d,t}$.

Following the same logic, the labor income of the a, d group ($Y^L_{a,d,t}$) can be aggregated to obtain the aggregate labor income: $Y^L_t = \sum_{a=0}^{\bar{a}} \sum_{d=1}^{\bar{d}} Y^L_{a,d,t}$. The share of group a, d labor income in total per capita labor income is $\gamma_{a,d,t} = \dfrac{y^L_{a,d,t}}{y^M_t}$, and, therefore, the overall participation of labor in aggregate income will be

$$(7\text{-}87) \qquad\qquad \gamma_t = \frac{Y^L_t}{Y_t} = \sum_{a=0}^{\bar{a}} \sum_{d=1}^{\bar{d}} \gamma_{a,d,t}\, u_{a,d,t}.$$

The nonlabor income part of Market Income, in turn, will be $Y^A_t = \sum_{a=0}^{\bar{a}} \sum_{d=1}^{\bar{d}} Y^A_{a,d,t}$, and then it follows that

---

[19] The overall propensity to consume can also be expressed as $\varphi_t = \sum_{a=0}^{\bar{a}} \varphi_{a,t}\, \mu_{at} = \sum_{d=1}^{\bar{d}} \varphi_{d,t}\, u_{dt}$ where: $\varphi_{a,t} = \sum_{d=1}^{\bar{d}} \varphi_{a,d,t}\, \dfrac{x_{a,d,t}}{x_{a,t}}$ and $\varphi_{d,t} = \sum_{a=0}^{\bar{a}} \varphi_{a,d,t}\, \dfrac{x_{a,d,t}}{x_{d,t}}$.

$$(7\text{-}88) \qquad \varepsilon_t^p = \frac{Y_t^A}{Y_t} = \sum_{a=0}^{\bar{a}} \sum_{d=1}^{\bar{d}} \varepsilon_{a,d,t}^p u_{a,d,t},$$

with $\varepsilon_{a,d,t}^p = \dfrac{y_{a,d,t}^A}{y_t}$. One important implication of (7-93) and (7-94) is that labor and nonlabor shares are not independent of the demographic transition because of the influence of $u_{a,d,t}$.

Once we have $\varphi_{a,d,t}, \varepsilon_t^p$ and $\gamma_{a,d,t}$, it is possible to calculate the main demographic indicators—effective consumers, effective workers, and the lifecycle deficit—and to show the connections between them, on the one hand, and $\eta_{a,d,t}^D$, the fiscal deficit, sustainability and wealth, on the other. In order to do so we must proceed as we have done in the previous sections. It is also possible to evaluate the evolution of wealth.

The methodology may also help to call attention to the role of the labor market when interpreting the evolution of demographic variables in a process of development and structural change. The following two indicators are useful in this regard. The first is "employment intensity": $f_{a,d,t} = \dfrac{X_{a,d,t}^e}{X_{a,d,t}}$, where $X_{a,d,t}^e$ stands for the members of the a, d group who are employed. The second is a "wage correction factor": $\tilde{v}_{a,d,t} = \dfrac{v_{a,d,t}}{v_t}$, which shows the relation between the a, d group average wage ($v_{a,d,t}$) and the average wage of the economy (v_t). Using these variables, the per capita labor income of the a,d group can be expressed as $y_{a,d,t}^L = \tilde{v}_{a,d,t} v_t f_{a,d,t}$. The correction factor $\tilde{v}_{a,d,t}$ reflects wage differences between groups determined by disparities in human capital accumulation, labor market failures, and age-related factors, such as experience or the ability to work.

The variable $f_{a,d,t}$ can help examine many factors. The first is the economy's ability to create jobs for the different a, d groups. Second, owing to the influence of demographic factors, we expect $f_{a,d,t}$ to vary significantly across cohorts. But for a given cohort a, we also expect the employment intensity to be correlated with the income level, which in turn tends to be associated with access to the labor market. Third, the social security institutions that determine the retirement date will have a bearing on $f_{a,d,t}$ in the case of older cohorts. Monitoring the evolution of $f_{a,d,t}$ is critical if we take into account that being employed helps to reduce the probability of being poor and that unemployment is typically high in the case of some cohorts that are in a vulnerable position, as in the case of the young.

On the other hand, a favorable evolution of $f_t = \sum_{a=0}^{\bar{a}} \sum_{d=1}^{\bar{d}} f_{a,d,t} u_{a,d,t}$ can be interpreted as an indicator of "positive" overall structural change because it tells us whether employment is increasing faster than the working-age population. If the economy is able to maintain $\Delta f_t > 0$ for a sustained period, the growth process will probably be accompanied by the reduction of unemployment and informality, increasing women's participation and reductions in the share of population below the poverty line. During the so-called demographic bonus—when the growth rate of the working-age population is expected to reach a maximum—it is important that $\Delta f_t \geq 0$. However, a situation in which $\Delta f_t \leq 0$ may easily occur if the investment rate in physical and human capital is low, and it could have deleterious consequences for both inequality and poverty. The income share of the a,d group will increase if the group is doing well vis-à-vis job creation $\Delta f_{a,d,t} > \Delta f_t$ or its human capital endowment is improving fast (and, hence, $\Delta \tilde{v}_{a,d,t}$ is high). These factors can make a particularly important contribution to equity if the dependency rate corresponding to the group is high. Finally, a dynamic evolution of Δf_t can be a blessing for fiscal sustainability because new workers produce income, consume increasing tax revenues, and contribute to financing the social security system, depending on the degree of informality in the labor market. Indeed, it is because of the fact that $\Delta f_t > 0$ over a long period that the so-called demographic window of opportunity, as well as the reduction in economic duality, can contribute to accelerating growth.

4 Concluding Remarks

In this chapter we developed a methodological framework to study the linkages between fiscal redistributions, fiscal sustainability, and the government's wealth constraint. We included demographic factors and income strata and underscored the importance of increasing the availability of data that considers demographic and distributional features simultaneously. We made an effort to show the connections between the NTA and CEQ concepts and suggested possible synergies and directions for further data collection efforts. We also tried to illustrate the implications of the framework in terms of the research agenda on development. In particular, we underscored the importance of the analysis of fiscal sustainability including all public assets in the government's balance sheet, especially natural resources. This is functional to connecting the two usual conceptions of sustainability: the one that is focused on fiscal soundness (Escolano, 2010) and the one that is focused on development (United Nations, 2015). We believe, in this regard, that more research is needed about the role of public wealth including all assets in the government's balance sheet and about the distributional consequences—on income as well as wealth—of policies regarding fiscal sustainability, intergenerational transfers that finance the demand for lifecycle wealth, and the management of publicly-owned natural resources.

We have paid special attention to the case of natural resource–rich developing countries that are going through the first stages of the demographic transition or are enjoying the demographic window of opportunity. One issue that requires more research is volatility. When international prices of natural resources in such countries rise substantially, political forces are likely to press for an increase in N_t^D because of the increment in rents revenues, E_t^G. But prices are volatile and shocks are, more often than not, transitory. Therefore, in the phase in which prices drop, the primary balance will likely worsen, and the previous increases in redistribution policies, N_t^D, will ultimately result in a higher public debt/GDP ratio. Demography and wealth constraints, in turn, enter the picture because greater indebtedness means that the funds to finance fiscal redistributions will be provided by different cohorts, which are not typically favored in the same way by the increase in redistribution policies. The longer the duration of public debt is, the more probable it is that significant intergenerational distributions will be involved.[20] Besides, we have shown that the significance of the additional burden for each cohort will depend not only on the increase in the debt ratio but also on the size of each of the cohorts, the growth rate of the economy, and the proportion of taxpayers and beneficiaries of public spending in each cohort, which, in turn, will be a function of the stage of the demographic transition. Meanwhile, the specific combination of generations' debt burden and debt duration features will influence the market perception of the maximum level of the debt ratio that is considered sustainable and, hence, the government's ability to access credit markets. In order to reduce D_t^{PG} in a period of reduced revenues from rents and weakening fiscal sustainability, the government might try to increase E_t^G by increasing extraction (ΔQ_t^G). This, in turn, would result in a faster depletion of nonrenewable resources, making growth less sustainable.

On the basis of these issues, the following policy implications of the methodological framework deserve mention:

1. Fiscal sustainability tests should be part of any significant initiative involving fiscal redistributions. Policies that do not pass the sustainability tests could undermine the ability of the state to improve income distribution, protect the poor, and create a growth-friendly environment over time, thereby giving rise to socially disruptive phenomena, such as "lost decades."

2. In the case of natural resource–rich countries it is particularly relevant to consider that fiscal redistributions may ultimately deplete the stock of natural resources without ensuring a compensatory accumulation of reproducible capital if they do not take adjusted government savings and capital gains into account.

3. In the context of the ongoing demographic transition, even if the parameters of fiscal redistributions are maintained, the changes in the weight of the different cohorts in the total population will modify the size of fiscal redistributions. This is one important reason why demography must be taken into consideration when designing fiscal redistributions and assessing sustainability. It also matters to income and wealth distribution to the extent that income distribution differs among cohorts.

4. Transfers associated with the social security system are a substantial part of public redistributions and a key determinant of both the lifecycle deficit and the government deficit. The ways in which lifecycle deficits and the demand for the lifecycle wealth of each cohort are financed impinge significantly on the distribution of wealth between the public and the private sectors and across generations as well.

---

[20] See Fanelli (2015).

5. Whether we consider pensions as deferred income or not matters for the distribution of wealth between the public and private sectors and, probably, for public opinion's perception of the significance of public redistributions. Public opinion's misperception can easily result in a demand for lifecycle wealth that cannot be satisfied, given the economy's capacity to accumulate wealth and the restrictions imposed by sustainable development on the trajectory of natural capital.

Acknowledgments

This chapter has benefited from comments by an anonymous reviewer, Nora Lustig, Ramiro Albrieu, and the participants in the *CEQ Handbook* 2020 Workshop, CEQ-UNDESA, November 2017, and the LACEA-CEQ Panel, Latin American and Caribbean Economic Association, November 2017.

References

Dasgupta, P. 2009. "The Place of Nature in Economic Development." *Handbook of Development Economics*, vol. 5, edited by Rodrik D. and M. Rosenzweig. Amsterdam: North Holland.

De la Torre, A., P. Fajnzylber, and J. Nash. 2009. *Low Carbon, High Growth: Latin American Responses to Climate Change. An Overview*. Washington, DC: World Bank.

El Serafy, S. 1989. "The Proper Calculation of Income from Depletable Natural Resources." In *Environmental Accounting for Sustainable Development: A UNDP–World Bank Symposium*, edited by Y. J. Ahmad, S. El Serary, and E. Lutz, 141–62. Washington, DC: World Bank.

Escolano, J. 2010. "A Practical Guide to Public Debt Dynamics, Fiscal Sustainability, and Cyclical Adjustment of Budgetary Aggregates." Washington, DC: IMF Fiscal Affairs Department.

Fanelli, J. M., ed. 2015. *Asymmetric Demography and the Global Economy: Growth Opportunities and Macroeconomic Challenges in an Aging World*. New York: Palgrave MacMillan.

Fanelli, J. M., J. P. Jimenez, and I. Lopez Azcunaga. 2015. "La reforma fiscal ambiental en America Latina. *Documentos de Proyecto*. Santiago de Chile: CEPAL and EUROCLIMA.

Hamilton, K. 2008. "Wealth, Saving and Sustainability." Washington, DC: World Bank.

Hartwick, J. M. 1977. "Intergenerational Equity and the Investing of Rents from Exhaustible Resource." *American Economic Review* 67, no. 5, pp. 972–74.

Hotelling, H. 1931. "The Economics of Exhaustible Resources." *Journal of Political Economy* 39, no. 2, pp. 137–75.

Lustig, N., and S. Higgins (2022). "The *CEQ Assessment*: Measuring the Impact of Fiscal Policy on Inequality and Poverty," chap. 1 in *Commitment to Equity Handbook A Guide to Estimating the Impact of Fiscal Policy on Inequality and Poverty*, 2nd ed., Vol. 1, edited by N. Lustig, 3–55. Brookings Institution Press and CEQ Institute, Tulane University. Free online version available at www.commitmentoequity.org.

Lustig, N., F. Mabile, M. Bucheli, G. Gray Molina, S. Higgins, M. Jaramillo, W. Jimenez, V. Paz Arauco, C. Pereira, C. Pessino, M. Rossi, J. Scott, J. and E. Yañez Aguilar. 2014. "El impacto del sistema tributario y del gasto social sobre la desigualdad y la Pobreza en Argentina, Bolivia, Brasil, Mexico, Peru y Uruguay: un panorama general." Working Paper No 13, Commitment to Equity Institute.

Mason, A., and R. Lee. 2011. *Population Aging and the Generational Economy: A Global Perspective*. Cheltenham, UK: Edward Elgar.

Mason, A., R. Lee, M. Abrigo, and S-H. Lee. 2017. "Support Ratio and Demographic Dividends: Estimates for the World." Technical Paper 2017-1. New York: Population Division, Department of Economic and Social Affairs, United Nations.

Neumayer, E. 2010. *Weak versus Strong Sustainability*. Cheltenham, UK: Edward Elgar.

Piketty, T. 2014. *Capital in the Twenty-First Century*. Cambridge, MA: Harvard University Press.

Stiglitz, J. E. 2015. "New Theoretical Perspectives on the Distribution of Income and Wealth among Individuals: Part I. The Wealth Residual." NBER Working Paper w/21189. Cambridge, MA: National Bureau of Economic Research.

United Nations. 2015. *Transforming Our World: The 2030 Agenda for Sustainable Development*, A/RES/70/1. https://sustainabledevelopment.un.org/content/documents/21252030%20Agenda %20for%20Sustainable%20Development%20web.pdf.

Vincent, J. R., T. Panayotou, and J. M. Hartwick. 1997. "Resource Depletion and Sustainability in Small Open Economies" *Journal of Environmental Economics and Management* 33, no. 3, pp. 274–86.

World Bank. 2011. *The Changing Wealth of Nations: Measuring Sustainable Development in the New Millennium*. Washington, DC: World Bank.

Appendix 7A

Pensions as Deferred Income

The relation between the social security system and fiscal redistributions raises the issue of whether contributory pensions should be considered a form of fiscal redistribution or deferred incomes. Here, we investigate the consequences of conceiving pensions as deferred income. We begin by adding the contributory social insurance old-age pensions net of subsidies ($G_t^{A'}$) to Market Income. In this way we obtain a "corrected" version of Market Income ($Y_t^{M'}$). Two clarifications are in order. First, $G_t^{A'}$ is not considered a transfer from the public to the private sector but is the perception of deferred income by the private sector. For this reason, we do not include the subsidized part of pension transfers (Z_t^A) included in G_t^A, if any. This means, of course, that $G_t^A = G_t^{A'} + Z_t^A$. Second, when adopting this perspective, social security contributions (T_t^A) must be assumed to be mandatory savings. Corrected Market Income is then

(7A-1) $$Y_t^{M'} = Y_t^L + Y_t^A + G_t^{A'}.$$

To calculate corrected Disposable Income ($Y_t^{D'}$), contributions to social security are not deducted from labor earnings because, as was already mentioned, they are assumed to be mandatory savings. But we have to add the subsidized part of pensions to contributory pensions. Consequently,

(7A-2) $$Y_t^{D'} = Y_t^L + Y_t^A + G_t^O + G_t^{A'} + Z_t^A - T_t^Y.$$

Corrected Consumable Income (Y_t^C) is, then

(7A-3) $$Y_t^{C'} = Y_t^L + Y_t^A + G_t^O + G_t^{A'} + Z_t^A + G_t^I - T_t^Y - T_t^I,$$

while corrected Final Income can be stated as

(7A-4) $$Y_t^{F'} = Y_t^L + Y_t^A + G_t^O + G_t^{A'} + Z_t^A + G_t^I + G_t^E + G_t^H - T_t^Y - T_t^I - T_t^F.$$

This means that the corrected version of Disposable, Consumable, and Final Income will be higher than their noncorrected counterparts by an amount equal to $T_t^A + G_t^{A'} + Z_t^A - G_t^A = T_t^A$.

We should correct the expression for the distributive effects of fiscal redistributions in accordance with the new assumptions. In particular, there is now no redistribution via fiscal intervention concerning pensions, with the exception of their subsidized share. Therefore, we define

(7A-5) $$N_t^{D'} = G_t^O + G_t^I + G_t^E + G_t^H + Z_t^A - T_t^Y - T_t^I - T_t^F.$$

The relation between the two concepts, then, is

(7A-6) $$N_t^D = N_t^{D'} + G_t^A - Z_t^A - T_t^A = N_t^{D'} + G_t^{A'} - T_t^A.$$

This means that the fiscal and redistributive effects that will be attributed to fiscal redistributions under the assumption of deferred income may greatly differ from the effects under standard assumptions. The difference depends on the value of $G_t^{A'} - T_t^A$ and the distribution of $G_t^{A'}$ and T_t^A among income strata. The greater the subsidized part of contributory pensions is, the lower the difference between N_t^D and $N_t^{D'}$ will be. Likewise, the difference will be low when the deficit of the social security system ($G_t^A - T_t^A$) is low.

When we look at this issue from an intertemporal point of view, a conceptual discussion is in order. We are assuming that contributory pensions originate in deferred income when in reality social security follows a pay-as-you-go rule. If we cease to record current contributions as part of public revenues but the government still has to pay committed pensions, the current and future primary fiscal deficits will obviously increase. Since $G_t^{A'}$ is assumed to be the return to assets that were previously accumulated by the private sector on the basis of T_{t-m}^A, with $m > 0$, the present value of the future fiscal deficits associated with those payments must be added to the existing public debt. Three issues deserve mention. First, any future pension payment in excess of the normal returns on an annuity that the pensioner could buy in the markets with the funds accumulated at the date of his or her retirement should be considered a subsidy and imputed to Z_t^A. In other words, the payments that will be received in the annuitization phase should reflect only the amount of income that was deferred in the accumulation phase; any payment beyond this is a subsidy. Second, the costs of the increasing longevity risk that a defined payment pension system faces as a consequence of aging should also be considered a subsidy. Third, if we cease recording T_{t+m}^A in the government budget, the private sector will have to cover an increasing part of future pensions due to the fact that, from $t=0$ onward, they will begin to accumulate stocks in their portfolios based on their forced savings, which equals T_{t+m}^A at each period $m \geq 0$. The assets acquired with forced savings should be used, in turn, to buy the annuities at the date of retirement. In this sense, to consider contributory pensions as deferred income is analogous to simulating what the budgetary consequences would be if the government reformed social security and replaced the pay-as-you-go system with one based on the private capitalization of individual contributions. The reform experiences show that at the moment of the implementation of the reform ($t=0$) there is a substantial increase in the primary deficit, which subsequently and gradually disappears. That is, $G_t^{A'}$ shows a downward trend, whereas the assets accumulated in private portfolios on the basis of forced savings show an upward trend. Consequently, from $t=0$ onward, only the falling magnitude $G_{0+m}^{A'}; m \geq 0$ should be recorded in the budget.

To perform sustainability exercises, we need to create a public liability that reflects the present value of the stream of future $G_t^{A'} + Z_t^A$ payments from $t=0$ onward. Taking into account that Z_t^A is already included in $N_t^{D'}$ and that this variable excludes T_t^A, the intertemporal restriction will be

$$(7A\text{-}7) \qquad \tilde{b}_0 = \sum_{t=1}^{\infty}(1+\lambda)^{-t}\left(\varepsilon_t^G - \eta_t^{D'} - \frac{g_t^{A'}}{y_t} - \eta_t^R - \iota_t^G \right)$$

$$= -\sum_{t=1}^{\infty}(1+\lambda)^{-t}\left(\tilde{d}_t^{PG} + \frac{t^A}{y_t} \right),$$

where $\sum_{t=1}^{\infty}(1+\lambda)^{-t}\left(\dfrac{g_t^{A'}}{y_t} + \dfrac{z_t^A}{y_t} \right)$ is the present value of the government liability generated by pension transfers. The liabilities will increase the overall debt burden because the government ceases to receive social security contributions $\left(\dfrac{t^A}{y_t} \right)$. If the fiscal rule is $\tilde{d}^{PG^*} = -\lambda\tilde{b}_0$, the restriction on $\eta_t^{D'}$ will be

$$(7A\text{-}8) \qquad \eta_t^{D'} = \varepsilon_t^G - \tilde{g}^{A'} - \eta_t^R - \iota_t^G - \lambda\tilde{b}_0.$$

And, under the more usual sustainability condition $\tilde{b}_t = \tilde{b}_t^*$, at each point in time the government will have to respect the restriction $\eta_t^{D'} = \varepsilon_t^G - \tilde{g}^{A'} - \eta_t^R - \iota_t^G - \lambda\tilde{b}^*$.

To be sure, the public sector may have accumulated nonfinancial assets using previous contributions to social security. But it is very difficult to identify those assets because, for one thing, public assets are only partially registered and their market value is difficult to assess and, for another, more often than not public accounting does not register what assets—if any—are acquired with the proceeds from social security.

1 Income Strata and Deferred Income

The deferred income assumption may help uncover hidden subsidies. The following example may clarify the issue. Since the difference between $N_{d,t}^D$ and $N_{d,t}^{D'}$ originates in the treatment of contributory pensions, the relevance of such difference is a direct function of the proportion of the population older than 65 years in the income group. Note the $N_{d,t}^D - N_{d,t}^{D'}$ gap. If we consider that pensions are deferred income and group l is favored over group h by fiscal redistributions, it means that $N_{h,t}^{P'} < N_{l,t}^{P'}$. But this is compatible with a situation in which $N_{l,t}^{D'} - N_{h,t}^{D'} < (G_{h,t}^{A'} - T_{h,t}^A) - (G_{l,t}^{A'} - T_{l,t}^A)$. Under these circumstances, the net benefits that group h receives from social security more than compensates for the group's disadvantageous position concerning other transfers and taxes and the group becomes a net winner. If $G_{h,t}^{A'}$ does in fact have a large component of hidden subsidy not registered in $Z_{h,t}^A$, the situation will not be equitable. For example, let us assume that the l group is composed basically of young people and the average age of the h group is much higher. The positive effect of the conditional transfers favoring the young may be more than offset by the effect of pension transfers. If the older are richer than the younger, the overall result is regressive. This type of outcome can be seen in Latin America.

2 Private Wealth and Forced Savings

If we consider T^A as "forced savings," the present value of forced savings is part of the private sector wealth. Therefore, we can write

$$(7A\text{-}9) \qquad \kappa_0^P + \tilde{b}_0^P + \sum_{t=1}^{\infty} (1+\lambda)^{-t} \frac{T_t^A}{X_t y_t} = \sum_{t=1}^{\infty} (1+\lambda)^{-t} \left(\delta_t - \eta_t^{D'} - \frac{G_t^{A'}}{X_t y_t} - \eta_t^R \right).$$

Consequently, forced savings contribute to financing the demand for lifecycle wealth:

$$(7A\text{-}10) \qquad \pi_0 = \kappa_0^P + \tilde{b}_0^P + \sum_{t=1}^{\infty} (1+\lambda)^{-t} \left(\eta_t^{D'} + \frac{G_t^{A'}}{X_t y_t} + \eta_t^R + \frac{T_t^A}{X_t y_t} \right).$$

In turn, we have to subtract the present value of the contributions to the social security system from the fiscal budget. Given that the committed pension payments Z_t are already registered in $\eta_t^{D'}$, we can write

$$(7A-11) \qquad \kappa_0^G - \tilde{b}_0 - \sum_{t=1}^{\infty}(1+\lambda)^{-t}\frac{T_t^A}{X_t y_t} = \sum_{t=1}^{\infty}(1+\lambda)^{-t}\left(\eta_t^{D'} + \frac{G_t^{A'}}{X_t y_t} + \eta_t^R\right).$$

3 Demography and Wealth

In terms of pensions as deferred income, $Y_t^{F'} = Y_t^M + G_t^{A'} + N_t^{D'}$ and, consequently, corrected private savings is

$$(7A-12) \qquad \begin{aligned} S_{a,t}' &= Y_{a,t}^M + G_{a,t}^{A'} + N_{a,t}^{D'} + N_{a,t}^R + N_{a,t}^{P'} - C_{a,t} \\ &= Y_{a,t}^{F'} + N_{a,t}^R + N_{a,t}^{P'} - C_{a,t} = S_{a,t} + T_{a,t}^A. \end{aligned}$$

Current corrected private savings is higher than private savings because contributions to social security are considered mandatory savings. $N_{a,t}^{P'}$ are private transfers when pensions are assumed to be deferred income. However, after the current period, the relationship between forced savings and contributory pension payments must be adjusted for the reasons that we have already explained, associated with the fact that, from an intertemporal perspective, the government has a de facto liability that declines over time and the private sector should finance an increasing part of private pensions. Consequently, cohort's a savings ratio with pensions as deferred income will be

$$(7A-13) \qquad \begin{aligned} \sigma_{a,t}' &= r\,\omega_{a,t-1}^p\frac{(1+x_t)}{(1+g)(1+x_{a,t})} + \eta_{a,t}^{D'} + \frac{G_{a,t}^{A'}}{X_{a,t} y_t} \\ &+ \eta_{a,t}^R + \eta_{a,t}^{P'} - \delta_{a,t} = \sigma_{a,t} + \frac{T_{a,t}^A}{X_{a,t} y_t}. \end{aligned}$$

Wealth evolves according to

$$(7A-14) \qquad \begin{aligned} \omega_{a_0,N}^{p'} &= (1+\lambda)^N \omega_{a_0,0}^{p'} + \sum_{t=1}^{N}(1+\lambda)^{N-t} \times \\ &\times \left(\eta_{a_0,t}^{D'} + \frac{G_{a,t}^{A'}}{X_{a,t} y_t} + \eta_{a_0,t}^R + \eta_{a_0,t}^{P'} - \delta_{a_0,t} + \frac{T_{a_0,t}^A}{X_{a_0,t} y_t}\right). \end{aligned}$$

And the lifecycle demand for wealth should be expressed as

$$(7A-15) \qquad \begin{aligned} \pi_{a_0,0} &= \omega_{a_0,0}^p + \sum_{t=1}^{\bar{a}-a_0}(1+\lambda)^{-t}\frac{T_{a_0 t}^A}{X_{a_0,t} y_t} \\ &+ \sum_{t=1}^{\bar{a}-a_0}(1+\lambda)^{-t}\left(\eta_{a_0,t}^{D'} + \frac{G_{a_0 t}^{A'}}{X_{a_0,t} y_t} + \eta_{a_0,t}^R + \eta_{a_0,t}^{P'}\right), \end{aligned}$$

where $\eta_{a_0,t}^{D'}$ and $\eta_{a_0,t}^{P'}$ stands for government redistributions and private transfers adjusted to reflect the changes in the assumptions concerning the social security system. If the period of duration a_0 covers the entire period during which the a_0 cohort accumulated "forced savings" and received pension payments and payments were "fair," the pension payments that the a_0 cohort should receive should be in the amount of

$$(7A\text{-}16) \qquad \sum_{t=-a_0}^{t=0}(1+\lambda)^{-t}\frac{T^A_{a_0,t}-G^{A'}_{a_0,t}}{X_{a_0,t}y_t}=\sum_{t=1}^{\bar{a}-a_0}(1+\lambda)^{-t}\frac{G^{A'}_{a_0,t}}{X_{a_0,t}y_t}.$$

Three points deserve highlighting. First, the total amount of the subsidy in present value at time $t=1$ can be calculated as

$$(7A\text{-}17) \qquad \frac{Z^{A'}_{a_0,1}}{X_{a_0,1}y_1}=\sum_{t=1}^{\bar{a}-a_0}(1+\lambda)^{-t}\frac{G^{A'}_{a_0 t}}{X_{a_0,t}y_t}-\sum_{t=a_0,}^{t=0}(1+\lambda)^{-t}\frac{T^A_{a_0,t}-G^{A'}_{a_0,t}}{X_{a_0,t}y_t}.$$

Obviously, if $\dfrac{Z^{A'}_{a_0,1}}{X_{a_0,1}y_t}<0$, it will be a tax rather than a subsidy. Second, if $r>g$, and the public sector pays the market rate of return on forced savings, it follows that pension payments will absorb a growing amount of per capita income because, *ceteris paribus*, the demand for lifecycle wealth increases with λ. This will tend to crowd out other fiscal redistributions or create the need to increase the tax burden. Third, we are assuming that $\bar{a}$ is constant. However, if $\bar{a}$ increases because of an increase in longevity of the kind that is being observed in advanced economies, the probability that the social security system subsidizes future pensioners will be higher.

To illustrate the linkage between demography and wealth distribution, consider an extreme case in which cohort a_0 is comprised of two groups ($d=h, l$)—the wealthy who own all private wealth ($a_{0,h}$) and are formal workers, on the one hand, and the poor ($a_{0,p}$) who own no wealth at all and participate in the informal labor market because of a lack of human capital, on the other. If we consider that $T^A_{a_0,t}$ are forced savings, from (7-67) it follows that the demand for lifecycle wealth of the wealthy will be

$$(7A\text{-}18) \qquad \pi_{a_0,0,h}=\omega^P_{a_0,0,h}+\sum_{t=1}^{\bar{a}-a_0}(1+\lambda)^{-t}\frac{T^A_{a_0,t,h}}{X_{a_0,t,h}y_t}$$
$$+\sum_{t=1}^{\bar{a}-a_0}(1+\lambda)^{-t}\left(\eta^{D'}_{a_0,t,h}+\frac{G^{A'}_{a_0,t,h}}{X_{a_0,t,h}y_t}+\eta^R_{a_0,t,h}+\eta^{P'}_{a_0,t,h}\right),$$

and for the poor it will be

$$(7A\text{-}19) \qquad \pi_{a_0,0,l}=\sum_{t=1}^{\bar{a}-a_0}(1+)^{-t}\left(\eta^D_{a_0,t,l}+\eta^R_{a_0,t,l}+\eta^P_{a_0,t,l}\right).$$

Under these circumstances, the poor would depend entirely on public and private transfers to finance their demand for lifecycle wealth. But the bequests received by the poor in the form of assets and financing for the accumulation of human capital will probably be very low. Consequently, the members of $a_{0,l}$ could easily get caught in a poverty trap. They do not participate in the formal labor market because of the lack of human capital, and they cannot accumulate human capital and forced savings because they do not participate in the formal labor market and, as a consequence, their income is insufficient. If the coverage of the social security system were reduced or biased in favor of the richer—whose participation in the formal labor market is higher—the prospects for those elderly who are also poor would be discouraging. Forced contributions would accumulate in the pension accounts of the wealthy, increasing formal workers' wealth ($\omega^P_{a_0,t,h}$) over time. Furthermore, if $r>g$, the benefits of forced savings will increase at a higher path than income. The higher the difference between r and g, the lower will be the present value of the lifecycle wealth of the poor ($\pi_{a_0,0,l}$), while the opposite case will hold for the wealthy because, obviously, the value of $\omega_{a_0,0,h}$, will not be affected.

But even if the lowest strata have some wealth, if the poor's birth rate is higher, given the return on capital, the rate of growth of their per capita wealth will be lower (because the effective rate λ' would be lower. Remember that we are assuming $\lambda = \lambda^a$ to simplify). This factor will also favor the generation of poverty traps. Indeed, if $(\eta^{D'}_{a_0,t,h} + \eta^R_{a_0,t,h}) < 0$, a lower present value will favor the wealthy.

Appendix 7B Nomenclature

a	subscript that identifies the cohort
$'$	superscript that states that pensions are considered deferred incomes
$\bar{a}$	oldest cohort
B^G_t	stock of public debt (net)
b_t	government bonds per capita
$\tilde{b}^G_t = \dfrac{B^G_t}{Y_t}$	
B^P_t	public bonds held by the private sector
$\tilde{b}^P_t = \dfrac{B^P_t}{Y_t}$	
$C_{a,t}$	consumption of cohort a
$c_{a,t}$	cohort a's per capita consumption
C^E_t	number of effective consumers in cohort a
d	subscript that identifies the strata
$\bar{d}$	highest strata
D^G_t	fiscal deficit
D^{PG}_t	primary fiscal deficit

$$\tilde{d}_t^G = \frac{D_t^G}{Y_t}$$

$$\tilde{d}_t^{PG} = \frac{D_t^{PG}}{Y_t}$$

E_t^G	total rents from natural resources
$\bar{E}_t^G$	deduction for depletion of natural resources
$f_{a,d,t}$	employment intensity
g	growth rate of GDP
g^n	nominal growth rate of GDP
G_t^A	pension transfers
G_t^E	expenditures in kind related to education
G_t^H	expenditures in kind related to health
G_t^I	indirect subsidies
G_t^R	other public goods
G_t^O	other transfers
h	high income
I_t^G	government investment
K_t^G	government's stock of capital
K_t^P	private stock of capital
l	low income
L_t	number of effective workers
$L_{a,t}$	number of effective workers of the a cohort
$lcd_{a,t}$	per capita life-cycle deficit of the a cohort
LCD_t	life-cycle deficit
m_t	proportion of natural resource depletion subtracted
N_t^D	fiscal redistributions
n_t^D	fiscal redistributions per capita
$N_{a,t}^P$	net transfers received by cohort a from other cohorts
N_t^R	net incidence of other budget items
p_t	natural resource rents
$\hat{p}_t$	rate of growth of rents
Q_t^G	government-owned reserves of natural resources
q_t^G	per capita government-owned reserves of natural resources
r	interest rate
$S_{a,t}$	savings of the a cohort

S_t^G	net government savings
s_t^G	per capita net government savings
S_t^P	private savings
$S_{a,t}$	cohort a savings
SR_t	support ratio
$SR_{a,t}$	cohort a support ratio
T_t^A	employee contributions to social security
T_t^F	fees
T_t^I	indirect taxes
T_t^R	other revenues (including corporate taxes)
T_t^Y	personal taxes
$u_{a,t} = \dfrac{X_{a,t}}{X_t}$	
$v_{a,t}$	average wage
$\tilde{v}_{a,d,t}$	wage correction factor corresponding to group a, d
W_t^G	government wealth
w_t^G	per capita government wealth
W_t^P	private wealth
$W_{a_0,t}^P$	wealth at time t of the cohort that was a_0 years old at time $t=0$
$w_{a,t}^P$	per capita wealth
X_t	total population
$X_{a,t}$	total population of cohort a
x_t	growth rate of the total population
$x_{a,t}$	rate of growth of the population of age a
$X_{a,d,t}^e$	members of the group who are employed
Y_t	GDP
y_t	per capita GDP
Y_t^A	income from accumulated assets
$Y_{a,t}^A$	cohort a income from accumulated assets
$y_{a,t}^A$	cohort a per capita income from accumulated assets
Y_t^C	Consumable Income
Y_t^D	Disposable Income
Y_t^F	Final Income
y_t^F	per capita Final Income
Y_t^L	labor income

$y_{a,t}^L$ cohort a per capita labor income

Y_t^M Market Income

z_t "extra consumption" financed by capital gains

Z_t^A subsidized part of contributory pensions

α_t benefits received from the government

$$\alpha_{a,t} = \frac{G_{a,t}^O + G_{a,t}^A + G_{a,t}^I + G_{a,t}^E + G_{a,t}^H + G_{a,t}^R}{X_{a,t} y_t}$$

$$\alpha_t^D = \frac{G_t^O + G_t^A + G_t^I + G_t^E + G_t^H}{Y_t}$$

$$\alpha_t^R = \frac{G_t^R}{Y_t}$$

β_t tax burden

$$\beta_{a,t} = \frac{T_{a,t}^A + T_{a,t}^Y + T_{a,t}^I + T_{a,t}^F + T_{a,t}^R}{X_{a,t} y_t}$$

$$\beta_t^D = \frac{T_t^A + T_t^Y + T_t^I + T_t^F}{Y_t}$$

$$\beta_t^R = \frac{T_t^R}{Y_t}$$

γ_t aggregate labor share

$$\gamma_{a,t} = \frac{y_{a,t}^L}{y_t}$$

$$\delta_t = \frac{LCD_t}{Y_t}$$

$$\delta_{a,t} = \frac{lcd_{a,t}}{y_t}$$

$$\varepsilon_t^G = \frac{E_t^G}{Y_t}$$

$$\bar{\varepsilon}_t^G = \frac{\bar{E}_t^G}{Y_t}$$

ε_t^p non–Labor Income share

$\varepsilon_{a,t}^p$ cohort a non–Labor Income share

ς depreciation rate of the capital stock

$$\eta_t^D = \frac{N_t^D}{Y_t}$$

$$\eta_t^R \;=\; \frac{N_t^R}{Y_t}$$

$$\iota_t^G \;=\; \frac{I_t^G}{Y_t}$$

$$\kappa_t^G \;=\; \frac{K_t^G}{Y_t}$$

$$\kappa_t^P \;=\; \frac{k_t^P}{y_t}$$

λ effective interest rate

λ^a effective interest rate with $x_t \neq x_{a,t}$

λ^* effective rate in terms of $\hat{P}_t$

$$\xi_t^G \;=\; \frac{Q_t^G}{Y_t}$$

π life-cycle wealth

$$\sigma_t^G \;=\; \frac{S_t^G}{Y_t}$$

$$\sigma_t^P \;=\; \frac{S_t^G}{Y_t}$$

$$\sigma_{a,t} \;=\; \frac{s_{a,t}}{y_t}$$

$$\varphi_{a,t} \;=\; \frac{c_{a,t}}{y_t}$$

ϕ_t aggregate propensity to consume

$$\psi_t^F \;=\; \frac{y_t^F}{y_t}$$

$$\psi_t^M \;=\; \frac{y_t^M}{y_t}$$

$$\omega_t^G \;=\; \frac{W_t^G}{Y_t}$$

$$\omega_t^P \;=\; \frac{W_t^P}{Y_t}$$

$$\omega_{a,t}^p \;=\; \frac{w_{a,t}^p}{y_t}$$

Chapter 8

FISCAL REDISTRIBUTION, SUSTAINABILITY, AND DEMOGRAPHY IN LATIN AMERICA

Ramiro Albrieu and Jose Maria Fanelli

Introduction

When discussing fiscal redistributions—that is, changes in income distribution caused by taxes and expenditures—policymakers tend to focus on two main factors: redistribution effects considering a cross-section of the current population's income levels and the short-run impact on the public budget. More often than not, the intertemporal implications are not systematically evaluated. Two dimensions are particularly relevant with regard to fiscal redistributions: the sustainability of public debt and the consequences for the distribution of wealth among present and future generations.

The literature that considers the intertemporal dimension argues that policy makers need sufficient budget "flexibility" to implement their policies and, in recent years, the concept of "fiscal space" has become increasingly popular to assess the degree of flexibility a government enjoys. Heller (2005) defined fiscal space as "room in a government's budget that allows it to provide resources for a desired purpose without jeopardizing the sustainability of its financial position or the stability of the economy" (p. 32). The UN's approach to the notion of fiscal space, in turn, explicitly considers the link between flexibility and fiscal redistribution (Roy, Heuty, and Letouze, 2007). Accordingly, fiscal space is needed in the first place to evaluate the extent to which a government can mobilize resources to combat poverty and achieve sustainable development goals. Ostry et al. (2010) focus on the financial side and define the fiscal space as the difference between an estimated upper limit of public debt (beyond which action would have to be taken to avoid default) and actual public debt, expressed as a percentage of GDP. The upper limit is estimated econometrically. The fiscal space so defined is routinely measured by Moody's Analytics (2011) for a set of developed economies, which are classified into three categories according to the availability of fiscal space.

The notion of fiscal space is useful to evaluate the financial dimension of flexibility, but it leaves aside two factors that are essential to measure the degree of flexibility that a government has to sustain a given fiscal redistribution structure in the face of a shock or to introduce changes in such structure.

The first factor is the combination of taxes and expenditures—that is, the fiscal redistribution structure—associated with the primary surplus required to ensure debt sustainability. This is crucial when evaluating the degree of flexibility to achieve the required primary surplus without jeopardizing the results sought concerning poverty or distribution. Under certain conditions, intertemporal financial stability restrictions and fiscal redistributions can interact perversely. On the one hand, when a negative shock occurs, say, a fall in the terms of trade, and debt sustainability is under scrutiny, the authorities may have to implement "adjustments" in taxes and expenditures to increase the primary fiscal balance and thus strengthen its creditworthiness. The adjustments often have a negative distributional impact that weakens the progressivity of the existing fiscal redistribution structure. This is why, in evaluating different options to ensure sustainability, it is crucial to include an assessment of the distributional effects of changes in the level and composition of the taxes and expenditures that make up the structure of fiscal redistributions. On the other hand, when launching an initiative to improve income distribution and/or combat poverty that changes the structure of fiscal redistribution permanently, the fiscal authorities should routinely check for debt sustainability. In the special case of natural resource–rich countries, it is important to consider the extent to which fiscal revenues depend on such resources. Marked budgetary imbalances may appear as a consequence of shocks in commodity prices that provide funds to finance the existing structure of fiscal redistributions. This is particularly so when symptoms of the so-called natural resource curse (the phenomenon of countries with an abundance of natural resources having worse development outcomes than countries with fewer natural resources) are present. Furthermore, it goes without saying that flexibility concerning the choice of the tax/expenditure mix has a bearing on the political economy equilibrium and, consequently, it matters to determine the maximum primary fiscal balance that is politically feasible.

The demographic transition is the second factor that matters to the link between intertemporal constraints and the fiscal redistribution structure. Unexpected, undesired redistributions of wealth across generations may occur when fiscal redistributions—especially those implemented through a social security system—do not properly consider the constraints posed by the demographic transition. One main reason for this is that as the demographic transition evolves and the weight of each cohort in the population changes, the overall tax/expenditure mix also changes because such mixes differ from one cohort to another. This induces endogenous changes over time, first, in the fiscal redistribution structure and, second, in the size of the primary fiscal balance, modifying the available fiscal space.

When the fiscal redistribution structure does not take demographic changes into account and, as a consequence, has a bias in favor of the current cohorts, market participants may foresee potential debt sustainability problems because of the difficulty of garnering political support for reforms that favor future generations to the detriment of the current ones. Consequently, the observed primary fiscal balance may tend to fall systematically lower than the one that is consistent with a sustainable public debt. This means that the fiscal space becomes partially determined by the stages of the demographic transition. Although that issue goes beyond the scope of this chapter, it is important to consider that demography can also change the upper debt limit and change the availability of fiscal space because of endogenous changes in the size and composition of private portfolios. For example, as aging approaches, the demand for financial instruments to allocate savings tends to increase.

In sum, we can say that a government has sufficient flexibility—or fiscal space—if it is able to run a primary surplus that is higher than the one required to ensure debt sustainability while maintaining a structure of fiscal redistributions that is consistent with its distributional goals. In assessing the degree of flexibility, it is crucial to take into account the endogenous changes in fiscal redistributions induced by the demographic transition.

The main purpose of this chapter is to investigate the links between fiscal space, fiscal redistributions, and distributional outcomes for the case of Latin America. We highlight two factors. The first is the intertemporal dimension. It plays an essential role because the definition of fiscal space introduces debt sustainability into the analysis, but we also take into consideration the demographic transition's influence on the fiscal redistribution structure. The second factor is the structure of fiscal redistributions, which is essential to evaluate the distributional effects of the intertemporal dimension of fiscal policies.

In the empirical work, we define fiscal flexibility following the fiscal space approach. To this end we state an exogenous debt to GDP limit and define the fiscal space as the difference between the primary fiscal balance/GDP ratio that is intertemporally consistent with such a limit and the observed primary fiscal balance/GDP ratio. By "observed" we mean either the actual balance or the one that results from a simulation exercise. We explore how the changes in the primary fiscal balance, the structure of fiscal redistributions, and the demographic transition influence government flexibility and impinge on income distribution as measured by the Gini coefficient.

To establish the links between the primary fiscal balance, the mix of taxes and expenditures that make up the fiscal distribution structure, and the effects of the demographic transition, we use the methodology presented in Fanelli (2022), which is designed to take advantage of the information provided by two relatively new sources of data developed by the Commitment to Equity (CEQ) Institute on fiscal redistributions and the National Transfer Accounts (NTA) project on the economic effects of the demographic transition. For fiscal data we use the International Monetary Fund (IMF) and Economic Commission for Latin America and the Caribbean (ECLAC) databases

(IMF, n.d; ELAC, n.d.). We work with a sample of 16 Latin American countries, which were chosen for the availability of the data.

The rest of the chapter is organized as follows. Section 1 defines the structure of fiscal redistributions and explores their relationship to income distribution in a set of Latin American countries. The main objective is to study the data provided by the CEQ database from a macroeconomic perspective that seeks to assess the empirical relevance of the issues that we raised previously and identify a set of stylized facts. Section 2 analyzes fiscal flexibility, discusses its linkages with the fiscal redistribution structure, and performs simulations to evaluate the impact of shocks and adjustment patterns on the fiscal space and the Gini coefficient. Section 3 examines long-term fiscal pressures via the changes in the population structure and its effects on the fiscal primary balance, fiscal sustainability, and income distribution. Section 4 concludes.

1 Fiscal Policy and Redistribution Outcomes

In this section, we first present a framework showing the relationship between the taxes and expenditures that make up the fiscal redistribution structure and the primary fiscal balance and then apply the framework to the case of 16 Latin American countries. We study the composition of the fiscal redistribution structures and the relevance in terms of the GDP and of the Gini coefficient.

1.1 Fiscal Redistribution, Primary Balance, and Fiscal Space

In what follows all variables are defined as ratios to GDP. We represent such ratios with Greek letters. The indicator of *aggregate fiscal redistributions* (η_t^d) that is presented in Fanelli (2018) is based on the CEQ approach (Lustig, 2022; Lustig, Lopez-Calva, and Ortiz-Juarez, 2015), and, consequently, it is defined as the difference between aggregate Market Income (γ_t^M) and aggregate Final Income (γ_t^F) in period t:

(8-1) $$\eta_t^D = \gamma_t^F - \gamma_t^M.$$

Market Income is the sum of market labor income (γ_t^L) and the Market Income stemming from previously accumulated assets (γ_t^A) before taxes. Income from assets includes private transfers such as private pensions and remittances. Hence, Market Income can be written as

(8-2) $$\gamma_t^M = \gamma_t^L + \gamma_t^A.$$

Final Income is calculated by adding the set of fiscal redistribution items as defined by Lustig (2018) to γ_t^M. Concerning the expenditure items, we add contributory pension transfers (ψ_t^A), other monetary transfers (ψ_t^O), indirect subsidies to energy, food, and other general targeted subsidies (ψ_t^I), and expenditures in-kind related to education (ψ_t^E) and health (ψ_t^H). For presentation purposes and owing to data limitations, in some cases we define $\psi_t^{OT} = \psi_t^O + \psi_t^I$. On the tax side, we subtract employee contributions to social security (τ_t^A), personal taxes (τ_t^Y), fees (τ_t^F), and indirect taxes (τ_t^I). We thus obtain

$$(8\text{-}3) \qquad \gamma_t^F = \gamma_t^L + \gamma_t^A + \psi_t^A + \psi_t^O + \psi_t^I + \psi_t^E + \psi_t^H - \tau_t^A - \tau_t^Y - \tau_t^F - \tau_t^I.$$

The *fiscal redistribution structure* can therefore be expressed as

$$(8\text{-}4) \qquad \eta_t^D = \psi_t^O + \psi_t^A + \psi_t^I + \psi_t^E + \psi_t^H - \tau_t^A - \tau_t^Y - \tau_t^I - \tau_t^F.$$

If $\eta^D < 0$, it means that fiscal interventions contribute to easing the budgetary constraint; in contrast, a positive figure indicates that the financing of the redistribution structure requires funds that will be obtained by running a surplus in the remaining budget items and/or increasing indebtedness. The rest of the elements that make up the primary fiscal balance are government investment (ι_t^G), the revenues from government-owned nonfinancial assets (ε_t^G), and a variety of miscellaneous items related to government revenues (τ_t^R) and the provision of public goods (ψ_t^R). For the sake of convenience, we define $\eta_t^R = \psi_t^R - \tau_t^R$. The primary fiscal deficit (θ_t^{GP}) can, then, be defined as

$$(8\text{-}5) \qquad \theta_t^{GP} = \eta_t^D + \eta_t^R + \iota_t^G - \varepsilon_t^G.$$

Note that the decisions concerning η_t^D directly influence the primary deficit. This deficit is a central determinant of debt sustainability to the extent that it equals the government's net borrowing, excluding interest payments on consolidated government liabilities. But, of course, to determine the impact on distribution, it is necessary to identify the value of η_t^D corresponding to each relevant stratum. If d stands for the stratum under consideration and the total number of strata is $\bar{d}$, we can write

$$(8\text{-}6) \qquad \eta_t^D = \sum_{d=1}^{\bar{d}} \eta_{d,t}^D = \theta_t^{GP} - \eta_t^R - \iota_t^G + \varepsilon_t^G.$$

For fiscal redistributions to have a significant impact on distribution, the tax burden and the portion of government expenditures that make up the $\eta_{d,t}^D$ corresponding to each stratum must differ substantially. With regard to $\eta_{d,t}^D$, the CEQ presents country-specific data for a base year. If we use a tilde for the ratio between government expenditures received by the stratum and total expenditures in the base year, $t = b$, and do the same with taxes, we can write

$$(8\text{-}7) \qquad \begin{aligned} \eta_{d,t}^D = {}& \tilde{\psi}_d^O \psi_t^O + \tilde{\psi}_d^A \psi_t^A + \tilde{\psi}_d^I \psi_t^I + \tilde{\psi}_d^E \psi_t^E + \tilde{\psi}_d^H \psi_t^H \\ & - \tilde{\tau}_d^A \tau_t^A - \tilde{\tau}_d^Y \tau_t^Y - \tilde{\tau}_d^I \tau_t^I - \tilde{\tau}_d^F \tau_t^F. \end{aligned}$$

We use this equation to evaluate the distributional impact of the fiscal redistribution structure. To distribute among the strata the amounts corresponding to each of the tax and expenditure items observed in the period under consideration, we will use the base-year coefficients corresponding to the d strata. Based on this, we can estimate approximately the simultaneous effects of shocks—for example, terms of trade shocks—on the fiscal space and income distribution.

As in Lustig (2022), we also use an alternative definition of fiscal redistributions according to which contributions to social security are forced savings rather than a tax, and, consequently, pension payments are considered to be the perception of deferred income rather than government transfers. In this case equation (8-4) becomes

$$(8\text{-}8) \qquad n_t^{D'} = \psi_t^O + \psi_t^I + \psi_t^E + \psi_t^H - \tau_t^Y - \tau_t^I - \tau_t^F = \eta_t^D + \tau_t^A - \psi_t^A.$$

The size of fiscal redistributions under the assumption of deferred income may greatly differ from the effects under standard assumptions. The difference depends on the value of $\tau_t^A - \psi_t^A$, but the redistributive impact, nonetheless, also depends on the distribution of ψ_t^A and τ_t^A among income strata.[1]

1.2 The Structure of Fiscal Redistribution in 16 Latin American Countries

We now use the framework to analyze the data on the structure of fiscal redistributions provided by the CEQ database.[2] Figure 8-1 presents the level and composition of fiscal redistributions as a percentage of GDP (that is, the right-hand side items of equations [8-4] and [8-7]) for the countries under analysis.

From figure 8-1 it follows that n^D is negative, as a rule. Only Argentina and Colombia show a positive value. This means that the structure of fiscal redistributions tends to make a positive contribution to the primary balance according to the CEQ sample.[3] The distributional impact, nonetheless, is largely independent of the value of

---

[1] See Fanelli (2022).

[2] Note that the CEQ data concerning the structure of fiscal interventions do not coincide with the aggregate data provided by the IMF and ECLAC databases on taxes and expenditures. The difference occurs because CEQ data are based on household surveys. In light of this, we have checked the stylized facts that we discuss in this section using the IMF and ECLAC data and find no substantial differences. We comment on any relevant difference. Given that the main goal of this part of this chapter is to examine the characteristics of the CEQ data, when we perform macroeconomic simulations using CEQ base-year coefficients to distribute taxes and expenditures among strata—deciles—we utilize IMF and ECLAC aggregate fiscal data.

[3] If we used FMI and ECLAC data in 10 out of 16 economies, the structure of fiscal redistribution would make a positive contribution to the primary balance, although the contribution is small in some cases.

FIGURE 8-1

Fiscal Redistributions in Latin America, ca. 2010 (% GDP)

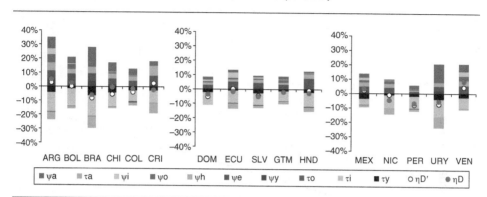

Note: Specific dates for countries are ARG: 2012, BOL: 2009, BRA: 2009, CHI: 2013, COL: 2010, CRI: 2012, DOM: 2013, ECU: 2011, SLV: 2011, GTM: 2011, HND: 2011, MEX: 2010, NIC. 2009, PER: 2009, URY: 2009, VEN: 2013.

η_t^D because a given value of this variable is compatible with different structures of taxes and expenditures. Poorer countries tend to show a negative n^D, as we can see in figure 8-2, although the correlation is low. This probably reflects the fact that expanding the fiscal space is more difficult for poorer countries not only because of the obstacles to increasing the tax burden but also because of the difficulties in accessing credit markets, which limit their ability to run a primary deficit and sustain a larger negative n^D. This suggests that poorer countries will have less ability to implement redistributive policies and to soften the effects of negative shocks while simultaneously sustaining the existing structure of fiscal redistribution. In the case of natural resource–rich countries, which are the richer ones in the sample, the revenues originating in such resources make it easier to finance fiscal redistributions.

In the economies of the sample, indirect taxes account for the largest part of fiscal revenues, and, therefore, they finance a good portion of government expenditures. In some countries, increases in indirect taxes have small effects, but the negative consequences for the poor may still be damaging.[4] Direct taxes, on the other hand, are generally less significant and in all cases much more progressive. On average, indirect tax revenues more than double the revenues from direct taxes.

What about the fiscal redistribution structure from the perspective of the demographic transition in Latin America? A first point to highlight in the CEQ sample is the absence of sizable differences between fiscal redistributions measured in terms of n^D and n^D (see figure 8-1). Nevertheless, in those societies that are undergoing the "bonus" stage of the demographic transition and must prepare for the aging stage—the case of all richer and larger Latin American economies—it is important to monitor closely the future evolution of the social security system deficit ($\psi^A - \tau^A$). Accord-

---

[4] See Lustig (2022).

FIGURE 8-2

Fiscal Redistributions and Per Capita GDP (PPP), ca. 2010 (% GDP)

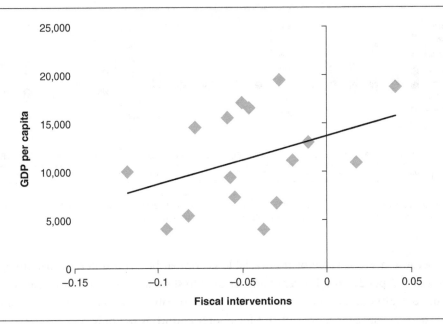

Source: Authors' calculations based on CEQ and World Bank data.

ing to the data, nine out of 16 countries show a deficit in the social security system $(t^A - g^A < 0)$. In addition, some countries, for example, Argentina and Uruguay, spend a significant amount on noncontributory pensions.[5] The consequences can be highly undesirable if the deficit of the social security system is financed by indirect taxes that may have a marked incidence on the poor's budget. In addition, as we will see in the next section, the redistributive effects of the social security system—in terms of the Gini coefficient—can differ substantially from one country to another, depending on the joint incidence of ψ_t^A and τ_t^A on each stratum.

A point that is highly relevant to our analysis of the role of demography in section 3 is that contributory pensions are an important part of government transfers in various countries, particularly in the cases of Argentina, Brazil, and Uruguay.[6] Figures 8-3 and 8-4 show the relationship between the dependency ratio, fiscal redistribution, and expenditures on contributory pensions.

---

[5] See Lustig and Pessino (2013).

[6] This is not surprising because these countries' per capita GDP is high in terms of our sample. We found a high correlation between development and pension expenditures (0.74) in the case of the IMF-ECLAC data.

FIGURE 8-3

Fiscal Redistributions and Dependency Ratios in Latin America, ca. 2010

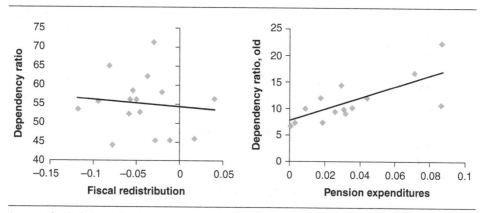

Source: Authors' calculations based on CEQ and World Bank data.

As can be seen, the relationship between fiscal redistribution and the dependency ratio shows no defined pattern, but the relationship between aging and pension expenditures is much clearer: the higher the old dependency ratio is, the higher pension expenditures are. One point should be highlighted: the countries that show a high level of expenditures on pensions are still undergoing the "bonus" stage of the demographic transition, which precedes the aging period. Therefore, the CEQ sample suggests that a problem of "premature" spending on social security may be present in Latin America. Pension transfers can displace other social expenditures that are of critical importance at the "bonus" stage, when the economy has to invest in human capital. Furthermore, we will see that the social security system can have deleterious effects on income distribution if pension transfers tend to favor the richer strata and the social security system runs a deficit, as seems to be the case in Brazil.[7] In fact, a bad combination will occur if fiscal redistributions and expenditures are low—as is the case in poorer countries—and the dependency ratio is high because the country is demographically young. Low government expenditures usually mean low investment in the younger generations' human capital, as well as low investment in infrastructure, which weakens productivity growth.

The CEQ database provides only the base year observation of η_t^D. Consequently, in what follows we use data from the IMF's Government Finance Statistics database and the ECLAC database to examine the evolution of η_t^D over time. Since the ability to sustain a given fiscal redistribution structure is not independent of the macroeconomic situation, and since the mix of taxes and expenditures that make up such

[7] As explained in Higgins and Pereira (2013).

FIGURE 8-4
Evolution of Fiscal Redistribution (% of GDP), 2000–15

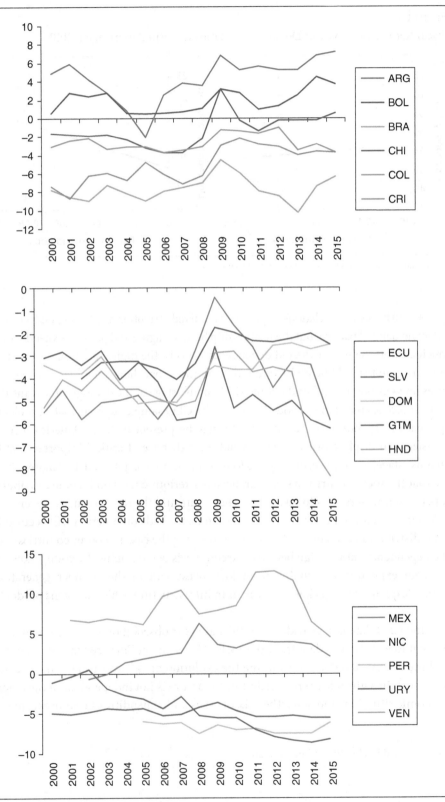

Source: Authors' calculations based on IMF and ECLAC data

structure is influenced by political economy factors, it is natural to expect the macro-economic relevance of η_t^D to vary across time. Figure 8-4 shows the year-by-year evolution of η_t^D from 2000 to 2015.[8]

From figure 8-4 it follows that, in fact, the value of n_t^D is rather volatile in many of the countries under analysis and that the range of variation can be of various percentage points of GDP. A better understanding of why n_t^D is volatile or why it is more stable in some countries than in others could greatly help to improve the sustainability of distribution policies. One aspect that complicates the matter is that n_t^D may change for different reasons. For example, as we will discuss later, n_t^D can change endogenously because of the demographic transition. Likewise, a change in the n_t^D ratio might be the result of initiatives that are not motivated by redistribution goals, such as expenditure cuts or tax increases aimed at reducing the deficit after the occurrence of a negative shock. But, beyond this, n_t^D can also change as a consequence of the implementation of new redistribution initiatives. And, indeed, in the case of Latin America, a positive shock often induces the implementation of redistributive policies, as was the case in the resource-rich countries during the 2000s commodities boom. If the change in the fiscal redistribution structure is permanent and the shock is transitory, the authorities will probably have to launch a fiscal adjustment. Our approach, which assesses debt sustainability and fiscal redistributions simultaneously, may help to avoid or to manage this kind of dynamic. In any case, in-depth understanding of the sources of shocks and the determinants of fiscal redistribution initiatives calls for detailed case studies that go beyond the goals of this study.

1.3 Fiscal Redistribution and Distributive Impact

We can evaluate the distributional impact of the structure of fiscal redistribution in greater detail using the CEQ data. In all the countries under analysis, the existing structure of redistribution improves the Gini coefficient, which is good news given the inequality that is observed in terms of Market Income. However, the magnitude of the reduction differs substantially among the economies in the sample. The maximum impact of the structure of redistribution is observed in Argentina and the minimum in Honduras. The effect observed in the first case is ten times higher. More generally, there is an association between the per capita GDP and the size of the redistribution (see figure 8-5). The correlation coefficient in our sample is 0.7.

The relationship between η^D and the improvement in the Gini coefficient is much weaker than the relationship between this last variable and expenditures. In the sample under consideration, the correlation coefficient is 0.25 in the first case and 0.88 in the second. Something similar can be found in the special case of contributory pensions

---

[8]Note that the CEQ estimates for aggregate fiscal redistribution as a share of GDP may differ from those estimated by the IMF and the NTA.

FIGURE 8-5

Fiscal Redistribution and GDP Per Capita (PPP), ca. 2010 (Contributory Pensions as Current Transfers)

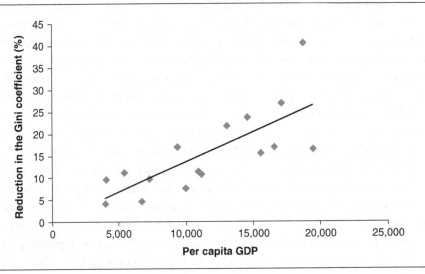

Source: Authors' calculations based on CEQ and World Bank data.

as deferred income (0.20 and 0.82, respectively). In line with these facts, figure 8-6B indicates that those countries that spend more as a percentage of GDP obtain better income distribution results as measured by the Gini coefficient corresponding to the Final Income. The association is weaker in the case of fiscal redistributions, as figure 8-6A shows.

The evidence, then, reveals two facts. First, those countries that have a higher per capita income and can spend more are in a better position to improve equity and combat poverty. Second, many of the countries that managed to increase the expenditure component of fiscal redistributions have also managed to increase tax collection. This follows from the fact that there is no high correlation between η^D and the redistributive impact. Of course, if the ability to match expenditures and tax collection were largely a consequence of the beneficial effects of the commodity super-cycle, we would observe a reduction in the fiscal space as the boom faded and/or a weakening in the positive distribution outcomes that have been observed in the region. In any case, we have shown that η_t^D has a degree of volatility that is macroeconomically significant.

Table 8-1 shows the results of simulating the relationship between the fiscal balance and n_t^D under different periods. For the simulations we draw on the observed changes in fiscal redistributions and the fiscal primary balance over two periods—2005–10 and 2010–15—using the results shown in figure 8-4 and the corresponding data on

FIGURE 8-6
Income Inequality and Fiscal Redistributions

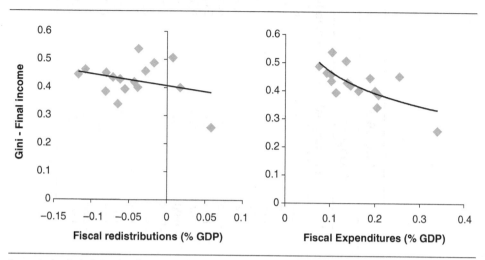

Source: Authors' calculations based on CEQ and World Bank data.

taxes and expenditures. We employ the CEQ base-year coefficients (the set of $\tilde{\psi}$ and $\tilde{\tau}$ in equation [8-7]) to allocate taxes and expenditures to the different strata. Based on this we calculated the Final Income of each strata (deciles) and the distributive impact as measured by the Gini coefficient. To isolate the effects of fiscal redistributions we kept Market Income inequality constant in the simulations. It goes without saying that the main purpose of these exercises is not to make a precise assessment of the actual evolution of income distribution but to illustrate the empirical relevance of one of the points that we have raised: fiscal flexibility, debt sustainability, and distributional impacts should be analyzed jointly.

Beyond the particularities of the relationship between the tax and expenditure components of fiscal redistributions in each of the economies under study, table 8-1 reveals a key stylized fact: changes in fiscal redistributions are quantitatively important. The changes in the components of the structure of fiscal redistribution and in the level of n^D may be of various percentage points of GDP and, therefore, can potentially affect the fiscal space. Nonetheless, empirically, the relationship is not simple. During the first period under consideration, five countries achieved a reduction of more than one point in the Gini coefficient and all of them experienced a significant worsening in the primary balance and an increment in n^D (with one exception in this latter case). In the second period, three countries experienced more than one-point improvement in the Gini coefficient and while two showed a worsening in the fiscal balance and an increase in n^D, one experienced a substantial improvement. For the sample as a whole, there is a low correlation between changes in the Gini Coefficient and the fiscal balance

TABLE 8-1
Fiscal Redistributions, Primary Fiscal Surplus, and Simulated Gini Coefficient

	2005–2010 Change in . . .				2010–2015 Change in . . .			
	Gini	Nd	Primary balance	Expenditures	Gini	Nd	Primary balance	Expenditures
ARG	-0.04	2.56	-2.97	7.39	-0.05	1.47	-4.14	6.45
BOL	-0.01	2.01	1.06	0.36	-0.01	-0.79	-5.01	2.47
BRA	-0.01	2.43	-1.13	1.89	0.00	-0.18	-4.22	2.19
CHI	-0.01	2.70	-5.45	2.41	0.00	0.67	-1.56	1.07
COL	0.00	-0.05	-1.54	-0.20	0.00	-3.18	0.87	-1.06
CRI	-0.02	2.28	-4.94	3.68	0.00	-1.45	-0.04	0.33
DOM	0.00	1.70	-1.72	0.68	-0.02	1.34	3.34	2.08
ECU	-0.03	2.42	-2.39	5.85	-0.01	-3.96	-3.09	0.36
SLV	0.00	-1.58	-1.52	-0.43	-0.01	-0.90	1.71	0.84
GTM	-0.01	2.11	-1.48	1.22	0.00	-0.38	1.93	-0.84
HND	-0.01	1.35	-2.92	1.50	0.02	-5.47	4.08	-2.74
MEX	-0.01	1.39	-1.85	1.47	0.00	-1.03	0.27	0.87
NIC	0.00	-0.70	0.29	0.30	0.00	-1.45	-1.25	0.71
PER	0.01	-1.38	-0.01	-1.23	0.00	0.52	-2.49	0.81
URY	-0.01	-2.35	-1.14	1.69	0.01	-2.60	-1.55	-1.11
VEN	-0.01	4.02	-14.49	2.88	-0.02	-4.94	-8.59	3.83

while the correlation with n^D is higher (0.58). In this regard, we should add that those countries in which the Gini coefficient worsened registered $\Delta n^D < 0$, suggesting that progressive distributional policies tended to be crowded out by other fiscal needs, especially in the cases in which expenditures fell.

The evidence in table 8-1 confirms the importance of public expenditures in accounting for changes in the Gini coefficient. With the exception of one country, expenditures fell in all of the countries showing regressive redistributions, according to our simulations. On the other hand, in the two periods without exception, expenditures increased, and substantially in some cases, in all those countries where the Gini coefficient fell. The case of Argentina is striking. Together with a sizable improvement in the Gini coefficient over the period 2005–15, there was an increase in expenditures of almost 15 percentage points of GDP, which in this case certainly affected the primary balance, although the degree of flexibility was favored by the fact that the debt/GDP ratio was low. There is a high correlation between changes in government expenditures and changes in income distribution. In this sample it is more than 0.9 in both periods.

The upward movements in the tax component of n^D are also important. These movements are especially marked in the period 2010–15. In both periods, all the economies showing more than a one-point improvement in the Gini coefficient experienced an increment in taxes (with the exception of Chile in 2005–10, when they remained constant). This suggests that the redistribution initiatives are bolder when the authorities perceive that it is possible to expand the fiscal space by increasing the tax burden. In those cases in which the change in the Gini coefficient was more modest, the picture is more diffuse.

2 Fiscal Redistributions and Debt Sustainability

In this section we introduce an upper limit for the public debt/income ratio to define an indicator of fiscal flexibility and evaluate its links to the fiscal redistribution structure and distributional outcomes.

If g and r, respectively, stand for the constant rates of growth of GDP and the interest rate on public debt, and we define $\dfrac{1+r}{1+g} = 1 + \lambda$, we can express the recursive equation governing the dynamics of the public debt to Market Income ratio as

$$(8\text{-}9) \qquad b_t = (1+\lambda)b_{t-1} + \eta_t^D + \eta_t^R + \iota_t^G - \varepsilon_t^g.$$

The solution to this equation in present value terms is

$$(8\text{-}10) \qquad (1+\lambda)^{-N} b_N = b_0 + \sum_{t=1}^{N}(1+\lambda)^{-t}(\eta_t^D + \eta_t^R + \iota_t^G - \varepsilon_t^G).$$

This is the intertemporal version of the government's budget constraint. This expression shows that future policies that impinge on the allocation of resources between

$n_t^D, n_t^R,$ and ι_t^G over time, together with the returns from state-owned assets, ε_t^G, will have a bearing on the trajectory of the debt/Market Income ratio. It also shows that the interest rate growth differential λ, which we call the "effective" interest rate, helps determine the path of the public debt. In the simulations we assume that these two variables are either constant at 2 percent and 4 percent, respectively, for all the countries in the sample, or that they equal the average country-specific values, depending on the purpose of the exercise.[9]

For the level of public indebtedness to be sustainable, it is necessary to impose the no-Ponzi-game condition $(\lim_{N \to \infty}(1+\lambda)^{-N} b_N = 0)$; under this condition, the present value of the surpluses that the government plans to run in the future must be equal to the value of the current stock of debt:

$$(8\text{-}11) \qquad b_0 = \sum_{t=1}^{\infty} (1+\lambda)^{-t}(\varepsilon_t^G - \eta_t^R - \iota_t^G - \eta_t^D).$$

In order to meet this constraint, if the government were to implement a fiscal rule to maintain the ratio between the primary deficit and Market Income constant, the primary deficit would have to be

$$(8\text{-}12) \qquad \theta^{PG^*} = -\lambda b_0,$$

because $\sum_{t=1}^{\infty}(1+\lambda)^{-t} = \dfrac{1}{\lambda}$. Under these conditions, at each point in time, the structure of fiscal redistributions that is consistent with the intertemporal budget constraint is

$$(8\text{-}13) \qquad \eta_t^{D^*} = \varepsilon_t^G - \eta_t^R - \iota_t^G - \lambda b_0.$$

At each point in time θ^{PG^*} can differ from θ^{PG}. Therefore, we can define the available fiscal space (χ_t) as

$$(8\text{-}14) \qquad \chi_t = \theta^{PG^*} - \theta_t^{PG}.$$

This means that the maximum flexibility to modify the fiscal redistribution structure is

$$\chi_t = \eta_t^{D^*} - \eta_t^D.$$

Of course, the authorities could set $b_t = b^*$ instead of $b_t = b^*$ as the politically feasible ceiling for the debt/GDP ratio. In the simulations we assume a 60 percent debt/GDP ratio, which is common in the literature (Fatas, 2010) and matches the Maastricht

---

[9]On effective interest rates, see Escolano (2010).

Criteria for the European Monetary Union. For an emerging economy, nonetheless, the World Bank (2017) suggests a limit at 45 percent of GDP.

If $\chi_t < 0$, it means that either the cost of the existing structure of fiscal redistributions or some of the other items in the budget must be reduced because otherwise the government would violate the restriction of keeping the debt/GDP ratio at the desired level. Following IMF (2011), which uses an adjustment threshold of 5 percent of GDP, we distinguish three cases:

- *Fiscal space available:* $\chi_t \geq 0$, (high flexibility to implement η_t^D);
- *No available fiscal space:* $-5\% \leq \chi_t < 0$ (required adjustment below 5 percent of GDP);
- *Unsustainable debt burden:* $-5\% < \chi_t$ (required adjustment above 5 percent of GDP).

Figure 8-7 presents estimates of the available fiscal space for the countries in the sample for three points in time: 2005, 2010, and 2015. We begin by assuming an effective interest rate of 2 percent—similar to that observed in France, Germany, Italy, and other countries in recent decades—and two debt ceilings: $b^* = b_0$ (figure 8-7a) and $b^* = 60\%$ of GDP (figure 8-7b).

By 2015, the only indicator in the unsustainable region corresponded to Venezuela. The rest of the countries were in a better position, although, on average, we can see a worsening in the degree of fiscal flexibility. The available fiscal space in 2005 was, on average, substantially higher than in 2015. Indeed, in 2015, only El Salvador showed some degree of flexibility. The result is basically the same independently of whether the fiscal balance required is calculated on the basis of a debt ceiling that equals the existing debt/GDP ratio or a 60 percent maximum.

How would these results change if we used country-specific effective interest rates in the simulations? In figure 8-8 we address this question. We set g at the country-specific average for 2010–15. For the interest rate, in turn, we calculate the 2010–15 average of the ratio between the interest paid and the stock of public debt of the previous period. Figure 8-8 shows the evolution of the fiscal space between 2010 and 2015. We used $b^* = 60\%$ of GDP.

If we consider the average degree of fiscal flexibility in the region in 2010, the situation concerning flexibility is much better under such metric, as can be seen in figure 8-8a. The fiscal space is much larger in 2010. However, the economies that show better debt-sustainability indicators are mostly those that are natural resource rich—with the striking exception of Venezuela. This may explain why important fiscal redistribution initiatives were launched in the 2000s in many resource-rich countries in the region. By 2015, nonetheless, the fiscal space shrank in a context of lower commodity prices. Fiscal flexibility has, however, improved in some Central American economies.

FIGURE 8-7
Available Fiscal Space (% GDP)

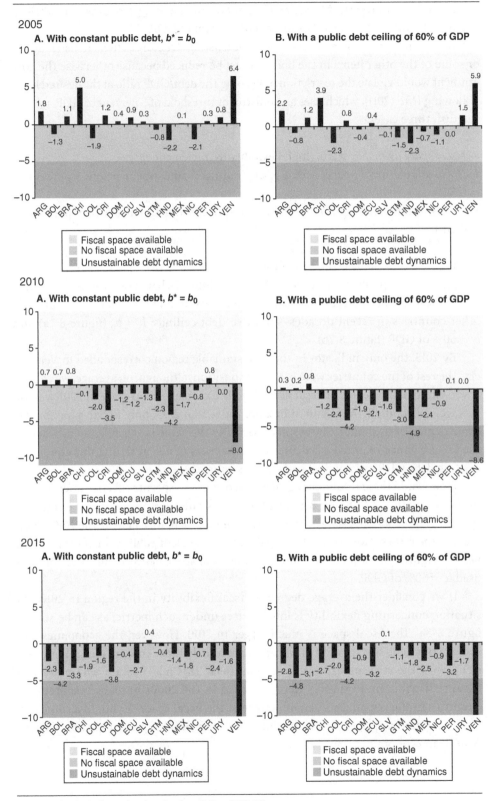

Source: Authors' calculations based on data from IMF and ECLAC.

FIGURE 8-8

Available Fiscal Space with Country-Specific $r - g$ (% GDP) (Public Debt Ceiling of 60% of GDP)

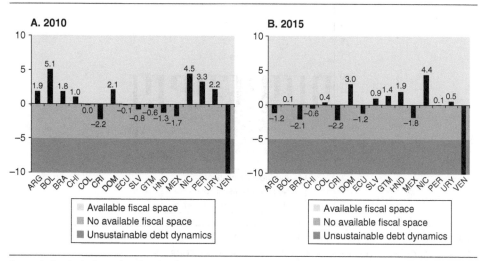

Source: Authors' calculations based on data from IMF and ECLAC.

An important conclusion that follows from these simulations is that we should not take fiscal flexibility for granted. When macroeconomic or financial conditions vary as a consequence of a shock, the size of the fiscal space may also vary substantially, making it necessary to adjust taxes and/or expenditures that are probably associated with fiscal redistributions. Since the adjustment could be of several percentage points of GDP, it is reasonable to conjecture that the distributional impact of fiscal adjustments can be significant.

For an idea of the empirical relevance of the distributional impact of shocks, we proceed as follows. First, we allocate prevailing taxes and expenditures corresponding to 2015 to each of the strata using the CEQ base-year coefficients (the set of $\tilde{\psi}$ and $\tilde{\tau}$ coefficients in equation [8-7]) and then calculate the Gini coefficient. Second, we simulate three shocks to evaluate the changes in the available fiscal space: a deceleration in the growth rate of 2 percent (figure 8-9); an increase in the interest rate of 1 percent (figure 8-10); and a fall in natural resource rents to its minimum in the period 2000–15 (figure 8-11). Third, we calculate the adjustment required in the primary balance to meet $\chi_t = 0$ and compare this to the maximum adjustment limit of 5 percent of GDP.

Low economic growth implies, *ceteris paribus*, a higher λ, and therefore, it is necessary to increase the primary fiscal balance. In the absence of an adjustment, several countries in the region have no available fiscal space and at least two face unsustainable debt dynamics. The results in figure 8-9 indicate that growth is a powerful tool to diminish fiscal risks.

FIGURE 8-9
Impact of Lower Growth Rates on the Available Fiscal Space (% GDP), 2015

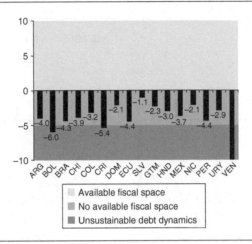

Source: Authors' calculations based on data from IMF and ECLAC.

Note: Scenario: Growth deceleration of 2% and public debt ceiling of 60% of GDP.

FIGURE 8-10
Impact of Higher Interest Rates on the Available Fiscal Space (% GDP), 2015

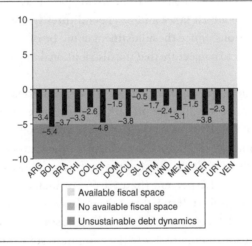

Source: Authors' calculations based on data from IMF and ECLAC.

Note: Scenario: A 1% increase in interest rates and public debt ceiling of 60% of GDP.

FIGURE 8-11

Impact of Lower Rents on the Available Fiscal Space (% GDP), 2015 (Public Debt Ceiling of 60% of GDP)

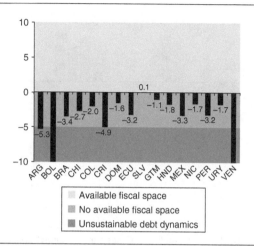

Available fiscal space
No available fiscal space
Unsustainable debt dynamics

Source: Authors' calculations based on data from IMF and ECLAC.

A higher interest rate operates similarly to low growth, that is, through a higher λ. The outcome shown in figure 8-10 is similar to the one observed in figure 8-9 and indicates that financial conditions matter significantly to the availability of fiscal space. Venezuela, Bolivia, and to a lesser extent Costa Rica are the most vulnerable cases. In the former two, a mild increase in the international interest rate may trigger a problem of debt sustainability.

The volatility of commodity revenues is represented in figure 8-11 by substituting the observed value of ε_t^G with its minimum value for the period 2000–15. Although the outcome is similar in the sense that the fiscal space shrinks, Bolivia and Ecuador are much more affected, while Honduras and Nicaragua are less sensitive under these metrics.

Bear in mind that the main purpose of these simulations is to show that shocks may significantly restrict fiscal flexibility and, hence, affect the government's ability to sustain a given fiscal redistribution structure. Historically, this seemed to be the case for Latin American countries. However, the exercise should not be interpreted as a description of the actual situation of the countries involved. For one thing, we have shown that the available fiscal space is larger when we take the actual rates of growth and interest into account. We use $\lambda = 2\%$ for all countries in order to facilitate within sample comparisons.

How does a post-shock adjustment affect distribution? Does the way in which the adjustment is implemented matter to the Gini coefficient? To address these questions, we simulate how much the Gini coefficient would change were the bulk of the adjustment to fall on a single item of the fiscal redistribution structure, leaving the rest

FIGURE 8-12

Impact of 1% of GDP Adjustment on the Gini Coefficient, 2015

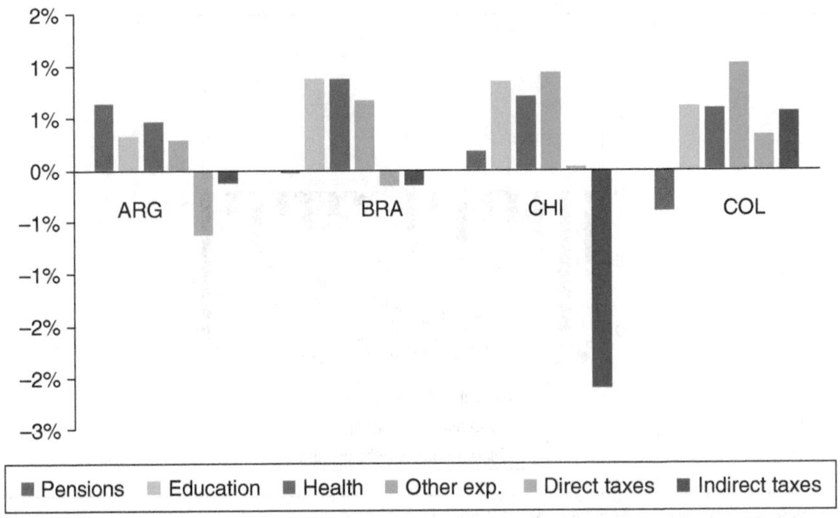

Source: Authors' calculations based on data from CEQ.

constant. Figure 8-12 shows the change in the Gini coefficient (multiplied by 100) per each percentage point of GDP of fiscal adjustment. We present the case of the only four countries from the sample that, given the standards of the region, present a developed fiscal redistribution structure.

Figure 8-12 indicates that there are marked cross-country differences concerning the impact on the Gini coefficient. Reducing expenditures on health and education always has a regressive effect, but it is higher in some countries than in others. There are some rather surprising results. In Argentina, the most regressive type of adjustment has to do with pension transfers and health expenditures. But in Brazil and Colombia, the effect of reducing pension transfers is progressive. The consequence of increasing taxes is, in general, progressive, but the results differ substantially from one country to another. In light of these differences, there is no one-size-fits-all when it comes to designing a fiscal adjustment.

3 The Future Sustainability of Fiscal Policy in Aging Societies

In this section we explore the role of the demographic transition in the evolution of the fiscal redistribution structure and its impacts on aggregate fiscal redistribution. We first briefly discuss a number of stylized facts that have to do with the stage of the demographic transition that Latin America is going through. Second, we examine the channels through which a changing population structure affects the size and components of the fiscal redistribution structures of a set of Latin American countries using information from the NTA and CEQ databases. Third, we analyze the way in which the demographic-driven changes in η_t^D affect the primary deficit and the availability of fiscal space. Finally, we examine the changes in the Gini coefficient that may occur as the demographic transition modifies the fiscal redistribution structure.

3.1 On the Demographic Transition in Latin America

According to the UN Population Division, in 2010 two out of three Latin Americans were adults aged 15 to 64 (UN, 2017). Latin America as a whole can be considered an "adult" region, younger than "old" Europe and older than "young" Africa. Thanks to their demographic structure, the richer and larger economies in the region—and in our sample—are enjoying the so-called demographic window of opportunity (DWO) stage of the demographic transition, but will abandon the DWO mostly during the 2030s.[10] This is the case not only for Argentina, Brazil, Chile, Colombia, Mexico, Peru, and Venezuela, but also for smaller Costa Rica and Uruguay. The poorer and smaller economies, on the other hand, are entering or preparing to enter the DWO (El Salvador and Ecuador are examples of the former, Bolivia and Guatemala of the latter). This means that in the next four decades the Latin American population structure will experience substantial shifts as the population gets older. As figure 8-13a shows, the proportion of the elderly will increase substantially, accompanied by a continuous fall in the share of the young. By 2050 the share of middle-aged adults is expected to remain roughly invariant but there will be one older adult for every child. The aging stage will come earlier in the older countries of the region (such as Uruguay, Chile, and Costa Rica) while younger countries (such as Honduras, El Salvador, and Nicaragua) will still be experiencing the demographic dividend (figure 8-13b).

The literature on the effects of demography on growth has shown that the DWO is a crucial period because the proportion of prime workers (aged 25–54 years) in the population reaches a maximum, and, as a consequence, it would be possible to increase per capita income even if productivity per worker remained the same (Lee and Mason, 2006, 2012; Bloom et al., 2015; Mason et al., 2017). This is the so-called "first growth dividend" that takes place during the DWO. There is also a "second growth dividend" originating in the fact that there is a rise in the proportion of "prime savers" to the extent that the prime workers exhibit the highest savings capacity hand in hand with the increase in the proportion of prime workers. This opens the way for faster capital accumulation and growth acceleration. The first dividend, nonetheless, will reverse as

---

[10] The UN Population Division has defined the DWO as the period in which the proportion of children and youths under 15 years falls below 30 percent and the proportion of people 65 years and older is still below 15 percent (See UN, 2004). Typically, the demographic window of opportunity lasts for 30–40 years depending upon the country. In our simulations we use the UN medium-variant projection of population growth and population structure.

FIGURE 8-13
Population Structure in Latin America

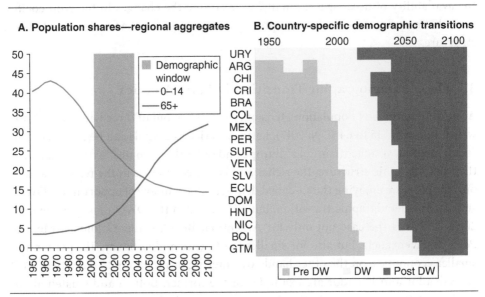

A. Population shares—regional aggregates

B. Country-specific demographic transitions

Source: Authors' calculations based on data from the UN Population Division.
DW = Demographic Window.

the DWO declines and the aging process deepens. This will be a more difficult period from the standpoint of growth because of the shrinking proportion of prime workers and the increasing number of retirees. However, the aging impact will be lower if real wages increase as a consequence of capital accumulation during the second dividend. In addition, as longevity steps up, workers may save more in anticipation of a longer retirement period, and this can help capital accumulation. Note, nonetheless, that the literature on the "demographic dividends" associated with the DWO (Mason et al., 2017) emphasizes that such benefits are not automatic; the DWO merely expands the opportunities for growth acceleration.

As Fanelli (2018) explains, the lifecycle deficit varies across cohorts, and, as a consequence, the transformations that accompany the demographic transition induce changes at the aggregate level in the relationship between labor income and consumption, as well as in the propensity to save and in labor and asset-income shares in Market Income. These changes, in turn, modify the structure of the demand for public transfers, public goods, and the tax base.

These developments may change the value of η^p markedly as well as the fiscal redistribution structure. In effect, first, the increase in the proportion of prime workers, prime savers, and, hence, growth opportunities during the DWO induces an expansion in the fiscal space. This is the consequence of the expansion in the tax base and in the demand for financial assets, which usually includes government securities. Second, the size and structure of the demand for transfers and public goods changes throughout the DWO. It is particularly important that the number of children in school peaks just before entering the DWO. The requirements of human capital accumulation during the DWO should be easier to finance given the parallel increase in government revenues associated with the first dividend. Afterward, nonetheless, the importance of investing in human capital does not decrease, as it is essential to enhance labor productivity for the post-DWO aging period, when the proportion of prime workers in the population begins to fall and the dependency ratio begins to increase, reversing the first dividend. Third, during the aging period, after the closing of the DWO, Latin American economies will experience a continuous growth in elderly demands for health services and pensions, which might be difficult to finance because of the weaker dynamics of tax collection. The costs of fiscal redistributions might exert a continuous pressure on the primary deficit. Under these circumstances, the fiscal space would be much more difficult to manage. The situation would be particularly complicated if the second growth dividend were not too large, employment rates were low, or informality were pervasive, as is the case in many Latin American economies. The intensity of the effects will depend on institutional factors, such as the generosity and the coverage of the social security system.

In sum, these facts indicate that the fiscal authorities should take into account demographic factors in evaluating the probable evolution of the cost of financing the structure of redistributions and of the impact on income distribution of changes in that structure. In what follows, we will use NTA, CEQ, and IMF data to evaluate the significance of these changes.

3.2 The Impact of the Demographic Transition on the Fiscal Redistribution Structure

In order to analyze the channels through which the demographic transition influences the fiscal redistribution structure, it is necessary to introduce the concepts utilized by NTA. The NTA database presents data on "age profiles" for the "tax burden" (T_a) and for the "benefits received" (G_a), where a stands for cohort. The parameter τ_a is defined as the ratio of the per capita taxes paid by cohort a normalized by per capita income, and ψ_a are the benefits (public goods and transfers) received by each cohort from the government normalized in the same way. We use the superscripts A, Y, I, F, and R with the same meaning as above. Hence, if $X_{a,t}$ is the total population of cohort a in year t, and y_t is the per capita income, for the base year b we can write

$$(8\text{-}15) \qquad \tau_a = \frac{T_{a,b}^A + T_{a,b}^Y + T_{a,b}^I + T_{a,b}^F + T_{a,b}^R}{X_{a,b} y_b}.$$

And, for the benefits received:

$$(8\text{-}16) \qquad \psi_a = \frac{G_{a,b}^O + G_{a,b}^A + G_{a,b}^I + G_{a,b}^E + G_{a,b}^H + G_{a,b}^R}{X_{a,b} y_b}.$$

FIGURE 8-14

Age Profiles of the Components of the Fiscal Redistribution Structure (as a Share of Per Capita Income)

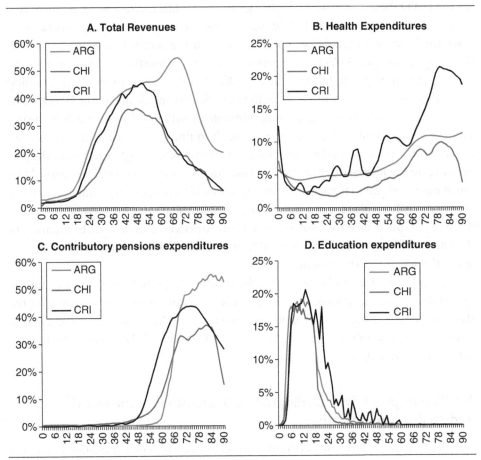

Source: Authors' calculations based on data from NTA.

Note: Specific dates are ARG: 2012, CHI: 1997, CRI: 2004.

Expressions (8-15) and (8-16) imply that demographic changes matter to the fiscal redistribution structure because each of the items that makes up such a structure is influenced by a specific per capita age profile, and, thus, the fiscal redistribution structure changes endogenously as the population structure changes. Figure 8-14 shows the tax and benefit profiles for the cases of Argentina, Chile, and Costa Rica, using the NTA profiles.

In light of our analytical goals, the following facts deserve mention. First, the top left-hand of figure 8-14 shows the tax profile. Fiscal revenues have a similar shape across countries in the sense that they have a bias towards middle-aged adults, who comprise the prime workers. Age-specific tax burdens across countries nonetheless differ in levels, as a quick comparison between Argentina and Costa Rica reveals. In addition, the bias toward middle-aged adults as taxpayers is stronger in some countries (e.g., Chile) than in others (e.g., Argentina). Second, the age profiles corresponding to different types of public consumption show very different shapes. In particular, figure 8-14C exhibits per capita fiscal expenditures in contributory pensions. As expected, this item of the fiscal redistributions has a bias toward the elderly. Yet again, there are important cross-country variations. Argentina shows the higher level of expenditures. Health expenditures, in turn, also present a pronounced bias in favor of the elderly. Finally, education benefits are concentrated in the younger cohorts, as was expected.

3.3 Simulations with Fixed-Age Profiles

From these facts it follows that the allocation of total expenditures will vary when the demographic structure changes and that the same will happen with the allocation of the tax burden. As a consequence, the value and sign of η_t^D are likely to vary. Likewise, if the allocation among deciles of different types of taxes and expenditures—say, education versus pension transfers—varies significantly, there will be modifications in the Gini coefficient calculated on the basis of Final Income.

If the older cohort is $\bar{a}$ and the participation of cohort a in total population is $\mu_{a,t}$, the aggregate tax burden and benefits expressed as ratios of Market Income at time t will be

(8-17)
$$\tau_t = \sum_a^{\bar{a}} \tau_a \mu_{a,t};$$

(8-18)
$$\psi_t = \sum_a^{\bar{a}} \psi_a \mu_{a,t}.$$

Note that in these simulations we are fixing the values of the age profiles—that is, we assume that behavior, rules, and institutions do not change in the future. Using estimated population dynamics from the medium-variant projection of the UN Population Division, figure 8-15 shows the demographic-driven evolution of τ_t until 2050. As we see, after the closing of the DWO in the older Latin American economies—such as Costa Rica and Uruguay—there is a flattening in the curve representing the tax revenues/income ratio, reflecting the reduction in the proportion of prime-age taxpayers. This is not the case of the younger and poorer countries, such as Bolivia or Nicaragua. This suggests that these two groups of countries will face very different fiscal challenges in coming decades: in the post-DWO countries the fiscal space will shrink and the opposite will happen in the economies enjoying the first dividend, opening an opportunity to take advantage of the larger fiscal flexibility to implement more aggressive poverty reduction initiatives.

FIGURE 8-15

Demographic-Driven Evolution of Fiscal Redistributions (i): Total Revenues (% GDP)

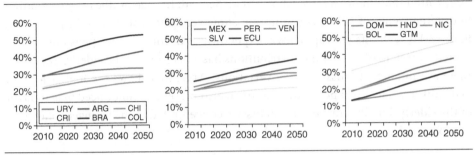

Source: Authors' calculations based on data from NTA, CEQ and UN.

The demographic-driven changes in pension expenditures ($G_{a,t}^A$) for the period until 2050 are presented in figure 8-16A. These types of transfers will increase in all countries. However, those that are more advanced in the aging process will face increased difficulties in keeping the primary deficit under control because of the combination of a less dynamic evolution of the tax revenues/income ratio with rising pension transfers/income ratio. The financial gap will grow as the initial level of transfers widens and the social security system is more generous—i.e., in terms of coverage, retirement age, and the level of the pension benefits. With respect to contributory pensions (figure 8-16A), the case of Brazil is striking and prone to generate sustainability problems. The evolution of contributory pension transfers also appears to be complex in Venezuela, Costa Rica, and Uruguay. Noncontributory pensions (figure 8-16B) can also trigger imbalances of great magnitude. The evolution of these kinds of pension transfers is clearly unsustainable in Argentina and Venezuela and to a lesser extent in Uruguay. The fast increase in noncontributory pensions in Bolivia is surprising, given that the country is undergoing an early stage of the demographic transition.

The path simulated for the demographic-driven educational expenditures shown in figure 8-17 differs markedly from the path of pension transfers. More advanced countries in the demographic transition will experience some financial relief stemming from the reduction in the demand for educational benefits, while such demand will move in the opposite direction in younger economies. This, of course, is not the case of Bolivia or Nicaragua, where demographics will push total education expenditures upward. The lower panel in figure 8-17 registers the paths simulated for health expenditures. It is interesting that expenditures in this case tend to increase in practically all countries, although the causes differ in young and adult countries. In particular, health expenditures in the latter countries are expected to increase because of the aging process. In some Central American countries, such as Costa Rica and Honduras, health expenditures will also be hard to finance in the not-so-distant future.

FIGURE 8-16
Demographic-Driven Evolution of Fiscal Redistributions (ii): Pensions (% GDP)

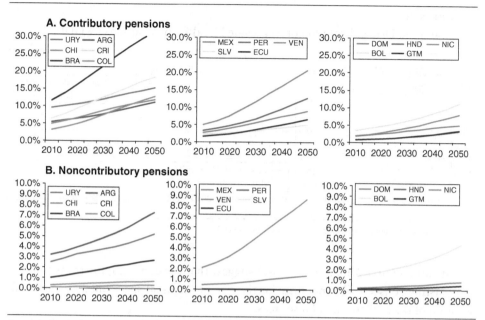

Source: Authors' calculations based on data from NTA, CEQ, and UN.

FIGURE 8-17

Demographic-Driven Evolution of Fiscal Redistributions (iii): In-Kind Transfers (% GDP)

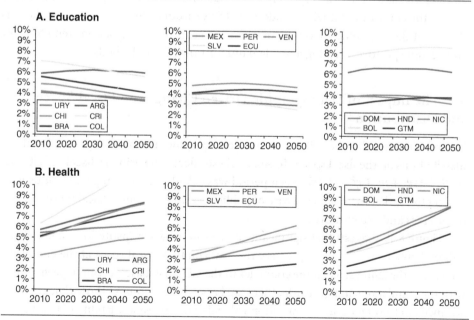

Source: Authors' calculations based on data from NTA, CEQ, and UN.

FIGURE 8-18

Demographic-Driven Evolution of Aggregate Fiscal Redistributions (% GDP)

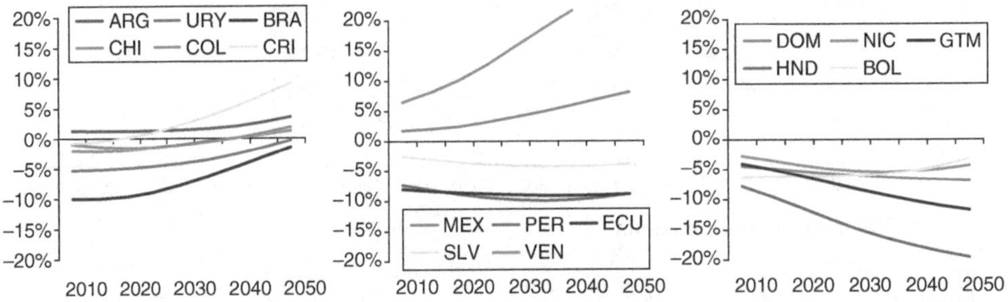

Source: Authors' calculations based on data from NTA, CEQ, and UN.

In sum, figures 8-15, 8-16, and 8-17 suggest that the demographic transition has long-lasting consequences not only for the size of the fiscal space but also for the allocation of the available fiscal resources.

Finally, figure 8-18 registers the demographic-driven changes in fiscal redistributions ($\psi_t - \tau_t = \eta_t^D$) that result from the diverging paths of taxes and expenditures. In the group of younger countries, the forces unleashed by the increase in the tax-paying proportion of prime workers dominate, and, as a consequence, fiscal redistributions are negative and decreasing. This suggests that it is reasonable to expect an expansion in the fiscal space, and, thus, more flexibility to implement redistribution policies. In these cases, demography favors sustainability. The opposite is true in the case of the countries that will abandon the DWO around the 2030s. The simulations show that demographic-driven changes in the costs of redistributions tend to grow and become positive, creating a net demand for funds from the budget.

3.4 The Impact of Demographic-Driven Changes on Fiscal Space and Distribution

Figure 8-19 exhibits the effects of the demographic-driven changes in fiscal redistributions on the fiscal space. To isolate these effects, the primary fiscal deficit (that is, $\theta_t^{GP} = \eta_t^D + \eta_t^R + \iota_t^G - \varepsilon_t^G$) for each period was calculated assuming fixed ratios with respect to Market Income in the case of public investment, nontax fiscal revenues, and other taxes and expenditures.

Figure 8-19 suggests that significant changes in behavior, institutions, and policies will probably be necessary to preserve the availability of fiscal space at the end of the bonus and the aging stage in the countries in the CEQ database. As can be seen, in line with the simulations in figure 8-18, there are basically two groups. Those that are more advanced in the demographic transition will enjoy much less availability of fiscal space as the transition evolves. The aging process is largely responsible for this: the fall in the

FIGURE 8-19

Demographic-Driven Changes in the Available Fiscal Space (% GDP)

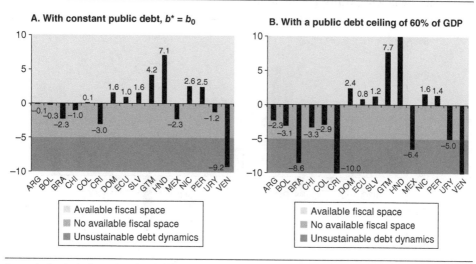

Source: Authors' calculations based on data from NTA, CEQ, and UN.

proportion of prime workers reduces the tax base, while simultaneously, the increase in the number of retirees augments the pension transfers. In this context, there will be a trade-off between equity-improving expenditures and policies aimed at ensuring public debt sustainability. The younger countries, in turn, will experience an expansion in the availability of fiscal space. These countries will be enjoying an increase in the tax base associated with the higher proportion of prime workers in the population. In this case, the most important challenge will be to achieve an allocation of the fiscal space that is both efficient and equitable. Undoubtedly, expenditures to accelerate human capital accumulation so as to improve the poor's endowment should play a key role.

To illustrate the effects of the demographic transition on income distribution, which operates through changes in the fiscal redistribution structure, we need to identify the groups in the population by cohort (a) and income stratum (d). The structure of fiscal redistributions can then be expressed as

$$(8\text{-}19) \quad N^D_{a,d,t} = G^O_{a,d,t} + G^A_{a,d,t} + G^I_{a,d,t} + G^E_{a,d,t} + G^H_{a,d,t} - T^A_{a,d,t} - T^Y_{a,d,t} - T^I_{a,d,t} - T^F_{a,d,t}.$$

Following Fanelli (2018) we define $\eta^D_{a,d,t} = \dfrac{n^D_{a,d,t}}{y_t}$, where $n^D_{a,d,t}$ is the per capita fiscal redistribution corresponding to the members of cohort a pertaining to stratum d. In this case, assuming time-invariant parameters for the distribution among cohorts and income strata, we can rewrite τ_t and ψ_t as

$$(8\text{-}20) \quad \tau_t = \sum_d^{\bar{d}} \sum_a^{\bar{a}} \tau_{a,d} \, \mu_{a,d,t};$$

FIGURE 8-20

Demographic-Driven Changes in the Fiscal Redistribution Structure and Changes in the Gini Coefficient (Multiplied by 100)

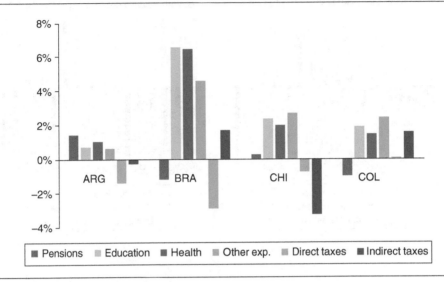

Source: Authors' calculations based on data from NTA, CEQ, and UN.

(8-21)
$$\psi_t = \sum_d^{\bar{d}} \sum_a^{\bar{a}} \psi_{a,d} \, \mu_{a,d,t};$$

and

(8-22)
$$\eta_t^D = \sum_d^{\bar{d}} \sum_{\bar{a}}^{\bar{a}} (\psi_{a,d} - \tau_{a,d}) \mu_{a,d,t}.$$

Regrettably, there is no information available on the parameters $\tau_{a,d}$ and $\psi_{a,d}$. Therefore, to simulate the evolution of Final Income, we follow a strategy that is similar to the one utilized in section 2. First, we project each of the components of η_t^D as the demographic transition evolves. Second, assuming that the parameters for the distribution of taxes and benefits among income strata remain invariant and equal to the ones provided by CEQ for the "base year," we distribute the demographic-driven taxes and expenditures corresponding to each year among the income strata. Third, we calculate Final Income corresponding to each income strata and obtain the Gini coefficient for each projected year. That is, the estimated share of expenditures allocated to stratum d at time t $\psi_{d,t}^*$ will be

(8-23) $$\psi_{d,t}^* = \tilde{\psi}_d \psi_t = \tilde{\psi}_d \sum_{a=0}^{\bar{a}} \psi_a \mu_{a,t} = \tilde{\psi}_d \sum_{a=0}^{\bar{a}} (\psi_a^A + \psi_a^Y + \psi_a^I + \psi_a^F + \psi_a^R) \mu_{a,t}.$$

Figure 8-20 plots the impact on the Gini coefficient (multiplied by 100) that would have the fiscal adjustment necessary to compensate for the endogenous changes induced by demography between 2010 and 2050 and achieve $\Delta\chi_t = 0$. As in figure 8-12, the graph shows what the impact would be if the bulk of the adjustment were to fall on only one of the components of the fiscal redistribution structure. We show four countries that will be affected by the aging process.

Figure 8-20 suggests that the worsening in the Gini coefficient as a consequence of aging could be important. The case of Brazil, where the aging process has been particularly rapid, can be very difficult to manage from a fiscal point of view.

4 Conclusion

In this chapter we have explored empirically the linkages between the fiscal redistribution structure, the fiscal space, and income distribution in a set of Latin American countries. The main purpose has been to take advantage of the new data provided by the CEQ and NTA databases from an intertemporal perspective, which includes demographic factors. To perform the simulations presented, we have had to make assumptions concerning the allocation of taxes and public expenditures to income strata and the behavior of the different cohorts; in particular, we have had to assume that the allocation and behavioral parameters will remain constant over an extended period, which are not uncommon in the literature on demography.

What is the value of the exercises? First, we hope that this work will contribute to highlighting how essential it is to produce the data that are necessary to fully evaluate the intertemporal consequences of fiscal redistributions. Second, we also hope that despite the data limitations, we have succeeded to a certain extent at showing that a unified methodology has the potential to reveal new aspects of the interactions between the fiscal redistribution structure, debt sustainability, demography, and income distribution. Third, we identified some stylized facts that, beyond the limitations of our data, may suggest future lines of research and restrictions that should be respected in designing fiscal and distribution policies. The following points deserve highlighting.

First, the notion of the structure of fiscal redistribution can be fruitfully used as a pivot to articulate the fiscal items of the budget that impinge on income distribution. We found that in the CEQ sample analyzed, those countries that show higher government expenditures/GDP ratios achieve better distributional outcomes. We also found a positive relationship between the expenditure ratio and the per capita GDP, which indicates that it will be more difficult for poorer countries to implement policies to improve income distribution, although demography may be an opportunity because of the expected increase in fiscal revenues in younger countries.

Second, an important point that follows from our analysis is that the way in which a given fiscal adjustment is implemented matters to income distribution. As a general rule, the downward adjustment of expenditures is regressive, although the importance of the impact varies from one economy to another. A reduction in pension transfers can be regressive (Argentina) or progressive (Colombia), but a cutback in education or health expenditures is always regressive. Meanwhile, the increase in income taxes is basically progressive, while the results concerning indirect taxes are mixed.

Third, we observed that, although fiscal expenditures in our sample are more correlated with distribution outcomes than fiscal redistributions, the latter are a better synthetic indicator of the "net budgetary costs" of achieving a given difference between Market Income and Final Income and, consequently, are a good indicator of the way in which the distributional dimension of the budget affects the primary surplus and thus public debt sustainability. Our exercises suggest that the modifications in the level and composition of fiscal actions required to achieve a given change in the Gini coefficient may amount to various percentage points of GDP and, under certain circumstances, may negatively affect either the required tax burden or debt sustainability.

Fourth, we believe that the methodological framework and the exercises are instrumental in showing that demography matters to the size and the allocation of the fiscal space because it impinges on the composition and the level of fiscal redistributions and on the primary surplus, which is a key determinant of debt sustainability.

Fifth, in the special case of Latin America the DWO is the key stage of the demographic transition. For younger countries it matters because they are entering the DWO and for the older ones because they have to prepare to abandon it and enter the aging stage. Using the NTA age-profiles, the exercises suggest that the DWO will probably help to create the fiscal space required to implement progressive policies in younger countries while the opposite will occur in the countries that will age. The simulations indicate that the demographic transition–driven effects on the items of fiscal redistributions are potentially very large and have substantial consequences for income distribution. If the allocation parameters corresponding to per capita expenditures and taxes remained unchanged, the net effects on the Gini coefficient would be mostly positive because the endogenous increments in expenditures induced by demography would exceed the increments in taxes. However, the bad news is that the evolution of the fiscal redistribution structure could render public debt unsustainable in the absence of appropriate fiscal policies. In particular, the likely evolution of contributory pension transfers might become worrisome in countries such as Brazil or Uruguay. Argentina, in turn, presents the problem that noncontributory transfers are already high even though the aging process is still ahead. Health expenditures will also exert pressure on the fiscal balance in some Central American countries.

Finally, we suggest that fiscal interventions are operating with a moving target. For one thing, the aging process might worsen the labor share along with income distribution. This would call for compensatory progressive fiscal interventions in a context in which the fiscal space will tend to shrink because of aging. The relative importance of alternative sources of income varies with age: the older people are, the higher will be the income from accumulated assets. But wealth distribution in older cohorts is likely to be rather unequal across the region. Therefore, new creative policies to fight inequality will be necessary as aging progresses.

Acknowledgments

We thank Nora Lustig, Jorge Paz, and Augusto de la Torre for their useful comments and suggestions. The study was made possible thanks to the generous support of the Bill & Melinda Gates Foundation.

References

Bloom, David E., Somnath Chatterji, Paul Kowal, Peter Lloyd-Sherlock, Martin McKee, Bernd Rechel, Larry Rosenberg, and James P. Smith. 2015. "Macroeconomic Implications of Population Ageing and Selected Policy Responses." *Lancet* 385, no. 9,968, pp. 649–57.

CEQ Standard Indicators Database. n.d. http://www.commitmentoequity.org/data/.

ECLAC. n.d. Bases de datos y publicaciones estadisticas. http://estadisticas.cepal.org/cepalstat/Portada.html.

Escolano, J. 2010. "A Practical Guide to Public Debt Dynamics, Fiscal Sustainability, and Cyclical Adjustment of Budgetary Aggregates." IMF Technical Notes and Manuals, 10/02. Washington, DC: International Monetary Fund.

Fanelli, J. M. 2022. "Inter-temporal Sustainability of Fiscal Redistribution: A Methodological Framework," chapter 7 in *Commitment to Equity Handbook: Estimating the Impact of Fiscal Policy on Inequality and Poverty*, 2nd ed., Vol. 2, edited by Nora Lustig. Brookings Institution Press and CEQ Institute, Tulane University. Free online version available at www.commitmentoequity.org.

Fatas, A. 2010. "The Economics of Achieving Fiscal Sustainability." Academic Consultants Meeting on Fiscal Sustainability. Board of Governors, Federal Reserve, April 9.

Heller, P. S. 2005. "Back to Basics—Fiscal Space: What It Is and How to Get It." *Finance and Development* 42, no. 2, pp. 32–33. https://www.imf.org/external/pubs/ft/fandd/2005/06/basics.htm.

Higgins, S., and C. Pereira. 2013. "The Effects of Brazil's High Taxation and Social Spending on the Distribution of Household Income." CEQ Working Paper No. 7.

IMF. 2011. "Modernizing the Framework for Fiscal Policy and Public Debt Sustainability Analysis." IMF Staff Note 805/11. Washington, D.C.: International Monetary Fund.

———. n.d. Government Finance Statistics Database. http://data.imf.org/?sk=a0867067-d23c-4ebc-ad23-d3b015045405.

Lee, R., and A. Mason. 2006. "What Is the Demographic Dividend?" *Finance and Development Magazine* 43, no. 3. https://www.imf.org/external/pubs/ft/fandd/2006/09/basics.htm.

———. 2012. *Aging, Economic Growth, and Old-Age Security in Asia*. Cheltenham, UK: Edward Elgar.

Lustig, N., ed. 2022. *Commitment to Equity Handbook: Estimating the Impact of Fiscal Policy on Inequality and Poverty*, 2nd ed., 2 Vols. Brookings Institution Press and CEQ Institute, Tulane University. Free online version available at www.commitmentoequity.org.

Lustig, N., L. F. Lopez-Calva, and E. Ortiz-Juarez. 2015. "Deconstructing the Decline in Inequality in Latin America." In *Proceedings of IEA Roundtable on Shared Prosperity and Growth*, edited by Kaushik Basu and Joseph Stiglitz. New York: Palgrave-Macmillan.

Lustig, N., and C. Pessino. 2013. "Social Spending and Income Redistribution in Argentina in the 2000s: The Rising Role of Noncontributory Pensions." CEQ Working Paper No. 5.

Mason, A., R. Lee, M. Abrigo, and Lee Sang-Hyop. 2017. "Support Ratio and Demographic Dividends: Estimates for the World." Technical Paper 2017-1. New York: Population Division, Department of Economic and Social Affairs, United Nations.

Moody's Analytics. 2011. "Fiscal Space." Special Report, December 20. https://www.economy.com/mark-zandi/documents/2011-12-13-Fiscal-Space.pdf.

Ostry, J. D., A. R. Ghosh, I. J. Kim, and M. S. Qureshi. 2010. "Fiscal Space." IMF Staff Position Note 10/11. September. Washington, D.C.: International Monetary Fund.

Roy, R., A. Heuty, and E. Letouze. 2007. "Fiscal Space for What? Analytical Issues from a Human Development Perspective." Paper for the G20 Workshop on Fiscal Policy, Istanbul, June 30–July 2.

UN, Department of Economic and Social Affairs. 2004. *World Population to 2300*. New York: United Nations. https://digitallibrary.un.org/record/538806?ln=es.

———. *World Population Prospects 2017.* New York: United Nations. https://esa.un.org/unpd/wpp/.

World Bank. 2017. "Debt Dynamics in Emerging Market and Developing Economies: Time to Act?" *Global Economic Prospects*, Special Focus 1, June.

———. n.d. *World Development Indicators*. https://data.worldbank.org/data-catalog/world-development-indicators.

Political Economy
of Redistribution

Chapter 9

ON THE POLITICAL ECONOMY OF REDISTRIBUTION AND PROVISION OF PUBLIC GOODS

Stefano Barbieri and Koray Caglayan

Introduction

The provision of public goods and services, taxation, and income redistribution are among the most important tasks of governments. Not surprisingly, the public economics and political economy literature dealing with these topics is very extensive, using both normative and positive approaches. While the normative approaches are well discussed, for example, in Boadway and Keen (2000), here we focus on a positive approach, i.e., one that determines the levels of the variables of interest as a function of political competition.

Even with this restriction, the political economy literature remains too vast to be fully considered here. We thus further focus our attention on the very prominent strand of the literature stemming from the seminal analysis of taxation and redistribution based on direct democracy and the median voter theorem.[1] Thus, by and large, we do not analyze models of representative democracy. We remand to the reviews of Borck (2007), Londregan (2006), and Persson and Tabellini (2002) for contributions covering the role of parties (Alesina, 1988), different political institutions (Persson and Tabellini, 2003), interest groups (Dixit and Londregan, 1998), political participation (Benabou, 2000), upward mobility in a dynamic model (Benabou and Ok, 2001), and social preferences for fairness (Galasso, 2003), among other topics.

Among median-voter theorem results, the work of Meltzer and Richard (1981) holds a special place of importance in the development of this literature, along with the contributions of Romer (1975, 1977) and Roberts (1977). In Meltzer and Richard (1981),

---

[1]See, e.g., Downs (1957); Black et al. (1958); Foley (1967).

287

individuals are faced with a labor/leisure decision. Further, the government uses a proportional tax on labor income to finance lump-sum redistribution. The model predicts that the political equilibrium will be determined by the preferences of the voter with median income, and in particular by the relationship between median and mean income.

While it is hard to overstate the contribution of the analysis of Meltzer and Richard, the subsequent literature pointed out the importance of two assumptions: (1) the fact that redistribution is narrowly defined as being in cash and not more broadly defined through the government provision of public goods, and (2) the linearity of tax rates. Indeed, we present an elaboration of Commitment to Equity (CEQ) data showing that, overall, tax systems are far from being proportional and that government-provided goods are a relevant part of government outlays.

The importance of the possibility that tax revenues are used to finance a public good is demonstrated by the analysis of Lovell (1975) and Kenny (1978) and summarized in Laffont (1999). We present this analysis in detail later, but, in summary, agents have exogenous income but decide how much public good to ask the government to provide. Again, taxes are linear, and the model's outcome is derived by applying the median voter theorem as in Meltzer and Richard (1981). However, the implications of the relationship between inequality and level of public goods provision turn out to depend on the form of the utility function, and in particular of the comparison between income elasticity of demand for the public good and its price elasticity. Indeed, it is easy to create examples in which the ratio of median to mean income has no effect on the public good level or precisely the opposite effect of that one might expect by simply applying the Meltzer and Richard framework without distinguishing cash redistribution and public goods provision.

The linearity of tax rates is important for two reasons. From the theoretical point of view, the linearity of tax rates is a key feature because through the budget constraint of the government, one can transform what is a two-dimensional decision problem (the level of the proportional tax t and the level of the public good or the lump-sum redistribution) into a one-dimensional problem. It is well known that, for even just two dimensions, one cannot expect a majority voting equilibrium to exist in general (due to Arrow's impossibility theorem [Arrow, 1951]). Therefore, being able to work with a one-dimensional problem solves an important technical issue. And under mild regularity conditions on utility, this problem satisfies either single-peakedness or the single-crossing condition (Gans and Smart, 1996), and therefore the median voter theorem applies. The second important consequence of assuming linear tax rates is that the level of government expenditures does not mechanically generate a change in Gini coefficients of post-tax income. This is not otherwise the case, in general. We demonstrate this with analytical derivations based on Lambert (2001) and simple examples that show how the mechanical effect on the Gini coefficients is complex. It depends both on the form of the tax system and the initial form of the income distribution.

An extension of the Meltzer and Richard (1981) model to quadratic tax rates appears in Cukierman and Meltzer (1991), under conditions that allow for a majority voting equilibrium to exist. Another interesting departure from linear tax rates in a taxation model with a fixed total revenue target is the majority voting analysis of a flat tax with exemption in Gouveia and Oliver (1996). However, we are not aware of a treatment of a public goods model using a flat tax with exemption.

This kind of model appears to be important for a variety of reasons. First, this framework allows for an immediate way to answer an important question: what are the consequences on the provision of public goods if we restrict the tax system to protect the poorest agents from taxation? In other words, if we increase the number of "net receivers," are there any unintended consequences on the provision level of public goods? Second, while remaining very clear that one should not interpret our results as causation, but simply as motivating correlational observations, we provide an analysis of CEQ data that shows the existence of relationships between the proportion of net receivers and the level of public goods provided. Third, the applicability of a flat tax with exemption goes well beyond the country level, and it appears to be a staple of local-level taxation in the United States.

Our analysis yields two main results. First, we obtain an expansion of the range of utility functions for which public goods provision increases with an increase in inequality, with respect to Lovell's (1975) and Kenny's (1978) analyses. Second, we find that the public goods level can *increase or decrease* in the proportion of "net receivers," according to the relationship between the income of the decisive voter and the average income in the population conditional on income being larger than the exemption. This suggests that to account for the richness of comparative statics we observe, the framework used should encompass additional considerations such as turnout (Larcinese, 2007) and the presence of substitutes for government-provided public goods, as in the "ends against the middle" framework of Epple and Romano (1996a).[2]

The rest of the chapter proceeds as follows. First, we present a summary and derive the main implications of the pure redistribution model of Meltzer and Richard (1981). Second, we describe empirical regularities from CEQ data showing that tax rates are not linear and that the public provision of public (or semi-public) goods is important. Further, in a flat tax with exemption regime, we formally present calculations and provide examples that show a relationship between tax rates, exemption amounts, and reduction in inequality of post-tax incomes. Third, we present a summary and derive the main implications of the public goods provision model of Lovell (1975) and Kenny (1978). Then, we present a picture analysis of CEQ data that shows a negative correlation between the proportion of "net receivers" and the amount provided for some public goods, and a positive correlation for others. We use this as motivation for and introduction to our theoretical results on a flat tax with an exemption. We show that an

---

[2]For a complementary result, see the description of "Director's law," in Stigler (2000).

increase in the exemption level can increase or decrease the amount of public good provided, according to the relative position of the income of the decisive voter and the mean income of the population, conditional on being above the exemption. It is worth pointing out that our analysis remains in a one-dimensional framework because we take the exemption size as given. We also consider the consequences of considering turnout and of the existence of substitutes for public provision. Finally, we briefly review papers that tackle taxation and redistribution without preventively assuming functional forms in a representative democracy framework.

1 The Meltzer and Richard (1981) Pure Redistribution Model

Before discussing the Meltzer and Richard (1981) model, it is opportune to describe the median voter theorem more generally. One can find a careful formal presentation of the median voter theorem in Austen-Smith and Banks (1999). More informally, a general version of that theorem is typically that if there is a unidimensional space of alternatives and individual preferences are single-peaked over the alternatives, then one majority equilibrium exists, and it is at the median of the ideal points of the individuals.

It is important to note that the median voter is not necessarily the individual with the median income, in general. For instance, consider a toy example with a society composed of three agents: Poor, Median Income (MI), and Rich. Suppose also that there are three possible tax rates, 10 percent, 20 percent, and 30 percent. Finally, suppose that Poor strictly prefers 30 percent to 20 percent to 10 percent, Rich strictly prefers 20 percent to 10 percent to 30 percent, and MI is ideologically opposed to taxation so that MI strictly prefers 10 percent to 20 percent to 30 percent. Then, if alternatives are ordered in the natural way, we see that preferences are single-peaked, and 20 percent is the median of the ideal points of the individuals. Therefore, 20 percent is the majority equilibrium. Note that 20 percent is the most preferred tax rate of Rich, and not of MI.

As we shall see below, the median voter theorem in its more restrictive interpretation—i.e., that the median voter is the individual with the median income—derives if we assume more stringent conditions on the homogeneity of utility functions. This most restrictive interpretation is convenient in deriving and specifying results, and is also what underlies many of the empirical investigations on the relationship between inequality and redistribution.[3] Therefore, in the majority of what follows, we focus on this most restrictive interpretation.

Meltzer and Richard (1981) define government size as the share of total income to be redistributed and build a model to explain it as the outcome of the utility-maximizing choices of fully informed rational agents. The decisive voter's preferred tax rate maximizes his or her utility, under a balanced government's budget. The decisive voter thus determines the size of the income redistribution and the size of the government through the political process, referred to as the "voting rule." Under majority rule, the voter with me-

---

[3] See, for example, Bénabou (1996) and references therein.

dian income (i.e., the median voter) is the decisive voter. The position of the decisive voter in the income distribution relative to the individual with average income plays an important role in determining the preferred tax rate. Out of this relation emerges the very well-known implication of the model that the higher the inequality (i.e., the ratio of the average income to median income), the higher the size of the redistribution (i.e., the tax rate). Because of its importance, we now describe the Meltzer and Richard model in detail.

All agents share the same utility function, $U(c, 1)$, where c denotes consumption and 1 leisure.[4] Utility is assumed to be strictly concave, and both consumption and leisure are normal goods. Agents differ in their level of productivity, x, in producing consumption goods and decide their labor supply $n = 1 - 1$ accordingly. The pretax income of an individual with productivity level x is given by $y(x) = x \, n(x)$.

The government runs a balanced budget and uses a linear tax schedule to finance lump-sum transfers as its only task. Here, there is no public goods provision. Each individual pays a fraction of his or her earned income in taxes, ty, and receives a fixed transfer r. Savings are assumed to be zero. The disposable income after taxes and transfers then becomes

$$c(x) = (1 - t)nx + r.$$

Each agent solves the following optimal labor supply problem by taking t and r as given:

$$\max_{n \in [0,1]} U(c, 1) = \max_{n \in [0,1]} U[r + nx(1 - t), 1 - n].$$

The solution of the maximization problem provides the optimal choice of labor supply, $n^*(r, x(1 - t))$ and the critical value of productivity x_0 below which an individual chooses not to work (i.e., for $x \le x_0$, $n = 0$ is the optimal choice).

Indeed, the first-order condition for the above-displayed problem is

$$\frac{\partial U}{\partial n} = U_c[r + nx(1 - t), 1 - n]x(1 - t) - U_l[r + nx(1 - t), 1 - n] = 0.$$

Using the concavity of the utility function and $n = 0$, one can establish that optimal labor supply is increasing in x around $n = 0$. Therefore, the agents with $n = 0$, i.e., the individuals who choose not to work, all have $x \le x_0$, where the critical productivity x_0 solves the first-order condition with $n = 0$. We then obtain $U_c(r, 1)x_0 (1 - t) = U_l(r, 1)$, so that the value of x_0 is given by

$$x_0 = \frac{U_l(r, 1)}{U_c(r, 1)(1 - t)}.$$

---

[4] The assumption that all agents share the same utility function has important consequences, and in particular, under some additional conditions, it allows the identification of the decisive voter with the agent with the median income, as we discussed with regard to the toy example at the beginning of this section.

Per capita income is given by

$$\bar{y} = \int_{x_0}^{\infty} x\, n(r,(1-t)x)\, dF(x),$$

where F represents the cumulative distribution of the productivity among agents. This implies that total and per capita income are functions of the values of x_0, t, and r. Furthermore, since x_0 depends only on t and r, the government's budget constraint implies that there is a unique amount of transfer consistent with each tax rate:

$$t\bar{y} = r.$$

This is because of the assumption that leisure is a normal good. Indeed, if we increase r, the right-hand side of the above-displayed equation increases, while the left-hand side decreases, given that labor supply decreases in r. Therefore, once either t or r is given, the other one can be determined, along with consumption, labor choice, and the size of the government.

At the voting stage, the decisive voter maximizes his or her indirect utility, considering the optimal labor supply choice, by choosing a preferred tax rate. Here, to apply the median voter theorem, Meltzer and Richard (1981) use a result by Roberts (1977) showing that if the ordering of individual incomes is independent of the choices of t and r, then the individual choice of the tax rate is inversely ordered by income. Meltzer and Richard (1981) accomplish this with two technical results, one showing that consumption increases in government transfers and one showing the ranking of pre-tax incomes is the same as that of productivities. (These are more technical derivations, and we include them in appendix 9A-1.)

Given these technical results, it turns out that the problem boils down to maximizing the Disposable Income of the decisive voter, $y_d(1-t)+r$, again given the optimal labor supply choice. The decisive voter's preferred tax rate maximizes the decisive voter's utility, taking into account the government's balanced budget:

$$\max_{t\in[0,1]} y_d(1-t)+r = \max_{t\in[0,1]} y_d(1-t)+t\bar{y}.$$

The first-order condition follows:

$$-y_d + \bar{y} + t\frac{d\bar{y}}{dt} = 0,$$

where $\bar{y}$ is a function of $\tau := (1-t)$ and r, as described above. In what follows, we let $\bar{y}_r$ and $\bar{y}_\tau$ indicate partial derivatives with respect to r and τ. Rewriting the government's budget as $t\bar{y}(\tau,r)=r$ and totally differentiating it, one obtains

$$dt(\bar{y}-t\bar{y}_\tau)+td\bar{y}+(t\bar{y}_r-1)dr = 0,$$

and eventually

$$\frac{d\overline{y}}{dt} = \frac{\overline{y}_r\overline{y} - \overline{y}_\tau}{1 - t\overline{y}_r}.$$

Substituting $\frac{d\overline{y}}{dt}$ into the first order condition of the decisive voter's problem,

$-y_d + \overline{y} + t\frac{d\overline{y}}{dt} = 0$, we obtain

$$-y_d + ty_d\overline{y}_r + \overline{y} - t\overline{y}\overline{y}_r + t\overline{y}\overline{y}_r - t\overline{y}_\tau = 0.$$

This can be rewritten as an equation that defines the equilibrium tax rate as

$$t = \frac{m - 1 + \eta(\overline{y}, r)}{m - 1 + \eta(\overline{y}, r) + m\eta(\overline{y}, \tau)}$$

where $m = \frac{\overline{y}}{y_d}$ is the ratio of average to median income and $\eta(\overline{y}, r)$ and $\eta(\overline{y}, \tau)$ are

partial elasticities with respect to r and τ, respectively $\left(\text{e.g.}, \overline{y}_r = \eta(\overline{y}, r)\frac{\overline{y}}{r} \right)$.

Under the common assumption of constant elasticities, the following derivative displays how the ratio of the average income to the income of the decisive voter affects the tax rate:

$$\frac{dt}{dm} = \frac{\eta(\overline{y}, \tau)(1 - \eta(\overline{y}, r))}{(m - 1 + \eta(\overline{y}, r) + m\eta(\overline{y}, \tau))^2} > 0.$$

Therefore, as the ratio of the average income to decisive voter's income increases (i.e., as the level of inequality increases), so do the tax rate and the share of income to be redistributed, and hence the size of the government.[5] However, a review of the empirical evidence in Larcinese (2007) shows very limited support for this implication.

2 Assumptions of Linear Tax Rates and the Importance of Public Provision

The details of the previous analysis of the Meltzer and Richard (1981) model clearly show the importance of assuming that tax rates are linear. This assumption, at least in terms of direct taxes as percentage of pretax Market Income, does not appear to be satisfied for a set of 26 countries for which we obtained CEQ data. Indeed, table 9-1 shows several notable departures. Focusing first on the patterns for the first 7–8

---

[5] For technical derivations of the Meltzer and Richard Model, please see Appendix 9A.1.

TABLE 9-1

Direct Taxes paid as a Percentage of Market (Pre-Tax) Income

Decile	ARG	ARM	BRA	CHL	COL	CRI	DOM	ECU	SLV	ETH	GHA	GTM
1	0.38	0.16	0.54	...	0.05	3.13	0.00	0.00	...	1.38	0.32	0.01
2	0.31	0.46	0.83	0.00	0.02	4.20	0.01	0.01	0.00	1.32	0.99	0.04
3	0.29	1.33	1.06	0.00	0.02	4.96	0.02	0.01	0.01	1.26	0.93	0.04
4	0.24	2.02	1.05	0.01	0.02	4.61	0.02	0.00	0.12	1.25	1.19	0.05
5	0.25	2.56	1.30	0.03	0.03	4.19	0.02	0.01	0.21	1.32	1.42	0.07
6	0.23	3.01	1.52	0.05	0.03	4.72	0.02	0.04	0.34	1.48	2.07	0.13
7	0.21	3.12	1.50	0.14	0.05	5.47	0.06	0.04	0.49	1.41	2.73	0.13
8	0.42	4.04	1.93	0.27	0.05	5.77	0.10	0.07	0.72	1.62	3.41	0.14
9	1.88	5.00	2.69	0.66	0.09	6.31	0.53	0.16	1.34	2.26	4.25	0.27
10	10.94	7.05	7.04	5.31	0.41	8.52	2.99	1.09	2.75	5.35	8.47	1.05

Note: The country codes are ARG (Argentina), ARM (Armenia), BRA (Brazil), CHL (Chile), COL (Colombia), CRI (Costa Rica), DOM (Dominica MEX (Mexico), NIC (Nicaragua), PER (Peru), RUS (Russia), ZAF (South Africa), LKA (Sri Lanka), TZA (Tanzania), TUN (Tunisia), UGA (Uganda

"..." = not available.

income deciles, most countries display an increase in average tax rates, but some, such as Argentina and Ethiopia, display "valleys," and others, such as Costa Rica, display "peaks." Quite clearly, one observes a marked increase in the percentage of pretax Market Income paid by the top 2–3 income deciles as compared to the bottom 7–8 income deciles.[6]

One should expect these different patterns to have importance for the ultimate voting outcome. For instance, if middle-income individuals pay the largest average tax, then middle-income individuals may also have the lowest demand for the size of government. The opposite pattern may be true if middle-income individuals pay the smallest average tax rate. In other words, changing tax rates may give another reason for non-monotonicity in income of the demand for government size, in addition to the differences in preferences already discussed.

Another key assumption is that the government redistributes only cash in this economy. This is a very useful simplifying assumption, but direct government provision is empirically important. Table 9-2 shows that direct government provi-

---

[6] Peaks and valleys appear also for the United States. For instance, Saez and Zucman (2019) document that in 2018, average tax rates display two peaks: one at the 80th income percentile, and another at the 99.99th income percentile, with the top 400 wealthiest households paying an average tax rate below the rates for almost everyone else.

HND	IRN	JOR	MEX	NIC	PER	RUS	ZAF	LKA	TZA	TUN	UGA	URY	VEN
...	0.61	0.03	0.03	...	...	2.81	0.03	0.00	0.00	0.80	0.00	0.44	...
...	1.09	0.03	0.33	0.03	...	4.10	0.14	0.01	0.00	1.52	0.01	1.02	0.00
...	1.48	0.03	0.52	0.11	...	4.44	0.31	0.01	0.12	1.69	0.02	1.57	0.00
0.02	2.38	0.03	1.02	0.03	...	4.43	0.48	0.01	0.04	3.35	0.01	2.04	0.00
...	2.96	0.02	1.39	0.14	...	4.82	0.77	0.03	0.22	4.16	0.19	2.42	0.00
0.02	3.29	0.10	1.70	0.17	0.06	6.08	1.36	0.05	0.48	5.02	0.24	2.92	0.01
0.04	3.26	0.12	2.16	0.77	0.14	6.59	2.68	0.05	0.71	6.14	0.36	3.69	0.02
0.15	3.34	0.19	3.12	1.53	0.16	7.66	5.00	0.10	1.36	7.72	0.74	4.62	0.06
0.31	3.55	0.32	3.87	4.07	0.49	8.20	9.91	0.22	2.16	9.22	1.34	6.18	0.09
0.95	3.32	4.25	7.63	7.68	3.35	8.75	19.80	1.30	12.86	11.80	6.65	9.85	1.99

Republic), ECU (Ecuador), SLV (El Salvador), ETH (Ethiopia), GHA (Ghana), GTM (Guatemala), HND (Honduras), IRN (Iran), JOR (Jordan),
URY (Uruguay), VEN (Venezuela).

sion of goods such as education and health is actually comparable to redistribution amounts.

The rest of this chapter analyzes the consequences of introducing both public goods and nonlinear taxation schemes in the economy.

3 The Provision of Public Goods Using a Median Voter Framework

We now consider a model of public provision of a public good. A model along these lines appears in Lovell (1975), Kenny (1978), and Laffont (1998). We will see that the basic message of Meltzer and Richard (1981) can be readily adapted to this framework, but also note important contrasts. Importantly, depending on the relation between income elasticity of demand for the public good and its price elasticity, inequality may increase, leave constant, or decrease the demand of the median voter for public goods provision.

We assume that all individuals have the same standard utility function over consumption c and public good G, u(c, G). For the sake of concreteness, we adopt a constant elasticity of substitution (CES) formulation, so

$$u(c, G) = (\alpha c^{-\beta} + (1-\alpha)G^{-\beta})^{-\frac{1}{\beta}},$$

TABLE 9-2
Relationship between Government Provision of Public Goods and Redistributive Measures

Country	Direct transfer (% GDP)	Education spending (% GDP)	Health spending (% GDP)	Decline in Gini (Gini points)	Decline in Gini (% change)	Net receivers (# of deciles)
Argentina	5.80	7.48	5.65	6.44	13.56	1
Armenia	2.52	3.52	1.68	2.85	7.08	2
Bolivia	2.05	8.27	3.60	0.02	0.04	2
Brazil	4.07	5.08	4.98	3.54	6.17	2
Chile	1.64	4.29	3.81	2.95	5.98	2
Colombia	0.46	3.34	4.98	1.16	2.01	6
Costa Rica	1.18	6.20	6.10	2.20	4.33	1
Dominican Republic	0.80	3.76	1.84	2.20	4.28	2
Ecuador	1.22	4.50	3.28	3.28	6.86	6
El Salvador	1.38	2.93	4.29	1.99	4.53	1
Ethiopia	1.35	4.62	1.25	1.98	6.15	2
Ghana	0.07	5.65	1.66	1.38	3.15	0
Guatemala	0.40	2.71	2.14	0.70	1.37	1

Honduras	0.40	6.08	3.53	1.23	2.18	2
Indonesia	0.39	3.40	0.88	0.76	1.92	10
Iran	3.99	4.48	2.50	5.73	13.38	9
Jordan	0.72	3.18	3.10	1.61	4.71	9
Mexico	0.96	4.54	3.06	2.98	5.84	4
Nicaragua	0.07	3.80	4.19	1.69	3.52	1
Peru	0.40	2.80	3.10	1.18	2.34	1
Russia	5.28	4.09	3.69	2.77	7.04	1
South Africa	3.81	7.00	4.11	7.66	9.93	5
Sri Lanka	2.00	1.94	1.48	1.15	3.09	3
Tanzania	0.15	4.60	1.56	4.00	10.47	0
Tunisia	0.83	6.26	1.59	4.95	11.49	2
Uganda	0.54	2.40	1.60	1.61	3.90	1
Uruguay	2.26	3.70	4.68	3.15	6.39	2
Venezuela	0.97	4.74	2.75	2.05	5.11	3

Notes: Direct Transfers refer to direct cash and near-cash transfers by the government. Education spending and health spending are indirect transfers (per CEQ methodology) and are considered as providing public goods in our models. The decline in Gini coefficient is measured by the difference in Gini coefficient calculated using Market Income (income before any taxes and transfers) and Consumable Income (income after taxes and direct transfers and before indirect transfers). This decline refers to the improvement in income inequality as a result of taxes and direct government transfers. An individual or household is a net receiver if the direct and indirect taxes paid are less than the direct government transfers received.

where $\beta > -1$ is a parameter affecting the elasticity of substitution between private and public good, and $0 < \alpha < 1$. As is well known, the restriction $\beta > -1$ makes the utility function strictly quasi-concave. Further, the limit cases of $\beta = -1$, 0, and $+\infty$ correspond to perfect substitutes, Cobb-Douglas, and perfect complements, respectively. The consumption of agent i depends on her exogenous income y_i and on the tax set by the government. We begin this section assuming that the government uses a flat tax with rate t. Therefore, the consumption of agent i follows:

$$c_i = (1 - t)y_i.$$

The amount of public good G and the tax rate t are related through the government's budget constraint. If we denote the total income in the economy with $\bar{Y}$, we obtain that, to be feasible, G and t must obey

$$G = t\bar{Y}.$$

We define a pair (G, t) as feasible if it satisfies the budget constraint displayed above, and if $0 \leq t \leq 1$ and $0 \leq G \leq \bar{Y}$. The amount of public good G and the tax rate t are chosen through the political process. In particular, we look for a feasible pair (G, t) that survives a pairwise majority-voting comparison with any other feasible pair. As in Meltzer and Richard (1981), the government budget constraint allows us to reduce the dimensions of the problem from two to one.

We assume that agents are aware of the government budget constraint and consider it in their choices. Expressing the tax rate as $t = G/\bar{Y}$ and substituting into the utility function and the budget constraint, we obtain that the most preferred amount of public good for agent i solves

$$\max_G v_i(G) \equiv u\left(\left(1 - \frac{G}{\bar{Y}}\right)y_i, G\right) = \left(\alpha\left(\left(1 - \frac{G}{\bar{Y}}\right)y_i\right)^{-\beta} + (1 - \alpha)G^{-\beta}\right)^{-\frac{1}{\beta}},$$

where $v_i(G)$ is the utility function of this agent expressed only in terms of the public good.

Any interior solution is characterized by the first-order condition, by strict quasi-concavity of the utility function. Assuming an interior solution and defining the most preferred amount of public good by agent i as G_i, the first-order condition $v_i'(G_i) = 0$ yields

$$\left(\frac{G_i}{\bar{Y} - G_i}\right)^{1+\beta} = \frac{1 - \alpha}{\alpha}\left(\frac{y_i}{\bar{Y}}\right)^{\beta}.$$

Note how the left-hand side of the above-displayed equation is increasing in G_i, by $\beta > -1$. However, the right-hand side may be decreasing, constant, or increasing in the ratio $y_i/\bar{Y}$, depending on whether β is negative, zero, or positive. In any case, the most preferred public goods amounts for agents are ordered by income. Therefore, the median voter theorem applies. If we denote with y_a the average income in the population, with y_m the median income, normalize the total population n to 1, and denote with G_m the most preferred amount by the median-income voter, the political equilibrium results in G_m as the unique value that solves

$$\left(\frac{G_m}{y_a - G_m}\right)^{1+\beta} = \frac{1-\alpha}{\alpha}\left(\frac{y_m}{y_a}\right)^{\beta}.$$

While the treatment above is similar to that of Meltzer and Richard (1981), the comparative statics regarding changes in median to mean income ratio now depend on β. If $-1 < \beta < 0$, then, for fixed y_a, the right-hand side decreases in y_m/y_a. Therefore, an increase in inequality (measured as a decrease in y_m/y_a, again for fixed y_a) increases the amount of public goods provided, just as in Meltzer and Richard (1981). But if $\beta = 0$, i.e., utility is Cobb-Douglas, then inequality does not affect public good provision. And if $\beta > 0$, then inequality decreases public good provision.

To illustrate the difference between $\beta > 0$ and $\beta < 0$, it is instructive to consider the extreme cases of perfect complements ($\beta = +\infty$) and perfect substitutes ($\beta = -1$). For perfect complements, agent i maximizes $\min\{\alpha c_i, (1-\alpha) G_i\}$, which leads to the condition $\alpha c_i = (1-\alpha)G_i$. If we pair this with the budget constraint $c_i = (1-t)y_i$ and $t = {}^{G_i}\!/_{\overline{Y}}$ we obtain

$$G_i = \overline{Y}\frac{\dfrac{y_i}{\overline{Y}}}{\dfrac{1-\alpha}{\alpha} + \dfrac{y_i}{\overline{Y}}},$$

so that the most preferred amount of public good by agent i increases in income y_i.

For perfect substitutes, agent i maximizes $\alpha c_i + (1-\alpha)G_i$, which, paired with the budget constraint $c_i = (1-t)y_i$ and with $t = {}^{G_i}\!/_{\overline{Y}}$, yields that i maximizes

$$\alpha\left(1 - \frac{G_i}{\overline{Y}}\right)y_i + (1-\alpha)G_i.$$

Therefore, $G_i = 0$ is chosen by agents with income $y_i > \dfrac{1-\alpha}{\alpha}\overline{Y}$, and the maximum feasible $G_i = \overline{Y}$ is chosen by agents with income $y_i < \dfrac{1-\alpha}{\alpha}\overline{Y}$. As expected, the most preferred amount of public goods by agent i decreases in income y_i, and it does show in an especially stark manner.

The monotonic relationship between income and the preferred amount of public good is a consequence of using a CES formulation in preferences. The CES formulation facilitates monotonicity by ensuring that income and cross-price elasticity balance each other. However, in general, the balance between income and cross-price elasticity might change with income level. Kenny (1978) shows how the relationship between income

FIGURE 9-1

Preferred Amount of Public Good with Different Levels of Income

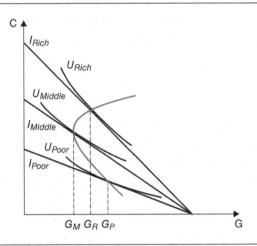

and the most preferred amount of public good generally depends on the comparison between income elasticity of demand and its price elasticity. Husted and Kenny (1997) exploit this fact in their econometric analysis on the effect of the expansion of the voting franchise on the size of government.

Suppose one does not assume a CES formulation but instead lets preferences be more general. In that case, it is possible to have a relationship between income and the preferred amount of public goods that is not monotonic. In this case, the equivalence between median voter and median income does not hold. This is the situation described in figure 9-1, which illustrates the preferred amount of public goods for three different income levels: poor, middle, and rich. The increase in income is given by the rotation of the budget constraint with slope $p_i = \dfrac{Y_i}{\bar{Y}}$, the price of the public good, where $\bar{Y}$ represents per capita income. As income increases, from poor to middle, the substitution effect dominates the income effect, resulting in a lower amount of preferred public goods; however, a further increase in income, from middle to rich, leads to an increase in the amount of preferred public goods, given that the income effect dominates the substitution effect at this level of income. More generally, the red line depicts the combinations of private consumption and public goods most desired for all income levels.

Note that if one builds a toy example based on figure 9-1 with three agents, poor, middle, and rich, the rich individual becomes the median voter.

The case presented in figure 9-1, where the rich individual becomes the median voter, also has implications for the equilibrium relationship between initial inequality and the preferred public goods amount. Consider an increase in inequality, caused for example by a decrease in the poor individual's income and an increase in the rich individual's income, while the income of the individual in the middle stays the same. The preferred amount of public goods for both the poor and the rich individual will increase, resulting in an overall increase in public goods provision at the political equilibrium since the rich individual is the median voter in this case.[7]

4 Extension to Nonlinear Tax Schemes

Here we maintain a median-voter framework as much as possible. We discuss abandoning this framework in Section 5.

We focus our analysis on the majority voting model of Gouveia and Oliver (1996) of a flat tax with an exemption.[8]

4.1 Gouveia and Oliver (1996)

There is only one good in this model, so the utility of agent i is identified with their after-tax income. In turn, after-tax income depends on the exogenous income y_i and on the total tax paid, $T(a, y)$. To capture the structure of a flat tax with rate t and exemption level a, we have

$$T(a, y) = \max\{0, t(y-a)\}.$$

Income in the economy is distributed with a cumulative distribution F with density f. Therefore, if we denote the total amount of resources collected by the tax system with $R(t; a)$, we obtain $R(t; a) = t\phi(a)$, where

$$\varphi(a) = \int_a^\infty (y-a)f(y)dy.$$

Note that

$$\varphi(a) = (1-F(a)) \int_a^\infty \frac{(y-a)}{1-F(a)} f(y) \, dy = (E(y|y \geq a) - a)(1 - F(a)).$$

---

[7] One can also imagine a toy model with one poor agent, nine middle-income agents, and one rich agent. In this case the median voter would have the middle income. Furthermore, imagine making the society more unequal by making one middle agent poor and another rich, without changing average income levels. This would not change the median voter nor his or her income, so the effect on public good provision would be zero. We can conclude that, for general preferences, inequality measures such as the Gini coefficient are not necessarily in a one-to-one relationship with public good levels.

[8] Another interesting avenue of departure from linear taxation is Cukierman and Meltzer (1991), who present a model of quadratic taxation and redistribution and characterize conditions that allow for a majority voting equilibrium to exist.

It is assumed that the government must raise a total amount of resources equal to an exogenously specified amount $\bar{R}$, which does not enter the utility of the agents. Therefore, the government's budget constraint then requires

$$R(t; a) = \bar{R},$$

and this equation can be used to express the rate t as a function of the exemption level a. Indeed, using this equation, it is possible to calculate that

$$\frac{dt}{da} = \frac{d}{da}\left(\frac{\bar{R}}{\varphi(a)}\right) = -\frac{\bar{R}\varphi'(a)}{(\varphi(a))^2} = \frac{t(1 - F(a))}{\varphi(a)}.$$

Not all exemption levels are consistent with $R(t; a) = \bar{R}$. Indeed, if $F(a) = 1$, then no revenue is collected from the tax. So, denote with $\tilde{a}$ the largest possible exemption amount, corresponding to a tax rate of 1.

Agents then decide with a majority voting election on the level of the exemption. Agents with income below a are indifferent to the level of the exemption. As for agents with income above the exemption level, what matters in their decision is how their post-tax income changes, as increases in the exemption level decrease the tax base and increase the tax rate, by the government's budget constraint. The change in post-tax incomes is given by the following:

$$\frac{d}{da}(y - t(y - a)) = +t - (y - a)\frac{dt}{da} = -\frac{t}{\varphi(a)}((y - a)(1 - F(a)) - \varphi(a))$$

$$= \frac{t(1 - F(a))}{\varphi(a)}(E(y \mid y \geq a) - y).$$

Therefore, we see that agents with income below the unconstrained mean $E(y)$ of the population would prefer to set a as large as possible, i.e., to $\tilde{a}$. Similarly, agents with income above $E(y \mid y \geq \tilde{a})$ always prefer smaller levels of the exemption. It turns out that agents with income between $E(y)$ and $E(y \mid y \geq \tilde{a})$ do not have single-peaked preferences, but under the assumption that the distribution of income is right-skewed, i.e., $F(E(y)) > 1/2$, the majority voting equilibrium is to select the largest possible exemption level, and completely expropriate any income over the exemption $\tilde{a}$.

4.2 Consequences of a Flat Tax with Exemption on Changes in Inequality

The conclusion of Gouveia and Oliver (1996) is, in a narrow sense, a commonsense one: in a pure endowment economy, i.e., without incentive effects, the poor "fully" expropriate the rich, of course within the limits imposed by the exogenous choice of fiscal instrument. However, the techniques they pioneer prove to be very useful.

In addition, it is worth pointing out that with a flat tax with exemption regime, the taxation regime itself tends to reduce inequality, measured for example with the

Gini coefficient. Following Lambert (2001) for the rest of this section, including his notation, one can express the Gini coefficient G as

$$G = \frac{2}{\mu} Cov[y, F(y)],$$

as we demonstrate in the technical derivation at the end of this chapter.[9] Changes in the Gini coefficient resulting from different combinations of rate t and exemption level a can be calculated only with reference to the whole distribution of income. In the formula above, income y is transformed to y-T(a,y), with $T(a,y) = \max\{0, t(y-a)\}$. Changes in a affect both the numerator, $Cov[y, F(y)]$, and the denominator μ in nontrivial manners.

The toy examples in table 9-3 show that, as soon as one abandons the no-exemption case, one should expect changes in the Gini coefficient from pretax to post-tax income. While increases in t tend to decrease the Gini coefficient (compare, e.g., tables 9-3B and 9-3C), increases in a first decrease, and then increase the after-tax Gini coefficient (see, e.g., tables 9-3A, 9-3B, and 9-3D).

Comparing tables 9-3B and 9-3C is also illustrative of another important fact. Suppose that the government needs to raise first $12 (9-3B) and then $18 (9-3C), because the size of expenditures has increased. This can be accomplished by leaving the exemption level at 10 and raising the tax rate from 20 percent (9-3B) to 30 percent (9-3C). Since the exemption level is not zero, this results in a reduction of the Gini coefficient for post-tax income from 0.2273 (9-3B) to 0.2134 (9-3C). In what follows, we refer to this fact as the "mechanical" reduction in inequality.

5 The Provision of Public Goods Financed with a Flat Tax with Exemptions

5.1 Empirical Patterns

We begin with a description of empirical patterns. We are interested in the relation between fiscal incidence/inequality reduction and the provision of public goods. We are not interested in the relation between initial inequality and redistribution or provision of public goods, in contrast with most of the empirical analysis conducted so far. Of course, our description has no pretense of establishing any causation relation. We just want to illustrate the kinds of patterns that may arise in the real world. The data used in the figures are from CEQ Standard Indicators and World Bank Development Indicators[10].

CEQ Analysis uses the income concepts shown in figure 9-2 to measure fiscal incidence.

---

[9] See appendix 9B for the technical derivation.

[10] For CEQ Standard Indicators, see https://commitmentoequity.org/datacenter/; for World Bank Development Indicator, see https://data.worldbank.org and World Bank (2017).

TABLE 9-3A
Toy Example: Exemption Level = 0, Tax Rate 20%

	1	2	3	4	Total	Gini
Original income	10	20	30	40	100	0.2500
After-tax income	8	16	24	32	80	0.2500

TABLE 9-3B
Toy Example: Exemption Level = 10, Tax Rate 20%

	1	2	3	4	Total	Gini
Original income	10	20	30	40	100	0.2500
After-tax income	10	18	26	34	88	0.2273

TABLE 9-3C
Toy Example: Exemption Level = 10, Tax Rate 30%

	1	2	3	4	Total	Gini
Original Income	10	20	30	40	100	0.2500
After-Tax Income	10	17	24	31	82	0.2134

TABLE 9-3D
Toy Example: Exemption Level = 20, Tax Rate 20%

	1	2	3	4	Total	Gini
Original income	10	20	30	40	100	0.2500
After-tax income	10	20	28	36	94	0.2287

In the current version of the *CEQ Assessment*, the allocation of in-kind transfers is based on productions costs, where the total government spending on a particular service, such as healthcare or education, is divided by the number of users of that service. If there are user fees or co-payments, they are subtracted to estimate the net benefit.

Once the in-kind transfers are added and the user fees or co-payments are subtracted, Consumable Income becomes Final Income in CEQ framework. The Gini coefficient declines further while moving from consumable income to final income, which implies that the in-kind transfers of education and health have an equalizing impact.

FIGURE 9-2
CEQ Core Income Concepts

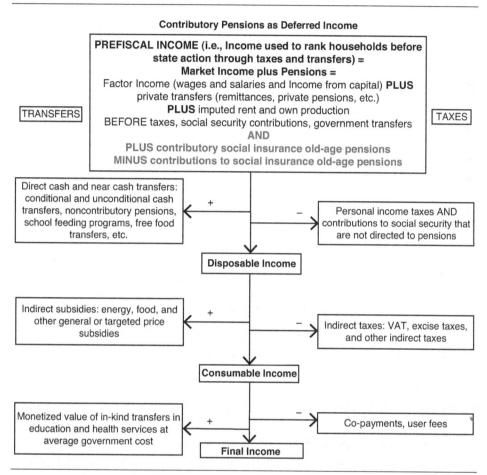

Source: CEQ Standard Indicators.

In figures 9-3, 9-4, and 9-5, fiscal incidence is represented by the number of deciles of net receivers, i.e. those with a higher Consumable Income relative to Market Income. Inequality reduction is given by the decline of the Gini coefficient from Market Income to Consumable Income. Education and health spending as a percentage of GDP represents the provision of public goods.

One common trend in the figures and the regression results in Table 9-4 is that the provision of the public good declines with the number of deciles as net receivers. At the same time, it increases with the reduction in inequality measured by the decrease in Gini coefficient. (The relationship between the provision of public goods and reduction in inequality is unaffected by the way we measure the decrease in Gini coefficient—namely, in Gini points or percentage change.) One exception to this trend

FIGURE 9-3A
Education Spending (% of GDP) and Number of Deciles as Net Receivers

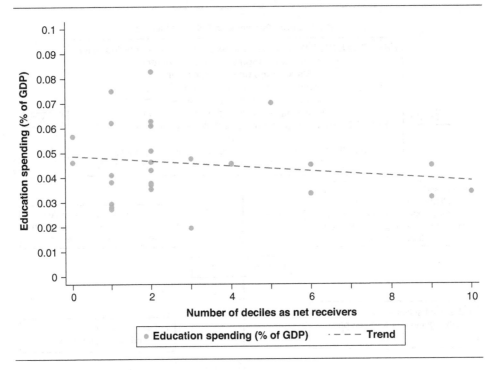

is tertiary education spending, measured by per-student spending as a percentage of per capita income.

The fact that more spending on public goods is positively correlated with a decrease in the Gini coefficient is easily interpreted in light of our discussion in section 4.2. Given the constraint of working with a flat tax with exemption and keeping the exemption level fixed, increases in public goods expenditures must result in a greater tax rate, resulting in a more progressive overall taxation scheme.

Therefore, in the model we develop in section 5.2, we focus on the effect of the number of deciles that are net receivers. This number is identified as the exemption level in a flat-tax-with-exemption taxation scheme in the model, as in Gouveia and Oliver (1996).

5.2 Theoretical Model

The framework we use combines the previous public goods model with the flat tax with exemption studied in Gouveia and Oliver (1996), so our tax scheme imposes average progressivity in the tax code.

Even before performing the analysis, we can immediately see countervailing forces at work when one changes the level of exemption and makes the tax system more progressive

FIGURE 9-3B

Education Spending (% of GDP) and Decline in Gini Coefficient

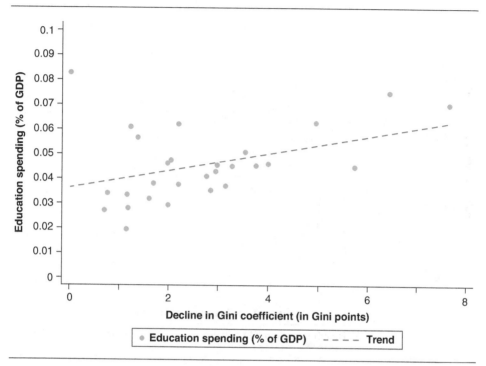

by considering the incentives depicted in figure 9-1. Starting from a proportional tax, a switch to a general progressive tax would rotate a high-income person's budget constraint down around its intercept on the vertical axis and rotate a low-income person's constraint out around its intercept. A middle-income person's constraint could rotate either way depending on where that income is relative to how the tax schedule is changed. To obtain a more precise answer, we, therefore, have to make several assumptions.

In our technical derivations, we assume as before that all individuals have the same utility function over consumption c and public good G, u(c, G). It is important to note that this assumption has bite. One can imagine why agents' preferences may differ in a manner correlated with income (for example, one can imagine that agents who value private consumption more may have invested more in a previous stage that is not modeled here). In that case, as we discussed in section 1, it may no longer be the case that the median voter is the voter with the median income. For simplicity, we abstract from these considerations in what follows. Furthermore, for technical tractability, we adopt the same constant elasticity of substitution formulation in the public good adopted earlier, so

$$u(c, G) = (\alpha c^{-\beta} + (1 - \alpha)G^{-\beta})^{-\frac{1}{\beta}}.$$

FIGURE 9-4A

Health Spending (% of GDP) and Number of Deciles as Net Receivers

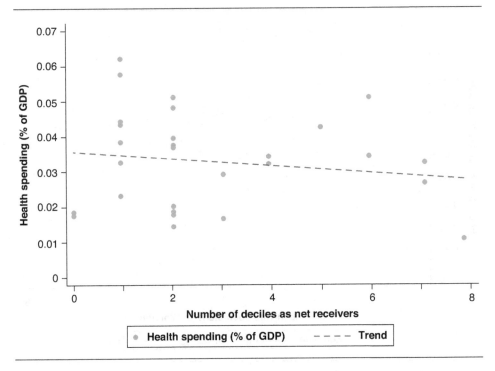

The consumption of agent i depends on his or her exogenous income y_i and on the tax set by the government. The difference from previous formulations is that now we consider the consequences of a government that uses a flat tax with rate t *and* exemption level a. In this case, the tax paid by agent *i* is zero if his or her income is below a, while it equals $t(y_i - a)$ if $y_i \geq a$. Therefore, the consumption of agent i is $c_i = y_i$ if $y_i < a$; otherwise it becomes $c_i = (1-t)y_i + ta$.

For simplicity, we conduct the analysis in a continuum of agents framework so that we can normalize the size of the population n to 1, and we describe the distribution of income in the economy with a cumulative distribution F with density f. The crucial assumption we make is that *a* is exogenous. This could be a restriction that arises for normative reasons on the number of agents that are net receivers. We then let the political process determine the level of the tax rate and of the public goods.

As in the previous formulation of the model, we can use the government's budget constraint to reduce the problem's dimensionality. If we denote the total amount of resources collected by the tax system with R(t; a), we obtain R(t; a) = tφ(a), where

$$\varphi(a) = \int_a^\infty (y - a) f(y) \, dy.$$

FIGURE 9-4B
Health Spending (% of GDP) and Decline in Gini Coefficient

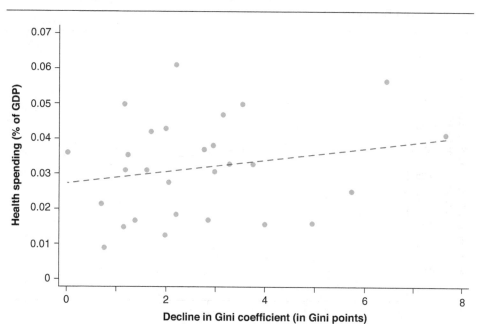

The government's budget constraint then requires $R(t; a) = G$. Solving this equation for the implied tax rate given the exemption and public good levels, we obtain

$$t = \frac{G}{\varphi(a)}.$$

We are now ready to find the optimal level of public good desired by agent i. If $y_i < a$, then this agent desires the largest possible level of the public good. This level is found where $G = \varphi(a)$, or, in other words, for a tax rate that equals 1. This will be the equilibrium if the exemption level is so large that $F(a) \geq \frac{1}{2}$. In this case, we observe the complete expropriation of all income above a minimum level a, with all the tax receipts devoted to the provision of public goods. In the more interesting case where $F(a) < \frac{1}{2}$, we can substitute the value of $t = G/\varphi(a)$ into the consumption level of agent i with income $y_i \geq a$ to obtain

$$c_i = \left(1 - \frac{G}{\varphi(a)}\right)y_i + \frac{G}{\varphi(a)}a = y_i - \frac{y_i - a}{\varphi(a)}G.$$

FIGURE 9-5A

Primary and Secondary Education Spending (% of Per Capita GDP) and Number of Deciles as Net Receivers

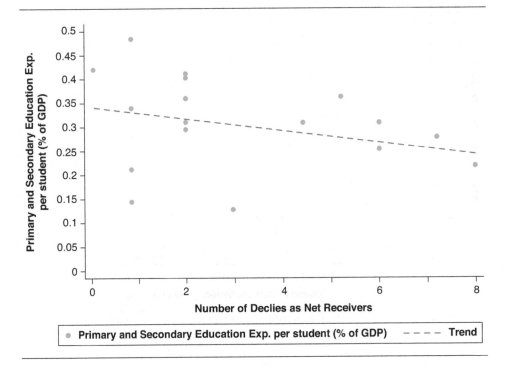

Thus, the most preferred amount of public good for agent i solves

$$\max_G v_i(G) \equiv u\left(y_i - \frac{y_i - a}{\varphi(a)} G, G \right).$$

Assuming an interior solution again and defining the most preferred amount of public goods by agent i as G_i, the first-order condition $v_i'(G_i) = 0$ yields

$$\frac{\alpha}{1-\alpha} \frac{y_i - a}{\varphi(a)} = \left(\frac{y_i - G_i \dfrac{y_i - a}{\varphi(a)}}{G_i} \right)^{1+\beta}.$$

This is a more complex equation than what we obtained for the linear tax case. But we can easily observe that changes immediately emerge for particular parameter configurations. For example, if we set $\beta = 0$, we recover the Cobb-Douglas case, but now this results in

$$G_i = (1-\alpha) \frac{\varphi(a)}{2} \frac{y_i}{y_i - a}.$$

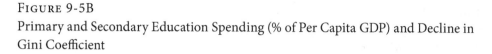

FIGURE 9-5B

Primary and Secondary Education Spending (% of Per Capita GDP) and Decline in Gini Coefficient

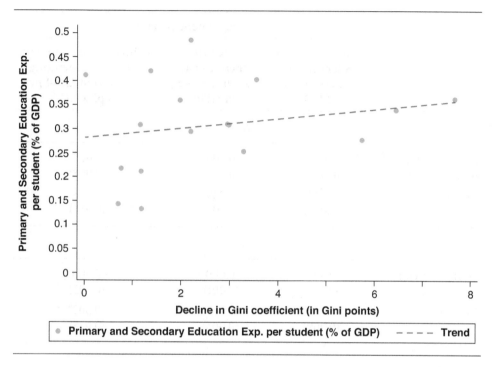

In the model without exemption, Kenny (1978) shows that the desired public good level is independent of income for the Cobb-Douglas utility, if taxation is proportional. Indeed, we can recover that result by setting a to zero in the above-displayed equation and noticing that income cancels out. However, as soon as $a > 0$, the above-displayed expression decreases in individual income; furthermore, one can show that the desired public good level is decreasing in income for any $\beta \le 0$. Therefore, by continuity, there must exist some $\bar{\beta} > 0$ such that if $\beta < \bar{\beta}$, then the desired public good level is decreasing in income. In other words, as compared to proportional taxation, a flat tax rate with exemption makes it more likely that the desired public good level is decreasing in income for agents with income above the exemption.

This is important because, as all agents with income below the exemption always vote for the largest public good amount in a pairwise election, if the desired public good level is decreasing in income for incomes above the exemption, then the median voter theorem applies. Otherwise, the situation is not so clear, and we may have the case of a coalition of poor and rich agents who want to spend large amounts on public goods, while the middle class wants to reduce public goods spending. This bears similarities and differences with the "ends against the middle" result of Epple and Romano (1996a), as we discuss at the end of this section.

TABLE 9-4

Correlations between Indirect Transfers (Provision of Public Goods) and Redistributive Measures

	Dependent variable		
	Total education spending as a percentage of GDP	Health spending as a percentage of GDP	Primary and secondary education spending as a percentage of per capita GDP
A			
Decline in Gini in Gini points	0.003 (0.002)	0.000 (0.001)	0.004 (0.008)
Constant	0.038*** (0.009)	0.020*** (0.005)	0.298*** (0.054)
B			
Decline in Gini in % Change	0.001 (0.001)	−0.000 (0.001)	−0.000 (0.005)
Constant	0.038*** (0.009)	0.022*** (0.005)	0.302*** (0.055)
C			
Net receivers in # of deciles	−0.00131** (0.00616)	−0.00127** (0.00725)	−0.0133** (0.0052)
Constant	0.045*** (0.007)	0.024*** (0.005)	0.352*** (0.058)

Notes: Each panel represents a set of regressions of a particular indirect transfer (education or health) on a redistributive measure as an independent variable—for example, the decline in Gini coefficient in Gini points. The outlier countries are excluded (i.e., South Africa in total education, Colombia in total health spending, and Guatemala in primary and secondary education spending) to have a better representation of the associations. The data regarding total education spending as a percentage of GDP and health spending as a percentage of GDP are taken from CEQ Indicators (https://commitmentoequity.org/datacenter/), whereas primary and secondary education spending as a percentage of GDP per capita is taken from World Bank Indicators (https://data.worldbank.org). Robust standard errors are in parentheses. * $p < 0.10$, ** $p < 0.05$, *** $p < 0.01$.

In general, however, we see that the public goods level now depends not simply on the ratio of median to mean income, but on a more complex formula that relates β, y_m, a and $\phi(a)$. To better understand these relationships, it is worth pointing out, as Gouveia and Oliver (1995) do, that

$$\varphi(a) = (1 - F(a)) \int_a^\infty \frac{(y-a)}{1-F(a)} f(y)\, dy = (E(y|y \geq a) - a)(1 - F(a));$$

i.e., $\phi(a)$ is determined by mean income conditional on income being larger than the exemption, the value of the exemption itself, and the proportion of agents whose income is above the exemption.

Another interesting question regards the equilibrium spending on public goods as the exemption level is raised. Assuming that the median voter theorem applies and recalling our first-order condition, we have

$$\frac{\alpha}{1-\alpha}\frac{y_m - a}{\varphi(a)} = \left(\frac{y_m - G_m\frac{y_m - a}{\varphi(a)}}{G_m}\right)^{1+\beta}.$$

Now applying the implicit function theorem, we see that the sign of the change in G_m with respect to a has the same sign of that of $\phi(a)/(y_m - a)$. We then obtain

$$\frac{d}{da}\left(\frac{\varphi(a)}{y_m - a}\right) = \frac{\varphi'(a)(y_m - a) + \varphi(a)}{(y_m - a)^2}.$$

Since $\phi'(a) = -(1 - F(a))$, the numerator of the above-displayed equation can be simplified as

$$\phi'(a)(y_m - a) + \phi(a) = (1 - F(a))(E(y \mid y \geq a) - a - y_m + a) = (1 - F(a))(E(y \mid y \geq a) - y_m).$$

So, if the distribution of income is right-skewed, so that the average income is above the median, increasing the exemption level *increases* the amount of public goods provided in the political equilibrium.

Indeed, this can be intuitively explained in a different way. Recall that agents are maximizing

$$u\left(y_i - \frac{y_i - a}{\varphi(a)}G, G\right),$$

so we see that $\frac{y_i - a}{\varphi(a)}$ acts as a public good price. Since this price decreases with a, if G is a normal good, then agents will demand more G.

Boix (2003) offers an interesting caveat, pointing out that turnout should be included in considerations such as ours.[11] Boix (2003) emphasizes the importance of turnout in determining the size of the public sector, and hence the level of redistribution. In his model, as turnout among the least skilled worker declines, the median voter's position gets closer to the position of the voter with average income, which results in a smaller public sector.

---

[11] See also Larcinese (2007).

In our model, what matters for electoral success is the income of the median *voter*, and it is well known that turnout is increasing with income.[12] We consider a scenario where the median voter is positioned above the voter with average income because of turnout. In the presence of such a turnout pattern, where the median income *among voters* is above the average of the overall population income, the sign of $\dfrac{d}{da}\left(\dfrac{\varphi(a)}{y_m-a}\right)$ reverses, and we obtain the opposite implication: increasing the exemption level *decreases* the public goods provided in the political equilibrium.

A second interesting caveat arises in the presence of private substitutes for the public good, as in the "ends against the middle" framework of Epple and Romano (1996a).[13] Epple and Romano (1996a) set up a voting model in which agents can opt out of consuming the public goods amount publicly provided and instead consume an amount that they privately acquire. Sufficiently rich agents may decide to do so at a discretely larger level than what is publicly provided. There are two interesting possibilities, and they are usefully described according to the analysis of Kenny (1978) of a public good financed with a proportional tax and without available substitutes. If agents' most desired level of publicly provided G decreases with income, then no changes arise when a substitute is present. The median voter remains decisive since richer voters demand fewer public goods, and the possibility of opting out only further reduces their demand.

In contrast, if agents' most desired level of publicly provided G increases with income, the availability of substitutes makes preferences not single-peaked, and equilibrium may fail to exist. When equilibrium does exist, the median voter is not decisive anymore since very high-income agents opt out and pool with very low-income ones to support a lower level of public expenditure. Therefore, the decisive voter has income below the median.

Combining this framework with our flat tax with exemption has two effects: first, as we demonstrated in our Cobb-Douglas example, it is now more likely that a utility function displays decreasing most desired levels of public goods in income, and so it is more likely that the usual median voter theorem applies. Second, if instead most desired public goods levels are increasing in income, then what matters in the comparative statics linking G and a is the sign of $\dfrac{d}{da}\left(\dfrac{\varphi(a)}{y_d-a}\right)$ at some decisive income level $y_d < y_m$. Therefore, even considering turnout effects, we tend to restore the implication that increasing the exemption level *increases* the amount of public goods provided in the political equilibrium. Of course, a definite prediction requires institutional knowledge of the patterns of income, turnout, and the presence of private substitutes for the public good.

---

[12] See, e.g., Wolfinger and Rosenstone (1980).

[13] See also Glomm and Ravikumar (1996); Epple and Romano (1996b); Gouveia (1996); Fernandez and Rogerson (1996); and the exposition of Director's law in Stigler (1970).

6 Taxation and Redistribution Models without Functional Form Assumptions

There are at least two strands of the literature that abandon the assumptions of a unidimensional policy space. Both strands have to contend with the problem that equilibrium in pure strategies does not exist. The problem arises because, given enough flexibility, for any tax/redistribution schedule it is always possible to reduce the tax paid by 50 percent of the electorate by a small amount, compensating this reduction by expropriating a small fraction of the electorate. The problem is similar to dividing a cake among three agents by majority voting. For any proposed division, it is always possible to find a coalition of two agents that does better by expropriating the third.

The first important strand stems from the seminal contribution of Myerson (1993), studying the implications of assuming that redistribution is perfectly targetable. These models are not models of direct democracy but models of representative democracy and tend to admit equilibria only in mixed strategies. Indeed, these equilibria resemble those of all-pay auctions. A very important contribution is that of Lizzeri and Persico (2001). They introduce a model with two competing, office-motivated politicians who can use the resources raised from taxation to either redistribute wealth or pay for the provision of public goods. The key assumption is that public goods are not easily targetable to a subset of voters. At the same time, redistribution can be (this notion of redistribution, therefore, captures both cash transfers and pork-barrel projects).

Indeed, in their model, there is no assumption at all on the shape of redistribution, and in particular, there is no restriction to linear tax rates and lump-sum redistribution. It is worth pointing out that in this framework, redistribution does not go from the rich to the poor. Rather, it is determined by the electoral incentive that office-motivated politicians have to aggressively tax a minority and redistribute the amount collected to a majority of voters, so this redistribution ends up increasing inequality. Politicians, therefore, face a trade-off: while the benefits from the public good may be higher for society as a whole, pork-barrel projects and cash redistribution can be targeted and therefore may end up undercutting the efficient choice. The main interest of Lizzeri and Persico (2001) is to compare the performance of different electoral incentives; indeed, they find that the under-provision problem is especially severe for winner-take-all systems. However, their equilibrium lends itself to a comparative statics analysis that relates changes in inequality brought about by taxation and redistribution and the level of public good provision. Equilibrium is in mixed strategies: with some probability, the public good is provided, and with the complementary probability targeted, inequality enhancing redistribution is implemented. Therefore, a positive correlation arises between observing the provision of public goods and a more equitable pattern of cash taxes and transfers. Crutzen and Sahuguet (2009) also contribute to this strand of the literature and consider the possibility that taxation can be targetable, in addition to redistribution. Further, they analyze the effects of distortions in taxes.

A second very important strand of the literature considers the problem of raising a fixed amount of revenue without imposing restrictions on the form of the tax schedule and tries to determine whether a progressive tax scheme emerges in equilibrium. Carbonell-Nicolau and Ok (2007) present a model of representative democracy with two office-motivated parties that compete against each other by offering tax functions that, in principle, are not restricted to be marginal-rate progressive. The only assumption they make is that income distributions are right-skewed; i.e., they assume that the median is below the mean. They investigate if this assumption is sufficient to generate an equilibrium in marginal-rate progressive tax schedules. Carbonell-Nicolau and Ok (2007) show that equilibrium exists, but only in mixed strategies. Generally, it is impossible to exclude the possibility that a marginal-rate regressive scheme is chosen in equilibrium with a positive probability. This result complements Marhuenda and Ortuno-Ortin (1995), who find that if the median voter's income is below the mean income and voting is self-interested, any marginal rate progressive (convex) tax schedule defeats any marginal rate regressive (concave) one. This shows how the possibility of tax schedules that are neither globally convex nor concave creates voting cycles.

To avoid mixed-strategy equilibria and restore a deterministic prediction, other papers in this strand of the literature introduce additional elements to the political process: uncertainty about abandoning the status-quo as in Marhuenda and Ortuno-Ortin (1998), policy preferences of the candidates and costs of participating in the election as in Carbonell-Nicolau and Klor (2003), and internal party dynamics as in Roemer (1999). These models deliver, in equilibrium, tax schedules with increasing marginal taxation rates.

7 Conclusion

We investigate the relationship between public provision of public goods and income redistribution using a median voter model. The fiscal incidence analyses conducted by the CEQ Institute suggest a negative association between the percentage of tax-exempt individuals ("net receivers" in our analysis) and the level of public provision of public goods. We start our analysis by reviewing the previous literature and then offer an extension of the classical framework of taxation and public goods provision that departs from the assumption of a simple proportional tax in favor of a flat tax with an exemption. Adjusting the exemption level, we capture tax schemes restricted to generating different numbers of net receivers. We then let voters decide on the tax rate and the quantity of public goods provided. Our model predicts that the level of public goods provision can increase or decrease in the proportion of "net receivers" depending on the relationship between the income of the decisive voter and the average income in the population, conditional on income being larger than the exemption. More specifically, if the distribution of income is right-skewed, so that the average income is above the median, increasing the exemption level *increases* the amount of public goods provided in the political equilibrium. We conclude by pointing out two caveats, which may change the direction of the model's prediction. If turnout patterns are such that the median income *among voters* is above the average of the overall population income, then increasing the exemption level *decreases* the amount of public good provided in the political equilibrium as observed in the CEQ data. Also, the presence of substitutes for government-provided public goods may result in agents opting out of consuming the amount of public goods publicly provided and instead consuming an amount that they privately acquire. Under certain conditions allowing the existence of an equilibrium, very high-income agents opt out and pool with very low-income ones to support a lower level of public expenditure, resulting in a negative relationship between the level of public goods provision and exemption level.

Acknowledgments

We would like to thank Nora Lustig and Steven Slutsky for their very generous comments on previous versions of this chapter. All remaining errors are our own.

References

Alesina, A. 1988. "Credibility and Policy Convergence in a Two-Party System with Rational Voters." *American Economic Review* 78, no. 4, pp. 796–805.

Arrow, K. J. 1951. *Social Choice and Individual Values.* New York: Wiley.

Austen-Smith, D., and J. S. Banks. 1999. *Positive Political Theory I: Collective Preference.* Ann Arbor: University of Michigan Press.

Bénabou, R. 1996. "Inequality and Growth." In *NBER Macroeconomics Annual*, vol. 11, edited by B. S. Bernanke and J. J. Rotemberg. Cambridge, MA: MIT Press.

———. 2000. "Unequal Societies: Income Distribution and the Social Contract." *American Economic Review* 90, no. 1, pp. 96–129.

Bénabou, R., and E. A. Ok. 2001. "Social Mobility and the Demand for Redistribution: The POUM Hypothesis." *Quarterly Journal of Economics* 116, no. 2, pp. 447–87.

Black, D., R. A. Newing, I. McLean, A. McMillan, and B. L. Monroe. 1958. *The Theory of Committees and Elections.* Cambridge: Cambridge University Press.

Boadway, R., and M. Keen. 2000. "Redistribution." In *Handbook of Income Distribution*, vol. 1, edited by A.B. Atkinson and F. Bourguignon. Amsterdam: North-Holland.

Boix, C. 2003. *Democracy and Redistribution.* Cambridge: Cambridge University Press.

Borck, R. 2007. "Voting, Inequality and Redistribution. *Journal of Economic Surveys* 21, no. 1, pp. 90–109.

Carbonell-Nicolau, O., and E. A. Ok. 2007. "Voting over Income Taxation." *Journal of Economic Theory* 134, no. 1, pp. 249–86.

Carbonell-Nicolau, O., and E. F. Klor, E. F. 2003. "Representative Democracy and Marginal Rate Progressive Income Taxation." *Journal of Public Economics* 87, no. 9, pp. 2339–66.

Crutzen, B. S., and N. Sahuguet. 2009. "Redistributive Politics with Distortionary Taxation." *Journal of Economic Theory* 144, no. 1, pp. 264–79.

Cukierman, Alex, and Allan Meltzer 1991. "A Political Theory of Progressive Income Taxation." In *Political Economy*, edited by A. Meltzer, A. Cukierman, and S. F. Richard. New York: Oxford University Press.

Dixit, A., and J. Londregan. 1998. "Ideology, Tactics, and Efficiency in Redistributive Politics." *Quarterly Journal of Economics* 113, no. 2, pp. 497–529.

Downs, A. 1957. "An Economic Theory of Political Action in a Democracy." *Journal of Political Economy* 65, no. 2, pp. 135–50.

Epple, D., and R. E. Romano. 1996a. "Ends against the Middle: Determining Public Service Provision When There Are Private Alternatives." *Journal of Public Economics* 62, no. 3, pp. 297–325.

———1996b. "Public Provision of Private Goods." *Journal of Political Economy* 104, no. 1, pp. 57–84.

Fernandez, R., and R. Rogerson. 1996. "Income Distribution, Communities, and the Quality of Public Education." *Quarterly Journal of Economics* 111, no. 1, pp. 135–64.

Foley, D. 1967. "Resource Allocation and the Public Sector." *Yale Economic Essays* 7, no. 1, pp. 45–98.

Galasso, V. 2003. "Redistribution and Fairness: A Note." *European Journal of Political Economy* 19, no. 4, pp. 885–92.

Gans, J. S., and M. Smart. 1996. "Majority Voting with Single-Crossing Preferences." *Journal of Public Economics* 59, no. 2, pp. 219–37.

Glomm, G., and B. Ravikumar. 1996. "Endogenous Public Policy and Multiple Equilibria." *European Journal of Political Economy* 11, no. 4, pp. 653–62.

Gouveia, M. 1996. "The Public Sector and Health Care." *International Tax and Public Finance* 3, no. 3, pp. 329–49.

Gouveia, M., and D. Oliver. 1996. "Voting over Flat Taxes in an Endowment Economy." *Economics Letters* 50, no. 2, pp. 251–58.

Husted, T. A., and L. W. Kenny. 1997. "The Effect of the Expansion of the Voting Franchise on the Size of Government." *Journal of Political Economy* 105, no. 1, pp. 54–82.

Kenny, L. W. 1978. "The Collective Allocation of Commodities in a Democratic Society: A Generalization." *Public Choice* 33, no. 2, pp. 117–20.

Laffont, J. J. 1999. "Competition, Information and Development." In *Annual World Bank Conference on Development Economics*, edited by B. Pleskovic and J. E. Stiglitz. Washington, DC: The World Bank.

Lambert, P. 2001. *The Distribution and Redistribution of Income*. Manchester: Manchester University Press.

Larcinese, V. 2007. "Voting over Redistribution and the Size of the Welfare State: The Role of Turnout. *Political Studies* 55, no. 3, pp. 568–85.

Lizzeri, A., and N. Persico. 2001. "The Provision of Public Goods under Alternative Electoral Incentives." *American Economic Review* 91, no. 1, pp. 225–39.

Londregan, J. 2006. "Political Income Redistribution." In *The Oxford Handbook of Political Economy*, edited by B. R. Weingast and D. Wittman. Oxford: Oxford University Press.

Lovell, M. C. 1975. "The Collective Allocation of Commodities in a Democratic Society." *Public Choice* 24, no. 1, pp. 71–92.

Marhuenda, F., and I. Ortuño-Ortín. 1995. "Popular Support for Progressive Taxation." *Economics Letters* 48, no. 3, pp. 319–24.

———. 1998. Income Taxation, Uncertainty and Stability. *Journal of Public Economics* 67, no. 2, pp. 285–300.

Meltzer, A. H., and S. F. Richard. 1981. "A Rational Theory of the Size of Government. *Journal of Political Economy* 89, no. 5, pp. 914–27.

Myerson, R. B. 1993. "Incentives to Cultivate Favored Minorities under Alternative Electoral Systems." *American Political Science Review* 87, no. 4, pp. 856–69.

Persson, T., and G. Tabellini. 2002. "Political Economics and Public Finance." In *Handbook of Public Economics*, vol. 3, edited by A. J. Auerbach and M. Feldstein. Amsterdam: North-Holland.

———. 2003. *The Economic Effects of Constitutions: What Do the Data Say.* Cambridge, MA: MIT Press.

Roberts, K. W. 1977. "Voting over Income Tax Schedules." *Journal of Public Economics* 8, no. 3, pp. 329–40.

Roemer, J. E. 1999. "The Democratic Political Economy of Progressive Income Taxation." *Econometrica* 67, no. 1, pp. 1–19.

Romer, T. 1975. "Individual Welfare, Majority Voting, and the Properties of a Linear Income Tax." *Journal of Public Economics* 4, no. 2, pp. 163–85.

———. 1977. "Majority Voting on Tax Parameters: Some Further Results." *Journal of Public Economics* 7, no. 1, pp. 127–33.

Saez, E., and G. Zucman. 2019. *The Triumph of Injustice.* New York: Norton.

Stigler, G. J. 1970. "Director's Law of Public Income Redistribution." *Journal of Law and Economics* 13, no. 1, pp. 1–10.

Wolfinger, R. E., and S. J. Rosenstone. 1980. *Who Votes?* New Haven, CT: Yale University Press.

The World Bank. 2017. "Adjusted savings: Education Expenditure (% of GNI)—Total Debt Service (% of GNI)." World Development Indicators. Washington, DC: World Bank Group. https://data.worldbank.org (accessed February 1, 2017).

Appendix 9A

Technical Derivations of the Meltzer and Richard (1981) Model

1 Response of Consumption to Government Transfers

Recall that individuals take both government transfers r and the tax rate t as given when making their optimal decisions. Therefore, although in equilibrium r and t are related to each other, here we are interested in changing r while keeping t constant.

For those who subsist on welfare (i.e., $n = 0$), consumption is equal to the government transfer (i.e., $c = r$).

$$\Rightarrow \frac{\partial c}{\partial r} = 1 \text{ for individuals who choose not to work.}$$

We now show that for individuals who choose to work, $0 < \dfrac{\partial c}{\partial r} < 1$. For these individuals, recall that $c = r + nx(1-t)$. Differentiating with respect to r, we obtain

$$\frac{\partial c}{\partial r} = 1 + \frac{\partial n}{\partial r} x(1-t) < 1,$$

as leisure is assumed to be a normal good. Therefore, the consumption of agents who decide to work reacts less to government transfers than that of agents who decide not to work. Furthermore, we have that

$$\frac{\partial c}{\partial r} = 1 + \frac{\partial n}{\partial r} x(1-t) \Rightarrow \frac{\partial n}{\partial r} = \left(\frac{\partial c}{\partial r} - 1 \right) \frac{1}{x(1-t)}.$$

Also, the second order condition of the maximization problem follows:

$$\frac{\partial^2 U}{\partial n^2} = \{U_{cc} x(1-t) - U_{cl}\} x(1-t) - U_{lc} x(1-t) + U_{ll}$$
$$= U_{cc} x^2(1-t)^2 - 2 U_{cl} x(1-t) + U_{ll} \equiv D < 0$$

since $U(c, l)$ is strictly concave. Now, differentiate the first order condition with respect to r:

$$\left\{ U_{cc} \frac{\partial c}{\partial r} - U_{cl} \frac{\partial n}{\partial r} \right\} x(1-t) = U_{cl} \frac{\partial c}{\partial r} - U_{ll} \frac{\partial n}{\partial r}$$

$$\Rightarrow U_{cc} \frac{\partial c}{\partial r} x(1-t) - U_{cl} \frac{\partial n}{\partial r} x(1-t) = \nu U_{cl} \frac{\partial c}{\partial r} - U_{ll} \frac{\partial n}{\partial r}$$

$$\Rightarrow \{U_{cc} x(1-t) - U_{cl}\} \frac{\partial c}{\partial r} = \{U_{cl} x(1-t) - U_{ll}\} \frac{\partial n}{\partial r}$$

$$\Rightarrow \{U_{cc} x(1-t) - U_{cl}\} \frac{\partial c}{\partial r} = \{U_{cl} x(1-t) - U_{ll}\} \left\{ \frac{\partial c}{\partial r} - 1 \right\} \frac{1}{x(1-t)}$$

$$\Rightarrow \{U_{cc} x^2(1-t)^2 - U_{cl} x(1-t)\} \frac{\partial c}{\partial r} = \{U_{cl} x(1-t) - U_{ll}\} \frac{\partial c}{\partial r} - U_{cl} x(1-t) + U_{ll}$$

$$\Rightarrow \{U_{cc} x^2(1-t)^2 - 2U_{cl} x(1-t) + U_{ll}\} \frac{\partial c}{\partial r} = -U_{cl} x(1-t) + U_{ll}$$

$$\Rightarrow D \frac{\partial c}{\partial r} = -U_{cl} x(1-t) + U_{ll}$$

$$\Rightarrow \frac{\partial c}{\partial r} = \frac{U_{cl} x(1-t) - U_{ll}}{-D} > 0$$

So all agents increase their consumption in response to an increase in transfers.

2 Response of Pretax Income to Productivity

Pretax income is a function of the tax rate, transfer, and the productivity level, $y(r, t, x) = xn(r, x(1-t))$. For individuals with $x \leq x_0$ (i.e., who not choose to work) $y = 0$ implying $\frac{\partial y}{\partial x} = 0$. For individuals for whom $n > 0$,

$$\frac{\partial y}{\partial x} = n + x \frac{\partial n}{\partial x}.$$

Differentiating the original utility maximization problem with respect to x,

$$(1-t)\left\{ \left[U_{cc}(1-t)\left(\frac{\partial n}{\partial x}x + n\right) - U_{cl}\frac{\partial n}{\partial x}\right]x + U_c\right\}$$

$$= U_{cl}\left\{(1-t)\left(\frac{\partial n}{\partial x}x + n\right)\right\} - U_{ll}\frac{\partial n}{\partial x}$$

$$\Rightarrow (1-t)\left\{ U_{cc}(1-t)\frac{\partial n}{\partial x}x + U_{cc}(1-t)n - U_{cl}\frac{\partial n}{\partial x}\right\}$$

$$x + (1-t)U_c = U_{cl}(1-t)\frac{\partial n}{\partial x}x + U_{cl}(1-t)n - U_{ll}\frac{\partial n}{\partial x}$$

$$\Rightarrow U_{cc}(1-t)^2 x^2 \frac{\partial n}{\partial x} + U_{cc}(1-t)^2 nx - U_{cl}(1-t)x\frac{\partial n}{\partial x}$$

$$+ (1-t)U_c = U_{cl}(1-t)\frac{\partial n}{\partial x}x + U_{cl}(1-t)n - U_{ll}\frac{\partial n}{\partial x}$$

$$\Rightarrow \frac{\partial n}{\partial x}\{U_{cc}(1-t)^2 x^2 - 2\,U_{cl}(1-t)x + U_{ll}\}$$

$$= -U_{cc}(1-t)^2 nx + U_{cl}(1-t)n - (1-t)U_c$$

$$\Rightarrow \frac{\partial n}{\partial x}D = -U_{cc}(1-t)^2 nx + U_{cl}(1-t)n - (1-t)U_c$$

$$\Rightarrow \frac{\partial n}{\partial x} = \frac{U_{cc}(1-t)^2 nx - U_{cl}(1-t)n + (1-t)U_c}{-D}$$

Substituting this back into the partial derivative of earned income with respect to productivity,

$$\frac{\partial y}{\partial x} = n + x\,\frac{U_c(1-t)x + n\{U_{cl}(1-t)x - U_{ll}\}}{-D} > 0.$$

So, $\frac{\partial y}{\partial x}$ is positive for all $x > x_0$.

FIGURE 9-B1

Typical Lorenz Curve

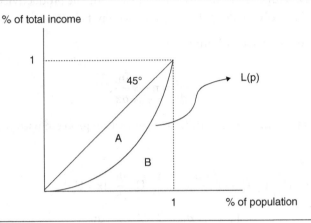

Source: Lambert (2001).

Appendix 9B

Technical Derivations of Lambert (2001)

The Lorenz curve, $L(p)$, represents the percentage of total income belonging to the poorest p% of the population and can be written as

$$L(p)=\int_0^y \frac{xf(x)dx}{\mu}=\int_0^{F^{-1}(p)} \frac{xf(x)dx}{\mu},$$

where $p=F(y)$ is the rank of an individual across income distribution (see Figure 9-B1). The Gini coefficient is given by

$$G=\frac{A}{A+B}=\frac{A}{A+\left(\frac{1}{2}-A\right)}=\frac{A}{A+\left(\frac{1}{2}-A\right)}=2A=2\left(\frac{1}{2}-B\right)=1-2B.$$

Substituting in the Lorenz curve,

$$G=1-2\int_0^1 L(p)dp$$

$$=1-2\left[(pL(p))|_0^1-\int_0^1 pL'(p)dp\right]$$

$$=1-2\left[L(1)(1)-L(0)(0)-\int_0^1 pL'(p)dp\right]$$

$$= -1 + 2 \int_0^1 p L'(p) dp$$

$$= -1 + 2 \int_0^1 p L'(p) dp$$

$$= -1 + \frac{2}{\mu} \int_0^1 p \frac{1}{f(F^{-1}(p))} F^{-1}(p) f(F^{-1}(p)) dp$$

$$= -1 + \frac{2}{\mu} \int_0^1 p F^{-1}(p) dp$$

$$= -1 + \frac{2}{\mu} \int_0^\infty F(y) y f(y) dy,$$

since $p = F(y)$ and $dp = f(y) dy$.

The covariance of y and $F(y)$ is given by

$$Cov[y, F(y)] = \int_0^\infty y F(y) f(y) dy - \mu \int_0^\infty F(y) f(y) dy$$

$$= \int_0^\infty y F(y) f(y) dy - \mu \frac{1}{2} [F(y)]^2 \big|_0^\infty$$

$$= \int_0^\infty y F(y) f(y) dy - \frac{1}{2} \mu$$

$$\Rightarrow \int_0^\infty y F(y) f(y) dy = Cov[y, F(y)] + \frac{1}{2} \mu$$

$$\Rightarrow G = -1 + \frac{2}{\mu} \left[Cov[y, F(y)] + \frac{1}{2} \mu \right]$$

$$\Rightarrow G = \frac{2}{\mu} Cov[y, F(y)].$$

ABOUT THE AUTHORS

RAMIRO ALBRIEU is a Principal Investigator at Centro de Implementación de Políticas Públicas para la Equidad y el Crecimiento's Economic Development Program leading the "Future of Work in the Global South" initiative, and a macroeconomics professor at the University of Buenos Aires (UBA). He is also an Associate Researcher at the Center for the Study of State and Society (CEDES) and at the Commitment to Equity Institute (CEQ) at Tulane University, as well as a member of the T-20 "Technological Change and the Future of Work" task force.

STEFANO BARBIERI is Professor of Economics at Tulane University, Co-Editor of *Economic Inquiry*, and Associate Editor of the *Journal of Public Economic Theory*. He is interested in cooperation broadly defined, with applications including public goods provision, fundraising, and group competition. He became a nonresident Research Associate of the CEQ Institute in 2016. His research has been published in the *Journal of Public Economics, Games and Economic Behavior* and the *RAND Journal of Economics*, among others. Dr. Barbieri received his PhD in economics from the University of Pennsylvania.

JEREMY BAROFSKY is the Vice President of Applied Research and Evaluation at ideas 42, a behavioral economics NGO, and a nonresident associate at Tulane University's Commitment to Equity Institute. Previously, he was the Okun-Model Fellow at the Brookings Institution and a postdoctoral research scholar at the Schaeffer Center for Health Policy and Economics at the University of Southern California. He holds a doctorate from Harvard University's TH Chan School of Public Health in Global Health and Population (Economics Concentration) and a masters in economics from Boston University.

KORAY CAGLAYAN is a Health Economist at the American Institutes for Research. He received his PhD in economics from Tulane University. His work concerns identifying the long-term effects of early-life health capital.

BERNARDO CANDIA is a PhD candidate in economics at the University of California, Berkeley. He received bachelor's and master's degrees in Economics from the University of Chile. He works on macroeconomics, economic history, and international economics.

EDUARDO ENGEL is Professor of Economics at the University of Chile and Director of Espacio Público, a Chilean think tank. He was President of the Latin American and Caribbean Economics Association (LACEA) during 2014 and 2015. He has published extensively in the areas of macroeconomics, public finance, and infrastructure economics. He recently coauthored "The Ways of Corruption in Infrastructure: Lessons From the Odebrecht Case," published in the *Journal of Economic Perspectives*. He holds an engineering degree from the University of Chile, a PhD in statistics from Stanford University, and a PhD in economics from Massachusetts Institute of Technology (MIT).

JOSE MARIA FANELLI is Senior Researcher at Universidad de San Andrés, Argentina and former Director of the Economics Department at the University of Buenos Aires (UBA). He has been actively involved in the establishment of research networks in Latin America. He has worked as a consultant for the Economic Commission for Latin America and the Caribbean (ECLAC), Inter-American Development Bank (IDB), The World Bank, Global Development Network (GDN), and International Development Research Centre (IDRC). He published extensively on macroeconomic and financial problems in Latin America. He has a PhD in Economics from the University of Buenos Aires (UBA).

CARLOS GRUSHKA is a Professor at the School of Economics, University of Buenos Aires (UBA), and of postgraduate studies at the National University of Lujan and Facultad Latinoamericana de Ciencias Sociales (FLACSO), as well as a consultant for national and international organizations (Economic Commission for Latin America and the Caribbean, Inter-American Development Bank, International Labour Organization, World Bank). He is author of numerous publications on demographic and social security issues in national and international books and journals. He is a member of the International Actuarial Association (IAA), the International Union for the Scientific Study of Population (IUSSP), the Latin American Population Association (ALAP), and the Association of Population Studies of Argentina (AEPA, former president). He is an actuary (UBA) and received a PhD in demography (University of Pennsylvania).

NORA LUSTIG is Samuel Z. Stone Professor of Latin American Economics and director of the CEQ Institute at Tulane University. She is also a nonresident fellow at the Center for Global Development and the Inter-American Dialogue. Her current research focuses on assessing the impact of taxation and social spending on inequality and poverty in developing countries and on the determinants of income distribution in Latin America. She is a founding member and past president of the Latin American and Caribbean Economic Association (LACEA) and was a codirector of the World Bank's *World Development Report 2000/2001: Attacking Poverty*. She is the editor of the Journal of Economic Inequality Forum, and she is a member of the Inter-American Dialogue, the G20 Eminent Persons Group on Global Financial Governance, and the Society for the Study of Economic Inequality (ECINEQ)'s Executive Council. She received her doctorate in economics from the University of California, Berkeley.

SERGEI SOARES is a Labor Economist at the International Labour Organization. He has previously worked at Instituto de Pesquisa Econômica Aplicada (IPEA), a research institute affiliated with the Brazilian government, as well as the World Bank. He works on labor markets and inequality. He holds a PhD in economics from the University of Brasilia.

SERGIO URZUA is an Associate Professor in the Department of Economics at the University of Maryland. He is a Research Associate at the National Bureau of Economic Research, Research Fellow at IZA Institute of Labor Economics, and International Research Fellow at Centro Latinoamericano de Politicas Economicas y Sociales. His research focuses on labor, development, and applied econometrics. His research agenda includes the evaluation of social/policy interventions in developing economies. He holds a PhD from the University of Chicago. He teaches in the areas of labor economics and econometrics.

STEPHEN D. YOUNGER is a consultant to the CEQ Institute and worked previously at Williams College, Cornell University, the Vrije Universiteit Amsterdam, the Facultad Latinoamericana de Ciencias Sociales (Quito, Ecuador), and Ithaca College. His research focuses on the distributional consequences of public policy in developing countries, especially the non-income dimensions of well-being, as well as multidimensional poverty and inequality. He earned his doctorate in economics from Stanford University.

INDEX